Environmental Ethics Today

Environmental Ethics Today

PETER S. WENZ

University of Illinois at Springfield

New York ❧ Oxford
OXFORD UNIVERSITY PRESS
2001

Oxford University Press

Oxford   New York
Athens   Auckland   Bangkok   Bogotá   Buenos Aires   Calcutta
Cape Town   Chennai   Dar es Salaam   Delhi   Florence   Hong Kong   Istanbul
Karachi   Kuala Lumpur   Madrid   Melbourne   Mexico City   Mumbai
Nairobi   Paris   São Paulo   Singapore   Taipei   Tokyo   Toronto   Warsaw

and associated companies in
Berlin   Ibadan

Published by Oxford University Press, Inc.
198 Madison Avenue, New York, New York, 10016
http://www.oup-usa.org

Oxford is a registered trademark of Oxford University Press

Library of Congress Cataloging-in-Publication Data
Wenz, Peter S.
  Environmental ethics today / Peter S. Wenz.
      p.   cm.
  Includes index.
  ISBN 0-19-513384-6
    1. Environmental ethics.   I. Title.
  GE42.W458   2001
  179'.1—dc21   000-058895

9 8 7 6 5 4 3 2 1
Printed in the United States of America
on acid-free paper

This book is dedicated to my wife
Grace,
Loving and well loved,
Whose name says it all

Contents

PART III   ENVIRONMENTAL SYNERGISM

PART IV APPLICATIONS

Preface

Human beings now manipulate the earth and its life forms as never before. Due to genetic engineering, the french fries you eat may contain the pesticide Bt, which kills potato beetles but is believed safe for people. The average American's body contains about 250 artificial chemicals, most created since World War II. They may be safe, but cancer occurs and kills more than ever. World food production increased dramatically in the twentieth century, largely through improved crop varieties and chemical inputs, but increases no longer keep pace with the world's growing population. Nearly a billion people go hungry now, and the human population is expected to grow from 6 to 9 billion by 2050. Can we, should we, try to end human hunger? Will this effort destroy rainforests, where human encroachments already cause many species to go extinct? Global warming may threaten coastal cities such as New York, Washington, D.C., and New Orleans, yet Third World economic development seems likely to increase emissions of greenhouse gasses. What kind of development is appropriate? Environmental ethics addresses these and other pressing issues.

This book introduces readers to current positions, controversies, and concepts in environmental ethics. Many people think of ethics as terribly abstract and unrelated to everyday life. But when ideas are presented in a clear, crisp, and sometimes humorous style that relates abstract matters to pressing personal and political concerns, ethics can be engaging and fun for students and general readers.

Each chapter begins with a real controversy or issue that readers might already care about, such as rising cancer rates, cruelty to domestic pets, cloning, prejudice against women, and road rage due to traffic congestion. Current information is cited from environmental journalists and other good writers. **Key terms** are placed in bold type and defined in the text as well as in a glossary near the back of the book.

Cases cited often center on particular individuals, because most people care more about individuals than about abstract ideas. One chapter contains a first-person account of a man running for his life to escape poison gas in Bhopal,

India. Another tells of a woman killing her newborn girl. Other stories record a zoo gorilla saving a man's life, successful surgery on a young girl made possible by medical experiments on animals, and the disappointment of a child when animal rights activists disrupt his first deer hunt. These personal stories are related to more general controversies, to abstract concepts employed in those controversies, and to ethical principles and theories.

Most textbooks introduce abstract ethical concepts and theories in the first chapter or two. Unfortunately, most students have insufficient context for the information to make sense, yet the books later refer to this material as if readers understood it, absorbed it, and can now apply it. This is like introducing people to a pile of engine parts, explaining in abstract terms what each part does, and then expecting folks weeks later to recognize the appropriate part and use it correctly to fix the engine.

The present text, by contrast, introduces abstract ideas, concepts, and arguments as needed to solve problems at hand. So philosophical material is spread throughout the book. This is like just-in-time delivery of parts in manufacturing. Chapter 1, for example, discusses psychological egoism and introduces the concept of human rights in the context of population pressures and the hunger of poor people around the world. Chapter 2 introduces contractarian support for human rights and explains cost-benefit analysis in a discussion that relates global warming to duties toward future generations. Chapter 5 explores more deeply the nature of rights and their relationship to hypothetical social contracts in connection with medical experimentation on animals. Chapter 4 discusses utilitarianism in connection with factory farming. Chapter 6 explains how metaphors support the preservation of species and ecosystems. Chapter 10 discusses hermeneutics, narratives, grand narratives, and worldviews to relate controversies regarding genetic engineering and cloning to different interpretations of Christianity. Chapter 5 introduces and uses the method of reflective equilibrium to discuss the justice of bullfights being illegal in a country where hunting and rodeos are legal.

Each concept, principle, and method aids the solution of some problems, so criticisms of concepts, principles, and methods indicate their limitations, not their elimination from further use. This makes the book incremental. Each chapter ends with "Judgment Calls," a series of issues and questions for further reflection. The incremental nature of the book enables readers to give increasingly sophisticated responses to these "Judgment Calls." Students obtain tools they can apply to new situations in life, not defeated theories they can forget after exams. Chapters 11 and 12 use these tools to weigh options in personal life and public policy.

Since this book covers the major twentieth-century thinkers and topics in environmental ethics, it is appropriate for courses on that subject. But its range extends much farther. It can be used with one or two other texts in general courses on contemporary moral problems because it discusses moral issues related to economics, business, government, and agriculture. The book's largest contribution, however, is likely to be outside of philosophy courses altogether.

Academics in many fields—business, government, environmental studies, architecture, city planning, women's studies, agriculture, religious studies, geography, biology, and more—find environmental ethics interesting and teach it to some extent in relation to their specialty. *Environmental Ethics Today* can aid all such courses because it gives an overview of environmental ethics with philosophical backbone, which complements the specialized expertise of academics in these fields.

Finally, of course, there is the general reader. If this book fulfills its promise, people who read for knowledge and fun will find it rewarding.

Acknowledgments

I would like to thank the University of Illinois at Springfield, especially the Center for Legal Studies and Institute for Public Affairs, and their respective directors Ernie Cowles and Nancy Ford, for years of support. I thank the University of Illinois also for support provided to me as a recently designated University Scholar.

I would like to thank the following people who read the manuscript in whole or in part. They are, in alphabetical order: Jose Arce, Harry Berman, Peter Boltuc, Meredith Cargill, Ed Cell, Albert Cinelli, Bernd Estabrook, Bob Fowler, Royce Jones, Bob Kunath, Richard Palmer, Marcia Salner, Larry Shiner, David Schmidtz, James Streib, Dan Van Kley, and Grace Wenz. Among these, as leaders among equals, I thank especially Ed Cell and Larry Shiner for their unswerving support over the many years we have taught together. Finally, I accept responsibility for any remaining deficiencies, but I would like to quote what Richard Nixon said about the Watergate scandal: "I accept the responsibility but not the blame." (What could that mean?)

Introduction

What Is Environmental Ethics?

I found this full-page ad by "America's Pharmaceutical Companies" in the September 7, 1998, issue of *Newsweek*:

CANCER.

IT'S A WAR.
THAT'S WHY WE'RE DEVELOPING
316 NEW WEAPONS.

America's pharmaceutical companies are developing 316 new medicines to fight cancer—the second leading cause of death in the United States. Gene therapies, "magic bullet" antibodies, and light-activated medicines are all new weapons in the high-tech, high-stakes war against cancer. Pharmaceutical company researchers have already discovered medicines that are allowing more and more cancer survivors to say, "I won the battle." We hope one day we can all say, "We won the war."[1]

Now there is progress for you, Progress (with a capital "P"). And that is not all. The American Geriatrics Society announces good news in the same issue:

The number of people aged 65 and older is larger than ever before. . . . The demographics tell the story. At the turn of the century, life expectancy was just 47 years. Today, the average American can expect to live to the age of 76, and the over-85 group is the fastest-growing segment of our population. . . . Medical breakthroughs are treating and delaying people's most fearful health problems; as we benefit from better diet and nutrition, more exercise, and reduced stress, we lessen chances of heart disease, osteoporosis, cancer, and other diseases.[2]

People not only live longer, their quality of life is improved. Electric lighting, for example, helps us to read at night, travel quickly in the dark in automobiles, and enjoy nighttime baseball and football. And now it is getting better, according to an ad in *The New York Times Book Review*. The Microsun Light Source claims to produce "light five times more efficiently than incandescent or halogen bulbs, with the vibrant quality of natural light, the light that people crave."[3] The same issue contains an ad for "Ordinary Couples, Extraordinary Sex—The Sex Education Videos that increase sexual pleasure for both partners."[4]

These ads illustrate our society's quest for improvement and our belief in progress. Scientists and engineers discover how nature works and manipulate it for human advantage. Their success is spectacular. Many dread infectious diseases, such as smallpox and polio, have been eliminated or greatly reduced, and average life spans have increased. Nutritious food is now abundant in industrial societies. Machines using the power of coal, oil, nuclear fission, and falling water relieve people of back-breaking labor on farms, in factories, and at home. We have new forms of communication and entertainment—radio, television, and computers. This is progress.

What does it have to do with **environmental ethics**? **Ethics** is *a reasoned account of how people should live their lives*. Environmental ethics exists because many people today question practices associated with progress. For example, the proliferation of synthetic chemicals in the environment appears to cause increases in cancer rates, cancer mortality, and diseases of the nervous system. Current agricultural practices in the United States, encouraged by world trade in food, may leave future generations of Americans unable to grow enough to feed themselves. Do we owe anything to these future people? What about poor people alive at this time? Worldwide, the human population continues to increase, while over 800 million people are already starving or malnourished. Can we, should we, help them? If so, how can we help them without degrading the environment? Many species of nonhuman animals are in danger of extinction due primarily to human activity. Do we have any obligations to nonhuman beings? These are among the questions that environmental ethics helps people answer.

I begin by considering the view that environmental ethics is unnecessary in the first place, because the normal course of progress takes care of all problems.

Environmental Ethics Under Attack

Economist Julian L. Simon has no need for environmental ethics because he believes that all is well. Progress continues. Rather than destroy the environment, progress actually improves it, Simon maintains. Big cities, such as London, were horribly polluted 100 years ago with the urine and feces of horses used in transportation. (No one ever steps in it in period romances.) Now the muck is gone because science and engineering harnessed the power of coal and oil for urban transportation.[5]

That solution created its own pollution problems. London fog became lethal smog that killed hundreds of people in the 1950s. Progress again solved the problem. Natural gas and electricity now heat homes, and electricity powers trains, replacing smog-producing coal. Pollution is declining further with tale-pipe emission controls on cars. Progress creates some problems as it solves others, but then it solves the problems it created, leaving humanity way ahead, according to Simon.

Simon cites a water pollution example in the U.S. Lake Washington near Seattle became severely polluted "soon after World War II when 10 newly built waste-treatment plants began dumping some 20 million gallons of treated effluents into its water every day. . . . The lake became cloudy and malodorous and the fish died."[6] The pollution problem resulted largely from technological success in aeronautics. Seattle's population was booming because Boeing Aircraft was thriving commercially, making planes that provide relatively safe, quick, and inexpensive air transportation. This is progress. But workers crowded into Seattle, and Lake Washington's pollution became a problem.

> Alarmed, the state legislature in 1958 created a new authority—the Municipality of Metropolitan Seattle—and charged it with sewage disposal for the Seattle area. With the support of local residents, Metro, as the agency soon became known, built a $121-million integrated system that funnels all of the area's effluents far out into Puget Sound. In that way, the wastes are dissipated by tidal action. . . . What Lake Washington demonstrates, of course, is that pollution is not irreversible—provided the citizenry is really determined to reclaim the environment, and willing to pay for past years of neglect.[7]

We can add to Simon's list of success stories. Lake Erie was dead, now it is alive. Buffalo were nearly extinct, now they are numerous. "In brief:" writes Simon, "Air and water are getting purer. And the public is being taken to the cleaners by such environmental groups as the National Wildlife Federation, which tell people just the opposite of the facts."[8]

My father, an engineer, also assumed that humanity would always be able to solve problems created by progress. He was a **technological optimist**. His favorite example concerned the building that housed his *alma mater*, Cooper Union, in New York City. Built in the 1840s, it was the first steel-frame structure in North America. When constructed, the technology to tear it down did not exist, but almost every building has to come down some time. Well, the problem of demolishing steel-frame buildings was solved long ago, and Cooper Union is still in use. The faith that scientists and engineers could solve the problem in time was justified.

But how do we know that the net effect of progress is positive? Where pollution is concerned, Julian Simon maintains that life expectancy is the best measure.

> How may we reasonably assess the trend of health-related pollution? It would seem reasonable to go directly to health itself to measure how we are doing. The simplest and most accurate measure of health is length of life, summed up as the average life expectancy. To buttress that general measure, which includes the effects of curative medicine as well as preventive (pollution-fighting) efforts, we may look at the trends in causes of death. . . . Nowadays, people die of the diseases of old age, which the environment does not force upon the individual—heart disease, cancer, and strokes.[9]

From Simon's perspective, then, new environmental ethics are unnecessary. Progress makes life longer and better.

Disturbing Trends in Human Health

A closer look reveals disturbing trends and alarming possibilities. We are not always able to solve problems in time. Consider cancer. *Overall cancer rates have been climbing for decades, and the trend continues.* Julian Simon wrote in 1981: "There seems to be no evidence that the increase in cancer is due to environmental carcinogens; rather, it is an inevitable consequence of people living to older, more cancer-prone ages."[10] He was wrong. Edward Goldsmith, co-editor of the journal *The Ecologist*, cites "official figures published by the National Cancer Institute (NCI). . . . According to these the age-standardized cancer incidence for all sites for the white population of the USA between 1950 and 1988 has increased by no less that 43.5 percent . . . and between 1950 and 1994, by 54 percent—and hence *by an average of 1 percent per annum.*"[11] The phrase "age-standardized" means that *none* of this increase is due to people living longer.

Dr. Samuel Epstein, professor of occupational and environmental medicine at the School of Public Health, University of Illinois Medical Center in Chicago, reports: "Increasing incidence rates have been accompanied by less sharply increasing mortality rates. From 1975 to 1984, overall age-standardized mortality rates increased by 5.5 percent. . . ."[12] In other words, *people are dying from cancer more than ever before, and none of this increase is due to people living longer.* However, the overall increase in cancer mortality is only about half the increase in cancer incidence because treatments for some cancers have improved. We are losing ground, but not as fast as we would be without sophisticated treatments for cancer.

This may surprise you. The media often report cancer cures, vitamins that may protect against cancer, and new treatments for vulnerable individuals. In 1984, for example, the NCI received good media coverage when it announced programs designed "to reduce the rate of cancer mortality to one half of the 1980 rate . . . by the year 2000." Soon, however, Epstein points out:

The NCI made the poorly publicized but startling admission that its objective of reducing cancer mortality was unrealistic. NCI now actually anticipates further *increases*, and not *decreases*, in cancer mortality rates. . . . This is a remarkable admission of the NCI's failure to even hold the line against increasing cancer mortality rates and the nation's second leading cause of death.[13]

But the media continue to emphasize the positive and ignore the negative. I do not know why. In many areas, their blare of sensational bad news drowns out the good. Not here, however. Consider this article entitled "Medical Progress: New Hope for Prevention, Treatment of Breast Cancer" in the "Harvard Health Letter" for August 1998. It begins:

Over the past few months, several unprecedented reports have indicated that breast cancer, the second leading cause of cancer death in women, can be delayed and possibly even prevented altogether by one of two drugs: tamoxifen or raloxifene. These synthetic compounds selectively block the action of the female hormone estrogen, which is thought to promote the growth of many breast tumors.

There is no hint in this statement that according to the NCI, our country's most authoritative source of information about cancer, past improvements in breast cancer treatment failed to kept pace with increases in breast cancer incidence.

In sum, *there are two disturbing trends regarding cancer. One is the increasing rate of cancer disease and death. The other is the public's misperception of the situation.*

❧   ❧   ❧

Why are overall, age-adjusted cancer rates increasing? *Industrial pollution and other aspects of industrial living seem to be major factors.* Cancer rates in pre-industrial societies were very low. Dr. Albert Schweitzer wrote in 1913: "On my arrival in Gabon, I was astonished to encounter no case of cancer."[14] *The Ecologist's* other co-editor, Zac Goldsmith, writes, "In 1915, the Prudential Insurance Company of America published an 846-page report on cancer, entitled, *The Mortality from Cancer Throughout the World*. Its author was Frederick L. Hoffman, chairman of the committee on statistics of the American Society for the Control of Cancer."[15] He concluded: "the rarity of cancer among native man suggests that the disease is primarily induced by the conditions and methods of living which typify our modern civilization."[16]

The increasing presence of artificial chemicals in the environment is a major factor. Dr. Epstein notes, for example, that American farmers have been exposed in recent decades to increasing amounts of pesticide. They used 50 million pounds a year in the 1940s, 600 million pounds in the 1970s, and over a billion pounds per year in the 1990s. Increasingly, during this period:

Farmers have experienced high rates of several cancers, including leukemia, non-Hodgkin's lymphoma and cancers of the brain and prostate. Animal and epidemiological studies have linked several of these cancers with exposure to pesticides or solvents.[17]

Farmers are not the only ones at risk from these chemicals. Epstein writes:

> Some 53 carcinogenic pesticides are registered for use on major crops, such as ap-
> ples, tomatoes and potatoes. Consumption of common foods with residues of 28
> of these pesticides have (sic) been associated with some 20,000 excess annual can-
> cer deaths. Some 34 pesticides are commonly used for professional lawn care treat-
> ment at rates up to five times greater than that used agriculturally. . . . Recent stud-
> ies have . . . demonstrated major excesses of lymphomas in dogs living in homes
> whose gardens receive regular lawn care treatment. . . . [18]

Children may be especially at risk, Epstein reports. "Some 20 US and international studies have incriminated parental exposure to occupational carcinogens
as major causes of childhood cancers, whose incidence has increased by 21 percent since 1950."[19] In sum, exposure to industrial chemicals seems to increase
the risk of death from cancer.

The health effects of industrial pollution may constitute problems that cannot be overcome by more of what we normally consider progress. Julian Simon is correct that in many ways the gains of progress outweigh losses. But
the losses are more than he acknowledges, and the disturbing trend in cancer
suggests that in the future losses may outpace gains if progress requires the
production of more artificial chemicals. We may do better with less progress,
or an entirely different kind of progress. *Environmental ethics investigates different conceptions of progress.*

Conceiving of the future with fewer artificial chemicals challenges our entire way of life, because artificial chemicals are integral to how we live. We use
them to make artificial fibers for our clothing; nitrogen fertilizers, herbicides,
and insecticides for agriculture; paints and varnishes; household cleaners and
sprays; carpets and upholstery to furnish homes and offices; and, just to cut
this list short, plastics for everything from Tupperware containers to medical
devices to automobile bodies (such as my Saturn's).

This may be why the NCI investigates cures instead of environmental causes
of cancer. They may consider it beyond their province to question our entire
way of life.

Botanist Sandra Steingraber, however, suggests a broader mandate for those
fighting cancer. She titled her book about causes of cancer *Living Downstream*
because the situation reminded her of "a fable about a village along a river."

> The residents who live here, according to parable, began noticing increasing num-
> bers of drowning people caught in the river's swift current and so went to work
> inventing ever more elaborate technologies to resuscitate them. So preoccupied
> were these heroic villagers with rescue and treatment that they never thought to
> look upstream to see who was pushing the victims in.[20]

The same concerns are raised by other health problems that industrial society
creates. Writing in *The Ecologist*, researcher Mark Purdey notes:

Degenerative nervous diseases are on the increase throughout the West. . . . There is considerable evidence that exposure to synthetic chemicals including solvents, organophosphates and pyridine compounds plays a role in the growing incidence of . . . Parkinson's disease, Multiple Sclerosis, Motor Neuron Disease (MND) and Myalgic Encephalomelitis (ME).[21]

Environmental researcher Jennifer Mitchell reports some of this evidence in the journal *WorldWatch*. "Worldwide, an average of two to three new synthetic chemicals—their effects largely unknown—are released into the environment every day. . . . Today, there are roughly 70,000 different synthetic chemicals on the global market, and many others are emitted as by-products of their production or incineration."[22] Some turn out to be toxic. Among these are polychlorinated biphenyls (PCBs).

Created in 1929, they were intended only for use in electrical wiring, lubricants, and liquid seals. But old buildings are demolished and old machines are junked, and the residues that remain in them—some proving to be dangerously toxic—often leach into ground water. Today, these PCBs—along with more than 250 other synthetic chemicals—can be found in the body of almost anyone who lives in the developed world. Furthermore, since a mother will pass some contaminants on to the developing fetus during pregnancy, even an unborn child is at risk. . . . [23]

It seems likely that "PCBs, DDT, and at least 50 other chemicals now at large in the environment may be harmful to reproduction and development—both

Reprinted by permission of John Branch

in wildlife and in people." They probably interfere "with the endocrine system which regulates growth and development as well as behavior and brain function."[24]

Here is evidence that children can be affected by their mothers' *lifetime* exposure, not just by exposure during pregnancy:

> A study by Sandra and Joseph Jacobson, psychologists at Wayne State University in Detroit, examined 242 children whose mothers had regularly consumed fish (two to three times a month or more for at least six years) from Lake Michigan— fish known to be contaminated with PCBs, mercury, organochlorines, and other pollutants. The more fish the mothers had consumed during their lives, the higher were the PCB levels in the babies' blood—and the smaller the babies' size at birth. . . . At age four, when compared to children whose mothers did not consume any fish from Lake Michigan, these children showed less cooperative behavior and poorer memories.[25]

At age 11, they had lower IQs and "exhibited deficits in both short-term and long-term memory, and difficulty in focusing or sustaining attention."[26]

Such health issues are largely ignored because new synthetic chemicals are essential to our society's view of progress, and because the chemical industry is powerful. It is dominated by large corporations whose campaign contributions influence legislation. Chemical company advertisements influence public opinion, and news organizations that depend on advertising revenue are reluctant to offend a major source of funds. Environmental researcher Ann Misch's findings are, therefore, not surprising. She reports in the magazine *WorldWatch* that "the U.S. Environmental Protection Agency (EPA) does not require that industrial chemical manufacturers run specific tests to determine any adverse effects of their products before putting them on the market. Most chemicals . . . are innocent until proven guilty."[27] The agricultural chemical atrazine, for example, has long been suspected of causing cancer, but the case against it is not yet strong enough to authorize a ban. Living in agricultural central Illinois, I receive my recommended daily allowance of atrazine every day as I drink the local water.[28]

Worse yet, proof of guilt is very difficult. Health problems can take many years to develop and, as we have seen, may appear only in the next generation. Furthermore, a chemical that is harmless by itself may be toxic in the presence of even trace amounts of other synthetic chemicals that are also harmless by themselves. These are synergistic effects that appear only when chemicals are tested in combination with one another. But such tests are impractical. Dr. Vyvyan Howard, a developmental toxico-pathologist at the University of Liverpool, points out in *The Ecologist*: "to test just the commonest 1,000 toxic chemicals in combinations of three (at a standardized dosage) would require at least 166 million different experiments."[29] The average person's body, however, contains not three, but 250 chemicals that did not exist 50 years ago.

In sum, progress has produced longer average life spans, but by-products of industry threaten these gains. Attempts to solve industrially created health problems with

*ever more surgery, chemicals, radiation, and other techniques common to modern med-
icine are only partly successful. Protecting our health may require reconsidering ideas
of progress and human fulfillment. This is a task of environmental ethics.*

Future Generations

People have long worried about health in modern industrial society, but not
about future generations. This may be tied to modern faith in progress. Assuming that science and technology make life better for people, future generations will benefit from progress now underway. On this assumption, we do
not have to worry about harming future generations because our progress helps
them.

Consider food production from this technological optimist perspective. During most of the twentieth century, yields per acre of farmland have increased
dramatically due to increased irrigation, and development of new crop varieties, synthetic nitrogen fertilizers, and powerful pesticides that reduce threats
from bugs, weeds, and fungi. Fewer and fewer people are now required in agriculture because technological progress has made it possible for one farmer to
feed more than 50 other people in the United States.

One measure of success is the cost of food, which has declined, leaving people with more money to spend on other consumer items. At the same time, the
variety of food produced domestically has improved, and world food trade
provides increasing variety in all seasons from around the globe. Other industrialized countries experience the same trends. So food prospects for future
generations seem excellent.

Unfortunately, this rosy picture is mistaken. The trend during the twentieth
century was toward more good food at lower prices produced by fewer people. But there are reasons to believe that this trend cannot continue. One reason is a shortage of fresh water, according to researcher Gary Gardner, writing in the journal *WorldWatch*. Much grain production in the United States, for
example, occurs in the High Plains between Texas and South Dakota. Yields
have increased in this area due largely to irrigation from the underlying Ogallala **aquifer**. This is an enormous underground reservoir 150 to 300 feet thick,
containing enough water "to cover all 50 states with a foot and a half of water."[30] However, writes Gardner, it is being pumped dry:

> Water level declines of more than ten feet have occurred in 29 percent of the Ogal-
> lala area, and declines of more than 50 feet are reported in about 7 percent of the
> region. . . . The first warnings were in evidence by 1980, when it was found that
> the state of Kansas had consumed 38 percent of its share of the Ogallala, and Texas
> had exhausted more than 20 percent of its share. . . . By the year 2040, the aquifer's
> volume is expected to fall by more than a fifth under the northern Texas High
> Plains, and by nearly half under the southern part—even assuming the use of strict
> conservation measures. In the southern section, irrigated cropland was cut by 2 to
> 4 percent per year between the mid-1970s and 1984, and the decline has continued
> since then.[31]

According to philosopher Charles V. Blatz, the Ogallala aquifer "is expected to serve us for only another forty years."[32] In short, *we may be jeopardizing the food security of future generations of Americans by exhausting reserves of fresh water needed to produce grain in our nation's breadbasket.* Food security is jeopardized further by the loss of prime farmland. Much land is degraded by soil erosion. Irrigation makes some parcels too salty for agriculture and waterlogs others, while suburban sprawl puts thousands of acres per year under asphalt and concrete.[33]

It may seem unrealistic that our society could undermine its ability to grow food. However, many civilizations before our own have flourished and then failed due to food insufficiency caused by ruined soils or insufficient water. North Africa, where Algeria is today, was once the breadbasket of the Roman Empire. Now it is mostly desert. Israelis and Palestinians currently dispute an area that the Bible describes as the land of milk and honey. News reports of the conflict show a bleak landscape.

Author Daniel Quinn, in his award-winning novel *Ishmael*, compares a society with unsustainable practices to a would-be airman with a pedal-powered contraption he thinks will fly.

> As the flight begins, all is well. Our would-be airman has been pushed off the edge of the cliff and is pedaling away, feeling wonderful, ecstatic. He's experiencing the freedom of the air. What he doesn't realize, however, is that this craft is aerodynamically incapable of flight, . . . but he would laugh if you told him this. . . . Nevertheless, whatever he thinks, he's not in flight. . . . He's in free fall. . . . In fact, the earth seems to be rising up toward him. Well, he's not very worried about that. After all, his flight has been a complete success up to now, and there's no reason why it shouldn't go on being a success. He just has to pedal a little harder, that's all.[34]

Current development of new seeds, pesticides, and fertilizers, not to mention deeper water wells, may be just "pedaling harder."

World Trade

Sandra Postel, director of the Water Quality Policy Project in Amherst, Massachusetts, notes that the water situation is similar in India. "In India's Punjab, for example, where a highly productive rice-wheat cropping pattern has turned the region into the nation's breadbasket, water tables are falling 20 centimeters annually over two thirds of the state."[35]

People may think that a water shortage in India, Libya, or South Africa will have little impact on food availability in the United States. Current trends in world trade suggest otherwise. Increased demand for food anywhere in the world can raise food prices and reduce availability here if people around the world are free to buy American food. Yet increased world trade is widely considered necessary for progress. It enables people in different parts of the world to specialize in whatever they can produce most efficiently. This product can then be traded for whatever is produced most efficiently elsewhere in the world. When all production is thus made efficient, there are more goods and services for people to enjoy. This is progress.

However, one of the specialties of the United States is food. If we are producing it inexpensively at the moment by running down our long-term supplies of fresh water and arable land, our current participation in world trade may be jeopardizing the welfare of future generations. *Two topics in environmental ethics are the wisdom of increased world trade in such items as food and our obligations to future generations.*

Population Growth and Obligations to the World's Poor

Worldwide, the prospects for fresh water are alarming due partly to population growth. In much of the world the climate is too dry for irrigation-free agriculture, so irrigation supplies about 40 percent of the water used to grow crops. But, Sandra Postel writes:

> If 40 percent of the water required to produce an acceptable diet for the 2.4 billion people expected to be added to the planet over the next 30 years has to come from irrigation, agricultural water supplies would have to expand by more than [the] equivalent to roughly 20 Nile Rivers, or to 97 Colorado Rivers. . . . It is not at all clear where that water could come from on a sustainable basis. Over the last five years . . . [the world's] per capita irrigated area . . . has continued to decline, having fallen 7 percent from its 1979 peak as population growth outpaced the spread of irrigation. As much as . . . nearly 1 percent of world irrigated area . . . comes out of production each year because of waterlogging and salinization of soils.[36]

Most of the increase in human population is expected in the Third World, where many people are too poor to pay market price for food grown here. So they will not deprive us of food through world trade. Does this mean we should ignore their plight, or should we help them? Eight-hundred-million people are currently malnourished.[37] Are they our brothers, and are we our brothers' keepers? If so, what kind of help should we offer? Should we give them food; assist economic development so they can buy food on the world market; and/or push for zero population growth? *These, too, are issues in environmental ethics, because our reaction to nutritional needs in an expanding human population affects the total impact of human beings on the environment.*

Obligations to Nonhumans

So far we have included only considerations of human welfare: our own health, the welfare of future generations in our country, and the needs of poor people around the world. These are called **anthropocentric** concerns because they are centered on human beings. The term comes from the ancient Greek "anthropos" which means human being. *"Anthropocentric" means "centered on human beings." Anthropocentrists adopt a perspective that includes only anthropocentric concerns.*

But human beings are only one species among an estimated 4 to 40 million species on planet earth. Our activities, especially those of industrialized people, seem to be pushing many other species to extinction, mostly through pollution, habitat destruction, and/or direct exploitation, such as hunting and fishing. John Tuxill and Chris Bright report in *State of the World 1998*:

> Like the dinosaurs 65 million years ago, humanity now finds itself in the midst of a mass extinction: a global evolutionary convulsion with few parallels in the entire history of life. . . . Examination of the fossil record of marine invertebrates suggests that the natural or "background" rate of extinctions—the rate that has prevailed over millions of years of evolutionary time—claims something on the order of one to three species per year. In stark contrast, most estimates of the current situation are that at least 1,000 species are lost a year—an extinction rate 1,000 times the background rate even with most conservative assumptions.[38]

The extinction rate of vertebrates, who are closer relatives in the genealogy of evolution than invertebrates, is also alarming. "About 25 percent of all mammal species are treading a path that, if followed unchecked, is likely to end in their disappearance from Earth,"[39] write Tuxill and Bright.

> While the drastic population crashes of great whales, elephants, and rhinos are well known, the long shadow of overexploitation actually reaches much further. For instance, only the most remote or best-protected forests throughout Latin America have avoided significant loss of tapirs, white-lipped peccaries, jaguars, wooly and spider monkeys, and other large mammals that face heavy hunting pressure from rural residents. . . . The real problem [for these species in recent years] occurs when hunting is done to supply markets rather than just for home consumption.[40]

The situation is similar for reptiles, amphibians, fish, and birds. For example, "one third of all fish species are already threatened with extinction,"[41] and "estimates are that at least two out of every three bird species are in decline worldwide, although only about 11 percent of all birds are already officially threatened with extinction."[42]

Concern about the extinction of nonhuman species is anthropocentric when it stems from worry that such extinctions diminish the quality or threaten the continuation of human life. Such anthropocentric concerns are justified. Miners used to take canaries with them underground because canaries were more sensitive than people to atmospheric pollution. When the canary died, miners knew the air was bad and they should leave. Analogously, the disappearance of many vulnerable species may signal that we are making the earth inhospitable to life as we know it. Because leaving is not practical, we may need to change our ways to safeguard the lives of ourselves and our progeny.

One issue raised in environmental ethics is whether these anthropocentric considerations should be supplemented by **nonanthropocentric** reasons. *"Nonanthropocentric" means "not centered on human beings." In this context it means concern for nonhuman lives and life forms for their sake rather than for our own.* Aldo Leopold, who helped found the science of ecology in the first half of the twentieth century, endorsed nonanthropocentric concern for species endangered or driven to extinction by human activities. One such species was the passenger pigeon, which thrived in the American Midwest until late in the nineteenth century. In 1947, more than 20 years after the last passenger pigeon died in the Cincinnati Zoo, a monument was erected to the pigeon in Wisconsin. Regarding that monument Leopold wrote:

> We have erected a monument to commemorate the funeral of a species. It symbolizes our sorrow. . . . It is a century now since Darwin gave us the first glimpse of the origin of species. We know now what was unknown to all the preceding caravan of generations: that men are only fellow-voyagers with other creatures in the odyssey of evolution. This new knowledge should have given us, by this time, a sense of kinship with fellow-creatures; a wish to live and let live; a sense of wonder over the magnitude and duration of the biotic enterprise.
>
> For one species to mourn the death of another is a new thing under the sun. The Cro-Magnon who slew the last mammoth thought only of steaks. . . . But we, who have lost our pigeons, mourn the loss. Had the funeral been ours, the pigeons would hardly have mourned us. In this fact, rather than in Mr. Du Pont's nylons . . . , lies objective evidence of our superiority over the beasts.[43]

A major topic in environmental ethics is whether or how such nonanthropocentric concern can be justified.

Preview of Chapters

As you can see, environmental ethics addresses many different issues and considers many different perspectives. This book offers a sample for beginners. Two perspectives have been introduced already—anthropocentric and nonanthropocentric. According to the anthropocentric perspective, only human beings are important in themselves. Other species and the physical environment are important only when they affect human well being. Most anthropocentrists aspire to manage resources for the general benefit of humanity.

The first part of this book examines anthropocentric environmentalism. The issues discussed include global warming, toxic wastes, overpopulation, and prostitution. Chapters 1 and 2 look at issues largely from an economic perspective, featuring market activity and cost-benefit analyses. This approach, **economic anthropocentrism**, fails to give enough weight to human rights and future generations. Chapter 3 retains the focus on human welfare exclusively, but maintains that many anthropocentric considerations cannot be captured adequately in economic calculations. These include values associated with aesthetics, the family, and our national heritage. This view is **non-economic anthropocentrism**. It fails to explain, however, why it is wrong to be cruel to animals.

The second part of the book considers nonanthropocentric perspectives. Nonanthropocentrists believe that human beings are important, but insist that other beings have independent value that people should respect. Some nonanthropocentrists focus on the treatment of individual domesticated (nonhuman) animals. This raises issues about wearing fur, eating meat, and using animals in medical experiments. I consider versions of utilitarianism and rights-based theories in this context in Chapters 4 and 5. These views are limited by their exclusive attention to individuals. They fail to account for the need to allow some animals to kill others in order that ecosystems function well.

Other nonanthropocentrists stress the importance of what they call **holistic entities**, *such as species, ecosystems, and life on Earth as a whole. Holists consider some wholes to be not only greater than the sum of their parts, but more important as well.* I discuss in Chapters 6 and 7 James Lovelock's Gaia hypothesis and Aldo Leopold's Land Ethic, as well as the nature and importance of metaphors and intrinsic values. I fault some interpretations of these views for sharing with many anthropocentrists the idea that promoting the good of nonhumans requires sacrificing overall, long-term human good.

In the book's third part I reject the idea of competition between human and nonhuman flourishing and adopt a third perspective, which I call "environmental synergism." In general, synergy exists when two or more "things" acting together produce results greater than the sum of the results of each acting separately. Basketball teams illustrate this. Some teams have great players who do not play as a team, so the team loses. Other teams with less talent play better due to better teamwork. This is synergy.

The two "things" involved in **synergistic environmental ethics** are respect for human beings and respect for nonhuman nature. Environmental synergists believe that overall, and in the long run, outcomes for both people and nature are better when both people and nature are considered valuable *in themselves*. As we will see in Chapter 9, valuing all human beings can promote pollution abatement and species preservation. Chapters 8 and 9 show that valuing nature tends to improve overall human welfare, so there is no *fundamental* conflict between human beings as a group and the rest of nature. The best life for human beings as a group preserves many individual and holistic nonhuman entities.

In may seem strange that valuing nature for itself can help human beings, but family life illustrates this aspect of synergism. Imagine people who have children for self-fulfillment. If they remain fixated on their own fulfillment, they will probably find parenthood unfulfilling, because good parents must often defer gratification to meet children's needs. Parents may need to wake up in the middle of the night to feed an infant, and play catch with a five-year-old instead of watching football. When self-centered parents fixated on their own fulfillment fail to alter their conception of fulfillment, they often meet children's needs poorly or grudgingly. The children often become whiney, loud, clinging, ill, and/or disobedient, making their parents' lives difficult.

Now imagine people who want children for self-fulfillment, but whose attention is diverted immediately from themselves to the children. They love and identify with their children, altering their values and their conception of the good life. Due to these changes, they find it easier than self-centered parents to wake up in the middle of the night to feed an infant. They value playing catch with a five-year-old instead of watching football. Their new values reduce, without eliminating, tensions between their needs and the children's. Children benefit from this, and usually thrive. These people get more from parenthood than those whose values make parenthood a heavy burden. Overall, for these people, in spite of the remaining tensions, life with children and transformed values is better than either life without children or life with children and their old, self-centered values.

Anthropocentrists and nonanthropocentrists who do not identify their own good with that of nature are like parents who fail to acquire a child-oriented conception of fulfillment. The resulting tension between human beings and nature detracts from the quality people perceive in their lives and/or from the well being of nonhuman nature.

Synergists, by contrast, are like parents who do identify with their children. Like nonanthropocentrists, they value (many aspects of) nonhuman nature for itself. But then they go farther. Just as good parents alter their ideas about self-fulfillment, synergists alter their ideas about human nature and about what constitutes a fulfilling human life. This reduces tension between human fulfillment and the well being of nature. While some tension remains, human life is better overall with these new values than with either anthropocentric or nonanthropocentric perspectives. I consider Deep Ecology, ecofeminism, biblically based ethics, the worldviews of some indigenous peoples, and (in a new light) the Land Ethic as synergistic environmental philosophies.

Part 4 of this book considers practical matters, addressing issues of personal character and life style, as well as public policy. Should I buy a sport utility vehicle? Should I become a vegetarian? Should the military buy organic food for soldiers? Should the government improve public transportation and/or fund political campaigns?

Throughout the book, proposals are evaluated partly by common sense and partly by philosophical principles introduced as needed. I explain these along the way and relate them to common sense. No prior knowledge of them is needed.

The book retains a plurality of perspectives. I introduce many views and endorse most of them because they have merit. They are proper ways to look at some things at some times. But they are limited. No one view provides an adequate perspective on all issues for all time. I criticize proponents of many views for applying them too broadly. It is like the fable of the blind people of

Hindustan. Several blind people were asked to describe an elephant. One touched a leg and said that an elephant is like the trunk of a tree. Another, who was beneath the elephant and felt the underside of the belly, said an elephant is like a big tent. A third touched the elephant's trunk and said an elephant is like a thick snake. Each was correct to a certain extent, but each was wrong to think that what she knew and experienced was a complete account.

This book does not offer a complete account, such as a final theory of environmental ethics. Instead, it introduces many concepts, values, perspectives, and considerations that can aid reflection. Each is good in its place, so the book is incremental. Readers become familiar with an increasing number of good ideas that can serve as tools for clear thinking. Judgment is required to determine which idea is most helpful in any given situation. This book is intended to help readers exercise good judgment. It provides intellectual training for people who want to straighten out or strengthen their thoughts on a variety of issues, from personal matters to public policies.

PART I

ANTHROPOCENTRISM

CHAPTER 1

Overpopulation, Markets, and Human Rights

Overpopulation and Scarcity

I received a letter in September 1998 from Paul Ehrlich, honorary president of "Zero Population Growth." "Dear Friend:" (He may have forgotten my name.)

Imagine your life a few short years from now. . . .

You're living in a world where fuel, food, jobs, housing, and health care are at a premium . . . where natural resources are severely depleted and cities horribly polluted, uncomfortably crowded, and plagued by crime.

Right now, we're heading on a collision course toward a population crisis that could deepen this nightmare—not only in the developing countries of Africa and Latin America, but right here in the United States.

With more than a 1% annual growth rate, the United States is still adding well over 2.5 million people yearly—making us the world's third-most populous nation.

ANY large population increase here puts a serious strain on our nation's reservoirs, sewers, roads, bridges, health facilities, and schools.

Increased congestion takes its toll everywhere, from urban gridlock to closed national parks to contaminated water.

While Ehrlich concentrates on the United States, journalist Gregg Easterbrook focuses on the Third World. The chapter on population in *A Moment on Earth* begins:

Once I took a walk through a poor neighborhood in New Delhi. . . . I'll skip the parts about the naked preschool children running through filth. I'll skip the parts about the aged beggars, meaning age 30 or more since a poor Indian of age 30 may appear by Western standards to be 65. I'll skip the parts about everyone grabbing my clothes and blocking my path to ask for rupees. I'll skip the parts about the human and animal feces on the curb, the cooking over open garbage fires, the children younger than ten employed in manual labor, the disease—I'll skip all that.[1]

He may have "skipped all that" to protect New Delhi tourism. I don't know. But he made his point. Like Ehrlich, Easterbrook recognizes a relationship between increases in human population and deteriorating environmental conditions and human standards of living. The issue is scarcity. In general, as populations increase each individual must share environmental amenities and resources with more people. At some point the environment may become horribly polluted and/or provide insufficient resources for everyone. Overpopulation is an environmental concern.

Because scarcity is involved, overpopulation is also an economic concern. Environmental economist Clement A. Tisdell writes: "The basic [economic] problem is considered to be how to manage or administer resources so as to minimize scarcity, that is, the 'gap' between individuals' demand for commodities and the available supply of them."[2] William F. Baxter, Professor of Law at Stanford University, broadens the concern about scarcity from economics to human life in general. He writes in his 1974 book *People or Penguins: The Case for Optimal Pollution*:

> The dominant feature of human existence is scarcity—our available resources, our aggregate labors, and our skill in employing both have always been, and will continue for some time to be, inadequate to yield to every man all the tangible and intangible satisfactions he would like to have.

Baxter concludes from this: "Waste is a bad thing. . . . None of those resources, or labors, or skills, should be wasted—that is, employed so as to yield less than they might yield in human satisfactions."[3]

Two ideas come together here. One is *anthropocentrism, the view that only human beings are important.* Baxter expresses this view explicitly. He notes:

> Recently scientists have informed us that the use of DDT in food production is causing damage to the penguin population. . . . My criteria are oriented to people, not penguins. Damage to penguins, or sugar pines, or geological marvels is, without more [of a relationship to human well being], simply irrelevant. One must go further, by my criteria, and say: Penguins are important because people enjoy seeing them walk about rocks. . . .
>
> It may be said by way of objection to this position, that it is very selfish of people to act as if each person represented one unit of importance and nothing else was of any importance. It is undeniably selfish. Nevertheless, I think . . . no other position corresponds to the way most people really think and act—i.e., corresponds to reality.[4]

I postpone until Part II any criticism of Baxter's anthropocentrism.

A second idea emerges from Tisdell's and Baxter's emphasis on scarcity and the environmentalist view that scarcity worsens as human populations increase. That idea is *efficiency. Scarcity calls for efficiency, because the efficient use of scarce resources allows for more human satisfactions than a wasteful use. So anthropocentrists, who favor maximum human satisfaction, value efficiency.*

But how can we promote efficiency? *In our society, many people think that free markets are the best means of maximizing efficiency.* In this chapter I explore the possibilities for handling environmental problems through market transactions. *I call the anthropocentric view that free markets (and simulated markets) can serve all genuine environmental values economic anthropocentrism.* This is the view discussed in the present chapter and the one to follow. In Chapter 3, I discuss an alternative anthropocentric view called *non-economic* anthropocentrism.

What Are Free Markets?

Free Markets are *rule-governed institutions for the exchange of goods and services, in which consumer demand significantly influences the nature, quantity, and price of what is produced.* Industrial societies like ours use money as the primary medium of exchange, so consumer demand is reflected in people's willingness to spend money.

Governments make the rules that create, sustain, and regulate free markets as we know them. They establish a common currency as legal tender. They create property in intellectual accomplishments through copyright and patent laws. Other laws permit the creation of corporations as perpetual persons with limited liability. Governments regulate investments in corporations with laws on the exchange of securities. Contract law allows private parties to make agreements that have the force of law, while government courts and sheriffs enable contract disputes to be officially settled and enforced. Laws forbid the sale of some items (sex and certain drugs) and limit buyers of others (no cigarettes or alcohol for minors, certain drugs require prescriptions, and so forth).

Because government involvement is integral to the free market as we know it, we can address many environmental problems through alteration of market rules. Such governmental activism is considered illegitimate encroachment on the free market only by those who do not recognize that governments make the rules that create, sustain, and regulate free markets in the first place. So long as consumer demand significantly influences the nature, quantity, and price of products, we have a free market.

Consider labor law, for example. Before the Wagner Act in the 1930s, employers in the United States could fire employees for attempting to form, or for being members of, trade unions. There was a free market in labor at that time, but the rules made it difficult for workers to unionize. This favored employers' attempts to keep down labor costs. With the Wagner Act, employees gained the legal rights to organize and belong to unions without employer retaliation. This changes the labor market because now workers can more effectively press for higher wages. But there is still a free market in labor, because consumer demand still significantly influences the price of labor.

Cornucopian Economics

Julian Simon is so enthusiastic about the potential for market activity to catalyze human ingenuity that he does not worry about human overpopulation resulting in scarcity. Human ingenuity is "The Ultimate Resource" (the title of Simon's book) that keeps scarcity at bay, and markets enlist human ingenuity in this cause.

Simon uses copper as an example. Imagine technologically unsophisticated people who use copper for cooking pots. The supply of copper that they have been using starts to run out. They can no longer get enough of what they want from the traditional source using traditional methods. So what do they do? Simon suggests the following:

> Perhaps they will invent better ways of obtaining copper from a given lode, say a better digging tool, or they may develop new materials to substitute for copper, perhaps iron.
>
> The cause of these new discoveries, or the cause of applying ideas that were discovered earlier, is the "shortage" of copper—that is, the increased cost of getting copper. So a "shortage" of copper causes the creation of its own remedy. This has been the key process in the supply and use of natural resources throughout history.
>
> This sequence of events explains how it can be that people have been using cooking pots for thousands of years, as well as using copper for many other purposes, and yet the cost of a pot today is vastly cheaper by any measure than it was 100 or 1,000 or 10,000 years ago.[5]

This kind of example supports one of Simon's major theses.

> Our supplies of natural resources are not finite in any economic sense. Nor does past experience give reason to expect natural resources to become more scarce. Rather, if the past is any guide, natural resources will progressively become less scarce, and less costly, and will constitute a smaller proportion of our expenses in future years. And population growth is likely to have a long-run *beneficial* impact on the natural-resource situation.[6]

Simon's view that there are no inherent limits to the human use of natural resources is called **cornucopian**, *after the legendary horn of Amalthaea, an emblem of abundance.* Although Simon does not explicitly discuss the role of markets in the process of human ingenuity creating abundance out of scarcity, he depends upon markets implicitly. Markets are needed in modern society to translate the scarcity of goods into higher prices for the people who wish to use those goods. These higher prices, according to Simon, catalyze innovations that ultimately reduce scarcity.

The Tragedy of the Commons

Garrett Hardin is the opposite of a cornucopian. He worries that overpopulation will get out of control and ruin humanity. He is called a **Malthusian** after the English cleric *Thomas Malthus, who predicted in 1798 that human popula-*

*tions, like those of many species, tend to grow too large, resulting in scarcity and, fi-
nally, widespread starvation.*

Although they have opposite views on the prospects for general affluence as
human populations increase, Simon and Hardin both believe that markets are
important. Hardin's worst fear is that markets will not be used to address problems of scarcity. The result, he predicts, is tragic. He calls it The Tragedy of the
Commons.

> The tragedy of the commons develops in this way. Picture a pasture open to all.
> It is to be expected that each herdsman will try to keep as many cattle as possible
> on the commons . . . [because] as a rational being each herdsman seeks to maxi-
> mize his gain. Explicitly or implicitly, more or less consciously, he asks, "What is
> the utility *to me* of adding one more animal to my herd?"[7]

Selfish logic convinces him to add that animal, Hardin reasons. Because all of
the other animals on the commons must share food resources with the new arrival, each has less to eat. This negatively affects all the animals equally and,
therefore, all the herdsmen. But the herdsman who puts the extra animal on
the commons gains as well as loses. He "receives all the proceeds from the sale
of the additional animal. . . ."[8] Whereas he shares the loss with everyone else,
he does not share the gain. He keeps the gain all to himself, and this leaves
him richer than he was before. Hardin continues:

> The rational herdsman concludes that the only sensible course for him to pursue
> is to add another animal to his herd. And another; and another. . . . But this is the
> conclusion reached by each and every rational herdsman sharing a commons.
> Therein is the tragedy. Each man is locked into a system that compels him to in-
> crease his herd without limit—in a world that is limited. Ruin is the destination
> toward which all men rush. . . .[9]

Too many cattle on the commons ruins the ability of the commons to support
any cattle at all, because overgrazing kills the grass. Hardin concludes: "Freedom in a commons brings ruin to all."[10]

How can this tragedy be avoided? Hardin writes, "The tragedy of the commons . . . is averted by private property, or something formally like it."[11] In
other words, privatize the commons. Suppose there are ten herdsmen using
the commons. Divide the commons into ten parcels with equal capacity to support cattle grazing and give one parcel to each herdsman. The herdsmen are
no worse off than they were before. Instead of having a one-tenth share of the
entire commons each has a full share of one-tenth of what used to be the commons. Now self-interest motivates people to protect the pasture.

The essence of private property is the ability to exclude others. My house is my
private property, so (except for police with valid search warrants) I can determine who is allowed to enter. The public park, by contrast, is not my private
property. It is a commons for everyone, so I cannot exclude people from entering and enjoying it.

The ability to exclude others that comes with **privatization** *of the commons motivates market activity that preserves environmental resources.* When people trade goods and services in markets they usually gain access to things they want or need, and would not have without the trade. They would not have these things without the trade because the things are held as someone else's private property. Those who buy copper, for example, want or need it and would not have it without the trade, because someone else owns it and demands payment for its use. The other party to the transaction has copper but wants or needs money, which she gets by selling her copper. She cannot get money from the other person without giving up the copper because the other person owns the money and will exclude her from its use unless she gives the copper in exchange.

In sum, people can use their private property to get what they want through market exchanges with others who also have private property. They cannot do this with public property, which is held as a commons. So people have selfish motivations to protect their private property in order to enjoy the privileges of using it and excluding others, or in order to exchange such privileges for other things. If a herdsman wants to put extra cattle on his private land and ruin it, he may do so. But I will not let him put extra cattle on mine. I thereby preserve my part of the pasture. Most others will act like me to protect their productive assets. Thus, self-interest leads to protection of the pasture when it is privatized. Privatization can protect environmental resources. Anthropocentrists favor using such protected resources for exclusively human welfare.

Public Goods, Externalities, and Government Coercion

It may seem that some environmental resources cannot be protected in this way, because they are **public goods**. *Public goods are goods whose benefits cannot be limited to a single owner. If anyone benefits, many others benefit as well.* National defense is the classic case. If the military protects anyone in a country from foreign invasion, it protects everyone else as well. National defense cannot be privatized as the pasture was. The essential attribute of private property, the ability to exclude others, is missing.

It seems that many environmental goods are like this. Clean air and, to a large extent, good water are public goods. For example, I cannot preserve the part of the Ogallala aquifer that lies beneath my farm by refusing to allow additional water wells on my farm. Water flows underground, so water that I refuse to pump, or allow to be pumped, on my land can be pumped by others from their land. Because I cannot exclude these others from use of the water, it is a public good rather than my private property, and if I want my share before others use it up, I have to take it right away. This reasoning leads to wasteful uses of the water and eventual exhaustion of the resource, without people receiving maximum benefit from it. Scarcity rears its ugly head.

Hardin notes that the tragedy of the commons applies to pollution:

Here it is not a question of taking something out of the commons, but of putting something in—sewage, or chemical, radioactive, and heat wastes into water; noxious and dangerous fumes into the air. . . . The rational man finds that his share of the cost of the wastes he discharges into the commons is less than the cost of purifying his wastes before releasing them. Since this is true for everyone, we are locked into a system of "fouling our own nest. . . ."[12]

Consider, for example, automobile exhaust fumes. Imagine that the catalytic converter had been invented but was merely optional on new cars. It adds an extra $300 dollars to the price of the car and reduces gas mileage by two miles per gallon, but it cleans up 90 percent of the pollution that cars otherwise emit into the air. Would a rational, selfish individual order her car with or without the catalytic converter? She would order the car without it, because with it she would only get the insignificant benefit of her car emitting less pollution. Others in her vicinity would automatically get just as much benefit as she, while she pays the entire expense. This goes against self-interest.

Economists call the addition to general pollution that my car makes an **externality**. It affects society through its effect on the commons much more than it affects me individually. So the effect is external to me; it is an externality. Externalities can be good or bad. People who walk to work to get exercise spare the rest of us the air pollution they would generate if they drove their cars. This is a positive externality. But people who save money for themselves by allowing their cars to generate extraordinary levels of pollution create negative externalities. According to Hardin and most economists, we can usually predict market outcomes by assuming market behavior is predominantly selfish. Here the assumption of selfishness leads to the prediction that people will be willing to create negative externalities whenever doing so is personally beneficial.

Of course, these same individuals would be happy if many other people refrained from producing externalities. Selfish economic individuals, in fact, would like it if everyone else were to use a catalytic converter (so she would benefit from cleaner air), while she alone drove a car without one (so she could avoid its cost). Everyone wants to be what economists call a **free rider**. This is *a person who benefits from public goods but does not contribute to their production or maintenance.*

However, when everyone tries to be a free rider, no one succeeds. The public good is degraded, so no one can enjoy it. To avoid this situation people must agree to pay for their use of public goods. When they pay individually for the damage they do to the commons, they have self-interested incentives to minimize that damage. In economic terms, such payments **internalize externalities**. The damage to public goods is no longer external to the individuals' economic calculations, because they have to pay for it.

But how can selfish individuals be brought to the point of internalizing their externalities? According to Hardin, "The social arrangements that produce responsibility are arrangements that create coercion, of some sort."[13] An example is the government requirement that new cars sold in the United States be equipped with catalytic converters. The law coerces people to internalize (in this case, pay the cost of avoiding) a negative externality—air pollution. This government requirement does not ruin the car market, but alters it much the way different labor laws alter the labor market.

Trading Pollution Permits

But mandating the use of a particular technology has the disadvantage of inflexibility. Will the government change the mandate as soon as a better technology is invented? Probably not, because governments tend to react slowly to technological change. As a result, inventors will be slow to develop new pollution-fighting technologies. They will fear that even if they do invent a "better pollutiontrap," the government will continue to require the old system. Investors will be slow to subsidize such inventions when commercial success requires convincing government bureaucrats to change direction. The result of discouraging innovators and investors is less technological innovation for environmental protection.

Protecting the environment for human good is an anthropocentric concern, and economic anthropocentrists often look to the free market. One approach is to provide market incentives for inventors and investors. Imagine an industrial area with poor air quality. Factories of many different kinds contribute to the pollution, which is composed of many different substances, such as nitrous oxides, sulfates, carbon monoxide, and ozone. The result is unhealthful, ugly smog. Government-mandated technologies like the catalytic converter are not likely to help here. The catalytic converter works on all cars with internal combustion engines because all these engines are similar to one another, and the type of pollution they produce is the same. But coal-burning electric power plants, steel factories, automobile assembly plants, and food processing facilities use different technologies and produce different types of pollution. No one technology will address this variety of problems.

An idea favored by many environmental economists is this: The government should issue **pollution permits** to industrial plants. Environmental journalists Thomas Michael Power and Paul Rauber reported in *Sierra* in 1993:

> One section of the 1990 Clean Air Act allows plants that pollute below certain levels to sell pollution "credits" to dirtier concerns; innovative, clean industries profit from their cleanliness, while the dirty industries pay for their sins until they can get around to cleaning up their acts. A market in these "pollution credits" has been established at the Chicago Board of Trade, where rights to emit tons of sulfur dioxide are bought and sold like pork bellies or soybean futures.[14]

Currently, permits relate only to sulfur dioxide. However, Dan Dudek, a senior economist at the Environmental Defense Fund, favors "the establishment of national markets for nitrogen oxides, and perhaps even global markets for CFCs and carbon dioxide."[15]

This sounds terrible at first, doesn't it? When pollution is already a problem the government should be forbidding it, not permitting it. But forbidding *all* pollution is unrealistic. *To live is to pollute.* Life processes all involve throughput of material substances. Resulting waste products can be harmful to self and others if they accumulate nearby. Hence the continuing popularity of toilets. Because life tends to create pollution, realistic goals are reduction and appropriate distribution of pollution so as to reduced harmful effects. This is what pollution permits do.

The government can start by issuing permits to all polluters in proportion to their current contributions to pollution. Suppose total air pollution in the area is 1,000 units, and this is considered too high. The government would issue permits that allow companies to pollute just this amount. But they would announce that in five years everyone's permitted level of pollution will be reduced by 10 percent. The total will be 900 at that time. Five years later air pollution will be reduced to 800, then in another five years to 700, and so on, until a level of 400 is reached. Violators face heavy fines.

Because it is total smog produced by the combined activities of various factories that is ugly and unhealthful, it does not matter much exactly which factories reduce their pollution. The important thing is to bring down the total. It would be unfair, however, to require that some factories or industries reduce their air pollution more than others, so reductions in pollution permits are made across the board. Every factory that was originally permitted 10 units of pollution will be permitted only 9 in five years.

But then a market can develop. Factories that reduce pollution more than required by law can sell their extra pollution permits to factories whose pollution exceeds their government allotment. For example, an iron smelting factory may start with 10 units of permitted pollution. A new technology developed for that industry enables Factory A to reduce its pollution to 5 units in just three years. The owners will have incentive to invest in this technology knowing that they will for many years have extra pollution permits to sell to other companies whose pollution exceeds permitted levels. Investors in, and developers of, innovative pollution-control technologies will be inspired to create such technologies, knowing that a good technology is likely to be bought by companies that can recover part of the cost through the sale of extra pollution permits.

If there were no market in pollution permits, for example, if the law disallowed the sale of such permits, outcomes would be worse. Without expected income from the sale of their extra pollution permits, the owners of Factory A might not find it economical to invest so heavily in pollution control. Rather than invest in innovative technology to reduce pollution, they may simply add new air filters to keep their levels just within permitted limits. Pollution abatement will suffer.

But what about companies that buy pollution permits? Aren't they getting off too easily? Shouldn't they, too, be required to reduce their pollution? Well, in the first place, if the goal is a better looking, more healthful environment, that goal is met under this system, even if some companies continue to pollute as before. Second, companies that continue to pollute as before have increasing incentives to reduce their pollution, because as permitted levels of pollution decrease, they have to buy ever more pollution permits to stay in business and avoid hefty fines. Also, the more such companies there are, the greater the demand for a limited number of pollution permits. This supply and demand situation will increase the market price of permits. So companies will be motivated to adopt new technologies that reduce their pollution. This, in turn, motivates investors in, and developers of, new technologies for those industries.

In sum, *a market in pollution permits reduces pollution to acceptable levels while encouraging maximum use of the most efficient pollution-control technologies available at any given time. It also encourages investment in new pollution-control technologies of many different types in many different industries. Government-mandated technologies evolve more slowly. Their efficiency at reducing pollution tends to fall behind technologies that must constantly meet market competition. Markets can be used to environmental advantage.*

A Market Approach to Overpopulation

Economist Herman Daly and theologian John Cobb recommend in *For the Common Good* that overpopulation problems be addressed, like pollution problems, through transferable government permits (certificates) to bear children.

> The right to reproduce can no longer be treated as a free good. It must be seen as a scarce good in a full world. As with other scarce goods, reproduction rights must be subject to distribution and allocation. . . . Initial distribution is on the principle of strict equality, but reallocation is permitted in the interests of allocative efficiency—in other words, providing a better match-up of rights to reproduce with desire to reproduce and ability to pay. It is the latter to which many people object—ability to pay should have nothing to do with reproduction, they think. This attitude is not supported in nature by territorial species, nor by human history where financial viability is often a precondition for marriage.[16]

There is an old saying, "The rich get richer and the poor get children." On this plan, however, it seems that the rich get whatever children they want as well, and the poor may get nothing. This does strike me as unjust, and Daly and Cobb's justifications seem unpersuasive. They cite the practices of other species, and maybe there are other species whose behavior resembles what Daly and Cobb propose. But do we generally aspire to imitate other species? I don't think so. Territorial female black widow spiders eat the male after he has impregnated her. Should this guide our treatment of deadbeat dads who fail to pay child support? I think most people prefer government distribution of cheese, milk, and peanut butter. Here is another example. Male seals are territorial animals. One male dominates the group, has a harem, and impregnates all the females. So should we let Donald Trump and Bill Gates father the next generation? I don't think so. The appeal to analogous behavior in other species makes a weak argument.

The other argument offered by Daly and Cobb concerns past practices in other cultures. Should we imitate these cultures? Probably not. Many cultures in the past have had slaves, killed religious heretics, treated women as property, and/or denied social mobility to peasants. The fact that other societies have done something does not, all by itself, suggest that we do likewise. Other considerations are needed.

Here is a consideration that I consider decisive against Daly and Cobb's proposal. It is "the problem of appropriate punishment for those who have children without the certificate. The alternatives range from ex post acquisition of certificate, perhaps on easy credit terms, to forced surrender of the child for adoption."[17] Forced surrender of the child for adoption suggests screenplays for movies about families living underground so their children will not be taken from them. Who would want to live in such a society?

Forcing parents to pay for a certificate after they have already had the child may be unrealistic given the financial situation of many poor families. And what if the couple has another child before they have paid off the certificate for the previous one? In addition, any required payment from poor families will detract from the material care those families can give to their children, who are innocent, even if born illegitimately. Why should they suffer? And if we force them to suffer as children, they may fail to acquire education and skills, making them misfits as adults who burden the rest of us. So let us look at another approach to overpopulation.

Lifeboat Ethics

Garrett Hardin claims that the tragedy of the commons applies to overpopulation, so we should resist appeals like this one from the organization, Bread for the World:

> Drought, overpopulation and civil war . . . are causing famine in southern Sudan. These combined factors have created a severe food shortage for at least 2.6 million people, according to United Nations officials. In some villages at least one in five children is severely malnourished. . . .
> The U.N. World Food Program is carrying out the largest airlift of food in its history, costing more than $30 million a month. Approximately 12,000 tons of food have already been shipped. Predictions of a poor harvest this fall have led relief officials to conclude that airlifts must continue for a year and a half in order to avoid a famine like the one in 1989 that killed nearly 250,000 people in the region.[18]

Bread for the World urges congressional support for the UN's efforts.

Hardin would urge the opposite. Just as too many cattle on a common pasture will ruin it and hurt all herdsmen, too many people on Earth will ruin the earth and hurt all people. In the one case, Hardin's solution is to privatize the pasture. When people own individual parcels of pasture, putting too many cattle on a parcel hurts only the owner of that parcel. Others avoid ruin by protecting their private property.

Hardin suggests a similar approach to problems of overpopulation. A country's food is like private property. America's food belongs to Americans. If we share it with people in poor, overpopulated countries, they will increase further in number and ruin the earth's capacity to support anyone. He compares people living in rich countries who have plenty of food to people in a lifeboat. You and I are in the lifeboat. Hardin writes:

> So here we sit, say fifty people in our lifeboat. To be generous, let us assume it has room for ten more, making a total capacity of sixty. Suppose the fifty of us in the lifeboat see 100 others swimming in the water outside, begging for admission to our boat or for handouts. We have several options: we may be tempted to try to live by the Christian ideal of being "our brother's keeper," . . . [and] take them all into our boat, making a total of 150 in a boat designed for sixty. The boat swamps, everyone drowns. Complete justice, complete catastrophe.[19]

Analogous considerations apply to food aid, according to Hardin:

> If poor countries receive no food from the outside, the rate of their population growth would be periodically checked by crop failures and famines. But if they can always draw on a world food bank in time of need, their population can continue to grow unchecked. . . . [20] [For example,] if rich countries make it possible, through foreign aid, for 600 million Indians to swell to 1.2 billion in a mere 28 years, as their current growth rate threatens, will future generations of Indians thank us for hastening the destruction of their environment?[21]

In sum, according to Hardin, we should not burden people starving in southern Sudan with our assistance. Nor should we let them immigrate to the United States. "World food banks move food to the people. . . . Unrestricted immigration . . . moves people to the food."[22] Environmentally destructive overpopulation results in either case. The same can be said for attempts to enable people to grow more food in their own countries. The result will be environmentally destructive overpopulation. Hardin cites the view of Alan Gregg, a former vice president of the Rockefeller Foundation, who compared the growth and spread of the human population on Earth to the spread of cancer in a person's body. "Cancerous growths demand food; but, as far as I know, they have never been cured by getting it."[23]

Several points can be made on the other side. First, when Hardin originally published "Lifeboat Ethics" in 1974, there was enough food to feed every human being on Earth. People were starving due to poor food distribution, not insufficient food production. So the lifeboat analogy is misleading. Due to its limited capacity, Hardin's lifeboat could not save everyone. The human ability to produce food on the earth is not similarly limited. In fact, in 1998, when

Bread for the World made its appeal, there was still enough food to feed everyone, including hungry people in southern Sudan.

But Hardin, like Gregg before him, assumes that the lifeboat situation will exist someday if we do not let people starve now. However, there is no reason to believe this. Historically, people do not tend to increase in numbers to the point of starvation the way, for example, deer do when wolves, people, and cold winters fail to kill them off. Many groups of human beings have maintained steady populations over long periods of time without starvation and without ruining the environment. Industrialized Western Europe is an example at the moment.

Currently, fertility rates in poor countries are declining. Environmental writer Bill McKibben reported in *The Atlantic Monthly* in May 1998:

> Population growth rates are lower than they have been at any time since the Second World War. In the past three decades the average woman in the developing world, excluding China, has gone from bearing six children to bearing four. . . . If this keeps up, the population of the world will not quite double again; United Nations analysts offer as their mid-range projection that it will top out at 10 to 11 billion, up from just under six billion at the moment.[24]

This good news seems to result from a combination of factors. More people around the world have access to reliable methods of birth control. According to Worldwatch research associate Jennifer Mitchell, "In the developing world, at least 120 million married women—and a large but undefined number of unmarried women—want more control over their pregnancies, but cannot get family planning services."[25] This is encouraging. We can help avert greater overpopulation by giving these women what they want. Also, economic development spurs interest in education for better-paying jobs. People often delay having families to pursue education. It is particularly important that women gain power and educational opportunities. Birthrates have fallen fastest under these conditions. So, in addition to their intrinsic merits, equal rights and equal opportunity for women around the world help curtail overpopulation.

In any case, the lifeboat analogy fails if the world will have "only" 10 or 11 billion people and the earth can feed that many. However, the matter is more complex. The ability of the world to feed that number of people depends on what people eat. Environmental researcher Gary Gardner reports: "The more meat, milk, and cheese people eat, the greater the demand for grain, because these products are grain intensive. For example, 2 kilos of grain are required to produce a kilo of chicken or fish, 4 kilos go into a kilo of pork, and 7 kilos are needed for a kilo of feedlot-raised beef."[26]

We saw in the introductory chapter that the world is running short of fresh water. Researchers Alan Durning and Holly Brough note:

> Feed-grain farming guzzles water, too. In California, now the United States' leading dairy state, livestock agriculture consumes nearly one-third of all irrigation wa-

ter. Similar figures apply across the western United States, including areas using water from dwindling aquifers. More than 3,000 liters of water are used to produce a kilogram of American beef."[27]

Water expert Sandra Postel adds: "With nearly two out of every five tons of grain going into meat and poultry production, individual choices about diet collectively can influence how much water is needed to satisfy future food demands."[28] Writing in 1991, Durning and Brough concluded:

> A meat-fed world now appears a chimera. World grain production has grown more slowly than population since 1984, and farmers lack new methods for repeating the gains of the "green revolution." Supporting the world's *current* population of 5.4 billion people on an American-style diet would require two-and-a-half times as much grain as the world's farmers produce for all purposes. A future world of 8 billion to 14 billion people eating the American ration of 220 grams of grain-fed meat a day can be nothing but a flight of fancy.[29]

It seems that the world food picture is not so rosy as cornucopian Julian Simon believes, because there are limits. On the other hand, they are not so bleak as Garret Hardin's lifeboat situation, because everyone can survive within those limits. But this requires that rich people not only share financial resources to help the poor gain access to contraceptives and education. We must also modify our diets—eat less beef, pork, poultry, eggs, and dairy products—to use the earth's food producing capacity efficiently.

Psychological Egoism and the Possibility of Sharing

If we look at matters purely from a market perspective, there is no reason to believe that people with money will alter their diets to provide food for the poor. Economic theory about the market assumes that people behave selfishly in market transactions. It may be unfair that people in some countries are rich and people in others are poor, but that situation developed historically. Perhaps no one alive today is responsible. Certainly, I am not. So if I buy food that diverts grains from feeding poor people in the world to feeding cattle for me, I am selfish. But there is a world food market, and selfish behavior is expected in markets.

Some proponents of markets as the best means of handling problems of production and distribution claim that selfish behavior in markets is beneficial. Robert L. Bartley, editor of *The Wall Street Journal* wrote: "The fundamentals of human nature are universal. . . . History suggests that economic development depends on harnessing the acquisitive instinct—greed, if you must, or as Adam Smith put it, self-love."[30] Bartley here suggests that selfishness is one of the fundamentals of human nature, and that it can be harnessed for good. It can promote economic development, given proper social arrangements. Environ-

*"And may we continue to be worthy of consuming a
disproportionate share of this planet's resources."*

mental economists Terry Anderson and Donald Leal agree. In *Free Market Environmentalism* they write:

> Free market environmentalism views man as self-interested. This self-interest may
> be enlightened. . . . But . . . good intentions will not suffice to produce good results.
> Developing an environmental ethic may be desirable, but it is unlikely to change basic human nature. Instead of intentions, good resource stewardship depends on how
> well social institutions harness self-interest through individual incentives.[31]

Like economists generally, they believe they can predict outcomes by assuming market behavior to be predominantly selfish. Some thinkers mistakenly equate this assumption about market behavior with the belief that people are capable of nothing but selfishness. This position, known as **psychological egoism,** is the view that everyone always behaves selfishly all the time. In the words of Archie Bunker, the leading character in a 1970s situation comedy, everyone is just "looking out for number one."

If this is correct, many poor people around the world today and in the future are doomed to starvation. Many rich people want meat, eggs, and cheese. If self-interest is their guide, they will buy grain to feed livestock while poor people starve.

But are people inevitably selfish in the long run? There seem to be exceptions, such as Martin Luther King, Jr., Mohandas Gandhi, and Mother Theresa.

They devoted their lives to helping others. Less famous people seem to do the same on a smaller scale all the time. People give up their seats on the bus to help strangers. They volunteer to coach Little League or participate in Big Brother/Big Sister programs. They help maintain their church buildings. Such behavior seems unselfish.

Defenders of psychological egoism reply that in each case the person gets a personal benefit and is therefore acting selfishly. The person who gives up her seat on the bus, for example, avoids pangs of conscience upon seeing old people fall down like pins in a bowling alley whenever the bus moves. Volunteers at Little League and Big Brother/Big Sister delight in making children happy. Unpaid workers at church enjoy the camaraderie of fellow church members, the knowledge that they are helping others, and possibly the promise of eternal reward in heaven. So all are acting selfishly.

This defense of psychological egoism is flawed because it attaches an unusual meaning to "selfish." Thinking of selfishness in its normal meaning, for example, I would not want to go camping with a selfish person. I fear that if I were accidentally to break my leg, she might leave me to suffer. It would depend on what she felt like doing in her own interest. So if a friend were to say: "Go camping with Jane. She's completely selfish, but you'll have a good time," I would express reservations. But then suppose my friend adds: "Don't worry about that. Jane has a strong conscience and good moral character. She always responds helpfully to the needs of others out of habit and to keep her conscience clear." Then I would ask why my friend called Jane selfish. He says: "Because she always gets some good out of it for herself, such as a clear conscience."

My friend has misunderstood the concept of selfishness. *We normally say that a person is selfish when she acts with insufficient regard for the welfare of others.* Jane is not like that at all. To say that she is selfish uses the word contrary to its normal meaning. What is more, my friend's use of the word makes it literally meaningless. Words have meaning by indicating that one state of affairs exists rather than another. A word that applies to absolutely every state of affairs in a certain context tells us nothing. For example, I had a kind friend who read my philosophy papers years ago. He said "Terrific!" to everything I wrote. That made me feel good at first. But when I realized that he said this about *everything* that any of his friends wrote, I knew his comment did not tell me which of my papers were better than the others, or whether any of them were any good at all. His comment was virtually meaningless.

The same is true of the word "selfish" when it applies to everything anyone ever does. The word is useful and meaningful when it helps us pick out, for example, good partners for camping. But if it applies to everyone, it cannot do this. It is meaningless, like my friend's "Terrific!" This is how I know the psychological egoist is not using the word in a normal fashion. Normally the word does have meaning and helps people pick friends and partners. Selfish people are those who pursue self-interest without sufficient regard for the welfare of others. But not everyone is like this. Most people pursue self-interest, but are not completely selfish. They gain some joy and meaning from helping others. Psychological egoism incorrectly denies this, or incorrectly calls it selfish.

Human Rights

But if people *can* care about, and be motivated to help, others, and they wish to do so, they need guidance about which acts of caring are appropriate in which circumstances. Moral training supplies this guidance, giving us many values and prescriptions (do's and don'ts). For example, we have all heard through the media that market economies meet economically oriented human needs and promote prosperity better than command economies, such as those of the former Soviet Union and its allies. Our training, which is largely anthropocentric, tells us that meeting human needs is important and that prosperity is necessary for the good life. We have been taught also that individual freedom is a good thing. Markets allow individual sellers and buyers a lot of freedom to determine what to manufacture, what to offer for sale, what to buy, and what to pay. Thus, we approach environmental philosophy with a positive attitude toward free markets as a means to prosperity. This gives us an initially positive attitude toward possible market approaches to problems of pollution and overpopulation.

We have seen that market approaches to pollution control can be very helpful. But overpopulation is a different matter. Other values seem more important. Consider the behavior we expect and respect in real lifeboat situations, such as the one dramatized in the 1997 movie "Titanic." Due to poor planning, there were not enough lifeboats to accommodate all passengers. Rich passengers received preferential treatment. Poor passengers were actually locked below deck to keep them away from lifeboats. This may make sense if we want to use markets to make such decisions. Rich passengers paid more for their tickets on the Titanic, so they should have greater access to its facilities.

The moral training of most people in the United States today leads them to reject this reasoning. Preventing poor passengers from coming on Titanic's deck was wrong, we think. In life-and-death situations, scarce resources should not go to the highest bidder. This view is reflected in laws governing the distribution of vital organs for transplant. By law in the United States people cannot buy hearts or livers for transplant. The demand exceeds the supply, so markets in these organs would result in high prices that only rich people could afford. Rich people would get the livers they need and all others in equal medical need would die of liver failure. We (the American public as represented by Congress and the president) do not allow this because we do not think it is right. But why? What other values taught in our culture conflict with, and in these circumstances override, the values associated with markets?

One such value is equality, based on belief in the equal worth of all human life. Religious training often includes this value in the saying that all people are equal in the sight of God. A secular way of putting the idea is that all people have equal human rights. Such ideas are now expressed in international documents endorsed by the United States. One of these is the Universal Declaration of Human Rights, which was adopted in 1948 by the General Assembly of the United Nations. Article 1 states: "All human beings are born free and equal in dignity and rights." Article 3 says: "Everyone has the right to life, liberty and security of person." Article 7 says: "All are equal before the law. . . ." And Article 25 states: "Everyone has the right to a standard of living adequate for the health and well-being of himself and of his family, including food, clothing, housing and medical care. . . ." We are taught in our culture that these are universal rights, and this may explain why we condemn trapping poor people below deck on a sinking ship. They are not treated "equal in dignity and rights" to rich people.

Human rights such as these are popular with the American public. Candidates for national office usually gain votes by opposing China's violations of human rights. We have welfare programs to secure everyone's "right to a standard of living adequate for the health and well-being of himself and of his family, including food. . . ." Taxpayers fund these programs, I assume, because they think no one should starve to death when there is enough food to feed everyone. This view may rest on belief in equal human rights.

Consider world hunger and overpopulation in this light. The world food situation now and in the foreseeable future allows everyone to be fed, even if the population increases to 10 or 11 billion, but only *if* rich people change their diets to include less meat, eggs, and dairy products. Should rich people do this? In other words, unlike on the Titanic, there are enough seats in the lifeboats for everyone. Should rich people make accommodation for the poor?

Imagine a lifeboat situation, unlike that on the Titanic, where there are enough seats in lifeboats for everyone. But imagine that people can buy lifeboat seats, and that some rich people can afford to buy two or more seats per person. They want additional seats because they want to save their stuffed animals, and they need a place to put them. But if rich people do this, there will not be enough seats for everyone. Because demand for seats exceeds supply, the price of seats rises dramatically and exceeds the means of many poor people. If decision is left to the market, poor people drown because they lack the money to buy seats at the elevated market price.

I assume that we reject this. We find a rich person's preference for saving stuffed animals morally inappropriate when it costs human lives. Universal rights to equality and to life require giving everyone a seat in this situation. We disallow a market in seats because it would needlessly sacrifice human lives.

Now let us apply this to the world food situation at present and in the expected future. Just as there are enough seats in the lifeboats for everyone, there is enough food in the world for everyone. But there is currently a market in food, and 800 million people in the world today are too poor to afford adequate diets. Due largely to the effects of malnutrition and poor water quality, almost 40,000 children die needlessly *every day*.[32] We in the United States and other First World countries, such as Western Europe, Japan, and Australia, have discretionary income that we spend on various consumer items (stuff). Are these expenditures like rich passengers purchasing extra seats for stuffed animals? Do poor children have lesser rights to life than poor passengers on the ship?

At present we can help poor people simply by giving money through private charities and supporting appropriate government initiatives. We do not have to give up much of our "stuff." In 1998, for example, Bread for the World urged Congress to pass a bill "to re-focus U.S. engagement in sub-Saharan Africa on programs that build self-reliance and support agriculture and rural development."[33] The expense for average taxpayers would be minimal. In the future, however, we may need additionally to alter our eating habits so enough food can be grown on Earth for everyone. I discuss this matter and other lifestyle issues in Part IV.

Because respecting human rights may eventually require us, people in rich countries, to give up some things we enjoy, we may be tempted to question the existence of human rights. Why should we think that there are universal human rights of the sort included in the UN's Universal Declaration of Human Rights?

Rights are not physical objects that we can detect by sense perception or scientific observation. We verify their existence largely by noting our own appraisals of various situations and scenarios. How do we make sense of our repugnance when a market in vital organs, or in lifeboat seats, allows the rich to live and leaves the poor to die? It seems that we believe everyone has an equal right to life.

In some respects this method of verification resembles the scientific method. We do not experience gravity directly. We know it by its effects on material things. We see the moon revolving around the earth, we experience the tides, we know that junk thrown from a window falls to the ground, and so forth. Scientists *infer* from this a force we call gravity. The inference is justified because the supposition of such a force explains so many different experiences. Similarly, the existence of human rights may be verified by inference because it explains a variety of experiences. The difference is that gravity explains diverse experiences of the material world, whereas human rights explain diverse experiences of our own approval and disapproval. In Part II, I consider scientific explanations, related to evolutionary theory, of the various evaluations people make.

Judgment Calls

It seems that the population situation is not nearly so desperate as Paul Ehrlich and Zero Population Growth would have us believe, but it is still a problem. Our views about human rights require addressing this problem more through sharing than through privatization and markets. Consider some practical implications.

- Eating meat is not necessary for human beings (except, perhaps, for those with special health problems). It is really a luxury. Perhaps there should be a luxury tax on meat. The higher price of meat will reduce overall consumption, which will improve the diet of most Americans. Less meat production will reduce the inefficient use of scarce agricultural resources, because more grain will go to people instead of livestock. Revenue from the tax could support international efforts that help poor countries grow more food for themselves. What do you think of this proposal?

- We saw in the Introduction that agricultural chemicals in the environment are probably responsible for some increases in cancer incidence and mortality. Organic agriculture avoids the use of such chemicals. Consider this market approach to encouraging organic agriculture. The government could phase in a program of buying only organic food for the military. This would create a large market for organically grown products that would stimulate increased production. As production increases and more farmers become familiar with organic techniques, the price of organic foods may come down, stimulating demand among ordinary consumers for these healthful products. What additional factors need to be considered?

- Through genetic engineering, the Monsanto corporation has created a new type of potato, New Leaf Superior, reports journalist Michael Pollan in *The New York Times Magazine*.[34] It can be grown without the usual pesticides because it contains the protein Bt in every cell, and Bt is poisonous to the Colorado potato beetle, the worst potato pest. The first large crop of New Leaf Superior potatoes appeared at stores in the fall of 1998. You may not have noticed this because stores are not required to label the new potatoes as containing a built-in pesticide. It is presumed safe, and may be safe, but its use in potatoes has not been thoroughly tested. Your french fries may be made from these potatoes. Do you think that labeling should be required? How does this relate to the way markets are supposed to work?

- Here is a more general issue. We have seen in this chapter that markets are helpful in avoiding wasteful uses of environmental resources and in curtailing pollution. But they curtail pollution only when governments alter the rules of the marketplace to accomplish this goal, as when they require catalytic converters on cars or pollution permits for factories. This raises a question. How does the government justify the particular alteration of the rules that it favors? How does it calculate the proper level of pollution abatement? How would we know, for example, if automotive pollution control ten times better than what we have at present is a good idea and should be required by law? (Look at the next chapter to find out.)

CHAPTER 2

Energy, Economics, and Future Generations

Global Warming and Future Generations

Environmental journalist Paul Rauber, writing in *Sierra*, imagines a nightmare resulting from runaway **global warming**, a general heating of the earth due to emissions of greenhouse gases:

> Slowly, almost imperceptibly, it starts to get hotter. The increase in average temperatures is gradual; what we notice are the scorching spikes, as heat records fall one after another. Winters are milder, but punctuated by deluges and blizzards. . . . Weather becomes more extreme—storms more powerful, hurricanes more damaging. . . . Ecosystems start to shift, subtly at first. Familiar trees, weakened by drought and disease, brown and burn in the more frequent fires. Grasslands replace what once were forests, and deserts replace grasslands. . . . Fewer songbirds visit your backyard feeder. Then, none. Species you never heard of are declared extinct. Then species you have heard of. . . . Melting icecaps and glaciers cause sea levels to rise; beaches erode and then disappear. . . . With warm winters and earlier springs, mosquitoes are everywhere. People get sick from diseases you thought occurred only in the faraway tropics. . . . [1]

Scientists claim that global warming is underway. In late November 1995, the Intergovernmental Panel on Climate Change (IPCC) declared by consensus: "The balance of evidence suggests that there is a discernible human influence on global climate."[2] The IPCC, first convened in 1988 by the United Nations, is composed of 2,500 scientists from around the world who study global warming. The earth is warmed principally by heat energy from the sun. When that energy hits the earth, most is absorbed and then re-emitted back toward space. Our atmosphere contains **greenhouse gases** that trap much of the heat before it reaches space, and this keeps the earth warm enough to support life. These gases are principally water vapor, carbon dioxide, methane, nitrous oxide, and chlorofluorocarbons. Colum Lynch, UN correspondent for *The Boston Globe* writes:

> Human industry has been stoking that natural heating system. Since the late nineteenth century, the global concentration of greenhouse gases has grown by 25 per-

cent, raising the average surface temperature around the world by 1 degree Fahrenheit. If the level of global emissions of greenhouse gases continues to increase at current rates, says the latest IPCC forecast, the average global surface temperature should rise between 1.8 and 6.3 degrees Fahrenheit by the year 2100. (The most likely increase is 3.6 degrees.)[3]

What does this mean in human terms? Paul Rauber's gloomy prediction is controversial. Journalist Gregg Easterbrook points out in his 1995 book *A Moment on Earth* that some global warming may be good. "What was the economic bottom line on the 1980s, the 'hottest years on record'?" he asks. "Agriculture was strong throughout the world. Most developing nations produced sufficient food for domestic consumption. . . . Energy consumption was soft, winter peak demand being a key variable in power needs. In turn, energy prices declined." Further warming could also be good, writes Easterbrook: "The Intergovernmental Panel on Climate Change has estimated that a 3.5 degree Fahrenheit warming would increase agricultural yields in the former Soviet Union by 40 percent, in China by 20 percent, in the United States by 15 percent."[4]

Simon Retallack, on the other hand, writing in *The Ecologist*, sees jeopardy to food security in the IPCC's report:

A clear danger to food security would be posed first, by proliferating droughts, which the IPCC's models suggest could lead, for example, to soils in Europe losing up to 50 per cent of their moisture . . . ; second, by proliferating floods as violent storms increase and as sea levels rise, drowning valuable arable land. . . . A startling indication of how vulnerable we are to climate change came in June 1991, when the worst flood so far this century burst across the Yangtze plain. China, which faces the challenge of feeding a quarter of the world's population with 8 per cent of the world's cultivable land, lost 20 per cent of its croplands.[5]

Floods in China were even worse in 1998.

What is more, global warming may be greater than the IPCC predicts. There may be positive feedbacks in the warming process. (Warming with a snowballing effect?) If forests die or burn due to droughts, they will decay and add more carbon dioxide to the atmosphere. The warming of tundra soils could release large amounts of stored carbon and methane. Methane traps 63 times more heat than carbon dioxide. In a warmer world there will be more water vapor in the air as heat evaporates more water from the ocean surface. This could form low clouds that block the sun and keep the earth cool. But they could form high cirrus clouds instead, which have the opposite effect. And water vapor itself is a greenhouse gas. A warmer ocean may also release more carbon dioxide and be slower to absorb it. In addition, "as snow and ice continue to melt, there will be fewer white areas on Earth to reflect the sun's heat directly back to space."[6] If some of these events occur, warming will be much worse than the IPCC predicts. It may be a nightmare.

Of course, we just don't know. Then why not play it safe and reduce emissions of greenhouse gases? It's the economy, stu. . . . Well, we emit these gases as by-products of burning fossil fuels, such as coal, oil, and natural gas, and these energy sources are pivotal to all industrial economies. Our cars and trucks run on gasoline. Most electricity and most energy used in heavy industries come from coal. This is why some business and manufacturing interests in the United States worry that bold measures designed to reduce greenhouse gas emissions could be economically disastrous.

William F. O'Keefe, executive vice-president of the American Petroleum Institute, addressed the International Conference on Climate Change in Washington, D.C. in May 1995. He said, "I have no doubt that if we tried to reduce greenhouse gas emissions by 20 percent over the next twenty years we would bring on a full-scale depression."[7] In July 1996, the CEOs of over 100 major American corporations sent a letter to President Clinton about upcoming negotiations on a treaty to limit greenhouse gas emissions. They wrote, "There remains great uncertainty about the extent, timing and effects" of global warming. They continued:

> The U.S. must take care to avoid commitments that will cost U.S. jobs, retard economic growth or damage U.S. competitiveness. Moreover, given the long-term nature of the issue, there is time to determine optimum strategies that are economically sound, comprehensive, market-driven and can be adjusted over time. . . . We urge you to ensure that the U.S. negotiating team recognizes that the unique needs of the U.S. economy are of the utmost priority and to adopt a negotiating position that protects U.S. interests.[8]

Others think the opposite. Gregg Easterbrook believes that energy efficiencies needed to combat global warming will improve our economy. Industry will save money on energy costs and become more internationally competitive. New industries based on energy-efficient technologies will create jobs.[9] Again, we just don't know.

The reason we don't know is that global warming problems are mostly in the future. Should we alter our lives right now on the real *possibility* that immediate action is needed to protect people in the year 2100, when none of us can expect to be alive? Why should we make sacrifices to help future generations? This is a philosophical question about the proper extent of anthropocentric concern.

Human Rights and the Futurity Problem

Economist Robert Heilbroner addressed this question in a 1975 *New York Times Magazine* article:

> By the year 2075, I shall probably have been dead for three-quarters of a century. My children will also likely be dead, and my grandchildren, if I have any, will be in their dotage. What does it matter to me, then, what life will be like in 2075 . . . ?

There is no rational answer to that terrible question. No argument based on reason will lead me to care for posterity or to lift a finger in its behalf. Indeed, by every rational consideration, precisely the opposite answer is thrust upon us with irresistible force.[10]

Heilbroner, an economist, associates rationality with limited concern for the welfare of future generations of human beings. We saw in Chapter 1, however, that rational people are often motivated by our cultural ideal of respecting human rights to help poor, starving people in overpopulated countries. Does the same apply to future generations? Should we help them out of respect for their human rights?

At first it seems that we should. Future generations will be as human as we are, so they should have the same rights as the present generation, including the rights to freedom from disease and to adequate nutrition, to the extent that these can be secured. Global warming threatens to unleash horrible diseases and make it difficult or impossible for future generations to grow enough food for everyone. So we violate their rights if we continue to create global warming by adding greenhouse gases to the atmosphere.

But then again, how can future generations have rights when they do not even exist? Consider this passage from Lewis Carroll's *Alice's Adventures in Wonderland*. Alice complained that the Cheshire Cat she was talking with kept "appearing and vanishing so suddenly."

> "All right," said the Cat; and this time it vanished quite slowly, beginning with the end of the tail, and ending with the grin, which remained some time after the rest of it had gone.
> "Well! I've often seen a cat without a grin," thought Alice; "but a grin without a cat! It's the most curious thing I ever saw in all my life!"[11]

Carroll is joking. Even if cats could grin, there could be no cat's grin without a cat that is grinning. Similarly, it seems impossible for human rights to exist without human beings who have those rights. But members of future generations do not yet exist. So how can they have rights?

One answer is that they do not have rights at the moment, but they will have rights when they do eventually exist. We should protect them from adverse effects of global warming out of respect for rights they will have when they exist. As Oxford philosopher Derek Parfit points out, "I am to blame if I leave a man-trap on my land, which ten years later maims a five-year-old child."[12] Similarly, it may seem, when people of the future are born into a world of disease, starvation, and harsh weather, they can claim legitimately that people of the past violated their rights. Respect for these rights requires that we act now to combat global warming.

Parfit points out a problem with this reasoning. Philosophers call it the **futurity problem**. The existence of the five-year-old-child in the earlier example did not depend on whether or not Parfit leaves a man-trap on his land. As

Parfit imagined the situation, she was going to exist anyway. So her rights are violated if Parfit leaves a trap that later injures her. But whether and how we address global warming affects both the conditions of future life and *the identity of future people*. This makes a difference.

Consider the actions we might take to combat global warming. We can subsidize urban mass transit, especially light rail, so people drive less. We can subsidize fast trains between cities to replace much travel by car and plane, which use more fossil fuel and emit more greenhouse gases. We can subsidize solar electricity to replace many coal-fired electric power plants.

In these cases and many more, the kinds of jobs people have will change. Many people who would have made cars if we did nothing about global warming will make solar collectors or trains instead. Commuting to work will change. Instead of driving, most people will take a train or bus. Neighborhoods will change because automobiles favor suburban sprawl. Light rail favors more compact residential areas along rail lines. One result is that different people will meet in high school, during daily commutes, and at work. Different people will fall in love and get married than would have met, fallen in love, and gotten married if we did nothing about global warming.

This means different people *will exist* in the next generation. To see this, consider the contingency of your own existence. If your parents had not met, each may have met someone else and had children. But none of those children would be you, because the uniqueness that is you depends in part on your genetic code. This code is a combination of your two parents' genes. Change one of the parents (unless the change is from one identical twin to another), and the same child cannot be produced, because different genes are put into the combination that is the child's genetic code.

My parents met at a fraternity party. My mother was dating Lindy, an old friend from Sunday school, who was attending the same college and joined the same fraternity as my father. Lindy took my mother to the party where she met my father. If my father had gone elsewhere to college, or my mother had not gone to religious school, or my father had not joined the fraternity, or Lindy had not gone to religious school, or Lindy had met Edith (his eventual wife) sooner, or. . . . I would not exist. Neither would my brother and sister. If we did not exist, neither could our children, grandchildren, etc.

The contingency of our existence is even greater. Our genetic codes are combinations of our two parents' genes, but the same two parents do not produce child after child with the same genetic code. Except in the case of identical twins, siblings have different genetic codes. Ova and sperm each contain one-half the genetic code of the parent, but each ovum and sperm contains a different 50 percent selection of the parent's genes. So for someone to be produced with exactly the genetic code that you have, the very same ovum had to be fertilized by exactly the same sperm.

If your parents had waited another month for pregnancy, the ovum would have been different. Your existence would have been impossible, as would the existence of your biological children, grandchildren, great-grandchildren, forever and ever, because a different ovum would have contained a different selection from among your mother's genes. If your parents had delayed even half an hour, to watch a TV show, for example, it is highly unlikely that the same one among the 20 to 60 million sperm in an ejaculation would have fertilized the ovum, and again, you, your children, etc., would not exist. Of course, you may exist because your parents *did* watch that extra sitcom on TV. Consider this before commenting on your parents' TV watching habits.

Now think again about policies designed to combat global warming. Different people will meet; different people will be born into the next generation. Any different person in the next generation will produce children in the third generation who would not have existed without the policies designed to combat global warming. After 100 years, in the year 2100, for example, almost none of the people who exist will be the same people who would have existed if different energy and transportation policies had been pursued.

Imagine, then, that we do nothing to alter our way of life or technologies to halt global warming. The earth is hotter, the weather is more violent, agriculture is impaired by bad weather and drought, and infectious disease is rampant, all because we did nothing about global warming. Could a person living at that time reproach us for our failure to act? Could she say her rights had been violated? It does not seem that she could. If we had acted to combat global warming, she would not exist. Someone else would exist instead. In other words, the alternatives are *not* a good environment for her or a bad environment for her. The alternatives are a good environment *for other people*, or a bad environment for her. Unless she finds the environment so bad that she would rather not exist at all, she must thank us for continuing selfishly to emit greenhouse gases for our own convenience, because that policy was necessary for her to exist at all.

This is the futurity problem. *It seems that our long-term environmental policies cannot violate the rights of future generations, because the existence of particular future people depends on what we do. Unless they would prefer nonexistence, future people are in no position to complain that we behaved badly.* The way we behaved was the best thing we could have done for them because it alone allowed them to exist. If we are doing the best thing possible for future people, how can they say we violated their rights?

Something seems amiss here. It seems that if we mess up the earth through global warming or in any other way, and human life is worse than it could have been, we have done wrong and future people should be able to blame us. But direct appeals to individual human rights do not allow this. Accordingly, Parfit introduces a new principle of morality: "*The Person-Affecting Principle*, or PAP." According to this principle, "It is bad if people are affected for the worse . . ." in these kinds of situations.[13] But this new principle is just another way of saying it is wrong to mess up the earth for future generations. It does not explain *why* it is wrong. To understand why it is wrong, we need to connect our views on this matter to some other moral principles that we respect.

Fair Contracts and Future Generations

One such principle is fairness. We test for fairness by putting ourselves in the position of other people and judging our actions from their perspective. If others find our actions acceptable, we usually think we are being fair. We approve most market transactions for this reason. If a person trades willingly, she is probably getting what she wants. The trade is fair to her because it is acceptable from her point of view.

In exceptional cases, however, we think that people are treated unfairly in market transactions. Through ignorance, impulse, economic desperation, or for some other reason a person may agree to a trade against her interests. Consider this case: A woman dies and the sight of her jewelry makes her daughter sad. Even though the daughter needs money, she offers to sell the jewelry to a dealer for whatever price the dealer names. The dealer takes advantage by offering a tenth of the jewelry's real worth. We know the financially strapped daughter will later regret this trade.

We often think it is immoral to take advantage of people in these situations. Why? Because our concept of fairness is guided by the Golden Rule: "Do unto others as you would have others do unto you." We assume that others are like ourselves, so whatever we would like if we were in their position is what they would like. We would not like someone taking advantage of our grief and underpaying us for heirlooms when we need money. So we think it is wrong for us, or for anyone else, to do this.

Harvard philosopher John Rawls used ideas about fairness and the Golden Rule to explain the nature of social justice. I modify his ideas to explain why we think it unjust for one generation to mess up the earth for future generations.

Rawls says that social rules are just when they are what all people would freely accept when they are thinking rationally about their own interests. He compares such voluntary acceptance to contractual agreements. A just society's basic social rules are ones people would accept contractually when they are free, well-informed, and rationally guarding their own interests. This is a **social contract view of justice**.[14]

For the contract to be fair, no one can take advantage of anyone else the way the dealer took advantage of the grieving daughter. The Golden Rule must be respected. To accomplish this, Rawls asks us to imagine a hypothetical situation. Imagine that the people making a contract that sets up society's rules do not know the roles they will play in that society. They do not know if they are rich or poor, male or female, religious or secular, etc. Under these conditions, "behind a **veil of ignorance**" Rawls calls it, people will respect the Golden Rule. Each contractor will favor rules that treat everyone fairly, because if the rules are unfair to anyone, that contractor might be among the people treated unfairly. For example, a contractor who accepts rules that are unfair to women might find out later that she is a woman who must, then, suffer injustice.

This "hypothetical contract" perspective reinforces some moral judgments discussed in Chapter 1. We think it is wrong for people to buy extra seats for their "stuff" in a lifeboat situation, resulting in needless human death. We think people have a right to life in such situations. A hypothetical contract would also rule out needless human death.

Imagine that a plane is going down in the South Pacific. The plane has life rafts with enough room for everyone. The rafts are parachuted down and deploy upon hitting the water. The passengers, who also have parachutes, wait in the circling plane as the rafts deploy. While waiting, they discuss whether people who parachute right into a life raft have any obligation to help those who land in the water. Not knowing which, if anyone among the passengers, will be so lucky as to parachute into a life raft, the passengers will choose to be fair to everyone. They will agree to treat everyone as they would want to be treated. They will agree that people who land in life rafts should not just row away. They have an obligation to help those who land in the water. Each agrees to this out of fear of being one of those who lands in the water and needs help. Thus, the hypothetical contract situation leads to a moral rule that satisfies common sense and the sense of justice in our culture.

However, the contract does not lead exactly to human rights. We said earlier that people have a *right* to seats in lifeboats when there are enough for everyone. The contract says that people in a position to help others have a *duty* or *obligation* to do so. This alteration from rights to duties can be helpful where future people are concerned. It seems paradoxical to say that people have rights when they do not yet exist. It is not paradoxical to say that we have duties to help them, or at least to avoid harming them, even though they do not yet exist.

Thus, hypothetical contracts can help explain why it is wrong to jeopardize future generations. John Rawls, a major champion of the contracts view, assumed that his contractors were all of the same generation, so he thought contracts could establish only limited obligations to future people.[15] But we can imagine that one of the things people do not know when they are setting up society's rules is their own place in history. They do not know if they will exist before or after the massive use of fossil fuels; before or after the use of nuclear fission to generate electricity; before or after plans to cut down rainforests, and so forth. They will be ignorant also of which policies are necessary for them to be born, so they will not favor policies that degrade the earth simply because these are needed for their parents to meet.

Under these conditions people will agree to rules that require those who live earlier in time to consider the welfare of those who live later. Each will fear that without such rules, earlier generations will degrade the earth and make life hard for those who live later, and she may be one who lives later. Thus, all agree that earlier generations have an obligation to safeguard the environment so later generations can have decent lives. This view, endorsed by our common sense and moral training, is here tied to another aspect of our training, i.e., our positive attitude toward bargains struck freely under conditions in which each party has a fair chance to secure her own well being.

Environmental Tradeoffs and Cost-Benefit Analysis

How far should our government go to safeguard the earth for future genera-tions? Decisions on this and many other environmental matters involve trade-offs. So we need a decision procedure that helps us determine how much of one thing should be traded for how much of another. For example, our burn-ing fossil fuels (let us assume) tends to warm the earth and jeopardize future generations. However, immediate and drastic reductions (let us assume) risk economic depression for people today. This suggests compromise. We should reduce somewhat to protect future generations, but not so much that our gen-eration suffers too much. But how much is too much? Similarly, the fewer ar-tificial, industrial chemicals in our air, water, and food (let us assume), the smaller the cancer risk to most people. But pollution-control devices cost money that could be spent otherwise. How much should we spend on pollution con-trol?

Again, consider the contribution of automotive exhaust fumes to unhealth-ful smog. We address this problem with catalytic converters. Requiring the con-verter on all cars reduces smog, but costs money, say, $300 per automobile. Without the converter requirement, people could spend this money on other consumer items or give more to charity. These opportunities are lost when the catalytic converter is required. Is it worth it? Should it be required at all? Would some cheaper, but less effective, pollution-control device be sufficient? On the other hand, perhaps we are not spending enough to reduce smog. Perhaps more pollution control is best. Economist William Baxter writes that our goal should be "optimal pollution:"

> The costs of controlling pollution are best expressed in terms of the other goods we will have to give up to do the job. This is not to say the job should not be done. Badly as we need more housing, more medical care, and more can openers, and more symphony orchestras, we could do with somewhat less of them, in my judg-ment at least, in exchange for somewhat cleaner air and rivers. . . . As a society we would be well advised to give up one washing machine if the resources that would have gone into that washing machine can yield greater human satisfaction when diverted into pollution control. . . . Trade-off by trade-off, we should divert our productive capacities from the production of existing goods and services to the production of a cleaner . . . nation . . . up to—and no further than—the point at which we value more highly the next washing machine or hospital . . . than . . . the next unit of environmental improvement. . . . [16]

Baxter acknowledges that figuring out the proper tradeoffs is not easy. "It assumes we can measure in some way the incremental units of human satis-faction yielded by very different types of goods."[17] How can we make such measurements?

Baxter does not tell us, but most economists favor **cost-benefit analysis** (CBA). CBA requires that all costs and benefits associated with a proposal be identified, and that dollar figures be attached to each. Adding up all costs and benefits enables economists to see if benefits outweigh costs. Unless there are other considerations, *CBAs recommend policies producing the greatest excess of benefits over costs as expressed in dollar terms. The use of dollar terms is crucial here, because it alone enables economists to arrive at mathematically defensible recommendations regarding tradeoffs "of human satisfaction yielded by very different types of goods." However, we shall see that expressing human satisfaction in monetary terms leads to controversy.*

CBA is not just a theoretical toy in economics departments. Government planners, including the Nuclear Regulatory Commission (NRC), use it regularly. The Solar Energy Research, Development and Demonstration Act of 1974 requires using CBA to measure the success of solar energy demonstration projects.[18] The National Environmental Policy Act of 1969 requires environmental impact statements for all "major Federal actions significantly affecting the quality of the human environment."[19] Such statements often use CBAs. On February 19, 1981, President Reagan issued Executive Order 12,291 requiring all executive departments and agencies to support every new major regulation with CBA.[20] In May 1999, a bill was debated in Congress that would require all new federal regulations to be accompanied by CBAs.[21]

So consider those catalytic converters from the cost-benefit perspective. The costs per year are, say, $300 per vehicle times the number of vehicles sold each year. The benefits are associated with reduced smog. These include lower rates of heart and lung diseases, lower medical costs to treat such diseases, and, therefore, reduced medical insurance rates. Due to improved health, people miss fewer days from work, and work more efficiently. Thus, reduced smog improves worker productivity. Lower mortality from heart and lung diseases helps people live longer, healthy lives than they otherwise would, and reduces life insurance rates. Smog has a corrosive effect on many buildings, so its reduction lowers the cost of building maintenance. Finally, a clearer atmosphere is more aesthetically pleasing than smog. People enjoy a clear day. There are other benefits, but these are enough to make the point.

In this case, the costs are easily computed. If, for example, one million cars are sold in a year, the cost of the catalytic converter requirement is $300 million. The benefits, however, are another matter. We know that smog impairs human health, but it is hard to say exactly how many fewer heart attacks, lung cancers, strokes, cases of emphysema, and so forth, result from a given reduction in smog. Let us assume, however, that this determination can be made with reasonable accuracy. Then a dollar figure can be given for associated savings in medical expenditures and related reductions in health insurance premiums. These calculations can be made because there are markets in medical services and health insurance, and these markets establish prices in these areas. Markets in life insurance and building repair similarly establish relevant prices and permit reasonable estimates of smog-reduction savings. Again, when people live longer they often work longer, and their extra income and other contributions to the economy during their longer lives can be measured in dollars.

But some benefits from smog reduction are non-monetary. People generally want to live longer, healthier lives for non-monetary reasons. They do not want to live longer primarily to earn money. Instead, they just enjoy life or fear death. There is no market to establish a dollar value for the satisfaction of this desire. We cannot directly buy longer, healthier lives, so we cannot compute this benefit of smog reduction from market values. Similarly, most people like clear days, but they cannot buy them with money, so there is no obvious monetary equivalent of this aesthetic benefit.

In cases like these, CBA requires what economists call **shadow pricing**. A benefit that can be bought with dollars is used to suggest appropriate dollar equivalents for benefits that cannot be bought. For example, the monetary equivalent of the aesthetic enjoyment of a clear atmosphere might be estimated from real estate prices where the air is relatively pure. In addition, economists can ask people on questionnaires how much they would be willing to pay for clearer air. Questionnaires can ask also what people would be willing to pay for additional years of life. The value of additional years expressed in dollar terms can be estimated also by observing how much people are willing to pay for services they believe likely to extend their life spans, such as regular medical checkups, organic vegetables, and memberships at health clubs.

The accuracy of shadow pricing is hotly debated. Critics of CBA maintain that such estimates are so inaccurate as to make the resulting CBAs worthless. But let us skip this issue for the moment in order to see how CBA might be used to determine whether present catalytic converters or some other technology should be required on automobiles. We see the cost of the converters, and estimate the value of the various benefits, using shadow pricing as needed. Suppose the benefits are $600 million per year, whereas annual costs are only $300 million. This justifies requiring some kind of converter, at least, but does not tell us if present converters are the best.

What about converters that clean exhaust emissions more thoroughly? Present converters costing $300 each may reduce emissions by 90 percent, whereas better converters costing $500 each may reduce them by 96 percent. With more powerful converters, the present yearly cost of $300 million would increase by $200 million to $500 million. But when the air is cleaner, the benefits of clean air generally increase. If the benefits with the present converter are worth $600 million, the total benefits from even cleaner air may increase by $150 million, to $750 million. Because the cost of this cleaner air is $500 million and the benefits are $750 million, the costs of the newer, more powerful, but more expensive converter may seem justified. However, the *marginal benefit*, which is the *extra* benefit of having the new converters, is only $150 million, whereas the extra cost is $200 million, so the more powerful converter is not justified by CBA. We are $50 million richer as a society by staying with the present converter.

Maybe a much cheaper converter, if it cleaned up 80 percent instead of 90 percent of auto emissions, would be better still. If we could save, say, $200 million on the converters and lose only $150 million of the $600 million benefits of the current converter, then CBA recommends the cheaper but less effective converter. CBA would not recommend, however, eliminating the converter requirement altogether. The cheap converter costs society only $100 million per year, and the benefits, which would be lost entirely if converters were no longer required, is still $450 million. Our society is richer by $350 million per year when we require converters on cars, and this is why they are good.

In sum, *economists using CBA want rules governing the market to protect public goods to an appropriate extent. Appropriate protection of the commons maximizes social wealth. Rules that protect the commons more than that protection is worth are not justified. Equally unjustified are market rules that allow the commons to be degraded by activities producing less wealth than the degradation costs.* This is the reasoning used by economists when determining not only the advisability of catalytic converters, but also, for example, how much factory pollution should be allowed in a given area.

We saw in the last chapter that governments can reduce air pollution from factories by issuing tradable pollution permits that allow less and less pollution over time. The fewer permits issued (the less pollution allowed) the more expensive permits become on the market. Reduction in supply raises the price. The higher price of pollution permits justifies costlier measures to reduce pollution.

But how much less pollution do we want? From a societal point of view, according to cost-benefit proponents, pollution permits should be used to maximize social wealth. They do this when any addition to their cost (due to limited supply so the air will be cleaner) results in greater increased benefits from cleaner air. If, on the other hand, added benefits from cleaner air are less than the additional cost of pollution permits, then rules to promote clean air have gone too far, and additional pollution should be allowed.

CBA and Increasing Scarcity

CBA is popular with some thinkers because it seems to permit rational decision making. All relevant considerations are put into the same units—dollars. This allows all considerations favoring pollution control to be added together to reach a sum total, and all considerations on the other side to be similarly summed. Then the sums favoring and disfavoring a given proposal can be compared mathematically. We do not have to add apples and oranges, as we say, because one unit of measure is used throughout. Decisions can be mathematically justified, and therefore rational.

Another point favoring CBA is wide respect for its goal—maximization of social wealth. Social wealth here means the dollar value of all the goods and services in the society, or the dollar value of all goods and services produced in the society during a given year (the gross domestic product or GDP).[22] In other words, the goal is the largest possible economy. This goal is so popular that every political candidate for national office, whether Republican or Democratic, endorses it. The goal is increasingly applied to the world economy. Economists and politicians often favor international trade agreements, for example, on the ground that they will foster global economic growth.

Economic growth means that people are producing goods and services of greater total monetary worth. Workers can receive higher salaries as they produce more goods and services for other people to buy. People can buy more of what they want because their salaries are higher and more goods and services are offered for sale. This makes the overriding aim of CBA, to recommend actions that maximize economic growth, very popular. We associate it with a higher standard of living and a better life.

However, these associations are deceptive. A country can have increased GDP (in constant dollars) as people get poorer. The reason is that dollar values generally reflect supply and demand in a market. Usually, increasing demand raises prices, whereas increasing supply lowers them. An item in ample supply has no price at all because all people can have all they want without paying for it. For example, air with sufficient oxygen content for normal human life is abundant near the surface of the earth, so it is free. It is essential for life and therefore very important. But it is free because supply exceeds demand. In other words, it is free because it is not scarce. In the Garden of Eden everything was free because nothing that people needed or wanted was scarce.

When something people need or want becomes scarce, it comes to have a dollar value. Imagine an area where there is enough farmland for people to grow all the food they want. Land would be as free among them as oxygen is among us. Now imagine that the population increases and there is no longer enough land to satisfy everyone's needs. Because it has become scarce, land acquires market value. It is worth money. People now have to do extra work to earn money to rent or buy land to grow crops. The dollar value of the area's assets has increased. The area has become richer. Its economy has grown, as measured by the total dollar value of all market items, including land. But people's (common sense, non-monetary) standard of living has not improved. It has gotten worse because now they have to pay for an essential item, arable land, that used to be free. Their lives are worse, but the economy is bigger. Thus, a bigger economy does not always mean a better life for anyone. It may just reflect increasing scarcity.[23]

This scenario is not just theoretical. The human population continues to increase while arable land is lost to soil erosion, salinization, road construction, and urban expansion. In the words of Lester R. Brown, director of the Worldwatch Institute: "The earth's capacity to produce enough food to satisfy our expanding demand . . . is now emerging as the overriding environmental issue as the world approaches the twenty-first century."[24] If growing the dollar value of the world's economy were our only goal, we would applaud food scarcity resulting from the earth's limited ability to feed a growing population. The monetary value of food and good cropland increase. But hunger increases as well. So *simply having a larger economy is not always good. CBA's goal of increasing the monetary value of social wealth is not always worthy.*

CBA and Political Equality

CBA also recommends policies in violation of the democratic maxim that the government should, in principle, give equal consideration to the interests of all citizens. CBA, as we have seen, recommends policies that maximize the dollar value of society's goods and services. These dollar values are determined in markets, except where shadow pricing is used for items that are not traded in any market. In these cases economists estimate the value people would place on things were they available in a market. In either case, dollar values represent what people are willing to pay for things. Consumer demand (hypothetical or real) is the foundation of cost-benefit analysis.

People's willingness to pay for things (the demands they place on the market) reflects their desires. People are generally willing to pay more for things they desire more. However, willingness to pay (consumer demand) also reflects people's *ability* to pay. A poor person and a rich one may equally desire a Lexus. But only the rich person can be willing actually to pay for it because only she has enough money. Due to lack of money, the poor person does not have an effective market demand for that kind of car. Markets are driven, then, not by desires alone, but by the desires of people who have enough money to combine desire with purchase. In other words, markets do not work on the principle "one person one vote" but on the principle "one dollar one vote."

CBA is supposed to identify policies that maximize the dollar value of goods and services. Dollar values represent the willingness to pay of people with money to spend, so people's impact on dollar values is greater as they become richer. Government policy guided by CBA therefore *legitimately* caters to the desires of the rich over the poor.

Consider, for example, disposal of toxic waste, such as low-level radioactive waste from nuclear power plants. This waste remains dangerously radioactive for many years, so Department of Energy (DOE) planners seek to bury it in stable geological formations where radioactivity will be contained indefinitely. Imagine that they have identified two equally suitable formations, but each is close to a city. Despite government assurances concerning safety, people will want to move away from whichever city is near the buried waste. Property values will plummet in that city.

Suppose one is a wealthy city with 100,000 people and the other is a poor community of 200,000 people. Even though it has fewer people, total property values in the first city are much higher than in the second. Because CBA recommends actions that maximize the total monetary value of society's assets, it recommends siting nuclear waste near the second, larger city. Its real estate values will be lowered considerably, but that loss will be less than if the waste were put near the smaller, wealthier community.

A less dramatic example may bring the issue of political inequality closer to home. Cities require landfill space to dump municipal waste. Most cities have poorer and wealthier areas. Having a landfill nearby will diminish property values somewhat, say, by 20 percent within a one-mile radius. Imagine that the wealthy side of town is less densely populated than the poor side because wealthy people have bigger houses and bigger lawns. Nevertheless, property values within a mile radius of a proposed site in a rich area are greater than those within a mile of a suitable spot on the poor side of town. According to CBA, a greater number of poor people should have their property values reduced in order to avoid greater monetary losses by rich people. Official municipal decision making, when guided by CBA, accords equal worth to each dollar, not to each human being. Following CBA *requires* that more people, rather than fewer, be harmed in this situation, and that those harmed be the poor, who are least equipped financially to absorb any loss.

People often complain that the government serves the interests of rich people over poor, and consider this reprehensible. Our government should have equal concern for every individual's interests, they think. Any other policy seems corrupt, possibly reflecting campaign contributions or personal friendships between rich people and politicians. But if growing the economy is our *only* goal, then preference for rich over poor is often proper rather than corrupt.

Why does this seem unfair? It goes against our ideal that government should care equally about the welfare of all citizens, and it conflicts with our ideal of a fair social contract. We saw earlier that one way to understand our obligations to others is to imagine that we make up rules of social behavior while unaware of our own places in society. Under these conditions, I want the rules to be fair to everyone because if anyone is treated unfairly, it might be me. This notion was used earlier to explain why I have an obligation to preserve the

Reprinted by permission of John Jonik

earth for future generations. If I do not know when I will exist, I will want the earth to support healthy human life indefinitely.

Here the hypothetical contract explains why I want the government to care equally about all citizens, rich and poor alike. If the government gives extra consideration to the rich, who are best able to take care of themselves anyway, and I turn out to be poor, I will be out of luck. So I would prefer social rules that require the government to care equally about all citizens. Rules guided by CBA do not do this.

In sum, those who believe that our government should give equal consideration to all people or citizens, rather than to each dollar, will not want government decision makers to rely exclusively on CBA.

By the way, where are the landfills in your part of the country?

CBA and Future Generations

We saw earlier that in our society we believe we have some obligations to future people. We should not serve our own interests at their expense. This obligation cannot rest on market relationships, because we can have no such relationships with people of the future. The obligation cannot rest on the rights of future people because it is strange that those who do not yet exist should already have rights. There is also the futurity problem. The identity of future people depends on our environmental policies. Whatever we do, people of the future owe their very existence to our having done exactly that and nothing different. If they are glad to be alive, they are in no position to complain about our treatment of the earth. So we based obligations to future generations on a hypothetical contract made under conditions that are supposed to be fair to all parties.

Now let us relate CBA to this obligation by considering some real cases. The nuclear power industry presents many. Nuclear power plants are built to last 40 years, by which time their walls become brittle and unsafe due to bombardment by subatomic particles. Old plants must be decommissioned. We cannot simply demolish them with a wrecking ball because, even when highly radioactive nuclear fuel is removed, the inside of the structure where nuclear fission took place is radioactive. Dismantling the structure must avoid exposing workers or the environment to this radioactivity. This is not easy or cheap. For one thing, any materials that come into contact with a reactor's low-level radioactivity become radioactive themselves. For this reason, writes Worldwatch associate Nicholas Lenssen:

> Dismantling these facilities can produce a greater volume of wastes than operating them: a typical commercial reactor produces 6,200 cubic meters of low-level waste over a 40-year lifetime; demolishing it creates an additional 15,480 cubic meters of low-level waste.[25]

No one has ever actually decommissioned a commercial-size nuclear power plant by dismantling it, so costs can only be estimated. Phillip A. Greenberg, an independent energy and environmental-policy consultant in San Francisco wrote in 1993:

> The utility that owns the comparatively small 175-megawatt (MW) Yankee Rowe plant has projected that decommissioning will cost $247 million, and recent estimates for dismantling the 330-MW Fort St. Vrain reactor stand at $333 million. . . . Indiana Michigan Power looks to spend as much as $550 million each to decommission its two 1,000-MW Cook reactors.[26]

This is a lot of money. Aren't there cheaper alternatives?

Probably the cheapest way to keep people safe from low-level radiation is to cover old reactors with concrete. This is literally billions of dollars cheaper than dismantling. The reactors will remain on the landscape and take up space, but concrete will protect people from its radiation *so long as the concrete remains intact*. But our best concrete may last only 500 years, and the radiation will be hazardous much longer. Burying reactors under concrete, then, amounts to sending a poisonous parcel to future generations, who may be better or worse equipped to handle it.

We saw earlier that our moral training includes obligations to future generations. These obligations explain why **decommissioning** is not by concrete burial. But this is what CBA would recommend.

CBA places all matters in financial terms. Future costs or benefits are discounted due to financial interest rates. Suppose that I will receive $100 inheritance in one year. What is it worth today? It is worth the amount of money someone would have to put in a secure bank today to get $100 in one year. At a 5 percent interest rate, for example, the $100 that I will receive in one year is today worth about $95, because if I put just over $95 in the bank today at 5 percent interest, it would be worth $100 in a year. If I had to wait two years for the money, its current worth would be less because there would be two years for bank interest to accumulate. Its current worth would be about $91.

This is why people can buy $100 U.S. Savings Bonds for only $45 or $50. Due to interest, the bonds will be worth $100 in a specified number of years. But they are not worth that now. Their future worth must be discounted in accordance with the interest rate and the amount of time until maturity to arrive at their current worth—$45 or $50. Because the interest rate is used to calculate how much to discount a future dollar benefit (or burden, such as a debt), the interest rate is here called a **discount rate**.

As we have seen, because CBA puts everything in the same financial terms, alternatives can be compared mathematically. This is considered good. But because *everything* is in financial terms, everything must be discounted in accordance with a discount rate, *even human lives*. Discussing radiation-induced deaths from the operation of nuclear power plants, energy economist Sam Schurr writes in *Energy in America's Future: The Choices before Us*:

> If all the predicted deaths over all future years were to be added up, the totals would be very large, 100 to 800 per plant. [We] propose discounting these effects

to yield their present-day equivalents, just as future incomes are discounted to represent the smaller value of future events in present-day calculations. If these effects are discounted at reasonable rates, such as 5%, contributions for each plant-year would be between 0.07 and 0.3 fatality.[27]

Proponents of CBA *must* discount human lives as we do financial rewards in order to put everything in mathematically comparable, financial terms. If this seems absurd or immoral, then we have reason to reject CBA and its identification of rationality with mathematical calculations of monetary values.

We have even greater reason where future generations are concerned. Consider future people who may be harmed by leaking radiation from old nuclear power plants covered with concrete that lasts only 500 years. How much are those future lives worth today at a 5 percent discount rate? Well, if you put a dollar away today at 5 percent interest, compound interest makes it worth about $16 billion in 500 years. (Too bad you didn't know that 500 years ago.) By this logic, one human life today is worth about 16 billion lives 500 years from now.

This suggests that we decommission nuclear power plants by burying them under concrete designed to last 500 years. We can save billions of dollars now. We can use part of this money to save human lives, such as by reducing pollution that causes cancer or by helping people in poor countries. Philosopher Peter Unger writes in *Living High and Letting Die:*

> For about $17 a head, UNICEF can vaccinate children against measles. On the positive side, the protection secured lasts a lifetime. . . . What is more, at the same time each child can be vaccinated for lifetime protection against five other diseases that, taken together, each year kill about . . . [a] million Third World kids: tuberculosis, whooping cough, diphtheria, tetanus and polio.[28]

With billions of dollars, it will be easy to save at least one human life.

Even if we save only one life today, and radiation leaks starting 500 years from now kill several *billion* people, CBA would recommend concrete entombment. One life today is worth 16 billion people. As long as fewer people than that are killed starting 500 years from now, the policy is mathematically justified.

Obviously, something is leaking here besides radiation. *Where future generations are concerned, CBA is not a reliable guide to reasonable policies.* Unfortunately, as noted already, the Nuclear Regulatory Commission, which licenses and oversees nuclear power plant construction and operation, uses CBA.

Some environmental issues concern human safety much farther in the future than 500 years. High-level waste from nuclear power plants will be toxic for 250,000 years.[29] Such waste is now stored around the country near nuclear power plants, but the Department of Energy (DOE) has a plan to bury it in a salt dome geological formation in Yucca Mountain, Nevada. "The big problem . . . is water," writes Nicholas Lenssen:

> In theory, the waste in Yucca Mountain's volcanic tuff bedrock would stay dry since the storerooms would be located more than 300 meters above the current wa-

ter table, and since percolation from the surface under current climatic conditions is minimal. But critics, led by DOE geologist Jerry Szymanski, believe that an earthquake at Yucca Mountain, which is crisscrossed with more than 30 seismic faults, could dramatically raise the water table. If water came into contact with hot radioactive wastes, the resulting steam explosion could "blow the top off the mountain."[30]

This would spread radioactivity to a wide area. "In 1990," Lenssen continues:

> Scientists discovered that a volcano 20 kilometers from Yucca Mountain erupted within the last 20,000 years—not 270,000 years ago, as they had earlier surmised. . . . It is worth remembering that less than 10,000 years ago volcanoes were erupting in what is now central France [and] that the English Channel did not exist 7,000 years ago. . . . [31]

Stanford University geologist Konrad Krauskopf summed up a 1990 article in *Science*: "No scientist or engineer can give an absolute guarantee that radioactive waste will not someday leak in dangerous quantities from even the best of repositories."[32]

I raise this issue here because most people have some concern for future generations living thousands of years from now. Writing in *Sierra* in 1992, environmental journalist William Poole notes, "most Nevadans—75 percent at last count—are repulsed by the idea" of high-level nuclear waste burial in Yucca Mountain.[33] CBA finds this concern to be absurd. From a CBA perspective, we should save billions of dollars on burial of high-level waste, as well as billions on decommissioning. Just put it all under concrete that lasts 500 years. When that much time has gone by, according to CBA's accounting method, there is no real loss even if radiation leaks kill billions of people.

The negative effects of global warming may occur sooner, perhaps in 100 years. At a 5 percent discount rate, one life today is worth about 120 lives in 100 years. This is better than 16 billion, but do we really think it proper for 120 people in the future to sacrifice their lives so that we can, at our economic convenience, save one life today?

Judgment Calls

The last chapter and this one show that market activity can be environmentally beneficial. When it is not beneficial, cost-benefit analyses often indicate changes in rules governing the market that rectify the situation. However, we found that recommendations based on CBA conflict at times with our strongly held moral opinions about human rights, equality among citizens, and obligations to future generations. But if we do not use CBA to determine appropriate tradeoffs, how can we rationally handle decisions regarding, for example, global warming and municipal waste facilities?

- Instead of putting municipal waste facilities on the poor side of town, a committee of people from different economic groups could identify all the practical sites for the next facility. Then, a random selection device, such as throwing dice, could be used to determine the actual site. What are the pros and cons of this approach?

- In November 1998, the California Air Resources Board voted to impose the same clean air standards on sport utility vehicles, minivans, and light trucks as they impose on passenger cars. This will make their exhaust fumes two-and-a-half times cleaner than at present.[34] How can this decision be justified? What CBA considerations suggest stronger standards for these vehicles than for most others?

- Global warming results primarily from using fossil fuels for energy. Americans use much more fossil fuel energy per capita than most other people. In fact, according to environmental journalist Bill McKibben, "an American uses seventy times as much energy as a Bangladeshi, fifty times as much as a Malagasi, twenty times as much as a Costa Rican." One result is this: "During the next decade India and China will each add to the planet about ten times as many people as the United States will—but the stress on the natural world caused by new Americans may exceed that from new Indians and Chinese combined."[35] In light of these facts, and the importance of mitigating global warming, maybe we should combat population growth in the United States. Currently, Americans can claim children as a tax deduction on income taxes. Perhaps this should apply only to the first two children. What do you think?

- Much of the population increase in the United States stems from the immigration of people from poor countries. These people soon live an American lifestyle and use much more fossil fuel energy than they would if they stayed in their native lands. Should we combat global warming by reducing immigration from poor countries? How does this proposal look when judged by rules of social justice that we would choose if we did not know whether we were born in the U.S. or Bangladesh?

We need some model of decision making to answer these and many other questions. But, as we have seen, CBA makes sense only some of the time. In the next chapter we explore anthropocentric environmentalism that allows for a *plurality* of values that accommodate more of our strongly held moral views. I call this *non-economic anthropocentrism*. It suggests a decision procedure that is less mathematical and more political, interpersonal, and conversational.

CHAPTER 3

Competing Human-Centered Values

Environmental Hazards in the Third World

Anthony Thomas Henriques ran for his life in the early hours of December 3, 1984, in Bhopal, India. An employee of the Greaves Cotton Company in Bombay, Mr. Henriques was in Bhopal on business. He later told *Society* magazine that when he left his hotel he was aghast:

> Oh my God! Why are all these people lying on Hamidia Road? They were dead, every one of them, hundreds of them—dead. They were all trying to get away from the gas. The dying were urinating, defecating, and vomiting. . . . I was choking because the gas was all around. . . . I ran to the lake. . . . Thousands of people were lying there. Some were alive, they were drinking water, they were vomiting in the lake and drinking the same thing. Many were dead, choked, dying bodies were heaped up . . . one dying on top of another. . . . In a few minutes I will be dead.[1]

Mr. Henriques managed to pick himself up and continue running. He survived. But many were not so lucky. Official figures put the number killed by one of the world's worst industrial accidents at 1,754, reports Ward Morehouse in an article in *The Ecologist* commemorating the tenth anniversary of the tragedy. But "circumstantial evidence based on the number of shrouds and the amount of cremation wood sold in the following weeks suggest that as many as 10,000 people may have died—a figure also put forward by senior UNICEF officials after a week-long investigation."[2] Another 200,000 to 300,000 were injured, many permanently with blindness and crippling respiratory problems. Spontaneous abortions and children born deformed became common.

Reactions to the Bhopal disaster illustrate tensions between economic and non-economic anthropocentrism. *Anthropocentrists care only about people. Economic anthropocentrists want to put all values in monetary terms so that people can use markets (or simulated markets) to choose actions and policies that promote maximum human well being. Non-economic anthropocentrists also want to promote exclusively human well being, but claim that some important values cannot be put in monetary terms. These values include some associated with human rights, aesthetics, national heritage, and opposition to the meaningless consumption of consumer items. Mathematical calculations of monetary costs and benefits ignore or distort these values, so people must discuss and weigh a plurality of competing values without translating them into comparable monetary units. The present chapter supports non-economic over economic anthropocentrism.*

No one tried deliberately to kill or injure people in Bhopal, but economic calculations could have justified actions that created the danger. The American-based multi-national corporation Union Carbide launched its Bhopal pesticide plant in 1969 to "import, dilute, package, and ship [the pesticide] Sevin,"[3] writes David Weir of the Center for Investigative Reporting. The corporation then proposed producing and storing MIC in Bhopal, a city of 800,000 people. MIC is a particularly dangerous substance of disputed chemical composition used in pesticide production. Because it is heavier than air, it stays close to the ground when it escapes. It is highly corrosive, boils at 39.1 degrees C (102.4 degrees F), and is prone to violent chain reactions producing great heat.[4]

Despite a government order in 1975 that the MIC facility be built 15 miles away, Union Carbide began producing and storing MIC in Bhopal in 1980. The plant was "just two miles from the Bhopal railway station, which was convenient for shipping, but disastrous . . . for travelers on the night of December 2, 1984." Also, the plant was "ringed with shantytowns, mostly populated by squatters, who are part of the mass migration from countryside to city taking place all over the Third World. Although Union Carbide has claimed the squatters arrived after it did, old maps of Bhopal indicate otherwise."[5]

The facility lacked state-of-the-art detection equipment. Union Carbide's factory in Institute, Virginia, which also used MIC to produce Sevin, had automated safety controls run by computers, whereas the plant in Bhopal had only a manually operated system.[6] Weir reports also that two years before the disaster:

> A three-member safety team from the Union Carbide headquarters in the United States visited the . . . plant, and submitted a revealing report on the safety dangers of the MIC section. . . . The report recommended various changes to reduce the danger at the plant; there is no evidence the recommendations were ever implemented. . . . In addition, the few systems present that could have slowed or partially contained the reaction were all out of operation at the time of the accident. Gauges measuring temperature and pressure in the various parts of the unit, including the crucial MIC storage tanks, were so notoriously unreliable that workers ignored early signs of trouble. The refrigeration unit for keeping MIC at low temperatures . . . had been shut off for some time. The gas scrubber, designed to neutralize any escaping MIC, had been shut off for maintenance.[7]

And the list goes on.

Warren Anderson, former chairman of Union Carbide Corporation, initially denied a double standard of safety between the facilities in the United States and India. But by March 1985, he admitted that the Bhopal plant operated in ways that would not be allowed in Virginia.[8] This kind of double standard is not unique to Union Carbide or India. Agrochemical plants are becoming common in the Third World. "During 1984, for example," Weir writes, "DuPont announced plans to build new pesticide plants in Indonesia and Thailand; Hoechst, in India, Pakistan, and Colombia; both Stauffer and Sandoz, in Brazil; and Monsanto, in Taiwan."[9] These countries need the money. But safety standards are seldom the same as in the First World. Contractors take shortcuts in construction. Government inspectors are too few, and their reports of safety hazards are often ignored. Workers are inadequately educated to handle dangerous chemicals. Corporations lack a culture of safety, and, typically, many people live in crowded conditions close to the facility. As a result, many Third World people are exposed to environmental hazards that we would not tolerate in our midst.

Manufacturing processes are not the only hazards. Their by-products often include hazardous wastes. Many people in poor countries are exposed to such wastes as incinerator ash, dioxin, and PCBs, which can cause cancer and other health problems. Worldwatch associate Jodi L. Jacobson reported in 1989:

> Thousands of tons of U.S. and European wastes have already been shipped to Africa and the Middle East. Some 3,800 tons of toxic waste from Italy dumped in the small Nigerian port town of Koko in five shipments between 1987 and 1988 contained at least 150 tons of PCBs—the chemical that put Love Canal on the map.[10]

Such shipments of toxic waste continued, reported Aaron Sachs in 1996. "Experts believe that at least 30 million tons a year cross national borders, with a high percentage going to poorer countries." The reason is this:

> In the late eighties, largely because of new laws, hazardous waste disposal prices in the United States climbed up to about $250 per ton. In Africa, meanwhile, where environmental regulations and appropriate disposal technologies were virtually nonexistent, the per-ton price was often as low as $2.50. Many African countries were willing to accept the toxic shipments because they were accompanied by much-needed foreign exchange.[11]

Again there is a double standard. The corporations involved may be acting from self-interest, but CBA allows them the justification of maximizing the world's wealth. So poor people live with life-threatening hazards that affluent people avoid. Is this right?

How Much Money Is a Human Life Worth?

We saw in the last chapter that if morality is determined by a hypothetical contract made behind a veil of ignorance, it includes equal human rights to life and to whatever is essential to life. If I were behind a veil of ignorance, I would not know whether I was rich or poor, so I would want the poor and rich to be protected equally from life-threatening chemical spills and toxic wastes. If the poor had a lesser right to protection than the rich, I might turn out to be a poor person exposed to chemical agents that shorten or impair my life, while rich people enjoy the benefits not only of their riches, but also of safer living conditions. This does not seem fair. When human rights are derived from the concept of fairness, then the exposure of so many people in poor countries to hazardous industrial processes and toxic wastes violates their human rights.

This is the view of many experts on human rights. Ward Morehouse reports that "The Permanent People's Tribunal on Industrial and Environmental Hazards and Human Rights in Rome . . ." addressed the plight of those killed and injured in Bhopal. They "concluded in October 1992 that the fundamental human rights of the victims . . . had been grossly violated by Union Carbide [and] the government of India. . . ."[12] A group of experts met in Geneva in 1994 to compose a more general document: "Draft Declaration of Principles on Human Rights and the Environment." It proclaims, among other things, a universal human right to a "secure, healthy, ecologically sound environment."[13]

But many economists give priority to economic growth because it leads to generally higher salaries and more spending power for average Americans. Market exchanges generally promote economic growth, except where public goods are concerned. In those cases, economists use cost-benefit analysis (CBA) to identify new rules of market exchange that maximize growth.

We noted problems with this approach. Economic growth does not improve human welfare if it merely reflects higher prices and longer working hours stemming from the increasing scarcity of essential items, such as land to grow crops. When governments use CBA they give equal consideration to each dollar rather than to each person. This goes against the ideal of equal government concern for all citizens. Also, CBA discounts the lives of future generations, as if people living later have fewer human rights than those living now. The situation in Bhopal highlights yet another problem. *CBA assigns different monetary equivalents for the lives of people living now.*

CBAs put all variables in dollar terms so that optimal policies can be identified mathematically. As we saw in the last chapter, shadow prices are assigned to whatever is not traded in markets, including human lives. Economists estimate how much people value their lives in monetary terms from how much they spend on life insurance and medical care, as well as how much extra pay they demand for dangerous work. Also, when people are killed in accidents caused by negligence, jury awards suggest common estimates of a life's monetary worth. The problem is that on such measures *an average human life in a poor country is worth much less money than an American, European, or Japanese life. This denies an equal human right to life.*

The denial could justify sending dangerous manufacturing processes and toxic wastes to poor countries. If people die in these countries due to accidents or ongoing environmental contamination, less money is lost than if people in rich countries are killed. Imagine what the jury awards would be if the Union

Carbide plant in Virginia had exploded instead of the one in Bhopal. It would run into the billions. Tobacco companies in the U.S. agreed in late 1998 to pay 46 states a total of $206 billion for medical costs associated with customers' voluntary use of cigarettes. Imagine the jury awards if people had been killed or permanently injured through no fault of their own!

Compare this with the compensation given victims of the Bhopal accident. Ward Morehouse reports in *The Ecologist* that after four years of litigation the Indian Supreme Court ordered Union Carbide Corporation to pay a total of $470 million.

> This sum, equivalent to only $793 for each of the 592,000 who had then filed claims, was not even sufficient to cover healthcare and monitoring of the gas-exposed population, which had been conservatively estimated at $600 million over the next 20 to 30 years. The settlement was so favorable for Union Carbide that its stock price rose $2 a share on the New York Stock Exchange the day it was announced.[14]

$793 per person! It is clearly cheaper to kill or maim an Indian than an American. And this is perfectly logical. Poor Indians buy less life insurance, earn less money during their lives, and require less extra pay for dangerous work. They also buy fewer treadmills and other equipment to prolong their lives. The shadow pricing used in CBA must conclude from such data that the monetary worth of a poor Indian's life is less than that of an American. The judgment of the Indian Supreme Court reflects this view.

The logic of this position had already been explained in 1992 by the World Bank's chief economist, Lawrence Summers, in an internal memo leaked to the press.

> Just between you and me, shouldn't the World Bank be encouraging *more* migration of the dirty industries to the LDCs [least developed countries]? I can think of three reasons:
>
> 1. The measurement of the costs of health-impairing pollution depends on the forgone earnings from increased morbidity and mortality. From this point of view a given amount of health-impairing pollution should be done in the country with the lowest cost, which will be the country with the lowest wages. I think the economic logic behind dumping a load of toxic waste in the lowest-wage country is impeccable and we should face up to that.
>
> 2. The costs of pollution are likely to be non-linear as the initial increments of pollution probably have very low cost. I've always thought that under-populated countries in Africa are vastly *under*-polluted. . . .
>
> 3. The demand for a clean environment for aesthetic and health reasons is likely to have very high income-elasticity. The concern over an agent that causes a one-in-a-million change in the odds of prostate cancer is obviously going to be much higher in a country where people survive to get prostate cancer than in a country where under-5 mortality is 200 per 1000. . . .
>
> The problem with the arguments against all of these proposals for more pollution in the LDCs (intrinsic rights to certain goods, moral reasons, social concerns, . . .

etc.) could be turned around and used more or less effectively against every Bank proposal for liberalization.[15]

Every such Bank proposal uses strict economic logic, which ignores all non-monetary concerns about intrinsic rights, moral reasons, and social concerns.

The Summers memo embarrassed the World Bank. It seems that many people are not economic anthropocentrists. They resist translating all moral values into monetary terms. The World Bank soon claimed that Summers was not serious. But he expressed consistently the logic of economic anthropocentrism, which puts all values in monetary terms and favors the largest accumulation of wealth. Indira Gandhi, the late prime minister of India, expressed similar views. She said, "Environmental safeguards are irrelevant: poverty is our greatest environmental hazard."[16] *The Economist* contained an article in 1995 that said Summers' "outspokenness annoyed many . . . especially environmentalists. . . ." He should not be blamed for his view, however, because he is right. His memo "pointed out—correctly but too frankly—that pollution had lower social costs in poor countries than in rich ones."[17] In 1999, Summers became United States Secretary of the Treasury in the Clinton administration.

What should we think? Are economic anthropocentrists correct and non-economic anthropocentrists just foggy-headed sentimentalists who fail to understand how to promote genuine human welfare? Or are non-economic anthropocentrists correct in their view that some important values are lost or distorted by purely economic calculations, so different methods of moral reasoning are needed in order to serve humanity best?

This issue has practical importance. It underlies a controversy that could jeopardize international efforts to combat global warming. Some economic anthropocentrists submitted a report in late 1995 to the Intergovernmental Panel on Climate Change (IPCC). It calculated the costs of global warming to determine how much should be spent combating it. Sociology Professor Steven Yearly writes:

> In making their calculations for this report the economists had put a price on the various sorts of loss likely to arise from climate change and sea-level rise, including the loss of human life. These values, together with the cost of preventative policies could then be used in a cost-benefit analysis to compute the optimal course of action. They calculated the "value" of human lives by reference to such things as how much people would be willing and able to pay to avoid environmental hazards. Accordingly Northern lives [in the First World] appeared far more valuable than those of citizens in the South [the Third World].[18]

Third World delegates objected. Who wants to be a cheap date to a global warming?

Such objections cannot be ignored. According to environmental journalist Bill McKibben, the IPCC "projects that an immediate 60 percent reduction in fossil-fuel use is necessary just to stabilize climate at the current level of disruption."[19] But, *The Atlantic Monthly's* Gregg Easterbrook noted in 1995, "if all

First World countries reduce their greenhouse output by 20 percent . . . while the Third World nations merely continue on their current rate of increase in power output, early in the next century the net global carbon dioxide output will increase 15 percent."[20] According to Easterbrook, the IPCC projects that "at current rates of increase in Chinese coal-power production, by the year 2025 China alone will emit more greenhouse gases than Canada, Japan, and the United States combined."[21] *Third World cooperation is essential, then, to combat global warming, and we can hardly expect their cooperation with plans that place less worth on their lives than ours. Economic anthropocentrism will not do.*

Some reasons for and against legalizing prostitution suggest that non-economic anthropocentrism is better.

Should Prostitution Be Legalized?

Prostitution is illegal almost everywhere in the United States, whereas in Great Britain it is legal but open solicitation by prostitutes is criminal, and in the Netherlands prostitutes can legally ply their trade and advertise their services. Why is prostitution illegal in the United States? Philosopher Jacques Thiroux expresses the thoughts of many in *Ethics: Theory and Practice*:

> Prostitution fosters a lack of respect for the prostitute (usually a woman) and for human sexual activity itself, which is supposed to enhance the intimacy of a relationship between partners. . . . Prostitution instead lowers human sexuality to an animalistic act of lust. . . . Prostitution is a big business and is usually managed and run by the criminal element in the United States. Prostitutes are often treated like animals by their pimps and customers; many are beaten, and some are ultimately killed. In addition, many prostitutes have been addicted to drugs by their pimps to keep them dependent. . . . There is no faster or more certain way of transmitting social diseases and AIDS than prostitution, for in addition to its being transmitted sexually, prostitutes may also become infected by needles as drug abusers. . . . Further, because prostitutes and their clients may have many partners, the chances of spreading these diseases are multiplied. . . . Because of all this, prostitution . . . should be eliminated from our culture. . . . [22]

We should continue to have and enforce laws against prostitution.

Notice that some of the considerations against legalizing prostitution can be put in monetary terms. The risk of spreading social diseases and AIDS, for example, can be translated into related costs for medical treatments and insurance premiums. When prostitutes die from violence or drugs the money they might have earned lawfully during a much longer life is lost. But is money foremost in people's minds when they decry the spread of AIDS and drug abuse through prostitution? I don't think so.

Other considerations raised against legalizing prostitution feature non-monetary ideals. Prostitutes are not respected as persons. Human sexual activity, which is supposed to foster intimacy between partners, is degraded to the point of animal lust. These considerations depend on *ideals* of how people should treat one another, and how sex should fit into human life. People who oppose prostitution on these grounds would not care if legalization increased GDP or generated taxes.

Now let us consider the other side. Conservative columnist George F. Will argued in 1974 that prostitution should be decriminalized. He wrote:

> This is not apt to happen soon, given the instinct of state legislators to recoil in horror from any idea that has only reason on its side. But the reasons for decriminalizing prostitution are impeccably conservative, involving respect for privacy, liberty, the Constitution, the law and the police. Prostitution is immoral, but it is not a threat to the fabric of society. Because prostitution is private sexual conduct between consenting adults the state should not proscribe it unless the state can demonstrate that it involves substantial harmful public consequences. But the harmful public consequences associated with prostitution are either unaffected by attempts to proscribe it or are produced by those attempts. . . . Anti-prostitution laws invariably violate the right to privacy. . . . Usually in their words and invariably in their application [they] violate the equal protection provision of the Constitution by discriminating against women.[23]

Will emphasizes non-monetary considerations. Americans have rights to liberty, equal protection of the laws, and privacy. These are social ideals whose monetary worth cannot be calculated. What is more, even if they could be calculated, Will favors them not because upholding these ideals makes the country *richer*, but because it makes the country *better*. So *the argument for legalizing prostitution, like the argument against it, presupposes aspects of morality that monetary considerations fail to capture. Both sides reject economic anthropocentrism.*

Non-economic vs. Economic Anthropocentrism

Scholar Mark Sagoff explains why economic anthropocentrism is attractive, but non-economic anthropocentrism is correct. People are both citizens and consumers.

> As a *citizen*, I am concerned with the public interest, rather than my own interest; with the good of the community, rather than simply the well-being of my family. . . . In my role as a *consumer* . . . I concern myself with personal or self-regarding wants and interests; I pursue the goals I have as an individual. I put aside the community-regarding values I take seriously as a citizen, and I look out for Number One.[24]

The arguments we have reviewed both for and against legalizing prostitution adopt the standpoint of the citizen, not the consumer. In general, consumers want the economy as big as possible because this maximizes employment possibilities, incomes, and product choice. Yet neither side in the prostitution debate mentions these considerations. Their views reflect what they think will make the society *better*, not *richer*.

How could so many economists miss this obvious point? A major goal of economists is to predict what people will do in market transactions. Predictions are generally best that assume people usually act selfishly in market contexts. Selfish behavior in markets is considered economically rational.

Many economists assume further that people think in economic terms, and therefore act selfishly, whenever their economic interests are affected, and this is where they go wrong. People often adopt a citizen perspective and endorse policies that adversely affect them economically. For example, many people of comfortable financial means favor regulation of working conditions to ensure worker safety. Neither these people nor their close family members are likely to work in coal mines or factories where conditions would be hazardous in the absence of such regulations, so they do not benefit personally. Instead, these regulations make mining and manufacturing processes more expensive and drive up the price of many consumer goods. This worsens the market position of these affluent consumers. As consumers we generally prefer lower to higher prices. So why do affluent people favor legislation authorizing workplace regulation by the Occupational Health and Safety Administration (OSHA)? In Sagoff's words:

> Social regulation expresses what we believe, what we are, what we stand for as a nation, not simply what we wish to buy as individuals. Social regulation reflects public values we choose collectively, and these may conflict with wants and interests we pursue individually.[25]

Sagoff supplies additional illustrations of conflicts between our roles as consumer and citizen, and greater commitment to the citizen over the consumer perspective:

> Last year, I bribed a judge to fix a couple of traffic tickets, and I was glad to do so because I saved my license. Yet, at election time, I helped to vote the corrupt judge out of office. I speed on the highway; yet I want the police to enforce laws against speeding. . . . I love my car; I hate the bus. Yet I vote for candidates who promise to tax gasoline to pay for public transportation. . . . The political causes I support seem to have little or no basis in my interests as a consumer, because I take different points of view when I vote and when I shop. I have an "Ecology Now" sticker on a car that drips oil everywhere it's parked.[26]

Sagoff claims that people make a logical error, called a **category mistake**, when they treat public policy preferences as if they were consumer demands. A category mistake, he writes, "is the kind of mistake you make when you predicate of one concept another that makes no sense in relation to it."[27] For example, it is a category mistake to claim that the square root of two is blue, or demand the name and address of the average American. Similarly, anyone

who asks how much citizens would pay to satisfy opinions that they advocate through political association commits a category mistake. . . . Public "preferences"

involve not desires or wants but opinions or views. They state what a person believes is best or right for the community or group as a whole. . . . Those who argue in favor of or against a public policy . . . wish their views to be heard and understood; they seek a response to the arguments they make. . . . No one . . . contends
that the intensity with which people hold beliefs or the money they spend to pub-
licize them indicates the cogency of their intellectual position. It is the cogency of
the arguments, not how much partisans are willing to pay, moreover, that offers
a credible basis for public policy.[28]

The abortion debate illustrates the absurdity of treating people always as
consumers and never as citizens. Economists Hugh H. Macauley and Bruce
Yandle suggest in *Environmental Use and the Market* that the abortion controversy could be settled by establishing a market in abortion permits. They write:

There is an optimal number of abortions, just as there is an optimal level of pollution, or purity. . . . Those who oppose abortion could eliminate it entirely, if their
intensity of feeling were so strong as to lead to payments that were greater at the
margin than the price anyone would pay to have an abortion.[29]

Pro-life and pro-choice advocates would reject this reasoning as absurd. It commits the category mistake of treating policy preferences as consumer demands.
Willingness to pay measures consumer demands, not policy preferences.

Aesthetic Values

If the generation of maximum wealth is not the only basis for reasoned judgments about public policies, what other standards should environmentalists
use? We have seen that the right to life is one. It justifies condemning the export of dangerous manufacturing processes and toxic chemicals to poor people in the Third World. But there are many other environmental issues, and
they cannot all be settled by appeals to the right to life. For example, environmentalists often want to preserve wilderness areas and restore wild animals to
their natural habitat.

Purely economic appeals (the sort made by economic anthropocentrists) seldom justify preservation, because more money can be made by developing
wilderness areas. An example is Mineral King Valley, whose fate was in the
hands of the Supreme Court in 1972. Mineral King was in a National Forest
adjacent to the Sequoia National Park. Justice Potter Stewart described it as "a
quasi-wilderness area uncluttered by the products of civilization." It was used
"almost exclusively for recreational purposes. . . . Its relative inaccessibility and
lack of development . . . limited the number of visitors each year."[30] Justice
William O. Douglas had never visited the valley, but assumed it was "like the
other wonders of the Sierra Nevada . . . [where people can] hike, . . . hunt, . . .
fish, . . . or visit . . . merely to sit in solitude and wonderment. . . ."[31]

In 1969, the Forest Service granted a license to Walt Disney Enterprises to build a ski resort in Mineral King Valley. The plan was for

a $35 million complex of motels, restaurants, swimming pools, parking lots, and other structures designed to accommodate 14,000 visitors daily. . . . Other facilities, including ski lifts, ski trails, a cog-assisted railway, and utility installations, are to be constructed on the mountain slopes. . . . To provide access to the resort, the State of California proposes to construct a highway 20 miles in length. A section of this road would traverse Sequoia National Park, as would a proposed high-voltage power line needed to provide electricity for the resort.[32]

The Sierra Club, an environmental organization with special interest in the Sierra Nevada Mountains, objected. It claimed that the development "would destroy or otherwise adversely affect the scenery, natural and historic objects and wildlife of the park, and would impair the enjoyment of the park for future generations."[33] The Sierra Club did not claim that leaving Mineral King Valley a quasi-wilderness area would generate more revenue and maximize GDP. The opposite is obvious. Skiers' bank balances dip as fast as any ski run. And there were to be 14,000 visitors *per day!* How strong is the Sierra Club's non-economic appeal?

One concern they raise is aesthetic. The Disney plan would "adversely affect the scenery." Judge the strength of this kind of appeal by considering this description of a different wilderness area. Aldo Leopold, a founder of ecological science in the first half of the twentieth century, described the delta of the Colorado River early in the century:

On the map the Delta was bisected by the river, but in fact the river was nowhere and everywhere, for he could not decide which of a hundred green lagoons offered the most pleasant and least speedy path to the Gulf. . . . "He leadeth me by still waters" was only a phrase in a book until we had nosed our canoe through the green lagoons. . . . The still waters were of a deep emerald hue, colored by algae, I suppose, but no less green for all that. A verdant wall of mesquite and willow separated the channel from the thorny desert beyond. At each bend we saw egrets standing in the pools ahead, each a white statue matched by its white reflection. Fleets of cormorants drove their black prows in quest of skittering mullets; avocets, willets, and yellow-legs dozed one-legged on the bars; mallards, widgeons, and teal sprang skyward in alarm.[34]

I wouldn't know a widgeon from a willet, but Leopold's description makes me wish I could visit the green lagoons of the Colorado River delta.

Leopold continues: "Never did we plan the morrow, for we had learned that in the wilderness some new and irresistible distraction is sure to turn up each day before breakfast. Like the river, we were free to wander."[35] One day Leopold saw in the sky "a rotating circle of white spots, alternately visible and invisible. A faint bugle note soon told us they were cranes, inspecting their Delta and finding it good." He reports misidentifying their species, but it didn't matter. "What matters is that we were sharing our wilderness with the wildest of living fowl. We and they had found a common home in the remote vastnesses of space and time; we were both back in the Pleistocene."[36]

❧   ❧   ❧

Eugene C. Hargrove argues in *Foundations of Environmental Ethics* that such aesthetic considerations as these support environmental preservation. Eighteenth-century Europeans and Americans favored formal gardens, where plants are cut into geometrical shapes, to more natural landscapes. But then tastes changed.

> Nonformal gardens became popular at the same time that horticultural societies began to be organized in Europe and America. These societies sent agents to all parts of the world to bring back seeds and plants. The landscape garden naturally became the showplace for these botanical exhibits, and the introduction of these new plants into them produced a more relaxed attitude toward nature by forcing garden enthusiasts to accept new and wilder standards of beauty. . . . Since each individual plant was an emissary, so to speak, from some mysterious and bizarre corner of the Earth, the thoughts of the garden enthusiast inevitably turned to the contemplation of the natural and alien environment. . . . In this way, an interest in wilderness areas arose that helped prepare the way for their direct appreciation later, both scientifically and aesthetically.[37]

Hargrove recommends that we think of such wilderness areas the way we think of art works. Our lives are enriched by experiencing them. This is an anthropocentric reason. We want them preserved, however, not just to provide enriching experiences, but also because we believe the world is a better place with these entities than without them. In other words, we regard them as having **intrinsic value**. Because we favor above all their continued existence, we are willing to view only copies and photographs if viewing them directly tends to destroy them. Hargrove notes, "art objects are routinely removed from public viewing whenever such viewing starts to damage them."[38] The same is true of cave paintings, such as the famous one of a deer at Lascaux, France. The light needed to show the painting to tourists fostered growth of a destructive fungus, so there are no longer any tours. Instead, the nearby visitors center has a full-size scale model of the cave. For analogous reasons, a completely natural cave passage in Mammoth Cave National Park is off limits to aesthetic viewing. People can see photographs.[39] Similarly, I know that if the green lagoons of the Colorado River delta existed today, I would want them preserved even if I had no chance of visiting them personally.

The National Wildlife Federation makes aesthetic appeals to intrinsic values. A letter I received from them in December 1998 urged me to support continuation of the Yellowstone Wolf Recovery Program. Wolves are natural to the Yellowstone area, but were hunted to local extinction many years ago. They were re-introduced in 1994. However, recently "a federal judge has ordered the U.S. Fish and Wildlife Service to shut down the program and evict the wolves. . . . *The majesty of the Yellowstone wolf could disappear forever!*" Hargrove would consider this an aesthetic appeal to the intrinsic value of wolves inhabiting Yellowstone. There is no suggestion of tours to see the wolves, much less pet them. The argument is just that the world is a better place with than without wolves in Yellowstone.

I am not sure that Hargrove correctly classifies as anthropocentric people's concern either about the natural cave passage in Mammoth Cave National Park or about the wolves in Yellowstone. Valuing these things apart from any human interaction with them does not seem anthropocentric because people gain no benefit apart from the mere knowledge that they exist. Their existence seems to be valued *for itself*, and this is a nonanthropocentric rationale for preservation (or restoration, in the wolves' case). We examine nonanthropocentrism in the next four chapters.

National Heritage

National heritage is another reason for preservation. The Sierra Club maintained that development of Mineral King Valley as a ski resort would destroy "natural and historic objects." Part of our national heritage would be lost.

Eugene Hargrove claims, "In the United States . . . wilderness has been a matter of national pride for at least a century and a half, and wildness has been regarded as the special characteristic that sets the natural beauty of American scenery apart from that of Europe."[40] Mark Sagoff traces the relationship further back to the eighteenth-century theologian Jonathan Edwards. Sagoff attributes to Edwards the belief that "Americans could find in the experience of nature the condition of spiritual awakening. . . . Nature is a symbol of the divine; therefore, the wilderness assures Americans of their special relation to God."[41] Sagoff finds further support in the writings of Jefferson, Emerson, Thoreau, Melville, and Whitman for the view that "nature has sublime qualities that can be read or at least translated into the American national character. . . ."[42]

James Fenimore Cooper's *Leather Stocking Tales* were popular in the nineteenth century because they venerated wilderness areas and wilderness virtues as they were being lost to the march of civilization. American historian Perry Miller wrote, "The more rapidly, the more voraciously, the primordial forests were felled, the more desperately poets and painters—and also preachers—strove to identify the personality of this republic with the virtues of pristine and untarnished or 'romantic' Nature."[43] In sum, America's artists, writers, and preachers instilled in Americans belief in a covenant with nature. This covenant includes what Jonathan Edwards called benevolence. Sagoff writes:

> This benevolence respects things enough to let them be. It . . . appreciates the character of things and allows objects their own integrity by restraining the interfer-

ence of man. This is a reverence for all things on which we might base an accept-able environmental ethic: It respects nature enough to leave it alone.[44]

So *preserving wilderness areas can be done to further distinctly American values, as well as to retain aesthetic objects with intrinsic value.*

Sagoff reports that he and his students discussed the proposal by Walt Disney Enterprises to build a ski resort in Mineral King Valley. He found that many more of his students would expect to visit the area if it were a ski resort than if it remained wilderness. They would spend considerable sums of money, so the project would surely provide jobs and increase GDP. Nevertheless, the students disagreed with the initial Forest Service decision to allow the Disney development. According to Sagoff:

> The students believed that the Disney plan was loathsome and despicable, that the Forest Service had violated a public trust by approving it, and that the values for which we stand as a nation compel us to preserve the little wilderness we have for its own sake and as a heritage for future generations.[45]

I, for one, am willing to assume that Sagoff's students were not just sucking up.

The Mineral King story ends favorably for preservationists. Congress rescinded Disney's lease. Their decision, Sagoff writes, was

> based on aesthetic and historical considerations such as the argument that a majestic million-year-old wilderness is objectively *better* than a commercial honky-tonk. In this way, Congress responded to the opinions citizens backed up with arguments in public hearings and not to the wants individuals might back up with money in a market. . . . [46]

In other words, people made the decision as citizens, not as consumers. If their only concern was human well being, this was non-economic anthropocentrism at work.

Transformative Values and Future Generations

Bryan Norton claims that encounters with nature can transform people's values away from materialistic consumption and toward a more fulfilling life. Many children are bored and unhappy while surrounded by toys and other "stuff" that are supposed to make life good. Norton imagines the following transformation of such a child:

> Suppose an adult comes upon a child playing in the woods. The child is gleefully destroying eggs from the nests of groundbirds. The adult gently explains to the child that eggs are necessary to hatch baby birds and shows the child baby birds in another nest. The child is fascinated, watches the baby birds being fed by the

mother, and loses interest in his destructive game. Now he begins to show solicitous concern for the welfare of birds and asks many questions. . . . The initial appeal of the destructive felt preference and the demand value represented has now been transformed.[47]

If a life of genuine interest in nature is better than one of mindless destruction, this transformation constitutes improvement. Norton imagines a similar transformation of a young adult who starts attending meetings of a conservation organization:

She realizes that, since her first attendance at the conservation meetings, *she* has changed. She has begun studying ecology texts and now finds a walk in the woods stimulating and satisfying. . . . A day of shopping, once her favorite activity, leaves her less satisfied than a day working as a volunteer for a conservation cause. Without really thinking about it, she has realized that there are more important things than material possessions. . . . And she believes that she is a better person for these changes.[48]

Norton writes that this sort of transformation is a reason to preserve wilderness areas and endangered species. The transformation is good, he thinks. "But it will not occur if nature is so altered that encounters with wild species become unlikely. Species preservationists should emphasize the value of wild species, especially endangered ones, as catalysts for the reconsideration of currently consumptive felt preference."[49]

In sum, *if you think that people in our society are generally too materialistic, you will want policies that help to combat materialism, and these include policies that preserve and protect wilderness areas and endangered species. Such policies may not maximize economic growth, so any argument for them based exclusively on human well being rests on non-economic anthropocentrism. The policies make society better, not richer.*

❧   ❧   ❧

Non-economic anthropocentrism supports many preservationist arguments concerning future generations. We saw in Chapter 2 that we have obligations to avoid messing up the earth for future generations. Economic anthropocentrism fails to accord with our beliefs about these obligations because it requires discounting the lives of future people.

A second problem bedevils economic anthropocentrism. Even if it treated future people as our equals, it could not tell us how to fulfill obligations to them. Its goal is maximizing consumer satisfaction. But in many areas, the consumer demands of future people will depend on the kind of world we leave them. The goal of satisfying their consumer demands puts the cart before the horse. It is like trying to buy furniture to fit your living room before you have designed the house. Sagoff writes in his colorful way:

> If we leave [future generations] an environment that is fit for pigs, they will be like pigs. . . . Suppose we destroy all of our literary, artistic, and musical heritage; suppose we left to future generations only potboiler romances, fluorescent velvet paintings, and disco songs. We would then ensure a race of uncultured near illiterates. Now, suppose we leave an environment dominated by dumps, strip mines, and highways. Again, . . . future individuals will be illiterate, although in another way.
>
> Future generations might not complain: A pack of yahoos will *like* a junkyard environment. This is the problem. That kind of future is efficient. . . . But it is tragic all the same.

Sagoff concludes that we have an "obligation to provide future individuals with an environment consistent with ideals that we know to be good."[50]

In sum, *our society will do justice to all our values only if our judgments reflect not only economic concerns, but also our standards of aesthetics, our notion of the nation's heritage, and our sense of equal human worth.* As in the case of prostitution, the issues cannot be meaningfully addressed, much less settled, by economic appeals alone.

Moral Pluralism

Cost-benefit analysis, which relies completely on consumer demands in real and hypothetical markets, puts all considerations in monetary terms. Mathematics determines the best course of action if the goal is maximum economic growth. We have seen, however, that CBA does not always produce acceptable results. CBA encourages harmful scarcity, and condones favoritism toward the rich over the poor, the current generation over future generations, and the First World over the Third World.

An alternative to CBA is **moral pluralism**, which is guidance by a variety of competing moral principles that cannot be boiled down to any one principle. We can, for example, be guided by considerations of aesthetics, national heritage, and various views about the best life for human beings. But then how can we settle conflicts among them? Suppose, just for the moment, that the best life for human beings includes hunting wild animals, but this requires building some roads that impair the beauty of wilderness areas. How would we know which consideration should prevail? Some philosophers claim that moral pluralism is unacceptable because it lacks a clear decision procedure.[51]

But this is not a serious problem. *People often make acceptable decisions by juggling competing values without any mathematical procedures or fixed priority rules.* Consider, for example, some vital issues of crime, personal security, and political freedom. Generally speaking, I favor the suppression of serious crimes. I want criminals to be caught, prosecuted, and punished. But I also value my privacy and political freedoms. I would not want the police barging into my home and searching through my papers and effects for no good reason. I must admit, however, that giving police the right to search and seize at their discretion would help to suppress serious crime. The police would be able to act quickly on the slightest tip and would sometimes find evidence of serious crimes (not at my house, of course!) that would put the bad guys away.

But instead of acting on a good tip, they may be responding to an inaccurate rumor that I have a stash of drugs. (I did go to graduate school in the 1960s). Worse yet, the police may be friends of the mayor who objects to my views about sex education in the public schools. In order to silence me at school board meetings, and intimidate others with my views, the mayor may have asked the police to search my home for embarrassing information that could discredit me. Even if the search turns up nothing, it is an ordeal. My sex education views may lose supporters among those who want to avoid that ordeal, or who do harbor embarrassing secrets at home. In sum, the principle that police should be allowed to do all they can to suppress crime conflicts with the principles that people should be secure in their homes and politically free.

Moral pluralists maintain that these principles cannot all be boiled down to any one principle. We cannot, for example, put all variables in monetary terms and adopt the principle of wealth maximization. Then how do we decide what to do? One principle suggests unlimited police searches and the others suggest no home searches at all.

Opponents of moral pluralism claim that there is no reasonable solution to this kind of conflict. But a solution is contained in the Fourth Amendment to the United States Constitution: "The right of the people to be secure in their persons, houses, papers, and effects, against unreasonable searches and seizures, shall not be violated, and no Warrants shall issue, but upon probable cause, supported by Oath or affirmation, and particularly describing the place to be searched, and the persons or things to be seized." This solution is a compromise. People can generally be secure in their homes. But the police can search a home if they have convinced a judge that the home probably contains particular pieces of evidence of certain crimes. Is this a *reasonable* compromise? It is not derived from a mathematical calculation, so it is not reasoned in that way, but most people think it is reasonable.

The conflict remains, of course. Should automobiles be treated the same as homes? Not entirely. Because they are mobile, it is impractical to require police to get a judicial warrant in all cases. But they are personal property that people want secured from arbitrary searches, so police must generally have probable cause to believe that they will find evidence of a crime before they search a car.

There are exceptions to this, too, however. The Supreme Court established in 1973 in *United States v. Robinson*[52] that searches can be conducted without probable cause whenever an arrest is made. The reasons are to protect the safety of the arresting officer and to preserve evidence of criminal activity. Iowa law went even further, allowing full searches whenever motorists are stopped for traffic violations.

The constitutionality of this law was at issue in *Knowles v. Iowa*.[53] A police officer clocked Patrick Knowles driving 43 miles per hour in a 25-mile-per-hour zone in Newton, Iowa. Besides issuing a citation for speeding, the officer acted on a "hunch," which he acknowledged was not probable cause, and searched the car. He found marijuana and a small pipe, so he arrested Mr. Knowles for violating the state's controlled substances act. Is this violation of privacy unacceptable?

The Supreme Court thought so. At oral argument in November 1998, Justice Stevens noted that Iowa police officers can issue warnings instead of citations when they stop someone for a traffic violation. Justice Kennedy concluded from this that Iowa's law would allow an officer who lacked probable cause, and had no intention of issuing a citation, to search a car and then arrest people if incriminating evidence were found. Justice Ginsburg remarked that this gives police officers "an enormous amount of authority."[54] The next month, Chief Justice Rehnquist, writing the opinion of a unanimous court, noted that the two reasons to allow searches without probable cause do not apply in this case. Searching the car cannot turn up additional evidence of speeding. Also, in situations of traffic citation or warning "the concern for officer safety is not present to the same extent" as when arrests are made.[55]

The moral is that *when principles and values conflict, discussion can generate compromises that most people find reasonable.* The probable cause rule is such a compromise. Exemption in cases of arrest is a compromise within that compromise. But exemption in cases of mere traffic citations or warnings is just going too far. So Patrick Knowles' conviction for possessing marijuana was overturned. Still, it is best not to speed with marijuana in the car (or to marijuana with speed in the car).

These are the kinds of discussions and compromises that Mark Sagoff counts on to guide public policy in environmental matters. Advocates of preserving a wilderness area may present aesthetic, historical, and educational justifications for their position. Developers will present conflicting considerations, such as the value of meeting consumer demand and making the economy grow. Most people think our government should help individuals get jobs and earn money so they can buy what they want. Money isn't everything, but it is something. *Considerations of money should inform, but not preclude, discussion.* For example, people may agree that making money justifies opening a national forest to selective logging, but that aesthetic considerations rule out clear cutting and Disney-type development.

Monetary concerns bear on environmental policies in another way as well. Political discussions using a variety of principles and values may result in the decision, for example, that the United States should reduce to a certain extent its emission of greenhouse gases to reduce global warming. As we have just seen, monetary considerations may legitimately influence, but not dictate, that decision. Now we come to implementing the desired reduction. *All other things being equal, it is usually best to reach our goals with minimum cost. While cost considerations alone did not set the goal (as CBA would require), they may legitimately guide strategies to meet the goal.* This use of economic reasoning is called **cost effectiveness analysis** (CEA). Unlike CBA, which sets the goals of public poli-

cies through monetary considerations alone, CEA merely indicates how to meet
goals with least cost.

Moral Relativism

Here is a problem. Sagoff recommends that we make decisions after discussing
competing values and principles. The problem is that the decisions will likely
be bad if the culture's values and principles are defective. Consider the case of
People v. Kimura.[56] A Japanese-American woman killed her two children while
attempting

> to commit oyakoshinju—parent-child suicide—after learning of her husband's ex-
> tramarital affair. According to the defense attorney and members of the Japanese
> community, in traditional Japanese culture, the death ritual was an accepted means
> for a woman to rid herself of the shame resulting from her husband's infidelity.[57]

If that were the American custom, few would envy the children of prominent
American politicians in the late 1990s. In another case "a member of the Hmong
tribe from the mountains of Laos living in the United States exercised his right
under Hmong culture to execute his adulterous wife."[58]

These are examples of decisions made on principle that we (I assume) consider wrong because we disagree with the principles and the values they em-
body. But we, too, may be guided by defective principles and values. To some
people, for example, hunting wild animals is part of the best human life. Others disagree.

Consider again Mineral King Valley. To some people, sequoia trees are beautiful and represent the majesty of our nation, so they should be preserved in
Sequoia National Park and Mineral King Valley for reasons of aesthetics and
national heritage. Others see the entrepreneurial spirit as the greatest gift of
America to the world, so they favor development of Mineral King as a ski resort not only for the money, but also as testament to the value of entrepreneurial excellence. Such people may find ski slopes bordered by trees more
beautiful than a mountainside of trees alone. This would be no surprise. Commercial advertisements influence aesthetic tastes, and most ads are designed
to generate revenue. Skiers pay to be on hillsides; trees do not.

In sum, leaving nature's fate to decisions based on our country's principles
and values may be no better than leaving the fate of an adulterous Hmong
woman to her husband's traditional conscience. We will consider this problem
later, beginning with the next chapter. I note here merely that the problem is
the same for economic as for non-economic anthropocentrism. The consumer
demands that ultimately determine the right course of action among economic
anthropocentrists are as culturally dependent as the principles and values employed by non-economic anthropocentrists.

Judgment Calls

- Many couples are infertile because the woman does not have viable eggs (ova). Some of these couples pay another women, a so-called surrogate, to be impregnated by artificial insemination with the husband's sperm, carry the resulting baby to term, and then relinquish the child to the couple. The couple pays all the medical bills and gives the surrogate $10,000 or $15,000 besides. How might you argue for (or against) giving full legal protection to surrogacy contracts? What part does the value of economic growth play in your reasoning?

- Many people in poor countries want consumer goods like those they see in ads from such corporations as Coca-Cola, Ford, and Nike. Like poor people in our country, they do things to earn money that richer people avoid, such as mine coal or wait tables. How might you argue that it is fair (or unfair) for Third World countries to accept manufacturing jobs and toxic waste dumps that are unacceptable here?

- In Bhopal, only poor neighborhoods were contaminated. The hill where middle-class people lived was untouched. How might your answer to the previous question be affected by who in the poor country actually receives most of the payment for the location of dangerous industrial processes in the country and who accepts most of the risk of eventual exposure to toxic substances?

- Do you feel better just knowing that some species of whale exists even though you have no particular desire to see them? If so, is this an aesthetic anthropocentric concern, as Hargrove suggests, or do you have nonanthropocentric concern for the whales themselves? Also, if you want whale species preserved, how much are you willing to pay in annual dues to an organization devoted to this purpose? How, if at all, does the introduction of money here make this an issue of economic, instead of non-economic, anthropocentrism?

PART II

NONANTHROPOCENTRISM

CHAPTER 4

Animal Liberation and Utilitarianism

Cruelty to Animals

Anthropocentric concerns have so far dominated this book. We have considered only *human* welfare. But human beings are not alone on this planet, and many people have nonanthropocentric concerns, among these, concern for animals.[1] This chapter explores concern for animals from a utilitarian perspective and examines the adequacy of utilitarianism as an ethical theory. We begin by considering cruelty to animals.

The American Society for the Prevention of Cruelty to Animals (ASPCA) sent me a letter in fall 1998 that began:

> His belly was empty. So empty it hurt. The back door would open and shut, and Astro would hope for food. But his owner never brought any. In fact, he didn't even look at Astro as he came and went. Astro drank out of a puddle near the stake he was chained to. The dirty water kept him alive, but then the puddle dried up. Astro had only a few days to live.
>
> By the time a neighbor called us about Astro, the dog was nearly dead. . . . Astro was too weak to bark or even to stand up. . . . The officers knelt down, speaking gently to Astro.
>
> Then they saw it. Astro was wagging his tail. He was barely moving, but yes— the poor, sick dog was saying, "Welcome, friends!"
>
> Astro's owner was charged with animal cruelty. . . . He admitted that he was deliberately starving the dog to death.
>
> Fortunately, . . . Astro was adopted by a loving family. Today he's happy and healthy, well-fed and loved.

Most people oppose cruelty to animals. Anti-cruelty statutes exist in all 50 of the United States. Illinois' Humane Care for Animals Act (1973), a typical anti-cruelty statute, requires owners to give each animal "wholesome food and water; adequate shelter and protection from the weather; [and] veterinary care when needed to prevent suffering. . . ." In addition, "No person or owner may beat, cruelly treat, torment, overload, overwork or otherwise abuse any animal."[2]

Such laws make Astro's owner, already a creep, into a criminal. The American Humane Association (AHA) encourages strict enforcement of anti-cruelty laws. Their letter for fall 1998 details increasing punishment for animal abuse. One case involved

> the brutal torture and murder of "Duke," a Dalmatian. Three men in their twenties tied Duke to a tree, taped his jaws shut, then allowed their pit bull to massacre him. Near death, they then cut Duke's tail and ears off, and finally crushed his skull. . . . They were sentenced to up to three years in jail—and all ended up behind bars!

In another case, "a 42-year-old Fort Lauderdale resident placed nine live puppies in a paper bag and buried them in his backyard. Three died, six were miraculously saved." The perpetrator received "four months in jail and five years on probation."[3] A Pittsburgh teenager who hammered a goose to death also went to prison.

Why punish these people? *If morality were entirely anthropocentric, it would be hard to justify punishment in these cases, because people are not harmed, only animals.*

Of course, people may be harmed indirectly. For example, "a Houston man poisoned his girlfriend's two cats, then put them in the microwave oven and turned it on. The cats eventually died."[4] The man received two years probation and an $1,800 fine. Here the girlfriend is harmed, because her cats were killed. Assuming she is human, her property rights are anthropocentric reasons to prosecute the microwave man.

But property rights do not cover all cases. Astro's *owner* was starving him. Property rights would be on the owner's side, but the conduct was still illegal. Why?

One reason could be that Astro was tied up outside the house where the neighbor, who called the ASPCA, could see his sorry plight. Anti-cruelty laws protect neighbors and others from disturbing sights and sounds, and that may be their justification.

This rationale does not cover all cases, either. Starving a dog in a soundproof basement where no one else can see or hear is just as illegal as doing so out in the open.

About 200 years ago the philosopher Immanuel Kant gave a different rationale:

> If a dog has served his master long and faithfully, his service, on the analogy of human service, deserves reward, and when the dog has grown too old to serve, his master ought to keep him until he dies. . . . If . . . [he] shoots his dog because the animal is no longer capable of service, . . . his act is inhuman and damages in

himself that humanity which it is his duty to show towards mankind. If he is not to stifle his human feelings, he must practice kindness towards animals, for he who is cruel to animals becomes hard also in his dealing with men.[5]

According to Kant, even if you own the animal and are cruel secretly in a sound-proof basement, you impair your character, and this will eventually make you cruel to human beings. On this reasoning, anti-cruelty laws are really designed to protect people.

I do not know if cruelty to animals leads to cruelty toward people, and I do not think anyone else knows either, because no one has studied the subject systematically. For all we know, cruelty to animals may substitute for cruelty toward people. Kicking the dog may relieve tension and spare a child. Microwaving a girlfriend's cats may replace microwaving the girlfriend. (That couple had issues.) On the other hand, animal lovers are not always nice to people. Hitler, I am told, loved animals.

What is more, cruelty to animals is not the only activity accused of warping the human character. Many people think that football and boxing teach anti-social aggression. Some professionals in these sports are convicted of assault, yet, unlike cruelty to animals, the sports remain legal. What is the difference?

Perhaps it is this. Much more than football or boxing, cruelty to animals disturbs many people. Even when they do not have to witness it, they want it stopped. Anti-cruelty laws may be anthropocentric attempts to relieve such people of distress.

But this is not sufficient justification. Abortion disturbs many people, but we do not make it illegal for that reason. Our law respects individual choice. People opposed to abortion, moreover, want it illegal not because it disturbs them, but because it kills the fetus, which they think deserves protection. So if we were to criminalize abortion, it would be to protect the unborn, not to relieve pro-lifers' distress.

This is the key to understanding laws against cruelty to animals. *We criminalize cruelty to animals not to appease animal lovers, but to protect animals. Laws prohibiting cruelty to animals are not primarily anthropocentric. They are nonanthropocentric attempts to protect animals' interests.* This is a major point because it departs from the assumption that our society attributes moral importance only to human beings. The assumption is incorrect. Animals are morally important to so many people in our society that we deprive human beings of liberty to do as they please even with their own animals. Our views are so strong that we back up our disapproval with real punishment.

What justifies this extension of morality from anthropocentric to nonanthropocentric concerns? One way to explain and justify moral views is to relate them to an **ethical theory**. *Ethical theories explain in general terms what makes any action right or wrong, good or bad.* If the theory seems correct, and if it justifies the moral judgments under review, then people gain confidence in those judgments. This chapter introduces and criticizes one such theory, utilitarianism.

Utilitarianism

Utilitarianism is an influential ethical theory that can explain and justify laws against cruelty to animals. The theory is influential because it seems clear, simple, and comprehensive. Most important, it seems to follow from common sense. Notice the word "seems." Here we explore utilitarianism from its advocates' perspective. It seems best to them. Later in this chapter I discuss limitations and imperfections. I conclude that utilitarianism makes an important, but limited, contribution to our moral thinking.

Here is the nature and common-sense appeal of utilitarianism. It is common sense that if I take a hammer to an ordinary rock in my garden, no one protests on behalf of the rock, whereas if I do the same to a goose, as a Pittsburgh teenager did, I am a criminal. People object *on behalf of the goose*. What is the difference? The goose is alive and its life can be longer or shorter, better or worse, *for it*. The rock is not alive and nothing that happens to it can be better or worse *for it*. The goose has *interests*; the rock does not.

This suggests a general theory about moral judgments. *Moral judgments attach only to actions affecting beings with interests.* We can test this theory with other cases. Suppose that, without my permission and against my wishes, someone takes an ax to the wooden fence around my backyard. I would not protest and seek compensation on behalf of the fence itself, because it is just pieces of dead wood. It has no interests. But I do have interests, and one of these is to keep my in-laws' dogs outside when they visit so they do not pee on my carpets. (Call me narrow-minded.) For this reason, I consider the wanton destruction of my fence to be morally wrong.

In sum, it seems that only living things can have interests. The treatment of all other things matters morally only if it directly or indirectly affects the interests of something alive. But what are those interests? Many interests are what living beings think about and want. I, for example, have an interest in pee-free carpets, low tax rates, and word processors, to name but a few. Many other people have interests in fashionable clothes, reliable cars, and the protection of bald eagles. Astro craved food and water. But some interests are not the object of conscious desire. The goose has an interest in not being bashed in the head, and puppies have an interest in not being buried alive. But they probably did not consciously think about these things. Is there a common thread here?

Utilitarians think that experience is the common thread. Why do I object to dogs peeing on my carpet? I do not like the smell or the look of the stain. What interest do I have in word processors? They make it easier for me to write books. Why do I have an interest in lower taxes? Lower taxes leave me more money to enjoy myself. I can take trips to France and support my favorite charities. Experience seems central here.

What if I were in a persistent vegetative state with no chance of ever recovering conscious experience? Thousands of people actually exist in this condition. I could be transported to France, but I could not know about, much less enjoy, the trip, so it would do me no good. Dogs peeing on the carpet would not bother me because I would never see or smell the stain. Word processors could improve or break down without affecting me. Utilitarians conclude that experiences alone make things good or bad for us.

People interested in high fashion enjoy seeing themselves looking good in the mirror or in photographs. They enjoy anticipating the new fashion season and discussing fashion with other connoisseurs. But if they were incapable of experience, how could fashion matter to them at all? The same is true for animals. We assume that being bashed in the head with a hammer was a bad experience for the goose, as was being buried alive for the puppies, and that is what made these actions wrong.

To test this view, consider a living carrot. Although it is alive and needs water and minerals to stay alive, it has no interests, according to utilitarians, because (people generally agree) *it cannot care* about its life. It cannot care because it has no consciousness and so no possibility of experience. Accordingly, we do not imprison people for bashing carrots with a hammer, or for microwaving ones that show signs of life. Without the possibility of consciousness and experience, it cannot matter to the carrot what happens to it. So it is treated morally like the rock and wooden fence. Actions regarding the carrot, whether alive or dead, are right or wrong depending on their effects on beings that can have interests. These are beings, like people and animals, who are not only alive, but can enjoy and suffer.

According to the utilitarian theory, then, actions are right or wrong, good or bad, according to how they affect the experiences of beings capable of experience. Here is some more common sense. What kinds of effects on experience make an action good or right? Good effects. Duh. Bad effects on experience make actions bad or wrong. The "granddaddy" of utilitarianism, Jeremy Bentham, who wrote about 200 years ago, called all good experiences "pleasure" and all bad experiences "pain." Pleasures and pains, according to Bentham, include mental as well as physical experiences, spiritual as well as secular experiences, auditory as well as gustatory experiences, and so on. "Happiness" is another word we might use for this.

In Bentham's view, then, the goal of morality is to promote good experiences and discourage bad ones, or, to use his terminology, to promote pleasure and discourage pain. Because he identified all good with pleasure, his version of utilitarianism is called hedonistic, **hedonism** being the view that *pleasure is the only good*. Actions are right, according to hedonistic utilitarianism, insofar as they produce pleasure and wrong insofar as they produce pain.

How much good should people try to produce? As much as possible, of course, but there are complications. The same action may have both pleasurable and painful effects. In these cases, we must subtract the pain from the pleasure to get a net pleasure score. For example, firing employees is painful to them. But if this is needed for corporate competitiveness that keeps a larger workforce employed, utilitarians may agree that it is the right thing to do. In the long run it produces maximum net pleasure.

Two things should be emphasized. First, *long-term effects are just as important as more immediate effects*. We should always try to produce the best net pleasure. It does not matter whether the pleasures come first or the pains. Pleasures and pains are of equal importance whenever they occur.

Second, *it is irrelevant who receives the pleasure and pain. Pleasure is good, and pain is bad, regardless of who experiences it. The goal of utilitarians, to produce maximum net pleasure, is not selfish.* It is **altruistic.** Altruists count their own good and that of others as equally important. Selfish people, by contrast, place more importance on their own good than on that of others, whereas self*less* people count the good of others but not their own. Being altruists, *utilitarians try to produce maximum pleasure and minimum pain, counting their own pleasure and pain as no more or less important than anyone else's.* Utilitarian corporate managers would willingly reduce their own pay if necessary to promote overall pleasure.

Clearly, no one always acts like a utilitarian. We saw in Chapter 1, for example, that people are altruistic (unselfish) only some of the time. At other times they are selfish. So utilitarianism does not *describe* how people behave. But it does *prescribe* how people *should* behave, and these prescriptions seem to accord with our ordinary judgments of right and wrong. We praise people who put the good of others over their own personal good to produce the best net effect. We praise war heroes for giving their lives for their country, for example. In other cases, we praise people whose lives are probably enriched by unselfish behavior. We praise unselfish basketball players who show more interest in team success than in their own personal scoring statistics. We praise successful people who "give back to the community," and so forth. Utilitarianism could be the official ethical theory of The United Way.

In some respects, utilitarianism is like cost-benefit analysis (CBA). Both recommend actions that maximize net good and rely on mathematical calculations to identify those actions. Both endorse maximizing the *total* net good (happiness in one case and wealth in the other) without concern for how the good is distributed. This raises the possibility in both cases that some people will not get their fair share of the good. We consider problems of utilitarian justice near the end of this chapter.

In some other respects, however, utilitarianism differs from CBA, and these differences enable utilitarianism to avoid some pitfalls of CBA. We saw that CBA discounts future effects, including the future loss of human life. Utilitarianism, by contrast, does not discount the future at all. It does not favor immediate over long-term effects, so it does not recommend, for example, sacrificing sixteen billion people in the future to save one person's life today.

Another problem with CBA is the lesser value it places on the lives of people in poor countries. From the utilitarian perspective, because all normally conscious people can experience similar amounts of pleasure and pain, all are (roughly) equal. Any inequality stems from differences, if there are any, in abilities to experience pleasure and pain, and this has nothing to do with the wealth of individuals or their societies. So hedonistic utilitarians are as concerned about the pleasure and pain of people in Bhopal, India, as in the U.S.A. Utilitarians value human well being regardless of race, religion, or nationality. Again, this accords with our highest moral aspirations.

Utilitarians claim that their theory eliminates the uncertainties of moral pluralism. Moral pluralism is the view that there are several basic moral principles, such as those favoring privacy, political liberty, and effective law enforcement. Because each is basic, none can be derived from any of the others.
When these principles suggest different courses of action, as we saw in Chapter 3 they sometimes do in law enforcement, there is no formal decision procedure. People discuss the matter and usually compromise. There is no way to
show mathematically that this compromise is really best.

Hedonistic utilitarians, by contrast, claim to have a mathematical procedure
to settle such issues. They have only a single good—pleasure—and a single
moral principle—that people should maximize net pleasure. They never have
to trade off one kind of good against another. What is more, this common currency can be quantified in what Bentham called "the **hedonic calculus.**" Here
is how Bentham imagined it working. People should review each of the conflicting alternatives that they face. They should calculate how much pleasure
and pain would result from following each, and then choose the path with the
greatest surplus of pleasure over pain. In principle, decisions reached through
the hedonic calculus should be justifiable mathematically.

Speciesism

Hedonistic utilitarianism helps to explain and justify the extension of morality
from human beings to animals. Many species of animals can experience pleasure and pain. *If the goal of morality is to maximize net pleasure regardless of who
has that pleasure, then the pleasures and pains of animals should be considered in the
hedonic calculus along with those of human beings.*

This explains why the Dalmatian named Duke should not have been tied up
to be massacred by a pit bull. Imagine the horrific experience for Duke. On the
other side, the pit bull and the three men who arranged the killing may have
enjoyed it. But Duke's pain, we assume, was worse than the pleasure derived
by the others. More important, the others could have had considerable pleasure in different ways. The pit bull might enjoy tearing up an appropriately
scented rag doll with regular dog food inside. The three men might enjoy a
Wild Kingdom video of a lion killing an antelope, or some other nature snuff
film. Even if the pit bull and the men derived less pleasure from these alternatives, the net good is better because Duke is saved all the pain of being bru-
tally massacred.

People accustomed to anthropocentrism may balk at extending morality to
animals. But customs often give way to logical consistency. For example, when
Jefferson wrote in the Declaration of Independence, "All men are created
equal," he owned slaves. Jefferson was troubled by slavery, but did not reject
it outright as obviously incompatible with human equality. The incompatibil-
ity became so obvious later that people eventually fought to end the practice.
We now condemn American slavery as exemplifying unconscionable *racism.*

American women remained second-class citizens even after slavery was abolished. They were denied the right to vote, denied equal educational opportunities, denied equal pay for equal work, and denied admittance to many professions, such as the law, regardless of their accomplishments. Today, American law and the morality of most American citizens condemn these past practices as unconscionable *sexism*.

Today's hedonistic utilitarians, following Jeremy Bentham's lead, claim that cruel treatment of animals is just like racism and sexism. Racists attribute more moral importance to people of their own race than to others. Sexists assign more moral importance to men than to women. So what do we call people who condone burying puppies and microwaving cats while they are alive? Utilitarian philosopher Peter Singer calls them speciesist. **Speciesism** is, according to Singer, *"a prejudice or attitude of bias in favor of the interests of members of one's own species and against those of members of other species."* [6] Speciesism is, Singer claims, analogous to both racism and sexism. Just as the logic of consistent thinking brought racism and sexism into disrepute, so it leads hedonistic utilitarians to condemn speciesism.

Of course, animals differ from people more than blacks differ from whites and women differ from men. This is because blacks, whites, men, and women are all members of one species, and many common traits belong to typical members of the same species. Normal human beings, for example, regardless of race or sex, are able to reason and speak complex languages. Animals either cannot do these things at all, or they do them with much less proficiency or sophistication. The philosopher Immanuel Kant thought the inability of animals to reason justifies what we now call speciesism.

Utilitarians object to speciesism. Different abilities and potentials often justify different treatment of individuals, but not different concern for their pleasure and pain. For example, because they cannot reason, debate, read, and write, the freedoms of speech and press are irrelevant to the treatment of animals, whereas denial of these freedoms would harm human beings. So utilitarians advocate such freedoms for people only.

However, there are many ways in which humans and animals are alike, and in these matters they should be treated with equal concern. Both can experience mental and physical pain and pleasure, so the hedonic calculus should include equal consideration of these pains and pleasures. This explains and justifies laws against cruelty to animals.

Jeremy Bentham summed up the utilitarian case for such laws. He was writing when slavery was still practiced in the United States, but had been abolished in France:

> The French have already discovered that the blackness of the skin is no reason why a human being should be abandoned without redress to the caprice of a tormentor. It may come one day to be recognized, that the number of the legs, the villosity of the skin, or the termination of the *os sacrum*, are equally insufficient for abandoning a sensitive being to the same fate.

Bentham concluded in 1789 with this comment on the abilities of people, but not animals, to reason and talk: "The question is not, Can they *reason*? Nor, Can they *talk*? But Can they *suffer*?"[7] Because they can suffer, we should protect them from cruelty. The ASPCA was established in 1866 to promote this cause, which is now supported by law.

Animal Husbandry

However, cruelty to animals persists in our society. Peter Singer's *Animal Liberation* documents cruelty in agriculture. Consider the pork industry. Singer writes, "the agribusiness lobby constantly assures us that only happy, well-cared-for animals can be productive."[8] But modern agriculture, which Singer calls **factory farming**, is cruel.

Commercial pigs are as intelligent and sensitive as pet dogs. Singer notes that when released to the wild:

> They form stable social groups, they build communal nests, they use dunging areas well away from the nest, and they are active, spending much of the day rooting around the edge of the woodlands. When sows are ready to give birth, they leave the communal nest and build their own nest, finding a suitable site, scraping a hole, and lining it with grass and twigs. . . . Factory farming makes it impossible for the pigs to follow these instinctive behavior patterns.[9]

They are crowded into small caged areas with concrete floors, instead of mud, dirt, and straw. Concrete floors are easier to clean. Conditions are crowded because the pigs are kept indoors. Using the space for the greatest number of pigs minimizes production costs. Also, Singer points out, "with less room to move about, the pig will burn up less of its food in 'useless' exercise, and so can be expected to put on more weight for each pound of food consumed." He quotes a pig producer: "What we are really trying to do is modify the animal's environment for maximum profit."[10] The animals have nowhere to go and nothing to do. The stress is obvious.

In 1987, I visited a model hog farm near my home in Springfield, Illinois. It was open to the public one weekend to show off its modern methods, which are now standard. My three daughters, twelve to fifteen years old at the time, made me promise to keep my mouth shut so they would not be embarrassed. I looked and listened. Pigs were literally climbing all over one another in caged areas with concrete floors. Some had distinctly wild looks in their eyes. The people in front of us and those behind expressed alarm and dismay at what they saw, and said they would give up pork, at least for awhile.

One sign of stress in the pigs is anti-social behavior. They bite one another's tails. Rather than recommend stress relief, the United States Department of Agriculture (USDA) suggests tail docking. "Cut tails $\frac{1}{4}$ to $\frac{1}{2}$ inch from the body with side-cutting pliers or another blunt instrument," the USDA recommends.[11] They do not recommend, much less require, anaesthetic. Singer quotes a hog farmer on the subject of docking:

> They hate it! The pigs just hate it! And I suppose we could probably do without tail-docking if we gave them more room, because they don't get so crazy and mean when they have more space. With enough room, they're actually quite nice animals. But we can't afford it. These buildings cost a lot.[12]

The stress causes many pigs to simply die from what is called "porcine stress syndrome." Singer quotes the journal *Farmer and Stockbreeder*: "These deaths in no way nullify the extra return obtained from the higher total output."[13] The agony of pigs is irrelevant.

Concrete floors damage the feet and legs of pigs. But Singer quotes a farmer: "We don't get paid for producing animals with good posture around here. We get paid by the pound." And *Farmer and Stockbreeder* adds, "The animal will usually be slaughtered before serious deformity sets in."[14] That's reassuring.

Actually, the pigs who die young may be better off than breeding sows who live longer. Singer writes:

> While pregnant they are usually locked into individual metal stalls two feet wide and six feet long, or scarcely bigger than the sow herself. . . . There they will live for two or three months. During all that time they will be unable to walk more than a single step forward or backward, or to turn around, or to exercise in any other way. . . .
>
> When the sow is ready to give birth she is moved . . . [and] may be even more tightly restricted in her movements than she was in her stall. . . . The ostensible purpose is to stop the sow rolling onto and crushing her piglets, but this could also be achieved by providing her with more natural conditions.[15]

Singer quotes a description of how sows reacted when first put in a stall with a tether:

> The sows threw themselves violently backwards, straining against the tether. Sows thrashed their heads about as they twisted and turned in their struggle to free themselves. Often loud screams were emitted and occasionally individuals crashed bodily against the side boards of the tether stalls. This sometimes resulted in sows collapsing to the floor.[17]

What is more, breeding sows and boars "are kept permanently hungry," writes Singer. They get "only 60 percent of what they would eat if they had more food available." Why is this done? "To give breeding animals more than the bare minimum required to keep them reproducing is, from the producer's point of view, simply a waste of money."[17]

In sum, Singer observes, *"an ordinary citizen who kept dogs in similar conditions for their entire lives would risk prosecution for cruelty. A pig producer who keeps an animal of comparable intelligence in this manner, however, is more likely to be rewarded. . . ."*[18] How can the pig producer get away with it?

Legally, the answer is simple. Illinois' Humane Care for Animals Act, which is typical, exempts "good husbandry practices." This includes all common agricultural practices, no matter how painful or stressful to animals.

Matters get worse when little piggy goes to market, because the yellow brick road between farm and market passes through a slaughterhouse. Gail Eisnitz, an investigator for the Humane Farming Association, documented cruelties in *Slaughterhouse*. She notes that a federal law, the Humane Slaughter Act, is supposed to protect animals from cruel slaughter. But the USDA, which joined the meat industry in opposing the law in the first place, is charged with enforcing it.[19] Violations carry no penalties anyway. Eisnitz finds the slaughtering process is cruel from start to finish.

The process starts with transportation of animals to slaughterhouses. Eisnitz interviewed workers at John Morrell and Company slaughterhouse in Sioux City, Iowa. Toby Glenn, a meatpacking employee for 10 years, discussed the transportation of hogs.

> In the summer they crowd them in trucks and run them clear from Canada. They don't stop and spray them to cool them down, so you get a lot of them that die from the heat.
> In winter after a long run like that, they always got ten to fifteen dead, frozen hogs laying around. . . . A lot of times there's live ones in there [with the frozen ones]. . . . You could see them still lifting their heads up, looking around.[20]

The dead ones are sent to rendering, where they are ground up for animal feed, fertilizer, and other products. But, Glenn told Eisnitz, "It's not uncommon to find a live hog in rendering, . . . buried under the pile of dead ones."[21] Such hogs are ground up alive!

So much for transportation. Upon arrival, hogs enter the slaughterhouse through lead-up chutes. Tommy Vladak, another Morrell employee, told Eisnitz:

> The hogs don't want to go. When hogs smell blood, they don't want to go. I've seen hogs beaten, whipped, kicked in the head to get them up to the restrainer. One night I saw a driver get so angry at a hog he broke its back with a piece of board. I've seen hog drivers take their prod and shove it up the hog's ass to get them to move.[22]

At this point the hogs are supposed to be electrically stunned unconscious for painless killing. But, Vladak continued, the stunning voltage is often too low:

> Management was constantly complaining to us about blown loins. They claimed that when the stunner voltage was set too high it tore up the meat. The supervisors always wanted it on low stun no matter what size hogs we were stunning. Then when you got big sows and boars in the restrainer, the stunner wouldn't work at all.[23]

The result was conscious hogs reaching the shackling table where hind legs are shackled so hogs can be hoisted upside down. Vladak complained:

> A lot of times hogs would jump off the shackling table and land in my little area. They'd been shocked, so they were vicious. They would be biting at anybody or anything that came near them.
>
> The foreman would be yelling at me, "Stick that hog before it gets away!" So I'd grab it by the front legs, roll it over on its back and stick it [in the neck], then just get out of there. 'Cause these hogs would spring back up after you stuck them. They would run around in a circle for about five minutes, just bleeding, trying to hold back everything they had.[24]

Other hogs were successfully shackled and hung upside down for killing while they were still conscious and literally kicking. The sticker, who is supposed to cut their arteries, often missed because the animal was moving. Also, when an animal is conscious it tightens its muscles and does not bleed as quickly. So instead of bleeding to death before immersion in scalding water, many remained alive to die from scalding or drowning.

Eisnitz found Morrell's transportation and slaughter of hogs to be typical in the industry. She also found the transportation and slaughter of cattle to be similar. During winter transport, some live cattle arrive frozen to the side of the truck. Once in the slaughterhouse, cattle are supposed to be stunned by be-

"You'll always be much more than a commodity to me."

ing knocked over the head before they, too, are shackled and hung upside down to have their throats cut. But the line often goes too fast, resulting in some cattle remaining conscious and kicking when the "sticker" tries to cut their throats. When the cut is poor, the bleeding is slow, and the line moves fast, some cattle reaching the end of the line are skinned alive!

Peter Singer details horrors, also, in the poultry and egg industries. He writes:

> The suffering of laying chickens begins early in life. The newly hatched chicks are sorted into males and females by a "chick-puller." Since the male chicks have no commercial value, they are discarded. Some companies gas the little birds, but often they are dumped alive into a plastic sack and allowed to suffocate under the weight of other chicks dumped on top of them. Others are ground up, while still alive, to be turned into feed for their sisters. At least 160 million birds are gassed, suffocated, or die this way every year in the United States alone.[25]

The female chicks are allowed to live, and this may be worse. They spend their lives in wire mesh cages much smaller than the average bird's wingspan. But each hen shares this cage with several others. Because crowding makes them anti-social, their beaks are cut off to prevent aggression, just as pig tails are cut on hog farms. Workers use no anaesthetic. The cages are built on a slant so eggs will roll to where they can be collected easily. Have you ever tried standing in one spot on a slant all day? Singer reports that wire floors are used so "excrement drops through and can be allowed to pile up for many months until it is all removed in a single operation. . . . Unfortunately, the claws of the hen are not well adapted to living on wire. . . . Without any solid ground to wear them down, the birds' toenails become very long and may get permanently entangled in the wire."[26] The air becomes poisonous as excrement builds up.

By this time you get the point. *Whether it is beef, pork, chicken, or eggs, what you find in the grocery store almost always results from revolting cruelty to animals.* We seem to be like those at the time of the American Revolution who claimed that all men are created equal, but failed to recognize blacks as men. We outlaw cruelty to animals, but fail to recognize that livestock are animals as sensitive to cruelty as domestic pets. What should we think? What should we do?

Vegetarianism

Should we extend the protections of anti-cruelty statutes to livestock? Many utilitarians think we should. If livestock were treated the way we require pets to be treated, enormous animal pain would disappear.

But what about human pains and pleasures? Livestock suffer for a reason. Their current treatment is the cheapest way to raise and kill them. *If these methods are disallowed, prices for meat and eggs will increase. This will reduce pleasure among people who want low prices on food so they have money left over to spend on other necessities, not to mention luxuries.*

There are two utilitarian responses to this. First, even if people were harmed by better treatment of farm animals, the benefit to the animals more than outweighs the harm to people. People usually lose pleasure when laws prevent them from doing as they please. Nevertheless, we disallow microwaving cats and burying puppies alive, because the animals' pain is greater than the humans' loss of pleasure. Similarly, laws protecting livestock would increase net pleasure. Animals may gain at human expense, but this would bother only speciesists—people who are prejudiced against animal welfare.

The second utilitarian response is that laws protecting farm animals would help people as well as animals. It is a win-win situation. Americans eat too much meat and eggs for their own good. If prices go up because animals must be treated better, Americans will consume less meat and eggs and eat healthier.

What is more, we saw in Chapter 1 that many poor people are starving around the world already, and the human population may nearly double from its present size. If Americans were to eat less meat and eggs, less grain would be fed to livestock, so less land would be needed to feed Americans. This would make possible international agreements that allocate some American food-producing capacity to alleviate world hunger. For example, poor countries may gain food credits for protecting their forests or native biodiversity, or for reducing emissions of greenhouse gases. But if Americans continue their meat-eating ways, and the American population doubles as expected in the twenty-first century,[27] such positive arrangements may not be possible.

So several considerations support extending anti-cruelty laws to farm animals and strictly enforcing anti-cruelty laws that already apply to slaughterhouses. If these measures push up meat prices, and Americans eat less of it, the overall effect is positive.

What should people do in the meantime, while animals are still treated cruelly on farms and in slaughterhouses? Imagine how it was for abolitionists during slavery. At a minimum, they refused to own slaves, because they wanted to minimize their personal involvement in the immoral institution. Similarly, Peter Singer claims, people opposed to cruelty toward animals should refuse to buy meat and eggs produced cruelly. They should become vegetarians if they cannot find alternate sources of meat.

Alternate sources of eggs are common. Eggs laid by humanely treated hens, called "free range" or "nest" eggs, are widely available. But commercial meat raised and killed humanely is hard to find, so Singer recommends **vegetarianism**, which is a diet that excludes animals killed for their meat. Vegetarians eat animal products, such as milk and eggs, but not the animals themselves. **Vegans** avoid eating animal products as well.

Are there utilitarian reasons *against* becoming a vegetarian? Yes, but they are not very strong. People who like meat will have less pleasure if they refuse to eat it. But most will find vegetarian dishes that they enjoy nearly as much. More important, refusal to eat meat will diminish demand and discourage farmers from raising livestock inhumanely. So net pleasure increases.

Some other reasons against vegetarianism are clearly bogus. People wonder if vegetarian diets are healthful. We now know that they are among the most healthful diets. I was Peter Singered into vegetarianism more than 20 years ago and have been healthier ever since. People wonder also what will happen to farm animals if no one eats them. Will they go wandering about farms unattended, or invade suburban backyards? No. As demand for meat diminishes, farmers, who control the number of livestock in the first place, will adjust their breeding. Unwanted livestock will not be conceived.

Rodeos and Bullfights

Utilitarians criticize many uses of animals, such as in rodeos and bullfights. Bullfights are generally illegal in the United States, whereas rodeos are an American institution. What is the difference? Is it a difference that utilitarians would accept?

Bucking broncos are major rodeo attractions. Did you ever wonder why they buck? Most horses I have ever seen just stand around and occasionally eat grass. Bucking broncos act wild and crazy because people organizing the rodeo have deliberately put them in pain. According to Friends of Animals, Inc., a "bucking strap [is] placed in the area of the small intestines and kidneys, then tightened unbearably to provoke tame horses to go 'loco' in excruciating agony." Also, "electric prods [are] used to agitate horses to a crazed state of pain and fear so they put on a 'good show.' "[28] Bulls are treated similarly to make bull riding a good show. What justifies this pain?

Spectators enjoy seeing rodeos, perhaps because they represent the eternal drama of man against beast. The rodeo business provides professionals with employment and encourages the development of courage and skill. Nevertheless, many utilitarians would say that rodeos are not justified because people can be entertained, employed, and challenged without hurting animals. There are health clubs, basketball games, bowling leagues, and other pursuits that could substitute for rodeos. All of these provide employment opportunities and encourage self-development. So if rodeos were made illegal, animal pain could diminish without any sacrifice of human pleasure.

Now consider bullfighting. It, too, is a spectator sport pitting man against beast. It provides job opportunities for professionals and encourages the development of courage and skill. As in rodeos, animals are caused pain to act ornery, but in this case they are all bulls, not horses as well. So what is the difference?

In bullfights bulls are killed, to the crowd's delight. Perhaps the difference is the bull's death. In Pennsylvania, Bravo Enterprises, Inc. decided to stage bullfights that eliminated the element of death. They called it American-style bullfighting. There would be a parade with a brass band and other pageantry typical of bullfights. The bull would be hurt to make it ornery. It would be jabbed in the back. It would charge matadors swinging red capes. In the end, however, it would be no more injured than a rodeo bull or bucking bronco. Pennsylvania's Society for the Prevention of Cruelty to Animals took Bravo Enterprises to court, claiming that their treatment of bulls would violate the state's anti-cruelty statute. The court agreed![29] Did we miss something here?

We failed to consider ethnic prejudice. We noted in the last chapter some risks of basing moral decisions on people's values. The values may be bad, like those of the Hmong man who thought it proper to kill his adulterous wife. This may be the problem here. The bad value is ethnic prejudice against Hispanic or Latin culture, as this seems to be the only reason why so-called American-style bullfighting is considered cruel to animals while rodeos are not.

The point here is that hedonistic utilitarianism does not contain such prejudice. It does not base moral decisions on people's values, but exclusively on pleasure and pain. *Many utilitarians would condemn both rodeos and American-style bullfighting, while others may approve of both, depending on their estimates of the pleasure and pain involved. But without differences between them regarding pain and pleasure, consistent utilitarians would judge them the same. Utilitarianism claims to provide a culturally neutral evaluation of actions, laws, and policies. This can be added to strengths noted earlier in this chapter. Utilitarianism does not discount the lives of future people. It does not discount the lives of people in poor countries. And, in principle, its hedonic calculus allows decisions to be justified mathematically.*

The Replacement Argument

Unfortunately, hedonistic utilitarianism has flaws. These do not stem from the principle that people should maximize net pleasure. This is a good principle. The problem is that utilitarianism claims it to be *the only principle*. Utilitarianism is a monistic theory. It says there is *only one basic principle of morality*. All other principles can be derived from this one principle. This is the problem. *The utilitarian principle is excellent when combined with other, independent principles of morality in a pluralistic theory. Then reasonable compromises can be made. But when the utilitarian principle is used alone it leads to absurd results.*

Some absurdities concern the size of animal populations. Because hedonistic utilitarianism advocates maximizing net pleasure in the world, it recommends in some circumstances increasing the population. Total net pleasure can often be increased by adding to the number of individuals (humans or animals) who can experience pleasure.[30] Now imagine the situation if and when humane animal husbandry and painless slaughter are finally established. Opponents of cruelty toward animals would welcome this, and it is not just a science fiction fantasy. If slavery could be abolished and women could be given the vote, animals can be raised humanely in a country as rich as ours.

Farm animals would then have pleasant lives. Their painless deaths would end their pleasure, but would not otherwise detract from the pleasantness of their lives. Should utilitarians oppose killing animals for food under these conditions because every death reduces the pleasure in the world by ending a pleasant life? I do not think so. If people stopped killing animals for food, farmers would stop rearing them. Livestock numbers would plummet and with it the pleasure that humanely reared livestock experience. Total pleasure in the world would diminish with reduction of pleasure among farm animals. Utilitarians advocate increases in pleasure, so under these conditions, they should oppose vegetarianism. Vegetarianism would reduce total pleasure in the world by diminishing the number, and thus the pleasure, of livestock.

According to this line of thinking, utilitarianism calls for people to raise animals humanely, kill them painlessly, enjoy the food, and then replace the animals killed with other animals leading pleasant lives. This is called the **replacement argument** because it says that happy animals should be killed painlessly and replaced by other happy animals.

Utilitarians, such as Peter Singer, who champion vegetarianism, are quick to point out that this argument does not apply here and now. Today, animals are raised and killed with great cruelty, so the fewer livestock the better. But we are examining utilitarianism for its guidance when cruelty to farm animals ends. Under such conditions we should eat meat. Go utilitarianism!

But wait. What about poor people in the world who do not have enough to eat? As noted in Chapter 1, when we eat meat we use the earth's food-producing capacity inefficiently. The earth could support more human beings if farmers grew crops for people instead of livestock. The human population continues to increase rapidly, and many are starving already. This suggests that utilitarians should push vegetarianism even when farm animals are treated well. Vegetarianism reduces human misery.

Another reason for vegetarianism follows from hedonistic utilitarianism's exclusive interest in maximizing net pleasure. Cattle and pigs are large animals. Each one eats a lot of what people and the earth can produce. The world could probably support a hundred times as many equally happy chickens, squirrels, rabbits, hamsters, and other little cuddly creatures, who could be bred for their tendency to be happy. (Unhappy neurotic ones could be killed painlessly before they reproduce.) Who is to say that a happy hamster adds less happiness to the world than a happy cow?

If this reasoning is sound, hedonistic utilitarians should either be vegetarians, or eat chickens, rabbits, and squirrels (that are bred to be happy, raised humanely, and killed painlessly). Utilitarians should also raise and care for small, happy pets, such as hamsters and gerbels. Even if this bores and annoys most people over the age of eleven, if the supreme good is maximum net happiness, raising these animals is a solemn duty. The pain of human boredom is less than the pleasure experienced by all those little critters.

But *it seems absurd to make raising small, happy animals an important duty. The problem stems from the hedonistic utilitarian view that pleasure and pain are the only good and bad, and that our greatest duty is to maximize net pleasure or happiness.*

Against Hedonism

One problem with hedonism is that pleasure cannot be measured accurately, making hedonic calculations unreliable. Do happy hamsters experience as much pleasure as contented cows? How could we ever know?

The problem is the same among human beings. Bentham held that the intensity of pleasures affect their quantity. Other things being equal, more intense pleasures are greater pleasures that should weigh more heavily in the hedonic calculus. But how can we measure intensity? Suppose a couple wants to buy a new house. She wants a single-level ranch-style, and he wants a multi-level Victorian-style house. How could either convince the other that maximum happiness results from buying the house of her or his preference? She says, "I'll be really pleased with a ranch-style house, because I hate to climb stairs. And you don't care about the house as long as the TV works." He counters, "I love to watch the birds in the trees from a second-story window, and I'm embarrassed by how plain and uninteresting ranch-style houses look."

Assuming that each is sincere, they cannot know how to maximize pleasure or happiness in this situation because neither can have the other's experience of the world and know directly the other's pleasure or pain. Our knowledge of others' experiences depends on our capacity for empathy, and empathy does not provide accurate enough information for mathematical calculations. In many cases, therefore, neither husband nor wife can judge that his or her pain from a disfavored choice would be greater or less (more or less intense) than the spouse's pain. Comparisons of pleasure are equally limited, so the hedonic calculus is impossible. Hedonistic utilitarianism claims to justify moral judgment mathematically, but cannot.

More important, *maximum net pleasure or happiness is not most people's goal in life.* Close personal relationships can ennoble and enrich life, but often cause more pain than pleasure. Consider Hamlet in Shakespeare's play. Hamlet's uncle killed Hamlet's father and then quickly married Hamlet's mother to become king of Denmark. Hamlet contemplates revenge on his uncle, but is tormented by an inability to act.

> O, what a rogue and peasant slave am I!
> . . .
> A dull and muddy-mettled rascal, peak,
> Like John-a-dreams, unpregnant of my cause,
> And can say nothing; no, not for a king
> Upon whose property and most dear life
> A Damn'd defeat was made. Am I a coward?
> Who calls me villain? Breaks my pate across?
> Plucks off my beard and blows it in my face?
> . . .

Why, what an ass am I? This is most brave,
That I, the son of a dear father murder'd,
Prompted to my revenge by heaven and hell,
Must, like a whore, unpack my heart with words,
And fall a-cursing, like a very drab,
A scullion![31]

Hamlet was one unhappy camper. Shakespeare's Othello was tormented as well. He thought his wife, Desdemona, was being unfaithful:

Ay, let her rot, and perish, and be damned to-night; for she shall not live: no, my heart is turned to stone; I strike it, and it hurts my hand. O, the world hath not a sweeter creature; she might lie by an emperor's side and command him tasks. [But] Hang her![32]

Would the world be better if society were organized to avoid such anguish? In one of the twentieth century's most important novels, *Brave New World*, Aldous Huxley explores this idea. He depicts a society arranged to maximize happiness. Aware that close personal relationships, like those between parents and children and husbands and wives, cause great misery, civilized society in the novel eliminates them. Human beings are produced in test tubes so that no one can identify mother or father. Marriage does not exist and sexual promiscuity is encouraged so that people will not develop deep emotional bonds. In such a society, the anguish of Hamlet and Othello are impossible.

Dull work also causes unhappiness in our society. In the novel, embryos are chemically altered to produce people of varying intelligence and imagination so everyone is happy with his or her work. Dull jobs go to suitable people. For any remaining stress in people's lives there is *soma*, a muscle relaxant that makes people happy without any long-lasting negative effects. Mustafa Mond, the society's Controller notes:

The world's stable now. People are happy; they get what they want, and they never want what they can't get. They're well off; they're safe; . . . they're plagued with no mothers or fathers; they've got no wives, or children, or lovers to feel strongly about; they're so conditioned that they practically can't help behaving as they ought to behave. And if anything should go wrong, there's *soma*.[33]

Would you want to live pleasurably in a society like that, without the liberty to make your own, possibly wrong, decisions? In such a society you would not be allowed the challenge of attempting major achievements. Failed attempts make people unhappy and sometimes anti-social, so the happiest society disallows attempting anything difficult. Missing, too, is the ability to form strong familial bonds. Such bonds occasion great suffering. In our society most interpersonal violence takes place within the family.

Finally, would you want drugs to keep you happy? When drugs are used to alleviate distress, people lose their distinctly human relationship with reality. According to a 1970 article in *The Christian Century* arguing against the use of drugs:

> When psychotropic drugs are ingested . . . the human is temporarily de-graded back toward the animal. . . . The brain . . . responds not to changes in its real environment, nor to the real needs of the self . . . but to toxic substances. . . . Such a condition may be pleasurable—indeed, that is precisely why it is sought. But in such a condition a man is less than fully himself. . . . Better the ambiguities and tensions experienced by a real man interacting with other real men . . . than the euphoria of chemically induced sensations of escape that do not let us escape from anything at all. . . . [34]

One reason many drugs are illegal in our society is the value people place on reality over pleasure. So the hedonist's goal of maximizing pleasure is not what people always prefer.

Preference Utilitarianism

Preference utilitarianism accepts the value of reality over pleasure for those who prefer reality. The goal of preference utilitarians is to maximize not pleasure or happiness, but the satisfaction of preferences.

Most utilitarians assume that animals generally prefer maximum pleasure, because animals do not develop commitments to abstractions. Animals would not, it is assumed, prefer a miserable life, just because it was a life of freedom, over a pleasant life of captivity. They would not prefer reality to illusion if the illusion contained more reliable, long-lasting pleasure. On these assumptions, preference utilitarianism leads to the same decisions regarding animals as hedonistic utilitarianism.

Similarly, for people who prefer pleasure, preference utilitarians try to secure pleasure because that is what those people prefer. For those who prefer strong personal ties, by contrast, preference utilitarians favor such ties even if they lead to emotional pain. "Love Hurts." In short, *preference utilitarianism allows people to define for themselves what they consider good, and then calls for actions that promote the maximum satisfaction of the various preferences that people happen to have.*

Preference utilitarianism has several problems. One concerns the measurement of preferences. *Because preferences often conflict, we need to evaluate their relative strength. We saw earlier that we cannot measure accurately one person's pleasure against another person's pleasure (or pain). The same is true for preferences when they are viewed as internal psychological states.* For example, I prefer Mind Extension University on my TV cable, whereas someone else prefers an extra shopping channel instead. How can we tell with mathematical accuracy whose preference is stronger? Suppose one of us shouts more than the other. That may reveal only different personal styles, social training, or manners, not different intensities of preference.

The extra shopping channel may be more popular in the viewing area than Mind Extension University. But this does not mean it satisfies preferences any better when intensities of preference are considered. Satisfying a minority's intense preference may be more preference satisfying than catering to the weaker preference of the majority. But, again, how can we measure accurately the relative strength of preferences?

One method favored by economists is to use consumer demand. They measure preferences by people's willingness to pay for things. This puts everything in monetary terms and converts preference utilitarianism into cost benefit analysis. We have seen that CBA often leads to bad results for poor people and future generations. But for animals it is absurd. How much can animals pay for better housing on the farm, more comfortable transportation, and more humane slaughter? Nothing. Hedonistic utilitarianism considers the welfare of animals. When preferences are judged by willingness to pay, preference utilitarianism does not.

Another problem with preference utilitarianism concerns its goal of satisfying preferences regardless of their nature and origins. Scholar Mark Sagoff points out:

> Many preferences—for example, . . . the urge for a cigarette—are despised by the very people who have them. Why should we regard the satisfaction of preferences that are addictive, boorish, criminal, deceived, external to the individual, foolish, grotesque, harmful, ignorant, jealous, . . . or zany to be a good thing in itself?[35]

Consider, for example, the preference of a healthy, attractive nineteen-year-old woman for breast implants. She wants to look more like models (many of whom have implants). Is the world a better place if her preference is satisfied? We cannot say the world is better because she will be happy. Getting what she wants may not make her happy, hence the saying: "Be careful what you wish for. You may get it." Also, if happiness is the general goal, we return to hedonistic utilitarianism with all its problems.

In my view, even if this woman has no medical complications, a better world is one where she accepts her healthy body without implants. Like Sagoff, I think that *in order to determine when and where preference satisfaction is good, we must judge which preferences are worthy and which are not.* Preference utilitarians disagree.

Hedonistic and preference utilitarianism may recommend trampling individual rights and ignoring justice. Consider, for example, the impeachment in 1998 of President William Jefferson Clinton for allegedly lying to a grand jury.[36] The testimony concerned sex with Monica Lewinsky. The alleged lying concerned who touched whom where and when. Personally, I do not want to know. But lying under oath is a serious offense because our system of justice often depends on the reliability of sworn testimony. Yet prosecuting someone for lying in these circumstances is rare because perjury is hard to prove and prosecutors have too many thieves, drug pushers, and murderers to deal with. Does this mean that Clinton should not be prosecuted?

From any utilitarian perspective, "high profile" cases should be treated differently from others, even if the perpetrator is no more guilty than others whose alleged crimes are ignored. The reason is deterrence. From a utilitarian point of view, we often prosecute and punish illegal acts primarily to deter others from committing similar acts. People who learn about the punishment are supposed to be scared off. Prosecuting a famous person generally provides more deterrence than prosecuting an unknown. More people learn about the prosecution, so more people are scared off. This makes the individual defendant an object lesson for others. The famous defendant is treated more harshly than others in identical circumstances. Many people think this violates individual rights and is unjust. But utilitarianism usually requires it.

Another kind of justice problem stems from cultural influences on preferences. Imagine a society where half of the population is socialized to *prefer* serving the needs of the other half. Their highest aspiration is to provide child-rearing, housekeeping, and emotional support services free to the other half. When they work outside the home, they generally expect to have positions with lower pay and less authority than people from the other half. They can advance to head secretary, but not chairman of the board.

People successfully socialized this way would get what they prefer, and this may also maximize net pleasure. Preference and hedonistic utilitarians would approve. But current American thinking finds such a society obviously unjust.

❧ ❧ ❧

The defects of utilitarianism need not affect our objections to cruelty toward animals. The world is better without unnecessary animal suffering because pleasure is generally good and pain is generally bad. But *maximizing net pleasure (or preference satisfaction) cannot be the basis of all morality, as utilitarians claim. We cannot measure pleasure (or preference satisfaction) to know when it is maximized; most of us do not think that all preferences are worthy of satisfaction; and we value individual rights and social justice, as well as pleasure and preference satisfaction. In sum, we should include pleasure and preference satisfaction in a pluralistic moral outlook, along with such values as liberty, privacy, political participation, and justice.*

Judgment Calls

- Assuming that the information from Peter Singer and Gail Eisnitz about animal husbandry and slaughter is current and accurate, how might one justify eating meat?

- Is eating fish morally proper? Where do the fish come from? How are they killed?

- Some people object to wearing fur more than they object to wearing leather. How can this distinction be justified?

- Should marijuana be legalized? What values are relevant besides pleasure and preference satisfaction?

- Jane Goodall wrote in her 1990 book *Through a Window* that "human DNA differs from chimpanzee DNA by only just over one per cent."[37] How might this justify using chimpanzees in medical research to combat such diseases as AIDS and hepatitis B? What reasons are there to avoid using chimpanzees in medical research? (See the next chapter for more on medical research.)

CHAPTER 5

Animal Rights and Medical Research

Introduction

Robert J. White, director of neurological surgery at Cleveland Metropolitan General Hospital, related the following story in a 1988 article in *Reader's Digest*:

> Four years ago I was part of a surgical team trying to remove a malignant tumor from the brain of a nine-year-old girl. The operation failed because we could not stem the hemorrhaging in the brain tissue. We were unable to separate the little girl from the cancer that was slowly killing her. To buy time, we put her on a program of radiation.
>
> Concurrently, we were experimenting in our brain-research laboratory with a new high-precision laser scalpel. Working with monkeys and dogs that had been humanely treated and properly anesthetized, we perfected our operating technique. Then, in July 1985, my associate . . . and I used the laser to remove all of that little girl's tumor. Now 13, she is healthy, happy, and looking forward to a full life. The animal experiments had enabled us to cure a child we could not help 15 months earlier.[1]

Dr. White does not mention what happened to the monkeys and dogs. Most likely they were killed, painlessly, I assume. Should we care? Many people think so, because they believe it is wrong to harm animals for human benefit.

In her 1990 book *Through a Window* veteran primate researcher Jane Goodall tells the story of a captive chimpanzee saving a man's life. Called Old Man, this chimp had been abused by people in a laboratory or circus until he was rescued at age eight and placed in a Florida zoo. There he lived on an island with three females. He was known to be ferocious, so when Marc Cusano was hired several years later to take care of the chimps, he was warned to stay away from Old Man. Obediently, Marc initially just threw food to the chimps from his boat, but later ventured onto the island and eventually could feed Old Man by hand and groom him. The females, one of whom was nursing an infant, remained more distant. Goodall writes:

One day as Marc was cleaning up the island he slipped and fell. This startled the infant, who screamed, and his mother, her protective instinct aroused, at once leaped to attack Marc. She bit his neck as he lay, face down, on the ground, and he felt the blood run down his chest. The other two females rushed to support their friend. One bit his wrist, the other his leg. . . . He thought it was all up for him.

And then Old Man charged to the rescue of this, his first human friend in years. He dragged each of the highly roused females off Marc and hurled them away. Then he stayed, close by, keeping them at bay, while Marc slowly dragged himself to the boat and safety. "Old Man saved my life, you know," Marc told me later. . . .

Were he human, we would praise Old Man as a Good Samaritan. Should we respect an animal whose acts resemble moral heroism? If so, should we use him for purely human benefit in medical experiments and other pursuits? This is the animal rights issue.

Animal rights differ from animal liberation because the underlying moral concern is different. Animal liberation rests on the utilitarian value of maximizing net pleasure or preference satisfaction. We should avoid behavior that hurts animals more than it helps people. Animal rights, by contrast, are claimed to be like human rights, which most people exempt from calculations of utility. *Advocates claim that many animals are similar enough to human beings to deserve similar rights.*

The Nature of Rights

Article 19 of the United Nation's Universal Declaration of Human Rights declares a right to freedom of speech: "Everyone has the right to freedom of opinion and expression; this right includes freedom to hold opinions without interference and to seek, receive and impart information and ideas through any media and regardless of frontiers." Even if exercise of this right lowers overall pleasure in the world, as it may if the speech convinces people to smoke cigarettes, it is immoral to stifle speech, as this violates a human right. The classic remedy to harmful speech is more speech, in this case, arguments against smoking cigarettes.

The Universal Declaration of Human Rights' Article 3 says: "Everyone has the right to life, liberty, and security of person." This disallows sacrificing one life to save several others, as in the following hypothetical presented by Leo Katz in *Ill-Gotten Gains*. Imagine a surgeon, Katz writes:

who has five patients, all of whom are at death's door. They are destined to die unless they receive transplant organs. Two need kidneys, two need lungs, one needs a heart. There is no donor to be found—except for a perfectly healthy patient who walks into the surgeon's office for his annual checkup. On seeing him, the surgeon realizes that he is a walking reservoir of useful spare parts, which, if judiciously redeployed, could save five lives at the cost of one. Suppose the surgeon were to quickly and painlessly kill his healthy walk-in and use his organs to save the other five?[2]

Would that be the right thing to do? Of course not. But why?

Utilitarians may say the surgeon is wrong to kill his walk-in patient because this will discourage people from getting needed medical care. (A doctor with cold hands is enough to discourage me.) In the long run, more people will suffer for lack of checkups, utilitarians maintain, than are saved by the occasional sacrifice of a healthy patient.

This long-run calculation may be correct, but is not why most people condemn the surgeon's action. We condemn it because it violates someone's right to "life, liberty, and security of person." If killing healthy patients were rare and kept secret, so others would not be discouraged from going to the doctor, we would still condemn it. As in the free speech case, total utility is irrelevant. Individual rights are more important.

Animal rights advocates claim that many animals, too, have rights, so even if more good than harm comes from killing an animal painlessly, it is wrong because it violates the animal's right to life. But why should we extend rights to animals? Animal rights advocates ask the same about human beings, saying that whatever justifies attributing rights to people justifies extending them to many animals as well.

They do not mean that animals and people have all of the same rights. It makes no sense to give a right of speech to animals who cannot talk. But where humans and (many species of) animals can benefit equally from the protection of individual rights, they are entitled equally to that protection. The issue boils down to whether human beings have attributes, lacking in animals, that justify recognizing rights, or whether, instead, many animals are equally deserving of rights that would benefit them.

Opinions about animal rights are often polarized. Some people say that animals have no rights at all, because they lack appropriate attributes. Others claim that when animals can benefit equally from the rights granted to people, they have exactly the same rights as people, because they have fully the attributes that justify human rights. A compromise view is that *many animals have attributes similar to those that justify human rights. But they have some of these in lesser degree than human beings. So animals generally have lesser rights than human beings. But they do have rights.*

I now discuss five justifications for human rights and relate each to the claim that animals have rights. The five are: people have immortal souls; people can speak and reason abstractly; people can act morally; people can make and abide by contracts; and people can benefit from basic human rights.

Immortal Souls and Rights

The seventeenth-century scientist and philosopher Rene Descartes considered the possession of an immortal soul to distinguish people from animals, and used this distinction to justify animal **vivisection**, the cutting up of live animals in biology experiments. Our immortal souls, he claimed, enable us to think, reason, and speak. Animals, by contrast, are like machines that cannot think, reason, or speak. Vivisection is like taking apart a clock or other mechanical device. No one objects to dismantling a clock. On the other hand, if animals are not machines and "had thought as we do, they would have an immortal soul like us. This is unlikely, because there is no reason to believe it of some animals without believing it of all, and many of them such as oysters and sponges are too imperfect for this to be credible."[3] In sum, "it is more probable that worms and flies and caterpillars move mechanically than that they all have immortal souls."[4] Without immortal souls, they have no rights against vivisection.

Claims about immortal souls are problematic, and philosophical opinions vary. The ancient Greek mathematician and philosopher Pythagoras, who lived in the sixth century before the common era (BCE), was reported by the Latin poet Ovid to believe that human souls enter animals upon death, making animals our relatives:

> We are not bodies only,
> But winged spirits, with the power to enter
> Animal forms, house in the bodies of cattle.
> Therefore, we should respect those dwelling-places
> Which may have given shelter to the spirit
> Of fathers, brothers, cousins, human beings
> At least, and we should never do them damage, . . .
> Wicked as human bloodshed, to draw the knife
> Across the throat of the calf, and hear its anguish
> Cry to deaf ears! And who could slay
> The little goat whose cry is like a baby's. . . .
> One might as well do murder; he is only
> The shortest step away.[5]

Today few people would base their opinion about human rights on uncertain and contested religious views about immortal souls. Whether they support or deny animal rights, people seek firmer foundations for general agreement.

Language, Abstract Thinking, and Rights

One traditional foundation of rights is human *language*, which helps people think in abstractions. Animals lack this kind of language, rendering them incapable of abstract thought. If the ability to think abstractly is the basis for recognizing "the right to life, liberty, and security," then people alone have this right, and animals can be subject to lethal experiments to help human beings. This was another of Descartes' considerations.

But language is not essential for abstract thought in animals or people. Steven Pinker, a linguist at Massachusetts Institute of Technology, gives a human example in his bestseller *The Language Instinct*. He discusses an experiment by developmental psychologist Karen Wynn showing that pre-linguistic five-month-old babies can do "a simple form of mental arithmetic." The experiment assumes that if a baby sees

> a bunch of objects long enough, . . . the baby gets bored and looks away. Change the scene, and if the baby notices the difference, he or she will regain interest.
>
> In Wynn's experiment, the babies were shown a rubber Mickey Mouse doll on a stage until their little eyes wandered. Then a screen came up, and a prancing hand visibly reached out from behind a curtain and placed a second Mickey Mouse behind the screen. When the screen was removed, if there were two Mickey Mouses visible (something the babies had never actually seen), the babies looked for only a few moments. But if there was only one doll, the babies were captivated—even though this was exactly the scene that had bored them before the screen was put in place. . . . The babies must have been keeping track of how many dolls were behind the screen, updating their counts as dolls were added or subtracted. If the number inexplicably departed from what they expected, they scrutinized the scene, as if searching for some explanation.[6]

Even without language, it seems, babies think about numbers and/or causality.

Some monkeys also appear capable of abstract thought and reasoning without language. Pinker discusses observations of vervet monkeys that primatologists Dorothy Cheney and Robert Seyfarth made in Kenya. The monkeys they observed divided themselves into extended families. On one occasion the families came into conflict:

> One juvenile monkey wrestled another to the ground screaming. Twenty minutes later the victim's sister approached the perpetrator's sister and without provocation bit her on the tail. For the retaliator to have identified the proper target, she would have to solve the following analogy problem: A (victim) is to B (myself) as C (perpetrator) is to X, using the correct relationship "sister of" (or perhaps merely "relative of . . . ").[7]

Time is another abstract consideration that many animals handle well. Philosopher Mary Midgley notes in *Animals and Why They Matter*:

> There is, for instance, plenty of evidence of the ability of domestic animals to follow a weekly cycle. Thus, Sheila Hocken's guide-dog quickly and spontaneously learned to take her every Friday, without needing to be told the day, to the places where she did her weekend shopping. More remarkably, feral cats which were fed once a week learned to turn up in advance on the day when the feeds were due.[8]

This demolishes the rationale behind the traditional language requirement for attributing rights. Descartes and others maintained that having language is a prerequisite for having rights because language is a sign of the ability to think abstractly, and only beings capable of abstract thought and reasoning are worthy of possessing rights. People have language and animals do not, they said, so people alone have rights. Now it appears that *language is not necessary for abstract thought by people or animals, so the fact that people have language and animals do not is irrelevant to the possession of rights.*

Differences between people and animals remain. Most people can express abstract thoughts in language, whereas animals express thoughts only in non-linguistic behavior. Also, many human abstractions, in mathematics and the arts, for example, are far more complex than any we can safely attribute to animals. Hence, if rights are based on the ability to think abstractly, people may have more or stronger rights than animals. But we cannot say on this basis that animals have no rights at all.

Moral Personality and Rights

Eighteenth-century philosopher Immanuel Kant, as was discussed in the preceding chapter, opposed cruelty to animals on the anthropocentric grounds that such cruelty ultimately harms people. He denied that animals have rights, claiming that only beings who can behave morally or immorally have rights. Animals, he thought, lack the reasoning ability and the freedom from instinctual compulsions required for moral (and immoral) actions. Animal parents, for example, often take good care of their children, but they do this without reasoning. They do it out of instincts that determine their behavior. They have no choice or freedom, according to Kant, so they deserve no moral praise for their actions. Good human mothers, on the other hand, deserve moral praise because they act with forethought and choose freely to act as they do.

We have just seen that many animals can think more abstractly than Kant realized. Now let us look at some animal behavior that seems to combine thought with moral sensibilities. The chimpanzee Old Man in the story told by Jane Goodall seemed to exhibit moral sensibilities when he saved Marc Cusano's life. It seems that he did so out of friendship. On what grounds can we say that Old Man acted out of blind instinct, whereas a human being doing the same thing made a free choice? I know of none. If the one deserves moral praise, so does the other.

Jane Goodall gives an example of a mother chimpanzee, Gremlin, whose care for her child Gimble was much more thoughtful than mere responses to his cries:

> Like a good mother she would anticipate trouble. Thus when Gimble played with young baboons Gremlin often watched closely and, if the game got the least bit rough, and long before Gimble himself seemed worried, she firmly took him away. Once, as she was carrying him along a trail, she saw a small snake ahead. Carefully she pushed Gimble off her back and kept him behind her as she shook branches at the snake until it glided away.[9]

Animals sometimes appear morally better than people. Sociologist Stanley Milgram and colleagues conducted a series of experiments at Yale University that show many people's willingness under orders to harm fellow human beings.[10] In a typical experiment, the subject was misled into thinking he was a teacher in a learning experiment. He was told to read lists of paired words to another person, the learner, who would try to learn them. The "teacher" thought he was then testing the "learner" by reading the first word in a pair and seeing if the "learner" would respond with the second word. The "teacher" thought he was required to administer progressively greater electric shocks to the "learner" for incorrect responses, supposedly to see the effect on learning.

The real experiment was to see how much harm the subject (the "teacher") was willing under orders to inflict on another person. The "learner's" responses were played on a tape recorder. No one actually received an electric shock. But the research subject (the "teacher") did not know this. In fact, he was told before giving any shock that the "learner" had a heart condition. In addition, some levers used to administer shocks warned that these shocks were severe and dangerous. The "teacher" could hear the "learner" scream in pain (only a recording), fear for his life, and demand release. Finally, the "learner" ceased to respond at all. Still, most subjects ("teachers") accepted reassurances from the administrative authority that no permanent harm would be done. So they continued giving shocks that the screaming, labels on the shock levers, and other sources of information suggested may be lethal. They did so because authority figures said that the experiment must proceed.

In *Created from Animals* James Rachels reports a somewhat similar experiment conducted in 1964 with rhesus monkeys at Northwestern University Medical School. Two monkeys were placed in a cage divided by a one-way mirror. One monkey, who could see the other through the one-way mirror, had been trained to obtain food by pulling either of two chains. The other was surrounded by wire mesh attached to electricity so he or she could be given inescapable electric shocks. After awhile, the first monkey's chains were attached to the electrical switch that caused the other monkey to be shocked. So when the first monkey obtained food by pulling either chain, the second experienced a severe shock. The monkey pulling the chain could see, and sometimes hear, the other's reaction to the shock. What did they do? Rachels writes:

> After numerous trials the experimenters concluded that "a majority of rhesus monkeys will consistently suffer hunger rather than secure food at the expense of electroshock to a conspecific." In particular, in one series of tests, 6 of 8 animals showed this type of sacrificial behaviour; in a second series, 6 of 10; and in a third, 13 of 15. One of the monkeys refrained from pulling either chain for 12 days, and another for 5 days, after witnessing shock to the [other monkey]—which means they had no food at all during that time.[11]

The willingness to shock others varied among the monkeys, but did not correspond to the monkeys' sex or to their relative positions on the social hierarchy. However, monkeys who had themselves been shocked in this apparatus were less willing to shock others, and monkeys were less willing to shock previous cage mates.

Rachels concludes that rhesus monkeys exhibit altruism, "the willingness to forgo some good for oneself in order to help others,"[12] much as people do. Members of both species vary in their altruism, and are more altruistic when they can empathize with the other's pain and when they know the other personally.

But experiments on people and monkeys suggest that social hierarchy and authority affect displays of altruism in people more than in some monkeys. This may be due to people's greater ability to think abstractly. We can identify with an abstract cause, such as scientific progress, which authority figures can invoke to reduce altruism. Thus, our intellectual superiority over animals in abstract thinking may sometimes lead to moral inferiority. In any case, *we can no longer say that human beings alone are entitled to rights because we alone exhibit moral behavior.*

Contracts and Rights

Defending vivisection in *The New England Journal of Medicine*, political philosopher Carl Cohen argues that animals cannot have rights. Cohen claims:

> Rights . . . are in every case claims, or potential claims, within a community of moral agents. Rights arise, and can be intelligibly defended, only among beings who actually do, or can, make moral claims against one another. . . . The holders of rights must have the capacity to comprehend rules of duty, governing all including themselves. . . . Only in a community of beings capable of self-restricting moral judgments can the concept of a right be correctly invoked.[13]

Cohen's use of "rights" is too restrictive. We normally say, for example, that infants have rights before they "do, or can, make moral claims . . ." and before they "have the capacity to comprehend rules of duty." Dead people retain rights after they have lost these abilities, for example, the right to have their wills honored. Severely retarded human beings who never have had and never will have these abilities also have rights.

It seems that Cohen has confused two groups. One is a smaller group whose members are part of the other, larger group. The smaller one is the group that *recognizes* or acknowledges the existence of rights. This group must consist of beings like ourselves who are capable of abstract thought beyond the reach of infants, the severely retarded, and (perhaps) all animals. But there is another, larger group that includes those to whom the first group accords rights. This is the group that *has* rights. Cohen assumes that members of the first group, the group that recognizes rights, will restrict such recognition to themselves the way that some exclusive country clubs admit members only; guests are not allowed. But the moral community is not like this. People who can "comprehend rules of duty" usually accord rights not only to themselves, the small group, but to others as well, such as infants and the severely retarded. Why not include animals, too?

An answer is given not by Cohen but by philosopher Peter Carruthers in *The Animals Issue*. Carruthers claims that all morality, and so all moral rights and duties, derive from a hypothetical contract made behind a veil of ignorance. We looked at this in Chapter 2. Carruthers assumes that the contracting parties are selfish, so they want to protect only themselves. They agree to respect the rights only of others who reciprocate by respecting their rights. Because only rational individuals can reciprocate, Carruthers believes that contractors would extend rights only to rational individuals, like themselves, who are capable of negotiating and adhering to a contract. He writes:

> Since it is rational agents who are to choose the system of rules, and choose self-interestedly, it is only rational agents who will have their position protected under the rules. There seems no reason why rights should be assigned to non-rational agents. Animals will, therefore, have no moral standing. . . . [14]

There are problems here. Why assume that morality should conform to a contract made by completely selfish people? As we have seen, most people are not completely selfish and consider those who are to be dangerous sociopaths. Imagine two people arguing about rights or duties. If they found completely ruthless behavior to be acceptable, one could say, "This is what they did in the movie 'The Godfather,'" and the other would reply, "Well, then, it must be right." Not many of us accept such a standard of conduct.

Carruthers actually assumes, inconsistently with his earlier assumption of complete selfishness, that people entering the negotiations to form a contract "share the aim of reaching free and unforced agreement."[15] In other words, they already believe that social arrangements should not be imposed by the strong on the weak. They seek a contract because they do not want might to be confused with right. But if they enter negotiations with this moral view, not all morality comes from the contract. Some morality pre-exists the contract, and that morality could include concern by many contractors for animal welfare. Such contractors could insist that society establish animal rights, including the right to "life, liberty, and security."[16]

Mary Midgley adds perspective to this consideration. Contracts specifying reciprocal rights and duties among selfish, egoistic individuals cannot possibly generate the whole of morality, she argues:

> Parental duty is not so much reciprocal as transitive—passed on. The parents pay to their children the care which they received from their own parents, who received it from theirs, and so on indefinitely. The main payment is never back to the giver, but always forward to the next receiver. . . . [17]

More important, parents care for children out of love. They view their children's welfare as good in itself. Midgley relates these facts to evolution:

> Parental motives should not puzzle anyone except a dogmatic egoist, and dogmatic egoists should only look around at the general parental behaviour of birds and mammals to see the implausibility of their dogma. Good egoists make bad parents, and . . . natural selection soon extinguishes their line. . . . The long childhood now characteristic of our species has been made possible only because selection has favored the emotional constitution which leads to very generous parenting.[18]

In sum, *morality contains more than what selfish hypothetical contractors would include in it. So animals may have rights regardless of what such contractors would say.*

An Animal's Right to Life

Do animals have "the right to life, liberty, and security?" The United Nation's Universal Declaration of Human Rights attributes this right to people. We have considered several ways in which people differ, or may differ, from animals, but none of these justifies attributing rights to people but not to animals. Claims regarding immortal souls are problematic. Only people have sophisticated languages, but this does not prevent animals from thinking abstractly, although to a lesser extent than people. Animals can act like moral beings, sometimes displaying a higher degree of morality than people. So why should people alone have the right to life, liberty, and security? Philosopher Tom Regan sees no reason at all.

Consider the right to life. Why do we attribute this right to people? We do so because an untimely death, even if it is painless, harms people. It deprives them of their memories, their friends, and their families. It deprives them of their future. It frustrates their plans and puts an end to their dreams. If this is the reason it is wrong to kill people painlessly, the prohibition against killing should apply to all animals who would be similarly harmed. Regan has a term that refers to people and to everyone else in this category. He calls them "**subjects-of-a-life**." He writes:

> Individuals are subjects-of-a-life if they have beliefs and desires; perception, memory, and a sense of the future, including their own future; an emotional life together with feelings of pleasure and pain; preference and welfare-interests; the ability to initiate action in pursuit of their desires and goals; . . . and an individual welfare [independent] . . . of anyone else's interests.[19]

Not all animals are subjects-of-a-life, so not all have a right to life, according to Regan. But all adult mammals are subjects-of-a-life. Consider, for example, chimpanzees. Jane Goodall describes the rise of one chimp, Figan, to the top of his social hierarchy. Figan showed the cunning and long-term strategy of a presidential candidate:

> When Mike deposed Goliath and rose to the top-ranking position of the community Figan was eleven years old and, clearly, fascinated by the imaginative strategy of the new alpha. For Mike, by incorporating empty four-gallon tin cans into his charging displays, hitting and kicking them ahead of him as he ran towards his rivals, succeeded in intimidating them all—including individuals much larger than himself. . . . Figan was the only one whom we saw, on two different occasions, "practicing" with cans that had been abandoned by Mike. . . . He did this only when out of sight of older males. . . . [20]

When age made Mike vulnerable, Humphrey succeeded as alpha. "Even during the early months of his reign," Goodall reports,

> Humphrey seemed to sense, in Figan, potential danger: he displayed, bristling and magnificent, much more often in Figan's presence than at other times. . . . Figan, for his part, . . . was still preoccupied with his long struggle to dominate [his early rival] Evered. Indeed, looking back on the events of the stormy period it seems probable that Figan, all along, realized that Evered, rather than Humphrey, was his most formidable rival.[21]

Eventually, Figan succeeded by gaining the reliable support of his brother Faben.

As you can see from this, an untimely, painless death would have harmed Figan much as Robert Kennedy was harmed by assassination. According to primatologist Frans de Waal, many animals have a comparable sense of self-identity. "Only two non-human species," he writes, "—chimpanzees and orangutans—seem to understand that they are seeing themselves . . ." when they look in a mirror.[22] But, de Waal continues:

> The mirror test provides a rather narrow measure of self-awareness. After all, such awareness may express itself in myriad other kinds of behavior and involve senses other than the visual. What to think of the dog's olfactory distinction between his own urine markings and those of other dogs; the bat's ability to pick out the echoes of its own sounds from among those of other bats . . . ?[23]

Sophisticated self-awareness is needed especially in social species.

> A macaque or baboon can hardly function without knowing the social position of each group mate, the kinship network, which individuals are likely to side with each other in a fight, the possible reactions of others to particular actions, and so on. How could a monkey ever reach such a grasp of social affairs without knowing its own capacities and limitations, and its own position vis-à-vis others? Understanding one's surroundings equals understanding oneself. . . . [24]

What does this have to do with a right to life? We saw earlier that people have a right to life at least in part to protect them from harm. Death harms people by depriving them of their memories, relationships, projects, and prospects, all of which are tied to their sense of self. Painless death might not harm a being totally devoid of such self-awareness, ergo the phrase, "slug today, gone tomorrow." But even painless death harms self-aware individuals, and we now see that this includes at least all (non-infant) mammals. *The same reasons for according people a right to life seem to apply to* these animals. They are all, in Tom Regan's term, *subjects-of-a-life*.

One implication is that mammals, at least, should not be raised and killed for food, even if they are reared humanely and killed painlessly, as this violates their right to life. This differs from the utilitarian view discussed in the last chapter. Utilitarians seeking to maximize pleasure may raise animals humanely, kill them painlessly for food, and then replace them with additional happy animals. This is the replacement argument discussed in Chapter 4. It does not apply to Regan's perspective, which ignores total net pleasure and preference satisfaction. We should not violate anyone's rights.

Other implications concern liberty. People and animals who are subjects-of-a-life are harmed by violations of their liberty, too. If we accord people the right to liberty to avoid such harm, we should extend this right to other subjects-of-a-life as well.

The Benefits of Experiments on Animals

According to the Department of Agriculture's Office of Technology Assessment, millions of mammals were used for research in the United States in 1986 alone. These include 49,000 primates, 54,000 cats, 180,000 dogs, and 12 to 15 million rats and mice.[25] Philosopher Sidney Gendin contends that the commonly accepted figure is much higher—between 70 and 90 million total animals per year.[26]

Whatever the number, it is not clear whether, or how much, people benefit from this research. Medical benefits are sought from three different, general types of research: basic biological science; the development of surgical techniques and medical devices, such as pacemakers and stents; and the testing of drugs, hormones, and other medications. The case for human benefits from medications testing is the weakest.

Jane McCabe is a mother with a positive view of the benefits:

My daughter has cystic fibrosis. Her only hope for a normal life is that researchers, some of them using animals, will find a cure. . . .

How has research using animals helped those with CF? Three times a day my daughter uses enzymes from the pancreas of pigs to digest her food. She takes antibiotics tested on rats before they are tried on humans. As an adult, she will probably develop diabetes and need insulin—a drug developed by research on dogs and rabbits. If she ever needs a heart-lung transplant, one might be possible because of the cows that surgeons practiced on. . . . [27]

The American Medical Association (AMA) agrees in its 1988 white paper, "Use of Animals in Biomedical Research: The Challenge and Response:"

> 54 of 76 Nobel Prizes awarded in physiology or medicine since 1901 have been for discoveries and advances made through the use of experimental animals. . . . In fact, virtually every advance in medical science in the twentieth century, from antibiotics and vaccines to antidepressant drugs and organ transplants, has been achieved either directly or indirectly through the use of animals in laboratory experiments.[28]

For example, "Primates played three different roles in the development of the poliomyelitis vaccines, all of them essential."[29] Polio is now rare in industrialized countries.

Others disagree. Stephen Kaufman, senior resident in ophthalmology at New York University maintains that "most of the key discoveries in several areas, such as heart disease and cancer, were made by clinical research, observations of patients, and human autopsies."[30] Kaufman quotes "renowned physician Paul Beeson" writing in the *American Journal of Medicine* on the history of hepatitis:

> Progress in the understanding and management of human disease must begin, and end, with studies of man. . . . Hepatitis, although an almost "pure" example of progress by the study of man, is by no means unusual; in fact, it is more nearly the rule. To cite other examples: appendicitis, rheumatic fever, typhoid fever, ulcerative colitis and hyperparathyroidism.[31]

Research on animals can actually hinder medical progress and endanger human beings, Kaufman claims, because people differ from animals:

> For example, research with the animal model of polio resulted in a misunderstanding of the mechanism of infection. This delayed development of the tissue culture, which was critical to the discovery of a vaccine. For [another] example, prior to 1963, every prospective and retrospective study of human patients, dozens in all, demonstrated that cigarette smoking causes cancer. Unfortunately, health warnings were delayed for years, and thousands of people subsequently died of cancer, because laboratory results were conflicting.[32]

Reliance on animal testing today, Kaufman contends, would expose people to additional risks of cancer. "Of the 19 known human oral carcinogens," Kaufman notes, "only seven caused cancer" in a National Cancer Institute (NCI) study of animals used in research. According to the NCI's figures, "a substance that did not appear to be carcinogenic in experimental animals could still cause cancer in up to one million Americans."[33]

Experts are clearly divided on whether medical research with animals provides net benefits to human beings. Besides different accounts of history that may show conflicting selective memories, there is a methodological reason why the net benefits of using animals to test medications cannot be settled. We generally test medications on animals before giving them to people to see if they are safe and effective. If the substance does not have the desired effect on the animals, or is toxic to them, it is not tried on human beings. This has probably spared people the experimental use of useless or toxic substances. This is the positive side. But is it greater than the negative side?

What is unhelpful to animals may be helpful to people, and what is toxic to animals may not hurt human beings. Because we use animal studies to protect people, we never give people what does not work, or hurts, animals. So people may be missing safe and effective medications. Sidney Gendin writes: "Penicillin is an interesting example of a drug that is fatal to guinea pigs even in very low doses. Other drugs useful to humans that are deadly to many animals include epinephrine, salicylates, insulin, cortisone, and meclizine."[34] Reliance on standard animal tests could have deprived people of the benefits of these substances.

We have no way of knowing how much benefit we are missing now due to required tests on animals, so we cannot know if people gain more than animals lose from such tests. Sarah McCabe, the mother of a girl with cystic fibrosis who thanks animal research for leading to medical help for her daughter may not realize that animal tests might have deprived her daughter of the insulin she may someday need. CF might be treated better now if reliance on animal tests had been eliminated long ago.

Animal Rights vs. Animal Research

But what if certain medical uses of animals do benefit people? Does this justify the way we use these animals? Chimpanzees are currently used in AIDS research. Jane Goodall describes the lab conditions in Rockville, Maryland:

> Young chimpanzees, two or three years old, were crammed, two together, into tiny cages measuring, I was told, 22 inches by 22 inches, and two feet high. They could hardly move. Not yet part of any experiment, they had already been confined there for more than three months. . . . And what was in the cage to provide occupation, comfort, stimulation? Nothing.[35]

Conditions worsen for chimps once they are infected with the AIDS virus. Because it is an infectious disease, they are isolated from other chimps. Goodall adds:

> Imagine being shut up in such a cell, with bars all around; bars on every side, bars above, bars below. And with nothing to do. Nothing to while away the monotony of the long, long days. No physical contact, ever, with another of your kind. Friendly physical contact is so terribly important to chimpanzees.[36]

Under these conditions chimpanzees, like most people, simply go insane.

Is such treatment of chimpanzees necessary and helpful in the fight against AIDS? Many human volunteers would willingly replace these animals, so it is not necessary. Is it helpful? Not likely, because people and chimpanzees are too different. Chimpanzees do not even get AIDS. When infected with the virus they contract a mild flu. Also, AIDS attacks the immune system, which we know is affected by stress. Because lab conditions are extremely stressful, immune responses from lab chimpanzees cannot be transferred to human beings leading normal lives.[37]

Much medical research that harms animals is unnecessary because we already have relevant information from observations of human beings. Many studies are designed to show that certain addictive drugs, such as cocaine, are bad for your health. Peter Singer describes an experiment in which

> rhesus monkeys were locked into restraining chairs. The animals were then taught to self-administer cocaine directly into the bloodstream in whatever quantities they wanted by pushing a button. According to one report, "the test monkeys pushed the button over and over, even after convulsions. They went without sleep. They ate five to six times their normal amount, yet became emaciated. . . . In the end, they began to mutilate themselves and, eventually, died of cocaine abuse."[38]

Lacking our superior linguistic abilities they could not "Just say 'No'." Did we learn anything from this experiment? Even if we did, was it justified?

Many animals die slowly to test the effect on them of excess heat. Here is Peter Singer's description of one experiment:

> In 1954 at Yale University School of Medicine, M. Lennox, W. Sibley, and H. Zimmerman placed thirty-two kittens in a "radiant-heating" chamber. The kittens were "subjected to a total of 49 heating periods. . . . Struggling was common, particularly as the temperature rose." Convulsions occurred on nine occasions. . . . Five kittens died during convulsions, and six without convulsions. The other kittens were killed by the experimenters for autopsies. The experimenters reported: The findings in artificially induced fever in kittens conform to the clinical and EEG findings in human beings and previous clinical findings in kittens.[39]

Is this any better than illegal cruelty to animals, such as burying kittens alive?

Similar horror stories with dogs, cats, rats, mice, monkeys, and chimpanzees abound. The American Anti-Vivisection Society cites studies in which

> guinea pigs were immersed for three seconds in 100 degree C water. This produced "full skin-thickness burns" over 50% or 70% of the body surface of each animal. In addition, the animals were conscious during these procedures; the only anesthesia being halothane during the scalding. In all three reports, the authors noted similar investigations by others; however, they have changed a few variables to justify their work. . . . With so many tragic cases of burn victims in the wards of hospitals around the world, it seems totally unnecessary to inflict such suffering on sentient animals.[40]

" THIS ONE WE GOT FROM THE COUNTY POUND IS HOUSEBROKEN AND
EVERYTHING. AND LOOK ... HE EVEN KNOWS HOW TO BEG ! "

How can we do this? Like utilitarianism, animal rights require that we avoid unnecessary animal suffering, and *we have found no good justification for denying rights to these animals. They have, although mostly in lesser degree, the characteristics that we say justify attributing rights to human beings.*

Richard C. Simmonds, a veterinarian who specializes in the care of laboratory animals, justifies research on animals this way:

> According to the natural order of life on earth, all living organisms exist at the expense of other organisms. . . . Nature imposes no limitations on how one species may exploit another for survival, and I submit that humans have a natural "right" to exploit other species for our survival and benefit. I include the development of medical cures and treatments as part and parcel of our survival.[41]

I think "nature imposes no limitations on how one species may exploit another for survival" means that might makes right—not a moral standard that most people admire. If might makes right, people are morally blameless not only for using animals in possibly useful experiments, but also for treating them cruelly in possibly amusing games. In fact, if might makes right, people are blameless for treating human beings cruelly, if they have might on their side. This justifies rapes during ethnic cleansing, for example.

Jane Goodall reflects on our acceptance of cruelty in experiments:

> If we, in the western world, see a peasant beating an emaciated old donkey, . . . we are shocked and outraged. That is cruelty. But taking an infant chimpanzee from its mother's arms, locking him into the bleak world of the laboratory, injecting him with human diseases—this, if done in the name of Science, is not regarded

as cruelty. Yet in the final analysis, both donkey and chimpanzee are being exploited and misused for the benefit of humans. Why is one any more cruel than the other? Only because science has come to be venerated. . . . [42]

Venerating science endangers people as well as animals. Stanley Milgram's obedience experiments showed that people were willing under the influence of scientific authority to administer what they had reason to believe were lethal electric shocks to human beings.

Limited Animal Rights in Reflective Equilibrium

In *A Sand County Almanac* ecologist Aldo Leopold invites readers to adopt the perspective of wild animals. He discusses snow and thaw in January.

> The mouse is a sober citizen who knows that grass grows in order that mice may store it as underground haystacks, and that snow falls in order that mice may build subways from stack to stack: . . . To the mouse, snow means freedom from want and fear.
>   A rough-legged hawk comes sailing over the meadow ahead. . . . Then drops like a feathered bomb into the marsh. . . . I am sure he has caught, and is now eating, some worried mouse-engineer who could not wait until night to inspect the damage to his well-ordered world.
>   The rough-leg has no opinion why grass grows, but he is well aware that snow melts in order that hawks may again catch mice. He came down out of the Arctic in the hope of thaws, for to him a thaw means freedom from want and fear.[43]

Has the hawk violated the mouse's right to life? No, because the hawk has no choice. It is by nature a predator whose life depends on killing other animals. Among wild animals we accept that might does make right.

But it does not where human beings are involved. When predators threaten human lives we do not hesitate to protect or rescue people when possible. If a bear threatens campers in a national park, we think it reasonable to rescue them by helicopter, if necessary. We do not try to protect the bear's other prey.

The difference is even greater where rights to receive assistance are concerned. The United Nation's Universal Declaration of Human Rights' Article 25 states: "Everyone has the right to a standard of living adequate for the health and well-being of himself and of his family, including food, clothing, housing and medical care. . . ." Nations typically have welfare programs for the poor to honor this right. When natural or human disasters overwhelm a nation's ability to respond effectively, the international community often responds with help from the United Nations, the International Red Cross, Physicians Without Borders, and so forth. We try to prevent mass human suffering.

However, *we seldom feed or shelter wild animals in need.* Why? Were we to feed all the deer who would otherwise starve during the winter, for example, deer would overpopulate and eat so much vegetation during the summer that plant life would suffer. With the decline of plants, many animals who depend on these plants, such as birds and squirrels, would lack food or shelter. Saving these animals, too, would require turning the wild into wildlife pet farms where naturally carnivorous predators eat veggie burgers. This repels most of us because we value the wildness of wild nature. This value and others that conflict with animal rights are discussed in Chapters 6 and 7.

There is a tension in our thinking here. On the one hand, we adhere to certain general principles about fundamental rights and the grounds for ascribing those rights to individuals. These principles suggest rights for both human beings and for many animals. These animals have the characteristics, although often in lesser degree, that we invoke to justify human rights. On the other hand, however, we have particular moral judgments incompatible with ascribing human rights fully to these animals. We believe that human rights require protecting people from predation and starvation, whereas animal rights often do not justify such protection. We often judge it better to let nature remain wild even though individual animals are killed by predators or starve.

When our thinking has this kind of tension, philosopher John Rawls tells us to seek what he calls **reflective equilibrium**. *We should try to bring consistency and coherence to our thinking by modifying our opinions about general principles and/or about particular situations.* In this case, we could change our view of particular situations and decide to eliminate carnivorous predators from the wild to protect their prey. We would then consistently advocate equal protection of human and animal rights.

On the other hand, we could modify our general principles about rights. We could say, for example, that animals have rights, but lesser rights than human beings. Their rights are less because they have in lesser degree the characteristics that justify ascribing rights in the first place. We could also say that we have special responsibilities to protect humans because they are members of our species. As a result, people have stronger and/or more rights than animals. In sum, we could say that human rights generally have greater moral clout than animal rights. This alteration of principle justifies our willingness to let animals be killed or starve in the wild.

However, the alteration of principle does not require abandoning animal rights altogether. Imagine that a person wanting to learn more about chimpanzees in the wild killed Figan painlessly as he struggled to become the alpha in his group. The person wanted to see the effect on the group's other members. I say this would be immoral. Why, if no pain was involved? It would violate Figan's right to life. If I could stop the inquisitive killer through peaceful means, I would do so to protect Figan. Why is it proper to protect Figan in this situation? Because he has a right to life.

If this is correct, we must reformulate the animal rights principle to attain reflective equilibrium. One possibility is that animals have rights against jeopardy from human beings, but not against jeopardy from other animals, the physical elements, bad weather, and so forth. That is why it would be wrong for a person to kill Figan painlessly, but we should not interfere if Evered were killing him (probably painfully).

Our distaste for converting a wilderness into a wildlife pet farm suggests another, perhaps complementary, idea. Rights are never absolute, because they often come into conflict with one another, and because we have other values besides rights. Consider our right to freedom of speech. It is illegal to shout "Fire!" in a crowded theater (unless there really is a fire), because the resulting panic jeopardizes human lives. In this case, the right to life limits the right to free speech.

Perhaps one of our animal rights principles should be this: Animals have rights as individuals, but the rights of wild animals are limited by the need to maintain the wildness of wild nature. Some reasons to maintain the wildness of wild nature are considered in Chapter 7. This is one way of reaching reflective equilibrium in our thinking about animal rights. Other ways of reaching reflective equilibrium are considered in Chapters 6 and 7.

❧   ❧   ❧

Let us relate animal rights to some issues discussed in the last chapter, with a view to reaching reflective equilibrium. Most people in the United States find bullfighting, even when the bull is not killed, more repellent than rodeo bronco riding. Yet the pain to the animals is similar. One way to reach reflective equilibrium is to say that each is as good or bad as the other. They are both morally permissible, or they are both morally wrong. But which is it?

Many people get upset if animals are treated cruelly in the course of making a feature film, such as one about Lassie. If such people generally oppose inflicting pain on animals as a means to human entertainment, consistency (reflective equilibrium) requires them to condemn also American-style bullfighting, rodeo bronco riding, and, if what I have read about animal abuse is correct, circuses and dog races as well.

On the other hand, some people may think circuses, dog racing, bullfights, and rodeos are fine. If they discover that such entertainment hurts animals, their continued support implies that they condone hurting animals to entertain people. Then do they oppose cruelty to animals at all? Would they condone backyard pin the tail on the donkey with a real donkey? They may not be able consistently to support both current laws against cruelty to animals and such amusements as dog racing, rodeos, and circuses.

Animal Research in Reflective Equilibrium

What does this tell us about medical research on animals? On the one hand, it is not done for entertainment. It is done to prolong and improve the quality of human lives. (We often say "to save human lives," but this misleads. We all die eventually regardless of medical advances. Salvation requires religion.)

Prolonging human life and making it better are lofty goals. If animals have fewer and/or weaker rights than people, perhaps we should use animals to further these goals. However, as we have seen, the historical benefits of medical research on animals is disputed, and such research hinders rather than furthers medical progress when, for example, it "protects" people from beneficial medications that harm research animals but not human beings. In addition, most improvements in human health in the last 100 years owe nothing to medical science. Better diet has improved people's resistance to disease, and public health measures have reduced exposure to disease organisms. Sidney Gendin writes: "It is generally conceded that progress made against infectious diseases owes most to personal hygiene and community-wide sanitation."[44] Finally, almost all benefits of animal research go to 10 or 12 percent of the human population rich enough to afford sophisticated health care. We could save more human lives by improving drinking water quality in the Third World instead of developing therapies for rich people through research on animals. These are anthropocentric reasons against such research.

But a promising research program in biological science is hard to resist. Paul Recer of the Associated Press reported in January 1999 that stem cell research on mice may benefit human beings. Researchers found that "the building-block cells that normally make brain tissue in adult mice could be changed into blood-making cells." If this can be done in human beings, it is possible that someday a person's own "stem cells could be used to grow new livers or skin, make cells to renew a failing heart, or replace nerve cells killed by Alzheimer's disease." This could prolong some human lives or improve their quality. Recer describes the experiment this way:

> In the experiment, researchers used mouse neural stem cells, which normally would develop into three types of brain and nerve tissue.
> They injected the cells into the blood stream of a second group of mice whose bone marrow had been killed with radiation. The cells migrated naturally to the void left by the killed bone marrow.
> Once there, they transformed from neural stem cells into blood-making cells—a complete change from their original role.[45]

Recer does not tell us what happened to these helpful mice. "Sacrificed" is the usual term. But these mice are as sensitive and intelligent, as much subjects-of-a-life, as most pets. Have they no rights? Can we justify hurting and then killing them to extend our own lives? How long do we think people should live, anyway? Is any justification we can offer better than "might makes right?" These are difficult questions. If I had Alzheimer's disease, I might welcome some fresh brain cells. Now, where was I?

Judgment Calls

- We saw that most rhesus monkeys would go hungry, at least for awhile, to avoid electro-shocking other rhesus monkeys. How altruistic are you? In what way would you be willing to forego some good for yourself to help fellow human beings? For example, how much money would you give each week to relieve poor people of hunger?

- How would you relate claims that animals have rights to the existence of zoos? What is your own position in reflective equilibrium?

- Compare and contrast animal rights and utilitarian reasons for becoming a vegetarian. Which are stronger and why? What is your own position in reflective equilibrium?

- Peter Singer and Tom Regan oppose speciesism, the unjustified preference for our own species over others. Relate this concept to our allowing many animals, but not people, to be killed by predators in the wild. What justifies this preference for our own species?

- Some people say that hunting deer, for example, helps preserve wilderness areas. Yet deer hunters deliberately kill subjects-of-a-life. How would you defend a consistent position on this issue, relating it to claims that animals have rights? See the next chapter for more discussion of hunting.

CHAPTER 6

Species Diversity and Gaia

Massive Extinction of Species

The last two chapters discussed the welfare and rights of individual animals. These are **individualistic nonanthropocentric concerns**, which arise when we value animals for themselves, not just for human satisfaction. This chapter and the one to follow examine competing **holistic nonanthropocentric concerns**, primarily regarding species and ecosystems.

In the late 1980s, author Douglas Adams and naturalist Mark Carwardine toured the world to see endangered species. Adams recorded their adventures in *Last Chance to See*. He writes of Mauritius, an island in the Indian Ocean that they visited:

> The most famous of all the animals . . . is a large, gentle dove. A remarkably large dove, in fact: its weight is closest to that of a well-fed turkey. Its wings long ago gave up the idea of lifting such a plumpy off the ground and withered away into decorative little stumps. . . . It didn't need to fly anyway, since there were no predators that wished it any harm and it, in turn, is harmless itself. . . . There's never even been any reason for humans to kill it because its meat is tough and bitter.
>
> It has a large, wide, downturned bill of yellow and green, which gives it a slightly glum and melancholic look, small, round eyes like diamonds, and three ridiculously little plumes sticking out of its tail. . . .
>
> None of us will ever see this bird, though, because, sadly, the last one was clubbed to death by Dutch colonists in about 1680. . . . And that is what Mauritius is most famous for: the extinction of the dodo.[1]

In 1973, the United States promoted species preservation by passing the Endangered Species Act. It was amended, but not weakened, in 1978, 1982, and 1988.[2] International treaties, such as the 1973 Convention on International Trade in Endangered Species (CITES), also protect species. One hundred thirty countries are now signatories.[3]

Why do we protect species? Clubbing helpless dodos to death seems cruel, and this may suggest that we protect species for the same reasons we protect individual animals from cruelty. We care about animals. However, the reasons for avoiding cruelty to animals cannot apply to species, which are **holistic entities**, not individual organisms. They cannot literally be pained, like individual animals, by confinement, clubbing, stabbing, and so forth. Only individuals can literally feel pain. Clubbing the last dodo caused extinction, but probably no more pain than clubbing a pig whose throat was imperfectly cut in a slaughterhouse. And yet, while people often object to this treatment of the pig, causing extinction strikes many people as worse or, at least, objectionable for different reasons. Extinction is bad even when the means used are painless.

Animal rights cannot apply to species either. Animals who are subjects-of-a-life are similar to people in having (at least some) self-awareness, plans, and social life. Killing them, even painlessly, harms them. But only individuals can be subjects-of-a-life. Species have no self-awareness, plans, and so forth. So why protect them?

Protection cannot be based on the idea that species are by their very nature eternal, an idea championed by the ancient Greek philosopher Aristotle and influential until Darwin's views took hold. Journalist Gregg Easterbrook notes candidly:

> To approach the topics of species preservation and its sibling issue, biodiversity, it is essential first to bear in mind . . . : Since nature began, 99 percent of all species called forth into being have eventually been rendered extinct. This estimate is almost universally accepted by researchers. . . . Extinction is nature's norm.[4]

So why do people now want to preserve species from extinction?

One reason is the dramatically increasing rate of extinction caused by humanity. Worldwatch researcher John Tuxill wrote in 1998:

> Examinations of the fossil record of marine invertebrates suggest that the natural or "background" rate of extinction—the rate that has prevailed over millions of years of evolutionary time—claims something on the order of one to 10 species per year. . . . Most estimates of the current situation are that at least 1,000 species are lost per year, an extinction rate 100 to 1,000 times above the background rate. . . . Like the dinosaurs 65 million years ago, human society now finds itself in the midst of a mass extinction. . . . Unlike the dinosaurs, however, . . . we are the reason for it.[5]

Among species currently threatened with extinction, many are vertebrates, our closest biological relatives—birds, mammals, reptiles, amphibians, and fish. Tuxill writes, "The best-known vertebrate groups are birds and mammals, of whose species about 10 and 25 percent, respectively, are threatened with extinction."[6] *The situation is worst among our closest relatives. About half of the world's primate species are in serious decline.*[7]

Causes of Extinction

The primary cause of extinction worldwide is loss of habitat. People have disrupted areas that animals depend on for food, shelter, mating, or spawning. The winter-run chinook salmon is an example. Susan Middleton and David Liittschwager described it in their photo essay in *Sierra* in 1996:

> After 5 million years of survival, many wild salmon are now—in our cataclysmic century—on the verge of extinction. In less than a single human lifetime we have so thoroughly dammed their rivers and transformed their spawning areas that more than a hundred populations of salmon and related seagoing fish are extinct and another two hundred are at risk in the Northwest. Northern California's winter-run chinook salmon, for instance, have dwindled from 117,000 spawners in 1969 to 1,000 or fewer in recent years.[8]

The desert tortoise is also threatened by habitat loss, as well as hunting, the second leading cause of extinction. Its numbers are down from 1,000 per square mile in the Mojave and Sonoran deserts to under 200 per square mile. Middleton and Liittschwager write: "Motorcyclists crush their shells and collapse their burrows. Gun nuts have riddled them with bullets. Ranchers' cattle and sheep mow down the plants they need to survive. Miners build tailings ponds in which they drown."[9]

Habitat loss and hunting decimate primate species, too. John Tuxill writes:

> Vietnam's Tonkin snub-nosed monkey may now be the rarest primate in the world. Hunting and the loss of nearly 90 percent of its lowland rainforest habitat since 1950 have reduced it to a handful of populations totaling fewer than 200 individuals, all of them living in forest patches . . . [near] nature reserves.[10]

A third leading cause of extinction is the introduction of **exotics**. *Exotics are species brought to an area by human beings, either deliberately or accidentally.* Pheasant, for example, come originally from Asia. Because they did not fly or walk to North America on their own, they are exotics in the United States.

Exotics can cause species extinction because ecological competition is a bit like commercial competition among companies trying to use the same raw materials, employ the same workers, and/or attract the same customers. Members of animal species, for example, have to perform certain basic life tasks to avoid extinction of the species. They must obtain suitable food and shelter and avoid becoming food for other animals before finding a mate, reproducing, and bringing their young to the point of performing these same tasks for themselves. **Fitness** *is a species' ability, through its members' activities, to remain in the environment indefinitely.* Exotics, which often have no natural predators in their new home, often out-compete native species, reducing their fitness and, possibly, leading to their extinction.

Many animals in relatively isolated environments, such as New Zealand, evolved without serious competition. *A species' evolution over generations to maintain or improve its fitness is called* **adaptation**. One species adapted to New Zealand's isolated environment is the kakapo, a night parrot. Douglas Adams describes its mating call:

> For thousands of years, in the right season, the sound could be heard after nightfall. . . . It was like a heartbeat: a deep, powerful throb that echoed through the dark ravines. It was so deep that some people will tell you that they felt it stirring in their gut before they could discern the actual sound.[11]

Although well adapted to an environment free of natural predators, this bird is now on the brink of extinction due to the introduction of predators. In 1990, only 43 remained. Adams gives this humorous description of its physical nature and activities:

> It is an extremely fat bird. A good-sized adult will weigh about six or seven pounds, and its wings are just about good for waggling a bit if it thinks it's about to trip over something—but flying is completely out of the question. Sadly, however, it seems that not only has the kakapo forgotten how to fly, but it has also forgotten that it has forgotten how to fly. Apparently a seriously worried kakapo will sometimes run up a tree and jump out of it, whereupon it flies like a brick and lands in a graceless heap on the ground.[12]

Adams explains how such an inept bird probably evolved. It adapted to an environment without predators.

> Until relatively recently—in the evolutionary scale of things—the wildlife of New Zealand consisted of almost nothing but birds. Only birds could reach the place. . . . There were no predators. No dogs, no cats, no ferrets or weasels, nothing that the birds needed to escape from particularly.
> And flight, of course, is a means of escape. It's a survival mechanism, and one the birds of New Zealand found they didn't especially need. Flying is hard work and consumes a lot of energy.
> Not only that. There is also a trade-off between flying and eating. The more you eat, the harder it is to fly. So increasingly what happened was that instead of having just a light snack and then flying off, the birds would settle in for a rather larger meal and go for a waddle afterward instead.[13]

Because the kakapos no longer flew, they ceased to develop wings that would enable them to fly and evade predators. But then people carried predators to the islands in boats. Kakapos are on the brink of extinction because they are such easy prey. Adapted to survive in an environment without predators, they cannot compete in one with predators.

Pursuing the analogy with commerce, Adams compares kakapos to an industry so long protected from foreign competition that it ceased to be competitive:

In fact, the kakapo is a bird that in some ways reminds me of the British motorbike industry. It had things its own way for so long that it simply became eccentric. . . . It built a certain number of motorbikes and a certain number of people bought them and that was that. It didn't seem to matter much that they were noisy, complicated to maintain, [and] sprayed oil all over the place. . . . The Japanese suddenly got the idea that motorbikes didn't have to be that way. They could be sleek, they could be clean, they could be reliable and well-behaved.[14]

At first, British manufacturers lost business. Fortunately, they responded to the challenge before going broke (becoming extinct), and now produce competitive motorbikes.

This is where the analogy breaks down. Industries can redesign and retool in a relatively short time, but many species take thousands of years to evolve. Unlike British motorbike manufacturers, kakapos cannot adapt fast enough. Adams observes:

The trouble is that this predator business has all happened rather suddenly in New Zealand, and by the time nature starts to select in favour of slightly more nervous and fleet-footed kakapos, there won't be any left at all, unless deliberate human intervention can protect them from what they can't deal with themselves.[15]

Why Do We Protect Endangered Species?

Kakapos are now protected through a program that relocates them to islands without predators, at considerable expense. Gregg Easterbrook writes of other efforts to save species from extinction and/or restore them to their natural habitats:

At least $25 million has been spent since 1983 to avert the extinction of the California condor. Hatchlings bred in captivity have been monitored around the clock, fed by hand puppets that suggest a mother bird, and allowed to find carcasses laid out for them, simulating wild feeding. In 1983 just 22 California condors were known to exist. Today about 70 live, with several having been reintroduced into the wild. . . .

U.S.-registered shrimping boats now have appurtenances called turtles exclusion devices to reduce deaths of sea turtles. These devices came too late for the Kemp's ridley sea turtle, which by 1985 . . . had been reduced to 200 known nesting pairs. The federal government has spent $4 million to airlift eggs of the Kemp's ridley to a laboratory in Galveston, Texas, where hatchlings are "head-started" . . . and then returned to the sea.

The Florida panther has declined to perhaps 50 creatures. Wardens from the Florida game commission now track the remaining panthers. When one is seen to have an injury it is flown to an animal hospital for treatment, then returned to the wild.

The National Zoo, in Washington, D.C., has experimented with employing female Siberian tigers, which reproduce readily in captivity, as surrogate mothers (via in vitro fertilization) for the endangered Sumatran tiger, which does not reproduce naturally outside the wild.[16]

Many other examples could be given. Why do people go to such trouble and expense?

Because people benefit from biodiversity, there are anthropocentric reasons to save species from extinction. John Tuxill writes:

> Biodiversity supports our health care systems; some 25 percent of drugs prescribed in the United States include chemical compounds derived from wild species, and worldwide the over-the-counter value of such drugs is at least $40 billion annually. Billions of people also rely on plant- and animal-based traditional medicine.[17]

One reason to preserve endangered species is the possibility that saved species will foster medical breakthroughs.

Biodiversity also improves agriculture. Wild varieties of rice, for example, were used to improve the disease resistance of domestic varieties. In addition, writes Tuxill:

> Insects, birds, bats, and even lizards provide pollination services, without which we could not feed ourselves. Frogs, fish, and birds furnish natural pest control; mussels and other aquatic organisms cleanse our water supplies; plants and micro-organisms renew and enrich our soils.[18]

In sum, we could not survive without other species helping us.

But these anthropocentric reasons do not account for many current preservation efforts. Humanity has flourished since the last dodo was killed. Does anyone think that if the 22 California condors alive in 1983 had been allowed to die, people would lack essential food, clothing, medicine, or housing? Certainly not. If the remaining 43 kakapos in New Zealand succumb to predation, will humanity go into decline? Of course not. Although people rely for essential services on a great deal of species diversity in nature, many efforts to avert extinction cannot be justified using this rationale.

We saw in Chapter 3 that Bryan Norton offers a different reason, which he considers anthropocentric, to preserve species. Natural variety, he says, has "transformative value." It helps us transform our values from unsatisfying consumption to more satisfying appreciation of nature and activities on its behalf.[19] This kind of beneficial transformation "will not occur," he writes, "if nature is so altered that encounters with wild species become unlikely. Species preservationists," he concludes, "should emphasize the value of wild species, especially endangered ones, as catalysts for the reconsideration of currently consumptive felt preferences."[20]

But this transformative value of species diversity is not really anthropocentric. The continued existence of natural variety transforms my life for the better, on Norton's model, only if I come to appreciate biodiversity as good in itself. But at that point I care about endangered species for the sake of those species, or for the sake of biodiversity in general, not for my own sake, or for the sake of any other human beings. My values are no longer merely anthropocentric. I now have nonanthropocentric concerns that serve, if Norton is correct, also to improve human life. This illustrates what I call environmental synergy, which I discuss in Chapters 8, 9, and 10.

Animal Rights vs. Species Preservation

Caring about other species for themselves is a *holistic nonanthropocentric concern*. But, as noted earlier, this is different from concern about the welfare or rights of *individual* animals. The difference stands out sharply in cases of conflict.

Consider again New Zealand's kakapos, birds that cannot escape predation because they are adapted to an environment without predators. The remaining kakapos are being relocated to islands where there are no predators. But as there were no such islands, people cleared Codfish Island and Little Barrier Island of its predators to make a safe haven for kakapos, and this is where species preservation clashes with animal liberation and animal rights. Mark Carwardine notes: "Codfish Island was infested with feral cats. In other words, cats that have returned to the wild." The New Zealand Department of Conservation decided to kill them:

> Kill them. Every last one. And all the possums and stoats. Anything that moved and wasn't a bird, essentially. It's not very pleasant, but that's how the island was originally, and that's the only way kakapos can survive—in exactly the environment that New Zealand had before man arrived. With no predators.[21]

The hunt for any remaining predators is constant, because one can never be sure they are all gone and that none have arrived again by boat. Animal rights advocate Tom Regan would condemn such deliberate killing of subjects-of-a-life, and animal liberation advocate Peter Singer would object to any killing that caused pain. These philosophers stress individualistic against competing holistic nonanthropocentric concerns.

Individualism and holism compete often. On Round Island near Mauritius in the Indian Ocean, Adams is told:

> There are more unique species of plants and animals . . . than there are on any equivalent area on earth. About a hundred, hundred and fifty years ago, somebody had the bright idea of introducing rabbits and goats to the island so if anybody got shipwrecked there, they'd have something to eat. The populations quickly got out of hand.[22]

Again, eradication was the only solution.

Subjects-of-a-life are also used as food in programs of species preservation. Members of endangered species must often be bred in captivity before being returned to the wild. While in captivity they have to eat. Once returned to the wild they may also need extra food to increase their rate of reproduction.

Richard Lewis, who is working to preserve the kestrel, a kind of falcon, on Mauritius, explains: "Conservation is not for the squeamish. We have to kill a lot of animals, partly to protect the species that are endangered, and partly to feed them. A lot of birds are fed on mice. . . ."[23] Adams describes the feeding of wild kestrels to increase the number of eggs they lay:

> Richard lobbed the small mouse high up into the air . . . The mouse reached the top of its steep parabola, its . . . weight turning slowly in the air.
> At last the kestrel dropped from its perch and swung out into the air. . . . The arc it described intersected sweetly with that of the falling mouse, the kestrel took the mouse cleanly into its talons, swept on up into another nearby tree, and bit its head off.[24]

Adams describes another case that might disturb animal rights advocates even more, because members of the species being saved, the komodo dragon, are not subjects-of-a-life. The komodo dragon is a giant lizard whose few remaining members live on a small island near Bali in Indonesia. Lizards and other reptiles are too intellectually primitive to be subjects-of-a-life. Nevertheless, efforts to save them include slaughtering goats to give them fresh meat. Goats, mammals like us, are subjects-of-a-life.

In sum, many efforts to save endangered species lack anthropocentric reasons, and individualistic nonanthropocentric reasons related to animal welfare do not apply, because species cannot feel pain and are not subjects-of-a-life. What is more, efforts to preserve species conflict with animal liberation and animal rights when individual animals suffer painful death to protect or feed members of endangered species. What holistic nonanthropocentric reasons justify protecting these species?

Species as Individual Living Things

Philosopher Lawrence Johnson offers holistic nonanthropocentric reasons to preserve endangered species. He argues that species are individual living things. To see his point, consider what makes a material object a unique individual. An inanimate object, such as a bowling ball, pen, chair, or rock, is different from all others, that is, it's a unique individual, due to its matter. However similar in color, shape, size, weight, and so forth, one rock is to another, each is differentiated from the other, in the last analysis, by the fact that different bits of matter are in the one than are in the other. One is composed of this group of molecules and the other is composed of that group of molecules.

I know this now because when I was about four years old my mother pulled a fast one on me. I had this pillow that I carried around the way many children carry around a blanket that is familiar from infancy. The pillow was filthy and my mother wanted to get rid of it, but I refused. So she told me that she just wanted to put new feathers in it. I agreed to this. But when I got it back it was yellow instead of gray. She said that as long as the pillow was getting new feathers, it might as well have a new cover and lining as well. Even then I was skeptical that this was still the same pillow.

If my mother had replaced relatively few feathers, or only part of the cover, we would say it was the same pillow. My car remains the same when I replace the oil filter. But if I replace the whole engine and someone says, "You're still driving that old thing," I'd quickly point out its new engine. It is not exactly the same old car anymore.

Living things are different. An organism's molecules change and are constantly renewed, even as the individual retains its identity. Individual cells of multicellular plants and animals die regularly and are replaced by other cells that perform the same function. If the replacement is gradual and the organism retains all functions needed to maintain its form of life, we say that individual identity is preserved. Lawrence Johnson puts it this way: "*A living system, such as a human or a tree, is not a concrete thing, like a tractor, but is a life process that takes place through concrete things.*"[25] The individual remains materially the same not because the material remains the same, but because the gradually changing material continues the life process without interruption.

In the last chapter, we discussed living things that are conscious and self-aware, which Tom Regan calls subjects-of-a-life. Philosopher Holmes Rolston, by contrast, discusses *all* living things, including those lacking consciousness and self-awareness. All organisms, he maintains, even the simplest, "have self-generating, self-defending tendencies."[26] Although a plant, for example, is not a subject-of-a-life because it lacks consciousness, it is "an evaluative system. . . . It grows, reproduces, repairs its wounds, and resists death. We can say that the physical state the organism seeks . . . is a valued state. . . . Every organism has a *good-of-its-kind*; it defends its own kind as a *good kind*."

Philosopher Paul Taylor puts the same point this way:

> Organisms like trees and one-celled protozoa do not have a conscious life. . . . They have no thoughts or feelings and hence no interest in anything that happens to them. Yet they have a good of their own around which their behavior is organized. . . . Each is a unified, coherently ordered system of goal-oriented activity that has a constant tendency to protect and maintain the organism's existence.[27]

Due to their nature, organisms can be harmed in ways that inanimate objects cannot. When organisms are killed, they lose *a good that is their own*. When a car is "totaled" in a crash, by contrast, we may say it is harmed, but we mean merely that a *person* who uses the car loses some good. Being inanimate, the car, unlike the organism, has no good of its own. It cannot be harmed like an organism.

Taylor and Rolston conclude that killing any organism requires justification, because causing harm requires justification. They have different views about which justifications are adequate. The point here is that many of the same points can be made about species. They are living systems, with their own tendencies and welfare.

A species typically has many members. These are the individual organisms of the past, present, and future that belong to the species. But the species is more than just a collection of individuals that fit into a certain category or class. Species differ from mere collections or classes, such as my old record albums, the pieces of wood that compose my backyard fence, and the leaves on my gingko tree. Lawrence Johnson quotes David Hull, who wrote in the journal *Philosophy of Science* in 1981: "The characteristics usually attributed to species make no sense when attributed to classes. . . . Species are the sorts of thing which evolve, split, bud off new species, go extinct, etc. Classes are not the sort of things which can do any of the preceding."[28] Johnson concedes that "the theoretical battle is not over though the tide seems definitely to be moving toward the view that species are entities rather than classes."[29] So let us examine the implications of this view.

In this view, species are related to their member organisms much as individual organisms are related to their constituent molecules. Just as individual organisms differ from the molecules that are in them at any given time, species differ from the organisms that are its members. This is because both organisms and species are involved in goal-directed processes. The goal itself (survival) is more central to the nature of organisms or species than the materials or individuals through which the goal is being accomplished. The main goal of organisms is to stay alive. The goal of species, by contrast, is to maintain genetic continuity.

Species adapt to their environment over generations to make better use of resources. Kakapos adapted to an environment without predators by losing the ability to fly. They traded this for the ability to eat more and grow heavier. This helped them get more for themselves from that environment. Rolston puts it this way:

> A form of life reforms itself, tracks its environment, and sometimes passes over to a new species. There is a specific groping for a valued *ought-to-be* beyond what now *is* in any individual. Though species are not moral agents, a biological identity—a kind of value—is here defended.[30] A specific life form urges survival of "its" kind, defends "its" life form. The "it" is a historic process with vital individuality, though it is not a single organism.[31]

This value defended by a species is independent of the goals of its individual members. Rolston gives this example:

> Predation on individual elk conserves and improves the species. . . . When a wolf is tearing up an elk, the individual elk is in distress, but the species is in no distress. The species is being improved, as is shown by the fact that wolves will subsequently find elk harder to catch.[32]

In this view, *species are similar to individual organisms. Each is a form of life with its own good. Unlike inanimate objects, therefore, each can be harmed by events that interfere with attainment of that good. Because harming anything requires justifica-*

© 2000 by Sidney Harris

tion, according to Rolston and Johnson, extinguishing a species, like killing an organism, requires justification.

Of course, we attribute action to individual organisms, whereas entire species do not literally act on their own behalf. Species "act" only through the actions of individual members. So species are not exactly like individual living things. But the similarities between individual organisms and species are striking and may animate efforts to avert the extinction of such species as the kestrel, the kakapo, and the California condor.

However, the analogy to individual organisms still leaves open the question of why people go to such trouble and expense to save these species. According to the analogy, killing one plant deprives a non-conscious being of its good, just as extinguishing one species deprives a non-conscious being of its good. The analogy suggests that extinguishing a species is just about as morally serious as killing an individual plant. But this does not seem right. We kill individual plants for relatively trivial reasons, for example, to improve home landscaping. We take extinguishing a species much more seriously. Many people think it is positively indecent to extinguish a species. We need to look beyond the analogy to individual organisms to justify this view.

The Gaia Hypothesis

One ancient, yet alarmingly novel, perspective is that Earth as a whole is alive, and that individuals are somewhat like cells in a living organism. Species resemble tissues, groups of similar cells with functions that maintain the system. This is the Gaia hypothesis, first put forth by James Lovelock in the 1960s. Gaia was the ancient Greek goddess that we might call Mother Earth. Thinking of ourselves as part of a larger living entity may suggest humility and inspire caution in our treatment of the earth and of other species. It may also help to justify holistic nonanthropocentric concerns and thus costly attempts to avoid extinguishing species. But the Gaia Hypothesis is first and foremost science, so let us look at the science of Gaia before considering its moral implications.

Why should we think that the earth is alive? Earth acts in some ways like a living thing. Consider temperature control. Warm-blooded animals such as ourselves maintain relatively constant temperatures while ambient temperatures fluctuate. When the temperature is hot, we perspire, and the evaporation of liquid from our skin cools us. We also tend to avoid strenuous activity, because such activity burns calories in our muscles and generates heat. When we are cold, however, we tend to move our muscles to generate heat. We shiver or jump up and down. In conditions of greater cold, we put on sweaters, coats, and hats. Other warm-blooded animals grow fur and/or layers of fat to maintain a constant internal body temperature during cold winters.

Cold-blooded animals must also maintain their temperatures within a certain range because the chemical reactions necessary to life occur with sufficient rapidity only within that range. For this reason, cold-blooded animals cannot live in cold climates. In warm climates they regulate their internal temperature in part by exposing themselves to the sun when they are too cool and entering the shade when they are too warm.

The tendency of animals to maintain internal body temperatures within a narrow range is part of what biologists call **homeostasis**. *Homeostasis is the tendency toward constancy of all living things.* Living things require certain internal conditions to maintain their lives, so they react to changes in the environment to maintain these internal conditions. They manage to stay (the "stasis" part) in the same (the "homo" part) condition while outside conditions change.

The earth, too, seems to have homeostatic tendencies regarding its temperature, the chemical composition of its atmosphere, and the salinity of its oceans. Consider temperature. The earth has had a relatively stable climate for over 3,500 million years. This is odd because the sun's output of heat has increased by at least 30 percent during that time.[33] A mere 2 percent change in one hemisphere makes the difference between normal weather and an ice age.[34] Assuming that the earth's temperature was suitable for life eons ago when life began, and the sun's output has increased 30 percent, why has the earth not become too hot? Lovelock does not know the details of the answer, but considers the earth's stable temperature to be evidence that it is alive:

> If the earth were simply a solid inanimate object, its surface temperature would follow the variations in solar output. No amount of insulating clothing will indefinitely protect a stone statue from winter cold or summer heat. Yet somehow, through three and a half aeons, the surface temperature has remained constant and favourable for life, much as our body temperatures remain constant whether it is summer or winter and whether we find ourselves in a polar or tropical environment.[35]

Lovelock offers a model to show how the living components of Earth could react to changes in the sun's output to maintain steady temperatures. Like most scientific models, it is purposely simplified to highlight important features.

Imagine Daisyworld, a world with only species of daisies. Its "daisies range in shade of color from dark . . . to light." Dark daisies absorb more heat than light ones, which reflect heat away from the earth. Suppose that daisies grow best at about 20 degrees C. Below 5 degrees it is too cold and above 40 too hot.

Imagine a time in the distant past of Daisyworld. The star that warms it was less luminous, so that only in the equatorial region was the mean temperature of the bare ground warm enough, 5 degrees C. Here daisy seeds would slowly germinate and flower. Let us assume that in the first crop multicolored, light and dark species were equally represented. Even before the first season's growth was over, the dark daisies would have been favored. Their greater absorption of sunlight . . . would have warmed them above 5 degree C.[36]

The light daisies would remain too cold to flourish because they reflect the sun rather than absorb its heat. So dark daisies flourish and make the surface of the earth as a whole darker than it used to be. This warms the earth *as a whole* and makes daisy life possible in regions far removed from the warmest areas near the equator. Thus, daisy life alters the climate of the earth to make more of the earth hospitable to daisy life.

As dark daisies cover more and more of the earth, however, Earth's temperature approaches the upper limit of the daisies' temperature range. Under these conditions, lighter daisies do better than dark ones, because the dark ones absorb more heat and get too hot, whereas the light ones reflect more heat and stay cool enough to thrive. So more and more of the earth's surface becomes covered with light daisies. This reverses the tendency of the earth to get too hot, initiating a swing toward a cooler Earth. As the earth becomes cooler, however, more of its surface favors the growth of dark daisies. In sum, daisy growth brings the earth's temperature into the center of the range that is best for daisy life, and keeps it there. If the external source of heat increases its output, as our sun has, an increase of light daisies can keep temperatures steady.

"Daisyworld proved to be a turning point in Gaian science," writes biologist Lynn Margulis in her 1998 book *Symbiotic Planet*. "Stephan Harding, professor at Schumacher College in Devon, England, now models Daisyworlds with twenty-three different colored species of daisies as well as herbivores that eat the daisies and carnivores that eat the herbivores."[37] The results are what James Lovelock predicted. Like many living things, the earth maintains its temperature. Margulis concludes:

Temperature regulation is a physiological function not only of Daisyworld but of the bodies and the societies of life. Mammals, tuna, skunk cabbage plants, and bee-hives all regulate their temperatures to within a few degrees. How do plant cells or hive-dwelling bees "know" how to maintain temperature? Whatever the answer in principle, the tuna, skunk cabbage, bees, and mouse cells display the same sort of physiological regulation that prevails across the planet.[38]

The earth is in this respect like a living thing.

However, the earth also resembles certain mechanical devices, such as refrigerators and ovens, which maintain (relatively) constant internal temperatures. Such devices are invented and constructed by human beings. Comparing the earth's temperature constancy to an oven's suggests that some powerful being or beings—a god or gods—established temperature-regulating processes on Earth as people do in ovens.

This is possible, but the earth is more like a living being than a machine. First, regardless of how the earth's system came into existence—by chance, design, or evolution—its operative parts, like the cells and tissues of plants and animals, and unlike the mechanisms of an oven, are living things. Second, machines are known to be designed by people, whereas the origin of Earth's homeostatic tendencies, like the origin of life itself, remains a matter of speculation.

Although Gaian science shows the earth to be very much like a living thing, this does not mean it is conscious, much less that it devises a conscious plan to maintain its temperature, any more than skunk cabbage plants do. Lovelock is clear: "In Daisyworld, one property of the global environment, temperature, was shown to be regulated effectively, over a wide range of solar luminosity, by an imaginary planetary biota without invoking foresight or planning."[39]

❧   ❧   ❧

The earth seems also to control the oxygen content of the atmosphere. When life began on earth there was little atmospheric oxygen. Then, in a process that persists today, water vapor in the upper atmosphere split into its component hydrogen and oxygen atoms. Hydrogen is so light that it escapes the earth's atmosphere, leaving a net increase of oxygen atoms that bond in twos (oxygen molecules) and threes (ozone molecules).

Lovelock claims that this source of oxygen is too meager to account for its current level in the atmosphere. Plant life is a more important source. Plants are composed largely of carbon, which they get from carbon dioxide (CO_2) in the air. Taking the C out of CO_2 leaves O_2, which is oxygen. Most of this oxygen converts back to CO_2 in oxidation—burning, whether in fires or as food. But a small portion, about 0.1 percent, of the carbon becomes unavailable for oxidation because it is buried in sedimentary rocks (some of which become carbon-based fossil fuels such as coal and oil). Oxygen that lacks carbon to burn remains in the atmosphere and tends to build up. This is primarily how oxygen attained, and retains, its present level of 21 percent of the atmosphere.[40]

Plant life thus creates the conditions for expanding life on Earth. When the oxygen content of the atmosphere approaches its present level, the environment is suitable not only for plants, but also for oxygen-breathing animals.

The air's oxygen content cannot, however, increase much above its present 21 percent without seriously endangering plant life. Lovelock writes:

The probability of a forest fire being started by a lightning flash increases by 70 per cent for each 1 per cent rise in oxygen concentration above the present level. Above 25 per cent very little of our present land vegetation could survive the raging conflagration which would destroy tropical rain forests and arctic tundra alike.[41]

So what keeps the air's oxygen content at a steady 21 percent?

One possibility centers on physical processes unrelated to life on Earth. For example, some oxidizing materials (materials that combine chemically with oxygen and thereby take oxygen out of the air) become available when weathering exposes them to the air. Also, volcanoes introduce oxidizing gases. However, the hypothesis that physical processes unaffected by life on Earth account for a billion years of constant oxygen levels is unscientific. It would be like saying that by pure chance these processes occurred at the right times and in the right amounts to keep oxygen at a constant level. Assuming a string of luck to persist for over a billion years is not scientific.

Lovelock considers life processes. We have just seen that plant life puts oxygen in the air. Another life form, however, anaerobic bacteria, produces methane that has the opposite effect. Anaerobic bacteria live in the intestines of cellulose-eating animals, from cattle to termites, but most anaerobic bacteria live in, and generate methane from, "the anaerobic muds and sediments of the sea beds, marshes, wetlands, and river estuaries where carbon burial takes place. The quantity of methane made in this way by micro-organisms is astonishingly large, at least 1,000 million tons a year."[42]

Methane affects the air's oxygen level through oxidation, Lovelock notes:

The oxidation of methane in the lower atmosphere uses up substantial amounts of oxygen, on the order of 2,000 megatons annually. This process goes on slowly and continuously in the air we live and move in. . . . In the absence of methane production, the oxygen concentration would rise by as much as 1 per cent in as little as 12,000 years: a very dangerous change and, on the geological time-scale, a far too rapid rise.[43]

Lovelock speculates:

The constancy of oxygen concentration suggests the presence of an active control system, presumably with a means of sensing and signalling any departure from the optimum oxygen concentration in the air; this may be linked with the processes of methane production and carbon burial. . . . It is an intriguing thought that without the assistance of those anaerobic micro-flora living in the stinking muds of the sea-beds, lakes, and ponds, there might be no writing or reading of books. Without the methane they produce, oxygen would rise inexorably in concentration to a level at which any fire would be a holocaust and land life, apart from micro-flora in damp places, would be impossible.[44]

Again, it seems that the earth has homeostatic processes similar to those of a living thing. These processes employ organisms, such as bacteria, plants, and animals, which keep conditions on Earth appropriate for the continuation, expansion, and development of these and other living things. Lovelock supplies additional evidence for this view of life on Earth. He discusses other atmospheric gases, the salt content of the seas, and acids. But we have already seen enough to understand his view and glimpse the science that backs it up.

This science is admittedly speculative. *For the most part we do not know exactly how the earth manages to maintain homeostasis: for example, relatively constant climate and atmospheric oxygen. The Gaia Hypothesis, that the earth is a living, self-regulating system, is a more plausible explanation for this homeostasis than a billion years of luck.*

From Science to Metaphor

Lovelock writes:

> The name of the living planet, Gaia, is not a synonym for the biosphere. The biosphere is defined as that part of the earth where living things normally exist. Still less is Gaia the same as the biota, which is simply the collection of all individual living organisms. The biota and the biosphere taken together form part but not all of Gaia. Just as the shell is part of a snail, so the rocks, the air, and the oceans are part of Gaia.[45] Gaia is the largest manifestation of life. [It is] the tightly coupled system of life and its environment.[46]

This means that Gaia may be thought of as one large living being. Margulis notes that reproduction is characteristic of life, and that Gaia can reproduce. She writes:

> If we define life as a reproducing system capable of natural selection, then Gaia is living. The easiest way to see this is through a simple thought experiment. Imagine that a spacecraft carrying microbes, fungi, animals, and plants is sent to Mars. Let it produce its own food and cycle its waste, and let it persist for two hundred years. Gaia is the recycling system of life as a whole. A budding off of one Gaia to produce two would have occurred. The construction of such a miniature Gaia would represent de facto reproduction.[47]

This would not be reproduction on the human model, but on the model of organisms that reproduce through division. And it is not exactly like that either. When a single-celled organism reproduces, the entire cell divides, whereas when Gaia reproduces in the manner described by Margulis, it is only a part of Gaia, human beings, who act. They alone gather life forms and send them to a new planet. Otherwise, Gaia reproducing in this way is similar to the reproduction of single-celled organisms.

As we have seen, Gaian science does not suggest that Gaia is conscious, much less that it has plans and purposes. Gaia is more like a tree than a mammal, so the term Mother Earth may be misleading. We usually think of mothers as conscious, caring, and attentive, whereas Gaia is none of these. On the other hand, the earth is somewhat like a mother to us. Although non-conscious, it is a living thing in which we developed and continue to live. Its life continues to support our lives much as a mother's life supports that of the fetus she carries. As a fetus lives in a mother, we live in Gaia. (We live *in* Gaia rather than *on* Gaia, because the atmosphere is a vital part of the earth, and we live surrounded by the atmosphere, not on top of it.) *Gaia is our mother only metaphorically.*

Metaphors and Moral Implications

What, if any, are the moral implications of the Gaia Hypothesis? *The Gaia Hypothesis influences morality primarily through its effect on the metaphors we use to describe nature and our relationship to it.* We use metaphors extensively in ordinary speech and writing because they can improve our grasp of reality. There, I just used one. Did you notice? The word "grasp" refers primarily to a physical relationship among material entities. "To grasp" is, according to my dictionary, "to take or seize eagerly." The noun "grasp" refers first to "forcible holding."[48] This means primarily that one physical entity, such as a person's hand, takes hold of another, such as a pen. Or a person forcibly holds her toddler to prevent the child from running into the street.

The word "grasp" has been extended metaphorically, however, to describe relationships between the mind and reality. When the mind grasps reality— whether that reality is a physical object, a social relationship, an abstract concept, or something else—it understands reality. Why is the word "grasp" used to indicate understanding? The reason is probably that understanding often provides the kind of control over reality that grasping provides over material objects.

Many mental concepts are drawn from terms whose original meaning described physical reality. She is "down in the dumps." He is "flying high" until he realizes that shoplifting is not such a "bright" idea. We use concepts that originally describe physical reality to describe mental reality because physical reality is accessible to our five senses and therefore better understood. We choose physical concepts that "illuminate" certain aspects of our mental life due to a shared property or relationship. For example, being in a garbage dump would make most people unhappy, so we say of unhappy people that they are down in the dumps. Most people are happy when they dream of flying like a bird, so we say happy people are flying high. Ideas are bright when they help people to recognize reality because bright light helps people to see (recognize) physical reality.

We also often express moral and legal concepts through metaphors drawn from physical reality. We say that people have "heavy" obligations. In criminal trials the state "carries the burden" of proof. The jury must "weigh" the evidence.

Metaphors are so common that it is hard to discuss them without using them. Terms used metaphorically typically have (here come some metaphors) a "home range," a more easily understood "area," in which the term is used non-metaphorically. For example, people weigh gold and silver to see how much money it is worth. George Lakoff, professor of linguistics at the University of California at Berkeley, refers to this as the word's source domain. Then there is its "target" domain, which is the area of the term's metaphorical application. For example, when juries weigh evidence they determine how much it is "worth," meaning, how convincing it is. Finally, there is a source-to-target "mapping," which is the structural or other similarity between the term's meaning in the source and target domains that justifies using the metaphor.[49] Convincing evidence is considered valuable, like weighty gold or silver.

People sometimes mistake metaphors for literal descriptions. They also sometimes turn metaphors into new literal meanings that enter dictionaries. The third meaning of "grasp" in my dictionary is "to lay hold of with the mind; comprehend." The term "virus" was originally used metaphorically to indicate a source of problems in computer programs. Now it is a new, literal meaning of the term.

But metaphorical meanings cannot become literal through metaphor simply by human choice if the association between source and target domains has limited basis in fact or science. The metaphorical association of minds with computers is often considered literal, but this is an error. We simply do not know enough about how the mind or brain works to take the computer metaphor literally. Taking the computer metaphor literally may lead people to believe, for example, that when computers become sufficiently complex, they will feel emotions the way people do. But this may be incorrect. It may be that non-living electronic devices, no matter how complex, are incapable of emotions. If we assume the brain to be just like a computer, we may be frustrated in attempts to understand the brain's role in generating human emotions.

Metaphors guide our actions when the source domain is action guiding. For example, Lakoff points out, "time is understood metaphorically as a money-like resource. Thus, time can be *saved, lost, spent, budgeted, used profitably, wasted*, etc."[50] Most people favor saving money over wasting it. So when time is associated metaphorically with money, people tend to think it better to save than to waste time. The metaphorical association of the mind with computers is also action guiding. It suggests certain research activities, such as the search for physical structures in the brain whose processes can be described in terms of binary logic. The metaphorical association of minds with ghosts or spiritual entities suggests different lines of inquiry.

In Chapter 1 we considered another action-guiding metaphor. Garrett Hardin quoted with approval a former vice-president of the Rockefeller Foundation, Alan Gregg, on the subject of feeding the world's starving poor people. Gregg described the growing human population as a cancer on the earth. The metaphor suggests that population growth is bad and should be stopped. As we saw in the Introduction to this book, pharmaceutical companies are conducting a "war" on cancer. Gregg's opposition to feeding poor people gets moral support from his cancer metaphor: "Cancerous growths demand food; but, as far as I know, they have never been cured by getting it."[51]

Mechanical and Organic Metaphors for Nature

We typically apply metaphors to nature as a whole because it is too vast and complex for literal descriptions to be adequate. These metaphors are often action guiding. Seventeenth-century philosopher and mathematician Rene Descartes thought that all material bodies in space operate mechanically. The stars, sun, moon, and planets seem to move around the sky like the hands of a mechanical clock keeping perfect time. The heart pumps blood the way mechanical pumps extract water from mines.

Descartes did not think he was using a metaphor. He thought that just as people construct clocks and pumps on mechanical principles to achieve desired effects, God made heavenly bodies and animal hearts on the very same mechanical principles to achieve His goals. The human mind, according to Descartes, is the only thing on Earth that is spiritual instead of mechanical, and the spiritual is the more valuable. The goal of all things mechanical, then, whether created by God or by people, is to serve humanity.

Although Descartes thought all of nature was literally mechanical, we now know that many natural things—magnetic fields, subatomic particles, and living organisms, for example—do not work entirely on mechanical principles. So now we consider Descartes' mechanistic view a metaphor.

This metaphor is action guiding. People take watches apart to learn how they work and to fix them when they break. The goal is to serve humanity better. Similarly, Descartes recommends vivisection on animals to understand their "mechanisms." This will enable doctors eventually to intervene mechanically to cure human beings who are sick. Doctors now do this in surgery. *In Descartes' hands, then, the mechanical metaphor for nature led to the view that nothing in nature is sacred. All of nature is like a watch that people can tear apart or build up to suit human purposes. People should have no moral qualms about altering nature any way they see fit to benefit humanity.*

The Gaia Hypothesis, by contrast, suggests an organic metaphor. Living things are different from mechanical devices. Holmes Rolston puts it this way:

> Cars have no self-generating or self-defending tendencies. . . . When a human steps out of a car, she takes all the purposes, needs, . . . [and] interests of the car away with her, all of which she gave to the car in the first place. . . . But none of this is true when a human walks away from a deer or a delphinium. . . . They have self-generating, self-defending tendencies. . . . [52] The organism is . . . an evaluative system. So it grows, reproduces, repairs its wounds, and resists death. . . . [53]

The Gaia Hypothesis says that the earth similarly has its own natural tendencies and its own good. Like a living thing, it is harmed when these are impaired. So whereas the mechanical metaphor implies that the earth is like a car that was made to serve human beings and cannot be harmed in its own right, the Gaia Hypothesis states that the earth can be thought of as having a life and a good of its own. Our actions can harm it.

The Gaia Hypothesis can guide action in two different ways. First, it under-mines the mechanical metaphor and its associated permissiveness. We no longer have good reason to treat the earth as though it were a mechanical de-vice designed to serve people.

Second, the Gaia Hypothesis inspires its own metaphor: that *the living earth is related to us as a pregnant woman is to the fetus she carries. Our lives developed in the earth's life, and the earth's life continues to support us.* We owe it big time.

But how do we discharge our duties toward Mother Earth? Well, we show appreciation for our mothers on Mother's Day by doing something that would please them. We have no reason to think that Gaia is conscious, but we can ob-serve the conditions that the earth tends to create and maintain. These are its values. One of these is species diversity. Although 99 percent of all species that ever existed are extinct, the earth tends to generate species faster than they go extinct. Except in periods of cataclysmic species decline, the total number of species becomes greater over time. So one way to respect Gaia is to resist species loss through human activity.

An explanation of our discomfort at extinguishing species and a justification for efforts to retain species can be given along these lines. We saw earlier that Gaia seems to retain its temperature within a relatively narrow range, much as people do. Part of the temperature control system in people is the sensation

*"I think we agree, gentlemen, that one can respect
Mother Nature without coddling her."*

of discomfort. Lovelock points out: "If shivering and cold were not unpleasant we would not be discussing them, since our remote ancestors would have died of hypothermia."[54] Pain is part of our survival kit. It motivates us to take care of such problems as hypothermia, which could threaten our lives.

Perhaps Gaia has a similar system. We are part of Gaia. Many human beings who learn about the massive human-caused extinction of species are morally outraged and highly motivated to avoid further species loss. Thus we have elaborate and expensive programs to save species. *This human reaction may be Gaia's reaction to the massive loss of species. We may be that part of Gaia that senses, through our moral discomfort, a deviation from one of Gaia's valued states. Just as our feeling cold is part of our body's system for maintaining its temperature, our moral discomfort at massive species loss may be part of Gaia's system for maintaining increases in species diversity.*

The next chapter considers other metaphors as bases for holistic nonanthropocentric concern. We will look at other reasons to retain species diversity, and other ways to account for our moral reactions.

Judgment Calls

- In February 1999, I received a letter from Care, a charitable organization, about the serious shortage of clean, safe water in many poor countries. Unsafe water causes "diarrhea, cholera and typhoid. The results can be catastrophic: 12 million children under the age of five die each year from diarrhea, malnutrition or related causes." They are among the "almost 1.2 billion people [who] do not have access to safe, clean water. . . ."[55] Care is appealing for money to continue their programs that have already brought safe water to about 10 million people since the 1950s. How much money should we spend saving the last 43 kakapos, the few remaining California condors, and other endangered species when money is needed now to save children's lives?

- Species are threatened primarily by habitat reduction caused by human land use, as when people cut down forests for agriculture. Many poor people live in countries where food is scarce and there is pressure to expand agriculture to feed people. Many environmental organizations, however, favor retention and expansion of nature reserves and designated wilderness areas where farming is prohibited. These are needed to save species from extinction. How can the conflict between these different needs be resolved in a way that is fair to everyone?

- If we view nature through the mechanical metaphor, what, if anything, is wrong with using the technology of genetic engineering to create chickens with no feathers (saves plucking them), human-like creatures with no heads or brains (so their organs could be used in transplants), or people with more intelligence (so they are easier to teach)? What do such issues suggest about the mechanical metaphor?

CHAPTER 7

The Land Ethic

Hunting Animals to Preserve Ecosystems

How does Gaia maintain the earth's temperature, the atmosphere's oxygen, and other requirements for life? We do not know the details. But we do know, in biologist Lynn Margulis' words, that "Gaia is [a] series of interacting ecosystems. . . ."[1] In this chapter we look at the nature and value of **ecosystem**s. They contain the habitats whose loss endangers many species. They are holistic entities, like species, that many people consider valuable in themselves. They are the context for biological evolution, including the evolution of our own species. And they are at the heart of pioneer ecologist Aldo Leopold's land ethic, the holistic nonanthropocentric view explored in this chapter.

Concern about ecosystems is central in debates about hunting, which pit individualistic nonanthropocentrists (who want to protect individual animals) against holistic nonanthropocentrists (who care more about holistic entities, such as species and ecosystems). Hunters often claim their sport is necessary to preserve ecosystems.[2]

In fall 1998, I received a letter about hunting from the National Rifle Association of America (NRA). It begins "Dear Mr. Shaffer" (I think he lives next door):

It was 11-year-old Mike's big day—the first time he would join his father and grandfather for a day of deer hunting. As the sun began to light up the eastern sky, the three hunters quietly slipped into the woods at the back of the family property.

Suddenly a band of wild-eyed intruders burst from the trees shouting "Barbarian!", "Murderer!" and "Hunt the hunter!"

Mike is doused with red paint. His elderly grandfather is pushed to the ground. Mike's father asks the trespassers to leave and is spat upon.

There will be no hunt today. A group of lawless animal rights extremists have halted one of America's oldest traditions and crushed the hopes of an eager young boy.

Here is a conflict. If animals, such as deer, are subjects-of-a-life with a right to life like ours, then hunting purely for sport resembles murder. A letter to Dear Abby expresses a mother's distress at her husband's desire to take their 12-year-old son hunting:

I don't feel that humans have the right to kill animals unless their lives are directly endangered, or unless they need the meat for survival. We are an upper-middle-class urban family, and neither of these situations is likely to occur.

My husband says that he wants our son to know the joy of our rapidly vanishing wilderness areas. I say "Fine, take him camping and teach him the craft of the woodsman."

He claims he wants our son to know the challenge of stalking . . . game.

I say, "Fine . . . let him stalk with a camera. And if he needs to have a trophy . . . bring home some pictures."

He says he wants our son to be skillful with a rifle. I don't mind that. We have access to an excellent skeet-shooting range and instructors.

Finally, and worst in my opinion, my husband says he wants our son to be a man. . . . Abby, to me a true man (or woman) is one who rejoices in the beauty of life, who works hard to preserve all of that beauty, who respects mankind and all animals, and who kills only as a necessity and never for pleasure or sport.[3]

"He was very old and quite sick."

In reply to this woman's kind of reasoning, hunters claim that hunting furthers holistic nonanthropocentric goals. It supports species diversity and
healthy ecosystems. For example, deer tend to overpopulate when predators—
wolves, coyotes, and human hunters—fail to thin the herd. Eventually, overpopulation results in death by starvation, which hunting advocates claim is
gruesome. So animals do not benefit when people fail to hunt, and ecosystems
are damaged. Before they starve, deer overgraze vegetation and degrade
ecosystems the way cattle overgrazing ruins a pasture. In both cases impover-
ished flora cannot support much animal life. In *A Sand County Almanac*, Aldo
Leopold describes the results of deer overpopulation on a mountain:

> I have seen every edible bush and seedling browsed, first to anaemic desuetude,
> and then to death. I have seen every edible tree defoliated to the height of a sad-
> dle horn. Such a mountain looks as if someone had given God a new pruning
> shears, and forbidden Him all other exercise. . . .
>   I now suspect that just as a deer herd lives in mortal fear of its wolves, so does
> a mountain live in mortal fear of its deer. And perhaps with better cause, for while
> a buck pulled down by wolves can be replaced in two or three years, a range pulled
> down by too many deer may fail of replacement in as many decades.[4]

In sum, predators, including hunters, often help to maintain healthy ecosystems.

The Nature of Ecosystems

Assessing this defense of hunting requires understanding ecosystems. Like
Gaia, ecosystems include living organisms that interact with one another and
with their inorganic surroundings. They differ from Gaia partly in being
smaller. Each one occupies only part of the earth. Gaia is their sum total, which
is the living Earth.

Life requires energy, and on Earth almost all energy comes from the sun.
Green plants transform the sun's energy into chemical energy through photosynthesis. The chemical energy contained in plants goes directly to animals
who eat plants. Animals (and some insect-eating plants) eat these animals. Aldo
Leopold compares this energy capture and transfer system to a pyramid, which
he calls the **biotic pyramid**:

> Plants absorb energy from the sun. This energy flows through a circuit called the
> biota, which may be represented by a pyramid consisting of layers. The bottom
> layer is the soil. A plant layer rests on the soil, an insect layer on the plants, a bird
> and rodent layer on the insects, and so on up through various animal groups to
> the apex layer, which consists of the larger carnivores.
>   The species of a layer are alike not in where they came from, or in what they
> look like, but rather in what they eat. Each successive layer depends on those be-
> low it for food. . . . Proceeding upward, each successive layer decreases in nu-
> merical abundance. Thus, for every carnivore there are hundreds of his prey, thou-

sands of their prey, millions of insects, uncountable plants. The pyramidal form of the system reflects this numerical progression from apex to base.[5]

Relationships of eating and being eaten among living things are sometimes called **trophic relationships**, but here Leopold calls them **food chains**:

> Thus soil-oak-deer-Indian is a chain that has now been largely converted to soil-corn-cow-farmer. Each species, including ourselves, is a link in many chains. The deer eats a hundred plants other than oak, and the cow a hundred plants other than corn. Both, then, are links in a hundred chains. The pyramid is a tangle of chains so complex as to seem disorderly, yet . . . it [is] . . . highly organized. . . . [6]

Leopold refers to the ecosystem as "land," and compares the circulation of energy through the **biota,** the land's living organisms, to a fountain. Energy is metaphorically water in the fountain. Just as there is more water at the base of the fountain than in the upper reaches of its spray, the land forms a biotic pyramid with more food energy in green plants at the base than in carnivores at the top. "Land, then," Leopold writes, "is not merely soil; it is a fountain of energy flowing through a circuit of soils, plants, and animals. Food chains are the living channels which conduct energy upward; death and decay return it to the soil."[7] **Niche** is another term for the role played by a given species in circulating the energy that comes ultimately from the sun.

Increases in **biodiversity**, the variety of species in a given system, usually lead to further increases in biodiversity. The greater the variety of species in the system, the greater the variety of things to eat. Additional species typically enter the ecosystem, or evolve within it, to exploit new sources of food. These species, in turn, become food for even more species, and so on. So *life on Earth becomes more varied over time. The biotic pyramid started out rather flat and has become taller. Leopold states: "In the beginning, the pyramid of life was low and squat; the food chains were short and simple. Evolution has added layer after layer, link after link. . . . The trend of evolution is to elaborate and diversify the biota."*[8]

The metaphor of commercial activity helps to explain why species diversity tends to increase. Imagine the old days when most people lived on farms and grew their own food. People needed to buy farm implements, cloth to make clothing, and a few food ingredients, but commercial activity was low because people were relatively self-sufficient. They did not buy and sell very much.

Then farming became more mechanized, enabling each farmer to cultivate more land. Other new technologies—artificial fertilizers and new kinds of corn, wheat, and other crops—increased yields per acre. New herbicides killed weeds with less human labor. The result was less farm work. Fewer farmers were needed to feed society.

But more specialized work increased elsewhere in the economy. Many non-farmers manufactured farm equipment, fertilizers, and herbicides. Increasing numbers of scientists and engineers worked to improve these products. More mechanical specialists were needed to service and fix increasingly complex equipment. Opportunities increased in the sale of the equipment, too. Because farmers required training in new techniques, there was more work for agricultural educators. As the farm (and the rest of society) used more internal combustion engines, opportunities in the petroleum industry increased. There was more work for geologists to find oil and for oil companies to market and distribute their products.

The commercial metaphor compares specialists like these to different species of plants and animals. The more specialized people become in what they do, the more they rely on others to meet all their needs. This reliance creates new commercial niches for additional "species" of specialists. The result is increased commerce, as more people buy from others more of what they need or want. The gross domestic product (GDP), which measures the flow of dollars through the economy, increases. This is metaphorically like an increase in the total energy flowing through an ecosystem.

In nature, the evolutionary development of a new strategy for living is like the development of a new technology in commerce that encourages or requires specialized employment. Mammals, for example, developed when dinosaurs strode the earth. Most dinosaurs concentrated their activity during warm daylight hours. Species that could operate in the cool twilight evening and morning hours could avoid most dinosaurs. The new strategy for living was the warm-bloodedness and better night vision of small mammals. These mammals expanded opportunities for predatory birds, such as owls and eagles, for insect parasites on mammals and birds, for birds that eat insect parasites, for scavengers who eat dead bodies, and for microbes that decompose the dead.

Species not only create niches for one another; they also hold one another in check. Rabbits, for example, eat oaks as they sprout from acorns. Leopold observes:

> Every surviving oak is the product either of rabbit negligence or of rabbit scarcity. Some day some patient botanist will draw a frequency curve of oak birth-years, and show that the curve humps every ten years, each hump originating from a low in the ten-year rabbit cycle. (A fauna and flora, by this very process of perpetual battle within and among species, achieve collective immortality.)[9]

Human beings are full participants, often without realizing it, in such contests among species. Consider, for example, the contest between prairie and forest in Wisconsin. Prairie grasses and forests are both suited to Wisconsin. Trees have the advantage of height over prairies, so they can prevent grasses from getting the sun that they need to grow. Why, then, was much of Wisconsin covered by prairie instead of forest? Fire is the answer. Fires started by lightning that burns the prairie actually favor the prairie over the forest. Prairie grasses can re-establish themselves quickly after a fire, whereas trees take many years to mature to the point where their height gives them a competitive advantage. Fires put all contestants in the race to the sun back in their starting blocks, and grasses do better than trees in the early stages of the race.

Agriculture had the unintended effect of favoring forests over prairie because farms carved out of the prairie had empty fields in April when fires used to rage. These empty fields acted like fire breaks that limited the extent of the fire. Many prairie areas did not burn because fire did not reach them, and burr oaks could establish themselves in these areas. Once established, these oaks can withstand prairie fires and make the land suitable for other tree species. So farmers unintentionally shifted the balance of power in many areas of Wisconsin from prairie to forest. Like squirrels who bury acorns (which favors oaks and forests) and rabbits (which eat oak sprouts and favor prairie), people play their part in the ecosystems they inhabit.[10] For the most part, however, we are unaware of our role because we have not read the entire play. Like squirrels, rabbits, and burr oaks, *we influence ecosystems in more ways than we realize.*

Does Hunting Help or Hurt Ecosystems?

As we have seen, hunters claim that their sport helps maintain ecological balances in healthy ecosystems. An ecosystem is sick, according to Leopold:

> When soil loses fertility, or washes away faster than it forms, and when water systems exhibit abnormal floods and shortages. . . . Other derangements are . . . the disappearance of plants and animal species without visible cause, despite efforts to protect them, and the irruption of others as pests despite efforts to control them. . . . [These] must, in the absence of simpler explanations, be regarded as symptoms of sickness in the land organism.[11]

Wilderness areas, by contrast, tend to be healthy, according to Leopold:

> Paleontology offers abundant evidence that wilderness maintained itself for immensely long periods; that its component species were rarely lost, neither did they get out of hand; that weather and water built soil as fast or faster than it was carried away. Wilderness, then, assumes unexpected importance as a laboratory for the study of land-health.[12]

Does hunting preserve and improve, or diminish and degrade, land-health? Hunters point out that one measure of hunting's positive influence is the recovery of many game species during the twentieth century. According to the periodical *Archery World*, at the beginning of the century beaver, for example, were "eliminated from states of the Mississippi Valley and all eastern states except Maine." By the 1980s, they were "common to abundant in nearly all states except Hawaii."[13] Similarly, "as recently as 1900, the total whitetail deer population of North America was estimated at about 500,000, following a study by the U.S. Biological Survey. . . . The deer population of the U.S. is now estimated at around 16 million."[14] Populations of wild turkey, trumpeter swan, wood duck, egret, and heron have also increased. In sum, advocates claim that hunting is good for ecological balances and wildlife populations.

Hunters remind us also that we all participate in the life of the ecosystems we inhabit. Non-hunting humans, no less than hunters, compete for environmental resources and cause other animals to die. Writing in *Sierra*, freelance journalist Margaret Knox quoted Kevin Lackey, "conservation programs manager of the Rocky Mountain Elk Foundation, a hunters' group based in Missoula, Montana." Lackey pointed out: "Even the vegetarian is partaking of food grown on wildlife habitat no longer available to wildlife—the corn we eat may have been planted in a former nesting site of wild birds."[15]

Patrick Scanlon of the Department of Fisheries and Wildlife at Virginia Polytechnic Institute and State University stresses that hunting exemplifies an honest and realistic relationship between people and nature:

> Many who fail to understand the human place in the global ecosystem fail to recognize its role as participant; rather they see humans as observers or somehow set apart as nonparticipants in the ecological scheme. But humans clearly are participants. . . . They consume, excrete, grow, reproduce, and die. To consume, they *compete* with other biological entities. Human consumption has impact on plant growth and succession. . . . Those who harvest wild animals *participate* in and exert humankind's role in ecology, at least to some extent.[16]

In short, people who think they are non-consumers and therefore innocent of causing animal deaths are self-deluded, according to Scanlon.

The story has another side, however. Relatively few of the 200 million animals that American hunters kill each year would otherwise ruin ecosystems through overpopulation.[17] Most birds, for example, limit their numbers through territorial behavior. Nesting pairs will not allow other birds of the same species to establish a nest within a certain distance of their already established nest. This limits nesting sites, nests, and therefore newborns in the area. Squirrels, on the other hand, are sometimes more cute than bright. They forget where they buried food and die of starvation or freeze to death without harming the ecosystem. Philosopher Robert Loftin writes:

> Most game animals . . . will not overpopulate. Most game animals are birds: quail, turkey, grouse, ducks, geese, doves, woodcock, snipe, rails, coots, and gallinules. None of these will overpopulate. . . . Nor will the smaller mammals, such as squirrels, raccoons, rabbits, or opossums.[18]

Where people are not integral to ecosystemic factors controlling animal populations, human hunting can impair ecosystems rather than help them. Margaret Knox quotes Raymond Dasmann's text *Wildlife Biology*: "Hunting, by [a] . . . species that does not [as predator] form an integral part of an ecosystem, removes the food supply of predators, parasites, scavengers, and all other organisms that are in turn affected by these species."[19]

Hunters damage ecosystems not only by taking food needed by wild species, but also by killing the wrong animals. Loftin writes:

> *Natural* predators benefit the prey population by eliminating the old, the very young, the sick, and the weak, simply because these individuals are easier to catch. Modern sport hunting, on the other hand, inverts the natural attrition and removes the largest and best conditioned animals from the herd. . . . The hunter deliberately selects the dominant male in the herd, the individual most fit to pass along the best genes.[20]

This impairs the species' evolutionary fitness, and may adversely affect breeding. Loftin reports that among Canadian bighorn sheep, for example, "the removal of older dominant rams by hunters . . . upset the social hierarchy of the herd, and resulted in excessive fighting and harassment of the ewes by younger rams, resulting in lower reproduction and scattering of the herd as well as actual physical injury."[21]

Even where predation is necessary to avoid ecological damage, hunting has generally been harmful. Aldo Leopold, an avid, lifelong hunter, explains why:

> It works thus: wolves and lions are cleaned out of a wilderness area in the interest of big-game management. The big-game herds (usually deer or elk) then increase to the point of overbrowsing the range. Hunters must then be encouraged to harvest the surplus, but modern hunters refuse to operate far from a car; hence a road must be built to provide access to the surplus game. Again and again, wilderness areas have been split by this process, but it still continues.[22]

The passage quoted from Leopold earlier, in which he writes that mountains are afraid of their deer, was not written in praise of hunting, but against the practice of killing wolves to make more deer available for hunters. *Reintroduction of natural predators, such as the recent re-introduction of wolves to Yellowstone National Park, preserves wilderness areas, ecological balances, and species of all types better than hunting*, Leopold thought.

Today's ecologists agree. Worldwatch associate John Tuxill wrote in 1998: "The extirpation of a region's top predators or dominant herbivores . . . can trigger a cascade of disruptions in the relationships among species that maintain an ecosystem's diversity and function."[23] Re-introducing such species, by contrast, benefits the entire ecosystem:

> Wolves had been absent from Yellowstone for about 50 years before they returned in 1995. . . . The wolves—now numbering nearly 100—have subsisted primarily on elk, a large deer that many biologists felt . . . was overbrowsing much of the park's best wildlife habitat. In order to elude the wolves, elk herds are now spending more time on higher ground where they can spot wolves more easily. Ecologists expect this shift will promote the recovery of rich river bottom stands of willows and aspens. . . . [24]

The benefits do not stop here. Wolves are reducing the coyote population that had been eating "about 75 percent of Yellowstone's voles, ground squirrels, and pocket gophers. . . . This rodent supply is now available to other predators, including eagles, hawks, owls, badgers, and pine martens—a change expected to promote a more balanced and thus more diverse ecological community."[25]

Coyotes also benefit from re-introduced wolves, Tuxill points out, because wolves eat only part of the meat on an elk carcass. The rest is left for coyotes and

> other part-time scavengers such as eagles, ravens, and Yellowstone's most endangered inhabitant, the grizzly bear. Scientists suspect that this newly abundant food source may even help grizzlies boost their population. Bear cubs are born during the mother's hibernation, and the number of cubs a female grizzly produces is directly dependent on her nutritional condition when she enters her winter den.[26]

Plant species can also depend directly on the continued presence of large mammals in the ecosystem, Tuxill wrote in 1997:

> In the American tropics, for instance, spider and wooly monkeys consume large quantities of wild fruit while foraging over wide areas of forest. Many tree species rely heavily on these monkeys to disperse their seeds. When the monkeys are hunted out of a forest, . . . the next generation of [some] tree species is in trouble— and so is the next generation of the birds, mammals, insects, fungi, and various other creatures that the trees support.[27]

Similarly, in parts of Africa, the Moabi tree, and all those who depend on it, may be endangered by the decline of gorillas and elephants. The tree's seeds may germinate only after being eaten by, and passing through the intestines of, these large animals.

In one sense, this is no surprise. We have seen that specialized species create niches for other species, so the more species in an ecosystem, the more opportunities for additional species. *Biodiversity has a snowballing effect. It is no surprise, then, that extirpating species would have the opposite snowballing effect of greatly reducing biodiversity.* In another sense, however, these drastic reductions are almost always a surprise because they depend on intricate, but largely unknown, interrelationships among life forms sharing an ecosystem. *One law of ecology is that you can't do just one thing because whatever you do alters many other things. What is more, we often cannot predict these effects because they depend on poorly understood interrelationships.* In sum, we cannot recommend on ecological grounds removing predator species to provide game for hunters. Ecology generally recommends the opposite.

This does not imply that all killing of wild animals is ecologically harmful. We saw in the last chapter, for example, that people must sometimes kill members of exotic species to preserve endangered indigenous species. But where animals must be killed to preserve species or healthy ecosystems, hunting as we know it is still bad. Such hunting requires roads in wilderness areas and allows killing the wrong members of target species. Professional culling is the proper response to such problems, according to biologist Ann Causey, writing in the journal *Environmental Ethics*. "If our purpose is to thin game herds, surely trained shooters using high-powered automatic weapons, and not restricted to certain seasons or times of day would be more effective than ordinary hunters who act in accordance with game laws."[28]

Promoting hunting to maintain land-health is like promoting amateur surgery for human health. People sometimes require surgery, just as ecosystems sometimes require the culling of species. But human health would not generally improve if we made a sport of surgery. Amateur surgeons would remove the wrong tissue, tie up loose ends badly, cause infections, and leave bad scars. Amateur hunters tend to do analogous damage to ecosystems. This is why Aldo Leopold, although he never renounced hunting, came to favor immersion in the wild through nature photography and wildlife research.[29]

Why Value Ecosystems?

We now know the nature of ecosystems and how they can vary in health, complexity, and richness. The question remains, Why should we care if ecosystems are more or less healthy, complex, or rich? Sickly, simplified ecosystems have less biodiversity and endanger the continuity of many species, so reasons to preserve species are reasons to favor healthy ecosystems. These are anthropocentric reasons when we value species merely for human enjoyment or health, and holistic nonanthropocentric reasons when we value species for themselves. Consider the holistic nonanthropocentric reasons. People have not always thought it worthwhile to preserve species or ecosystems as good in themselves. Why adopt such values now?

Addressing this issue requires confronting the fundamentals of ethics. In 1940, Leopold wrote: "To change ideas about what land is for is to change ideas about what anything is for."[30] According to philosopher J. Baird Callicott, Leopold saw in the theory of evolution ample reason to change ideas about what land and everything else are for.

Currently existing species have all competed successfully for the resources needed to meet life's basic needs. All animal species have evolved traits that enable its members to gather food, find mates, and escape predation long enough to rear progeny that do the same. This is the species' fitness.

Human beings, like many other species, are social. Our survival depends in large part on our ability to work cooperatively with other members of our species. This explains the development, for example, of our necks and larynx. They make us vulnerable to attack by leaving our windpipes unprotected by bone, and they allow food intended for the stomach to "go down the wrong way" toward our lungs. But they also enable us to make the sounds of speech.

Evolutionary theory suggests that speech improves overall fitness, otherwise only creatures with better-protected windpipes, like other primates, would exist. We would not. So what is the value of speech? Speech enables people to communicate more sophisticated thoughts to one another than would otherwise be possible. Perhaps this makes our species fit by enabling us to cooperate with one another in the performance of complex tasks. It also enables us to pass down abstract concepts and complex knowledge so that future generations can benefit from the wisdom of the past.

Cooperation requires more than speech, however. It requires also a disposition to cooperate. We saw in Chapter 1 that people are not always selfish. Instead, they often take pleasure in going out of their way to help others. Eighteenth-century philosopher David Hume, who lived before Charles Darwin put forth the theory of evolution, recognized that people have tendencies toward both selfish and unselfish behavior. He maintained that our tendencies toward unselfish behavior, which he referred to as our sentiments of sympathy, are the basis of all morality. We generally praise people as morally good when they help and cooperate with other people, rather than act selfishly.

Why do people act morally? Often it is because they want to. It makes them feel good. It satisfies their sentiment of sympathy, which is a tendency to be moved emotionally to work for the good of others. Without this sentiment, Hume thought, people would behave horribly to one another, and morality would be impossible. Hume is said, for this reason, to have a **sentiment-based ethics**.

Charles Darwin accepted this view of morality, Callicott tells us, and provided an evolutionary explanation for the sentiments that ethics and morality require. *The human species is more fit when its members generally have sympathetic sentiments. Humans depend on cooperation to accomplish life's basic tasks, and people with sympathetic sentiments cooperate better. Improved cooperation helps people get food and shelter; evade predators; find mates; and raise children to the point where they can do likewise. This improves the species' long-term prospects for survival. Cooperators passed their sympathetic tendencies on to their children. Thus, many people today have the sentiments that make morality possible.*

Few people extend sympathy to everyone equally. We generally have stronger sentiments of attachment, and willingness to help, people in our family, social group, or community, than strangers. Darwin remarked on this in technologically primitive people whom he referred to, following the usage of his day, as "savages." "A savage will risk his life to save that of a member of the same community, but will be wholly indifferent about a stranger."[31] This makes sense in light of the theory of evolution. People evolved in families and small communities, in which people depended on one another's cooperation. Relationships with human beings outside this group were often hostile. Certainly, fitness was seldom improved by feeling sympathy for and acting cooperatively with strangers. So the sentiment of sympathy extends naturally only to one's own community.

But the boundaries of community are not fixed. Callicott points out:

Human societies have grown in extent or scope and changed in form or structure. Nations—like the Iroquois nation or the Sioux nation—came into being upon the merger of previously separate and mutually hostile tribes. . . . With each change in society came corresponding . . . changes in ethics. The moral community expanded to become coextensive with the newly drawn boundaries of societies and the representation of virtue and vice, right and wrong, good and evil, changed. . . .

Today we are witnessing the painful birth of a human super-community, global in scope . . . [the] "global village." [And] a corresponding global human ethic—the "human rights" ethic, as it is popularly called—has been more definitely articulated.[32]

Again, this makes sense from an evolutionary perspective. Our sentiments of sympathy exist to foster cooperation with those in our communities. As technology increasingly brings all humanity together in mutual interdependence, strangers around the globe enter our community. They are people with whom we interact and must cooperate. The technology that fosters interdependence also allows us to see and get to know people of other cultures. The resulting sense of community leads naturally to sentiments of sympathy and caring. So we declare that all people have the same human rights.

Knowledge of ecology also enlarges our sense of community, Callicott notes. It teaches, as we have seen, that we humans are enmeshed in interdependencies with soil, water, microorganisms, plants, and animals in the ecosystems we inhabit. Presumably, most nonhuman members of ecosystems lack our scientific understanding of these interdependencies and do not think of themselves as members of communities that include both them and us. Nevertheless, they and we depend on one another to meet basic life needs in ways similar to mutual dependence within human communities. So one can say that ecosystems are at least metaphorically communities.

The land ethic is based on this metaphor. Leopold writes:

All ethics so far evolved rest upon a single premise: that the individual is a member of a community of interdependent parts. His instincts prompt him to compete for his place in the community, but his ethics prompt him also to co-operate. . . . The land ethic simply enlarges the boundaries of the community to include soils, waters, plants, and animals, or collectively: the land.[33]

Just as people feel moral obligations to their human communities and its members, they can come to feel obligations to the land and to members of the land community. "In short," Leopold affirms, "a land ethic changes the role of Homo sapiens *from conqueror of the land-community to plain member and citizen of it. It implies respect for his fellow-members, and also respect for the community as such."*[34] Leopold summarizes the land ethic in this maxim: "A thing is right when it tends to preserve the integrity, stability, and beauty of the biotic community. It is wrong when it tends otherwise."[35]

According to Callicott, people tend naturally to adopt this ethic when they become informed enough by "ecology's social representation of nature" to recognize the ecosystem (or land) to be their community. He writes, "A land ethic, . . . a moral response to the natural environment—[is] automatically triggered in human beings. . . . Therefore, the key to the emergence of a land ethic is, simply, universal ecological literacy."[36] In short, if people know the facts about ecology, they will recognize that the community includes the land, and will automatically adopt the land ethic.

Unfortunately, we cannot win general acceptance of the land ethic in this way. The community representation of ecosystems is a metaphor. It rests on real similarities between ecosystems and human communities, but there are differences as well. In most human communities people cooperate for the most part with others who consciously, purposely, and freely go out of their way to act cooperatively. We often act morally in reciprocation for acts that others perform out of conscious regard for morality. For example, we may tell the truth when a lie would be more convenient. We realize that others, too, often find lying convenient, but that social relations are impaired by general dishonesty. So we consciously forgo lying in expectation that others will do the same.

This element is missing in most ecological relationships. The bees are not putting themselves out to pollinate our crops, nor is alfalfa when it adds nitrogen to the soil. We benefit from what these organisms do, but one might say that we do not owe them reciprocation because they simply do what they must. They have no choice. They are not giving up anything to help us, so the ideas of community and sympathy do not entail an obligation for us to give up anything to accommodate them. We should go about our business of serving our own human good as they go about their business of serving their own good. Thus, contrary to the land ethic, we may reasonably decide to conquer nonhuman members of the land community to serve human purposes.

Another problem with the community-based justification of the land ethic is that within many human communities people do not recognize responsibilities to everyone. Slave societies, for example, generally denied basic rights to slaves, even though owners depended on their services.

In sum, extending community obligations to all aspects of the ecosystem is possible, but science does not make it inevitable. Even where human communities are concerned, our innate tendencies toward sympathy do not engender universal respect for fellow community members. *Cultural norms influence what constitutes a community, who belongs to the community, and what moral consideration community members can expect. These norms can differ from culture to culture.*[37]

Conflicting Moral Commitments

The land ethic's central maxim conflicts with many widely held moral beliefs. That maxim is: "A thing is right when it tends to preserve the integrity, stability, and beauty of the biotic community. It is wrong when it tends otherwise." This principle has the advantage and disadvantage of simplicity. There is just one rule to follow, one good to pursue—the good of the biotic community. The advantage is that it seems easy to determine the right thing to do in any situation. For example, if hunting deer in a given situation is needed to aid the biotic community, then hunting is morally required. However, if hunting involves the extermination of natural predators and the construction of access roads, then it is morally wrong because it harms ecosystems.

The disadvantage of this simplicity is conflict with common morality. For example, human populations have increased enormously in recent years. At the same time, habitat reduction is a major factor causing massive extinction of species and simplification of ecosystems. Habitat reduction stems largely from human overpopulation. If we cull deer in order to preserve ecosystems, and if our *only* moral guideline is to enhance the biotic community, we should cull the human population at this time. Most people find this immoral. It violates human rights. Animal rights advocate Tom Regan calls it "environmental fascism" because the group's good is considered more important than individual rights.[38]

Fortunately, the land ethic is not so simple. Leopold did not mean his maxim to constitute the whole of morality. He did not mean to cancel our normal moral obligations to family members, colleagues, and countries. Callicott understands Leopold to be saying this: Human morality evolved by adding new responsibilities without canceling the old. When people lived in extended families and then formed larger societies, for example, they did not eliminate all special obligations to family members. Family members legitimately remain more important to us than unknown members of our society. We are expected to feel more sympathy for them and go farther out of our way to help them. Nevertheless, obligations stemming from our membership in the larger society affect what we can legitimately do for family members. For example, the larger society must collect taxes from me to function well, so I must pay those taxes, even though I might prefer to spend the money on my children.

Thus, my obligations extend out from me in concentric circles. In the center, I must take care of myself and close family members. Then I must consider colleagues and my local community. Farther out are my country, then foreign people, then international institutions, and finally the nonhuman world. I should not condone culling the human population to improve the welfare of ecosystems because my obligations to human beings are greater than to ecosystems, on this view.

In the concentric circle approach, obligations to human beings do not always take priority over obligations to ecosystems. Just as I legitimately pay taxes rather than buy frivolous toys for my child, I legitimately subject my child to the relative discomfort of my small Saturn rather than buy a roomier minivan or sport utility vehicle. The small car's discomfort is trivial. Because it is more fuel efficient, it adds less carbon dioxide to the atmosphere, and so contributes less to ecosystem harm from global warming than gas-guzzling minivans and SUVs. Here, a person in the immediate circle of care takes a (buckled up) back seat to the nonhuman environment. So the land ethic is effective without jeopardizing human rights. Callicott acknowledges, however, that balancing these values sometimes presents "a difficult and delicate question."[39]

Tigers and Elephants in the Third World

What should we do when the lives of people come in direct conflict with efforts to save species from extinction? Philosopher Holmes Rolston, III addresses this issue:

> Ought we to save nature if this results in people going hungry? In people dying? Regrettably, sometimes, the answer is yes. In 20 years Africa's black rhinoceros population declined from 65,000 to 2,500, a loss of 97 percent; the species faces imminent extinction. . . . The primary direct cause is poaching, . . . for horns. People cannot eat horns, but they can buy food with the money from selling them. Zimbabwe has a hard-line shoot-to-kill policy for poachers, and over 150 poachers have been killed.[40]

Are such deaths justified? Rolston thinks so, citing the Bible's story of the flood:

> There, God seems more concerned about species than about the humans who had then gone so far astray. In the covenant re-established with humans on the promised Earth, the beasts are specifically included. "Keep them alive with you . . . according to their kinds" (Genesis 6.19–20). There is something ungodly about an ethic by which the late-coming *Homo sapiens* arrogantly regards the welfare of one's own species as absolute, with the welfare of all the other five million species sacrificed to that.[41]

Rolston strengthens his case for sacrificing people to save species by noting that we regularly choose our own pleasure or convenience over the needs of poor people:

> Every time we buy a Christmas gift for a wife or husband, or go to a symphony concert, or give a college education to a child, or drive a late model car home, or turn on the air conditioner, we spend money that might have helped to eradicate poverty. We mostly choose to do things we value more than feeding the hungry.
> If one were to advocate always feeding the hungry first, doing nothing else until no one in the world is hungry, this would paralyze civilization. People would not have invented writing, or smelted iron, or written music, or invented airplanes.[42]

Rolston assumes that we all value these developments enough to condone some humans starving to death, if necessary, so we can enjoy them. Even today we place some values above human life itself, Rolston claims: "Wealthy nations . . . put up borders across which the poor are forbidden to pass. If we believe in immigration laws at all, we, on the richer side of the border, think that protecting our lifestyle counts more than their betterment, even if they just want to be better fed."[43]

In the light of these priorities and the harm people have already done to other species and their ecosystems, Rolston concludes, we should now be willing to sacrifice human lives to protect endangered species and the ecosystems they require. Consider the endangered tiger, a large carnivore at the top of the biotic pyramid. The 40 tigers in the Ranthambhor National Park sanctuary in Rajasthan, India, are threatened by human population pressure that degrades the ecosystem. Rolston writes:

> There are 200,000 Indians within three miles of the core of the park—more than double the population when the park was launched, 21 years ago. Most depend on wood from the 150 square miles of park to cook their food. They graze in and around the park some 150,000 head of scrawny cattle. . . . The cattle impoverish habitat and carry diseases to the ungulates that are the tiger's prey base.[44]

Rolston claims that these people have not managed their resources intelligently. For example, replacing Indian with American cattle would result in much more milk, and the Indians could use cattle dung for heating. He wonders whether tigers, "these majestic animals," should be "casualties of human inabilities to manage themselves and their resources intelligently. . . ." It "leaves us wondering whether the tigers should always lose and the people win."[45]

But there is another side of this story. Indian writer and historian Ramachandra Guha claims in *The Ecologist* that the real problem concerns only 6,000 tribal people:

> who have been in the area longer than anyone can remember, perhaps as long as the tigers. The Karnataka Forest Department wants the tribals out, claiming they destroy the forest and kill wild game. In response, the tribals answer that their demands are modest, consisting in the main of fuelwood, fruit, honey and the odd quail or partridge. . . . [46]

Guha objects to the attitude of Western (First World) wildlife conservation officials toward such tribal (indigenous) people. Dr. John G. Robinson, for example, "works for the Wildlife Conservation Society in New York [which] oversees 160 projects in 44 countries." According to Dr. Robinson, tribals compete with tigers for food, thereby driving them to extinction, and "their extinction means that the balance of the ecosystem is upset and this has a snowballing effect."[47]

Rolston and Guha focus on different facts. Rolston writes about 200,000 tiger-harming people whose population is growing and who use the park wastefully for their entire sustenance. Guha writes about 6,000 tiger-friendly people whose population is steady and who use the park sparingly for essential needs. We should clarify the facts before sacrificing people for endangered species.

Values must also be considered, and one of these is justice. Guha notes:

> Tribals and tigers have co-existed for centuries; it is the demands of cities and factories that have put unbearable pressures on the forest, with species after species joining the endangered list. Tribals are being made the scapegoats, while the real agents of forest destruction—poachers, planters, politicians and profiteers—escape notice. As Dr. Robinson flies off to his next project, he might reflect on his own high-intensity lifestyle, which puts a greater stress on the world's resources than dozens, perhaps hundreds, of forest tribals.[48]

Rolston suggests that people make sacrifices to save other species, but are the right people being asked to make these sacrifices? Guha quotes ecologist Raman Sulumar:

> It is . . . unjust to expect only a certain section of society, the marginal farmers and tribals, to bear the entire cost of de-predatory animals. . . . There is urgent need to reorient management of our wildlife reserves so as to pass on economic benefits to local communities. . . . [49]

But obtaining such benefits may conflict with animal rights and species preservation.

Consider the African elephant. Worldwatch Institute staff researcher Cheri Sugal reported in 1997: "Unrestrained poaching for ivory would virtually assure the elephants' annihilation. Over just one decade . . . the total elephant population in Africa was cut by half—from 1.2 million in 1981 to 620,000 in 1989."[50] In 1989, an international ban on trade in ivory began under the Convention on International Trade in Endangered Species (CITES), and elephant populations recovered remarkably. Now there are too many.

In the past, elephants controlled their own population. Elephants ate the saplings, bark, and leaves of trees in the forests where they lived. They trampled and pushed over so many trees, which were later consumed in forest fires, that they converted woodlands to grasslands, and then the elephants moved on. Many died of starvation as they ranged far afield in search of food and water. In the meantime, the grasslands became woodlands again, which could feed more elephants. "In recent decades, however," Sugal writes:

> This cycle has been interrupted. Elephants confined to smaller ranges by the expansion of human development can quickly exceed their range capacity. Their sudden overcrowding is exacerbated by the fact that parks and refuges now offer a constant supply of water—greatly stabilizing the historically uncertain habitat and virtually ensuring uninterrupted reproduction. . . . This can set them up for rapid population increases—which sooner or later reach unsustainable levels.[51]

Local people can suffer when this happens, Sugal notes: "In 1995, for example, villagers living near Zambia's Bangweulu Swamp wildlife preserve nearly starved after elephants from the park began trampling farmers and destroying crops."[52] What should be done?

An approach being tried in Zimbabwe, the Communal Areas Management Programme for Indigenous Resources (CAMPFIRE), and funded with $28 million from the U.S. Aid for International Development (USAID), helps local people manage elephant populations for local benefit, the goal being eventual, local self-sufficiency. Currently, most revenue comes from granting hunting licenses:

> A typical package might include permits to shoot an elephant, a lion or leopard, a buffalo, and some antelope, on a 21-day hunt. The client pays $900 to $1,000 a

day, plus "trophy" fees for each animal shot—approximately $10,000 for an elephant, $3,000 for a lion, and $1,500 for a buffalo. . . . Village councils receive 33 percent, with costs accounting for 60 percent and the outfitter's profit 7 percent.[53]

More money would result if ivory from hunted animals could be sold internationally.

CAMPFIRE gives local people incentives to halt poaching. Hunting licenses are expensive. As a result, Sugal reports, "The program has reduced the number of elephants killed [annually] both by hunters and by poachers [to] about 1 percent." This is too small to curtail elephant overpopulation. If controlled ivory trade were resumed, there would be more incentive to hunt, and the population might stabilize.

But this solution conflicts with the rights of individual elephants and harms the elephant species. Hunting for elephant trophies, like hunting for deer trophies, takes the wrong animals, writes Wayne Pacelle, vice president of the Humane Society of the United States. "Trophy hunters . . . selectively eliminate the prime, breeding-age bulls with big tusks. Some call it evolution in reverse—with younger, less fit animals breeding in place of the most suitable reproductive males."[54] From evolutionary and ecological perspectives, **culling**, which kills an entire herd at once, is better than hunting. It also reduces elephant suffering because no survivors are left to mourn or starve.

But culling requires professionals and costs money, whereas hunting makes money. Where could money for culling come from? Some argue for resuming international trade in ivory. With the ivory ban only slightly relaxed in early 1999, the price of ivory is high, making poaching increasingly attractive at a time when unsold ivory stocks from culling and hunting are increasing. "Zimbabweans argue," Sugal reports, "that selling this ivory—thereby undercutting the poaching that would otherwise escalate—is a reasonable way to help finance sustainable local management."[55]

The U.S. Humane Society, which opposes killing elephants, started a pilot elephant contraception project in South Africa's Kruger National Park in 1996. The present method seems too expensive for widespread application, but should we hope for success? It would eliminate elephant overpopulation, thereby protecting people and ecosystems from too many elephants. But it would hamper the ability of local people to profit from the sale of hunting licenses and ivory. Does the U.S. Humane Society have alternate employment for these people?

Sugal concludes:

The debate over elephants is an emotional one, and often simplified in terms of a struggle between the advocates of a moral high ground (we shall not kill elephants) and the predatory forces of mammal-killers. But under its disputatious political surface, this isn't really about bad people versus enlightened ones; it's about stable systems (economic and ecological) versus unstable ones.

We see here the pull of the three different basic concerns discussed so far in this book. Anthropocentric concerns, discussed in Part I, suggest that local people make the most of local resources to provide for themselves and their progeny, such as by hunting elephants (and selling ivory) at sustainable levels, even though this involves not only killing individual elephants, but harming elephant evolution.

The animal liberation and animal rights (individualistic nonanthropocentric) concern alternatively suggests expensive contraception for elephants, and continuing the ban on selling ivory, because ivory sales could tempt poachers.

Finally, the holistic nonanthropocentric concern for species and ecosystems suggests, in conflict with anthropocentrism, professional culling instead of hunting, and, in conflict with animal liberation and rights, strictly managed ivory sales to bring down the price of ivory so that poaching will not become too lucrative to resist.

These three types of concern—anthropocentric, individualistic nonanthropocentric, and holistic nonanthropocentric—make environmental ethics, in J. Baird Callicott's phrase, "a triangular affair."[56] *Three different types or bases of concern compete for our consideration.* In Parts III and IV of this book we investigate synergistic views that lessen the tension among them.

Judgment Calls

- What should be done about tigers in India?

- What should be done about elephants in Africa?

- Hunters point out that all human beings, including vegetarians, consume food to live, compete with wildlife for scarce resources, and therefore cause wild animals to die. What is the best diet for us if we are "plain members and citizens" of the ecosystems we inhabit?

- One February, a bison fell through the ice in the Yellowstone River in Yellowstone National Park. When asked about helping the bison, "a park ranger replied that the incident was a natural occurrence, and the bison should be allowed to sink or swim on its own."[57] Some snowmobilers arrived, were incensed that the rangers were letting the struggling animal die, and tried unsuccessfully to extricate it. "The sad thing," a would-be rescuer said later, "is that he [the bison] knew we were trying to help. He laid his head at my feet just exhausted." That night was cold and by morning the animal was dead. Hearing about the incident, news commentator Paul Harvey decried what he called "knee-jerk ecologists." He said, "It is not a scientific question, it is a moral one. The reason Jesus came to earth was to keep nature from taking its course." What do you think about this case?

PART III

Environmental Synergism

CHAPTER 8

Human Rights, Agriculture, and Biodiversity

Poverty, Efficiency, and Human Rights

In 1993, John Ward Anderson and Molly Moore supplied the following account of a family in India to *The Washington Post* Foreign Service:

> When Rani returned home from the hospital cradling her newborn daughter, the men in the family slipped out of her mud hut while she and her mother-in-law mashed poisonous oleander seeds into a dollop of oil and forced it down the infant's throat. As soon as darkness fell, Rani crept into a nearby field and buried her baby girl in a shallow, unmarked grave next to a small stream.

This happens often, the authors explain: "For many mothers, sentencing a daughter to death is better than condemning her to life as a woman in the Third World, with cradle-to-grave discrimination, poverty, sickness and drudgery."[1]

Many girls who survive in the Third World are sold by their parents into prostitution. Freelance writer Germaine Shames gave this example in 1993: "Kham Suk, a delicate girl with fathomless eyes, hovers in the doorway of a Bangkok brothel in Thailand. Three months ago, on her 12th birthday, her mother walked her across the border from Myanmar (Burma), and sold her to a pimp for 2,000 baht."[2] Worldwatch associate Aaron Sachs supplied some general numbers in 1994:

> Brazil alone has between 250,000 and 500,000 children involved in the sex trade, and a recent study conducted by the Bogota Chamber of Commerce concluded that the number of child prostitutes in the Colombian capital had nearly trebled over the past three years. Similar increases have occurred in countries as geographically and culturally disparate as Russia and Benin. But the center of the child sex industry is in Asia: . . . about 60,000 child prostitutes in the Philippines, about 400,000 in India, and about 800,000 in Thailand. Most of the children are under 16 and most are girls. . . .[3]

There is a saying in Bangkok's red-light district, Sachs reports: "At 10 you are a woman. At 20 you are an old woman. And at 30 you are dead."[4]

What does this have to do with the environment? Hunger and poverty drive people to kill daughters or sell them into prostitution. These families are not getting enough of what they need from the environment to live decent lives. Anderson and Moore recount the story of another Indian woman:

> Amravati, who lives in a village near Rani, . . . says she killed two of her own day-old daughters by pouring scalding chicken soup down their throats, one of the most widely practiced methods of infanticide in southern India. . . . "My mother-in-law and father-in-law are bedridden," says Amravati, who has two living daughters. "I have no land and no salary, and my husband met with an accident and can't work. Of course it was the right decision."[5]

Such hunger and poverty results from government decisions about natural resources. Sachs explains that in rural Thailand, for instance:

> Many of the villagers, like the peoples of the Amazon rainforest, used to derive their income from forest products—charcoal, bamboo shoots, wild mushrooms, squirrels, even edible toads. Small-scale subsistence farmers also depended on the forests to provide breaks against soil erosion and to regulate natural irrigation systems. But logging projects . . . have laid waste to the area's hillsides over the last three decades. Economists often point to Thailand as a clear success—and the country's lucrative exports, consisting mostly of agricultural products grown on previously forested land, have certainly helped boost the Thai economy. . . . However, . . . the poorest people . . . lost . . . their livelihoods.[6]

Jodi Jacobson, senior researcher at the Worldwatch Institute, reports that this is common: "Throughout Africa, Asia, and Latin America, women are being muscled out of forests—and off croplands and grasslands—by governments and private interests. . . .' "[7]

The issue comes down to how people should use the earth. *Some believe that for people to get all they need and want from the earth they must exploit it maximally for human advantage. This is the only way to avoid human rights violations that stem from desperate poverty. These theorists maintain further that maximal exploitation requires concentration on monetary investments that generate cash.* Such investments are needed to develop and employ the most technologically sophisticated and efficient means of using the earth for human advantage. These efficient means must generate cash to pay off investments and provide salaries to workers, who can then buy whatever they do not produce for themselves. When technology maximizes efficiency and generates the greatest monetary rewards, humanity reaps the benefits, they say.

These thinkers consider the poverty of people displaced from forests and fields a regrettable, but fortunately temporary, part of the transition from less to more efficient uses of the earth. Everyone will eventually benefit from such efficiency, they believe.

This view is anthropocentric. Nature is merely a means to human well being, so people can use unlimited power over nature to achieve human goals. Anthropocentrists also often regard environmental decision making as, in J. Baird Callicott's phrase, "a triangular affair." There are inevitable tradeoffs between the well being of people, individual plants and animals, and such holistic entities as species and ecosystems. Each is served by sacrificing the others. For example, people gain by subjecting individual animals to horrific conditions on factory farms, because this results in inexpensive meat. Individual animals gain when people renounce gruesome medical experiments, but then people lose the benefits of medical advances. People gain lumber when they cut down old-growth forests, but individual animals lose their homes, species lose habitat, and the forest ecosystem is destroyed. Migrating birds and other species gain when developers are forbidden to fill in a wetland, but people lose the value of their property and a good place to build a house. In sum, *according to the triangular affair approach, environmental choices are predominantly win-lose situations that pit anthropocentric, individual nonanthropocentric, and holistic nonanthropocentric concerns against one another. Anthropocentrists willingly sacrifice all nonanthropocentric values.*

Environmental Synergism

The present chapter considers an alternative—environmental synergism. In general, synergy exists when the effect of things acting together is greater than the total effect of those same things acting separately. *Environmental synergists believe that synergy exists between respect for people and respect for nature. Overall and in the long run, simultaneous respect for people and nature improves outcomes for both.* This belief animates views discussed in this and the next two chapters, including those of Wendell Berry, ecofeminists, deep ecologists, some Native American religions, and some Christian theologians. I highlight the benefit to human beings of valuing nature for itself. *Respect for nature promotes respect for people, so the best way to serve people as a group is to care about nature for itself.*

The thesis may seem paradoxical. We often favor the direct approach to getting what we want. If we want the most from nature, we should subordinate nature as much as possible to human purposes. We should treat nature merely as a means to human ends. We should not be limited by concerns about ecosystems or individual animals for themselves, because such caring impedes actions that promote human welfare.

But the direct approach does not always work. Consider the **hedonic paradox**. Most people want to be happy, but those who aim directly at personal happiness seldom achieve it. For most people, happiness comes from involvement in pursuits that distract them from concern about their own happiness. People may construct model airplanes, sing in a choir, study a foreign language, work to protect animal welfare, or help maintain their church. When people "lose themselves" in these activities, that is, when they care about such goals for the sake of achieving those goals rather than for the sake of personal happiness, then they are most likely to find happiness in these pursuits.

Those, on the other hand, who retain a focus on their own happiness are unlikely to achieve it. They will often ask themselves: Will constructing this model airplane make me happy? Will learning to conjugate this verb make me happy? Will getting up early to help paint the church make me happy? Often the honest answer will be "no," so people focused exclusively on their own happiness will not pursue their goals consistently. Inconsistency leads to failure and frustration, not happiness. Hence the paradox. The best way to be happy is to find something that you care about *for itself*. Pursue that. Forget happiness, and you will be happy. This is the hedonic paradox.

But why think that the human relationship with nature is paradoxical in this way? Why think that the best way to get the most from nature for people as a group is to limit our activities out of respect for nature? The answer, in a word, is POWER. *People with unchecked power often misuse it.* An extreme example in the 1990s was Yugoslav President Slobodan Milosevic, who retained power by fomenting Serbian hatred of non-Serbs. In 1999, he promoted expulsion of ethnic Albanians from Kosovo Province, killing many in the process. Here is an Associated Press report from that conflict:

> Ten-year-old Dren Caka fingers the inflatable brace wrapped around his bulletshattered right arm. . . . Dren says he was shot as Serb police slaughtered his family. . . .
>
> It begins before dawn Saturday when they claim Yugoslav police began looting and burning homes on Milos Gjic street in Djakovica, in southern Kosovo. . . . Dren and 19 women and children, including his mother and three sisters, hide in a basement. But they are quickly discovered and accused of being supporters of the Kosovo Liberation Army, the ethnic Albanian separatists. . . .
>
> A 13-year-old girl is shot first, Dren says. Then, one by one, the police lower their guns and fire. It takes less than a minute.
>
> "I was hit in the arm, but I fell and pretended I was dead."
>
> The police set the home ablaze and move on, he says. Thinking everyone is dead, he starts to run. Then he hears moans from his baby sister.
>
> "I tried to pick her up, but . . . but," Dren says before breaking into tears and pointing to his arm. His uncle takes over: "He means he couldn't lift her because of his arm. She burned to death in the house."[8]

The inhumane use of unchecked power is, unfortunately, common. Consider the Nazi treatment of concentration camp inmates. Most people were simply killed at Auschwitz; others were starved and worked to death; still others were subjected to gruesome "experiments," such as immersion in cold water to time death by hypothermia.

Modern political organizations designed with "checks and balances" reflect our fear of unchecked power. We also favor representative democracies that require periodic election of public officials so the public can limit the terms of those who misuse power.

But we are ambivalent. While we fear unchecked political power, we crave unlimited power over nature and call its acquisition "progress." People in our society generally value such progress because they think it enables them to get more of what they need and want from nature. People want to travel, so invention of the steam locomotive and steam ship was progress. The use of internal combustion engines in cars and trucks is more progress. Jet planes are even better because they are faster, and if we had the ability of unlimited movement at the speed of light, that would be better still.

People want to see at night, so the invention of electric lights is progress. People want cheap entertainment, so radios, compact disks, and videos are welcomed. If unlimited quantities of electricity were available nearly free, as proponents of nuclear fusion energy used to claim it could be, that would be best. And if digitized signals could make radios and CDs sound exactly like live performances, that would be best.

People want to live long, healthy lives, so medical advances are welcome progress. The goal appears to be healthy lives of indefinite duration. In these cases, and many more, we celebrate using nature for exclusively human ends, and seek the kind of *unchecked power* that we fear in politics. With all its benefits, why fear this power?

According to synergists, unchecked human power over nature tends to be just as dangerous to people as unchecked political power. In general, harm to people results when those wielding power are not concerned about or aware of their actions' effects on people. Milosevic seems not to have been concerned about many untoward effects on people of his exercise of power. However, as we shall see in this chapter and ones to follow, many anthropocentrists are often concerned about people, but seem unaware of untoward effects on others. Occupational specialization, geographic distance, powerful technologies, and the ideology of progress combine to blind well-intentioned anthropocentrists to the human suffering caused by our power, and the quest for unlimited power, over nature. In sum, *like unchecked political power, unlimited power over nature endangers human beings. The most endangered are the least powerful—women, children, and poor people.*

This explains why her mother sold 12-year-old Kham Suk into prostitution. People with power over nature divert natural resources from feeding the Suk family to making money. They may have clear cut a forest to sell lumber or establish a coffee plantation. Well-intentioned anthropocentrists authorizing this action may live far from Thailand and be unaware of the misery such action causes. They specialize in businesses that supply timber or coffee, and consider land only from those perspectives. They have institutional responsibilities to maximize monetary returns for investors, and may believe that corporate profits foster the kind of economic progress that helps all people in the long run. But their power to bulldoze forests hurts people as well as nature.

Synergists believe that people will limit their use of power over nature, and so its oppressive consequences for other people, only when they adopt individualistic and holistic nonanthropocentric concerns. This means caring about the pain of individual animals, the disappearance of species, and the degradation of ecosystems for the sake of the animals, species, and ecosystems themselves, not for the sake of human beings. Such caring will limit humans' quest for, and exercise of, power over nature, which will, in turn, spare people a lot of misery. In sum, *people as a group get more from the environment by caring about nature for its own sake, which limits attempts to dominate nature, than by trying to manipulate it for maximal human advantage.*

The Benefits of High-tech Agriculture

Proponents of modern, powerful, high-tech agriculture can point to major successes. Lester Brown, Director of the Worldwatch Institute wrote in 1999:

> Technological advances have tripled the productivity of world cropland during this century. They have helped expand the world grain harvest from less than 400 million tons in 1900 to nearly 1.9 billion tons in 1998. Indeed, farmers have expanded grain production five times as much since 1900 as during the preceding 10,000 years since agriculture began.[9]

The result has been improved living standards for human beings. Brown writes:

> For the world as a whole, incomes have risen dramatically over the last century, climbing from $1,300 per person in 1900 to more than $6,000 per person in 1998 (in 1997 dollars). This rising economic tide has lifted most of humanity out of poverty and hunger. . . . [10] Over the last half-century, the share of the world that is malnourished has declined substantially. More than anything else, this has been due to rising food production per person.[11]

These advances stem from technological innovations. Increased *irrigation* results from better wells, stronger pumps, and larger dams that direct water to agricultural use. Brown notes the tripling of irrigated cropland in just 50 years: "The growth in irrigation has permitted the expansion of agriculture into arid regions, [and] increased multiple cropping in monsoonal climates by facilitating cropping during the dry season."[12]

Agricultural productivity has increased also due to dramatically increased use of *chemical fertilizers*. Agricultural crops need and take nutrition from the soil. The soil becomes depleted and crop yields decline unless nutrition is returned. One traditional method is to spread animal manure on the fields. However, as farming has become increasingly specialized (farmers who grow corn do not grow many animals) and mechanized (people use mechanical tractors instead of animals to till fields), the on-farm supply of manure has diminished. Another traditional method of returning nutrition to the soil is crop rotation. Some crops, such as legumes, take needed nutrition from the air. When they are grown on a field every third year or so and then plowed under, they help restore soil fertility. But this means that the field is not being used during that year to grow a cash crop, such as corn or wheat. Cash cropping has increased as artificial nitrogen fertilizers, derived from fossil fuels, have replaced crop rotation and manure as means of maintaining soil health.

A third technological spur to agricultural productivity was the development of *hybrid corn*. It "helped make corn one of the big three cereals, along with wheat and rice," Brown tells us.[13] Finally, wheat and rice fields have become more productive through the development of short-strawed varieties of those grains. These varieties are often called **high-yield varieties** (HYVs), because they

> increase the share of photosynthate, the product of photosynthesis, that goes into seed production. Originally domesticated wheats converted roughly 20 percent of photosynthate into seed, with the remainder used to sustain leaves, stem, and roots. . . . The more productive modern wheat varieties now convert . . . more than 50 percent of photosynthate into seed.[14]

Because it is the seed that people eat, this means more food from each field of wheat. The so-called **Green Revolution** stems from widespread adoption of HYV wheat and rice.

"When the last half of this century began," Brown concludes, "the average world grain yield per hectare was just over one ton—1.06, to be precise. By 1998, it had climbed to 2.73 tons per hectare."[15] This is certainly power over nature, but it does not seem malevolent. As world population continues to increase, climbing toward 9, 10, or 11 billion people, perhaps the lesson of twentieth-century agriculture contradicts the synergist thesis. Controlling nature in the human interest does not seem to harm humanity. Instead, it seems that companies like Archer Daniels Midland (ADM) are humanity's benefactors as they attempt to control nature and become "supermarket to the world."

Specialization Leads to Preoccupation with Money

Wendell Berry, author of the 1977 collection of essays *The Unsettling of America*, supports what I call synergism. He begins his attack on high-tech, power-over-nature agriculture by decrying the specialization that it requires. He writes, "the disease of the modern character is specialization." He acknowledges that from the social point of view its goals are good. "The aim is to see that the responsibilities of government, law, medicine, engineering, agriculture, education, etc., are given into the hands of the most skilled, best prepared people."[16] Specialization may also facilitate exploiting the earth maximally for human advantage. *Only specialists concentrating in narrow areas of inquiry can develop the most powerful technologies to serve humanity.*

There is a down side, however. Specialists do not think holistically. They are trained to concentrate on a narrow range of problems and develop solutions based on their expertise, ignoring all other considerations. This can be bad for people and the environment, Berry claims. He gives this example: "In 1973,

1,000 Kentucky dairies went out of business." United States grain sales overseas raised the price of cattle feed, and the importation of dairy products from abroad lowered the price farmers could get for milk. Berry writes: "An agricultural expert at the University of Kentucky, Dr. John Nicolai, was optimistic about this failure of 1,000 dairymen. . . . They were inefficient producers, he said, and they needed to be eliminated." Berry wonders about this:

> Did these dairymen have any value not subsumed under the heading of "efficiency?" And who benefited by their failure? Assuming that the benefit reached beyond the more "efficient" (that is, bigger) producers to lower the cost of milk to consumers, do we have any formula by which to determine how many consumer dollars are equal to the livelihood of one dairyman? Or is *any* degree of "efficiency" worth *any* cost?[17]

The problem is that in his specialized capacity, the agriculture expert thinks about only one thing, the "efficient," least-cost production of dairy products. Other considerations are out of his view because they are not part of his specialty. They are similar to what environmental economists call "externalities." They are external to the expert's calculations in the way that, as we saw in Chapter 1, costs associated with environmental degradation may be external to the financial calculations of a company that pollutes. So what is good from the specialist's point of view may be bad for society as a whole.

Another result of specialization is increasing dependence on commercial exchange with other people. When I specialize in one pursuit, such as teaching philosophy, I meet my various human needs—for food, housing, clothing, and so forth—through dependence on other people who specialize in providing these things. Because they, too, are specialists, they depend on others to meet most of their human needs. Each earns money from her specialty and gives money to other specialists to make a whole life possible. The result is that most people are insecure because they realize that their incompetence at providing life's necessities for themselves leaves them at the mercy of forces beyond their control. For example, as the year 2000 approached, people worried that they would lack food and fuel because computers had not originally been set up to recognize the new millennium. Berry imagines the average person this way:

> He does not know what he would do if he lost his job, if the economy failed, if the utility companies failed, if the police went on strike, if the truckers went on strike. . . . And for these anxieties, of course, he consults certified experts, who in turn consult certified experts about *their* anxieties. . . . The specialist system fails from a personal point of view because a person who can do only one thing can do virtually nothing for himself. In living in the world by his own will and skill, the stupidest peasant or tribesman is more competent than the most intelligent worker or technician or intellectual in a society of specialists.[18]

Because specialists depend on others who require money for their services, people in a specialized society tend to use money as the criterion by which they evaluate practices and policies. But thinking of human well being in strictly monetary terms is unrealistic, even in our specialized society, in which money is needed to live decently. Such thinking loses sight of how people flourish and what money is really for. The Beatles wrote: "Can't Buy Me Love." Nor can we buy personal accomplishments, such as the ability to play the piano, do a beautiful swan dive, or learn a foreign language. We cannot buy family ties. We can buy health care, but not good health, or rich people like Aristotle Onassis would never die of incurable diseases. In short, many of the things we value most cannot be bought with money, so focusing too much on money is unrealistic.

The same is true, Berry points out, with most human pursuits. Agriculture is the primary way that people gain food from the earth. It not only provides food, but can also foster good exercise, communal and family ties, a sense of accomplishment, a feeling of reciprocity with other life forms, a sense of rootedness in one's own corner of the earth, and commitment to sustaining the system for future generations. Money alone cannot measure, represent, or replace these values. Yet this is what prominent agricultural leaders advocate. Berry quotes former United States Secretary of Agriculture Earl Butz:

> . . . true agripower . . . generates agridollars through agricultural exports. . . . With additional income earned from exports U.S. farmers are able to purchase more household appliances, farm equipment, building supplies, and other capital and consumer goods. . . . Agridollars . . . [go] toward offsetting our petrodollar drain.[19]

Berry comments:

> "Agripower," it will be noted, is not measured by the fertility or health of the soil, or the health, wisdom, thrift, or stewardship of the farming community. It is measured by its ability to produce a marketable surplus, which "generates agridollars". . . . The income from this increased production, we are told, is spent by farmers not for soil maintenance or improvement, water conservation, or erosion control, but for . . . "household appliances . . . and other capital and consumer goods." The farmer does not prosper to become a better farmer, but to become a bigger spender.[20]

In sum, specialization harms people by making them dependent and insecure. It also encourages them to evaluate work and welfare in monetary terms, which impairs perception and appreciation of life's greatest gifts and treasures.

Fouling Our Own Nest

Specialization narrows people's vision and leads them to create dangerous environmental hazards. Earl Butz promoted specialization in agriculture because he believed it improved efficiency. Only specialists in large-scale operations can afford the most efficient high-tech equipment. He wrote: "Years ago, farm

operations were highly diversified, but today, farmers are concentrating on fewer and much larger crop or livestock enterprises."[21] Notice the "or," in "crop or livestock enterprises." Butz advocates farmers choosing between livestock and crop production. But then the same farm will not have both animals to generate manure and crops to use it, so farmers lose the advantage of using free manure as fertilizer. The result: Pollution happens.

Hog farming in the United States is increasingly dominated by giant enterprises that own large "mega hog farms." Pollution from animal waste threatens the health of nearby people and ecosystems. Attorney Jim Martin of the Environmental Defense Fund's Rocky Mountain office used the organization's newsletter to address the situation in Colorado:

> Industrial hog farming poses unprecedented and growing threats to our ground-water, air, soil, and ultimately our economy. Hog production is up almost 600% in Colorado since 1995, even as the number of farmers has declined dramatically. With factory farms producing the waste-equivalent of a city of as many as 250,000 people, we've got a huge environmental challenge.[22]

The newsletter points out in addition that "the factory farms, many directly above the Ogallala aquifer, threaten the lifeblood of Colorado's farm economy and the drinking water of its citizens."[23] Fortunately, according to the Environmental Defense Fund, Colorado voters passed Amendment 14 in the November 1998 election, which requires new hog farms to get permits and monitor water quality to prevent pollution.

Some residents in the neighboring state of Kansas live with hog pollution. *Time* magazine reported in November 1998 the plight of Julia Howell and her husband, who live near a mega hog farm in Kansas. It is owned by Seaboard Corporation:

> In a long barn that houses about 1,000 animals, the hogs spend their days jammed next to one another, eating constantly until they grow from about 55 lbs. to 250 lbs. They stand on slatted floors so their wastes drop into a trough below that is flushed periodically into a nearby cesspit. . . .

Julia Howell, 69, talks about her "40,000 neighbors" and explains why she seals the farmhouse windows, stuffs pillows into the chimney and seldom ventures outdoors without a face mask.

> It's the ever-present stench—the overpowering smell from Seaboard's 40,000 hogs closely confined in 44 metal buildings, where exhaust fans continuously pump out tons of pungent ammonia, mixed with tons of grain dust and fecal matter, scented with the noxious odor of hydrogen sulfide (a poisonous gas produced by decaying manure that smells like rotten eggs), all combined with another blend of aromas wafting from five cesspits each 25 ft. deep and the size of a football field. They are, in effect, open-air sewage ponds, and 75 ft. below lies the Ogallala aquifer, which provides drinking and irrigation water. . . .
>
>   The smell has forever altered the Howells' way of life. [Mrs. Howell reports:] "When the hog fumes come rolling in, you can't plan on anything. I haven't had people in for dinner [for two years] because I'd probably have to meet them out on the driveway with a mask for them to get to the house."[24]

Needless to say, the value of their property has plummeted.

Wendell Berry attributes this kind of situation to specializaton. Specialists do not live where they work, so they do not experience personally the environmental consequences of their business decisions. He commented in 1977:

> Once, . . . farmers . . . in Europe lived in their barns—and so were both at work and at home. Work and rest, work and pleasure, were continuous with each other, often not distinct from each other at all. Once, shopkeepers lived in, above, or behind their shops. Once, many people lived by "cottage industries"—home production. Once, households were producers and processors of food. . . . [25]

Now, however, people do not live where they work:

> They do not feel the effects of what they do. The people who make wars do not fight them. The people responsible for strip-mining, clear-cutting of forests, and other ruinations do not live where their senses will be offended or their homes or livelihoods or lives immediately threatened by the consequences. The people responsible for the various depredations of "agribusiness" do not live on farms.[26]

Corporate executives harm people in the name of progress because they do not have to live with the stench of "efficient" hog farms nor sell their daughters into prostitution when a forest is destroyed.

The current system is irrational. If hog farming were dispersed in small operations on diversified farms that raised livestock, grains, fruits, and vegetables, farmers could save money by fertilizing fields with animal waste instead of chemicals, thereby saving money and avoiding pollution. Instead, farmers incur debt and create pollution. Berry observes: "The genius of American farm experts is very well demonstrated here: they can take a solution and divide it neatly into two problems."[27]

Sustainability Problems

The good news that Lester Brown delivers about increased agricultural output in the twentieth century is tempered by the bad news that such gains cannot continue. Consider irrigation. Water is getting scarce. Brown writes:

> Water tables are falling on every continent—in the southern Great Plains of the United States, the southwestern United States, much of North Africa and the Middle East, most of India, and almost everywhere in China where the land is flat . . . For instance, . . . the water table under the north China plain is dropping an average of 1.5 meters, or roughly 5 feet, a year. . . . Underground water withdrawals in India are at least double the rate of aquifer recharge [and] water tables are falling 1–3 meters (3–10 feet) per year almost everywhere in India.[28]

In addition, "many major rivers run dry before they reach the sea," Brown notes:

> In the southwestern United States, the Colorado River rarely ever reaches the Gulf of California. . . . The Yellow River, the cradle of Chinese civilization, ran dry for the first time in China's 3,000-year history in 1972, failing to reach the sea for some 15 days. . . . Since 1985 [it] has run dry for part of each year. In 1997, it failed to reach the sea for seven months out of the year.[29]

Cropland, too, is needed to raise the grains on which most of the world's people depend for nutrition. However, it is shrinking. Brown writes:

> The world's grain harvested area increased from 587 million hectares in 1950 to the historical high of 732 million hectares in 1981. . . . Since then, however, the grain area has shrunk to 690 million hectares. . . . Heavy cropland losses during the next half-century are expected in countries such as India, where the construction of housing alone will claim a substantial area of cropland.[30]

Worldwatch research associate Gary Gardner points out: "China hopes to build 600 *new* cities by 2010, thus doubling the number it has now. Net losses [of cropland] in the United States between 1982 and 1992 totaled an area larger than the state of New Jersey."[31] Such losses continue with expansion of sub-urban housing, malls, and roads.

Cropland is lost also to environmental degradation caused by modern agri-culture. Irrigation tends to add salts to the soil. The land eventually becomes too salty for crops. Where drainage is poor, irrigation causes waterlogging, which deprives crops of the air they need in the soil. Many modern agricul-tural practices cause soil erosion as well. Gardner summarizes: "Between 1945 and 1990, erosion, salination, waterlogging, and other degradation eliminated from production an area equal to the cropland of two Canadas."[32] Such degra-dation continues, reducing cropland available for the future.

Artificial fertilizers are among the modern agricultural innovations respon-sible for increased productivity. But they reduce productivity in the long run when they replace manure, crop rotation, and other natural means of main-taining fertility. Gardner reports:

> The thin layer of earth we call topsoil is essential to land's fertility. Topsoil is a rich medium containing organic matter, minerals, nutrients, insects, microbes, worms and other elements needed to provide a nurturing environment for plants. While fertilizer offers a short-term fix to soil productivity, it replaces only the soil's nutrients, not the entire spectrum of elements that make up the soil community, all of which are needed for long-term health.[33]

Topsoil health is jeopardized also by insecticides and herbicides used in mod-ern agriculture to control insects and weeds. These chemicals kill not only the life forms that are their targets, but microbial life needed to maintain healthy soil.

Lester Brown reports, too, that productivity increases from the Green Revo-lution's high-yielding varieties (HYVs) cannot continue. These varieties of short-stemmed wheat and rice are high yielding because they put over 50 per-cent of the energy gathered from the sun into the seeds that people eat. Brown writes: "There is not much remaining potential for increase, since scientists es-timate that the absolute upper limit is 62 percent. Anything beyond that would begin to deprive the rest of the plant of the energy needed to function, thus re-ducing yields."[34] Yet hunger continues, Brown notes:

> The U. N. Food and Agriculture Organization . . . estimates that 841 million people living in developing countries suffer from basic protein-energy malnutrition—they do not get enough protein, enough calories, or enough of both. Infants and children lack the food they need to develop their full physical and mental potential.[35]

The Green Revolution

What should we do? Should we rely on specialized agricultural experts to de-vise additional miracles that overpower nature? They may extract food from the earth in ways only dimly imaginable at present, but, if the future is like the past, they will reduce biological diversity, jeopardize the world food supply, centralize power in fewer hands, and deprive poor people of their livelihoods. According to Vandana Shiva, physicist and director of the Research Foundation for Science, Technology and Natural Resource Policy in India, this is the legacy of the Green Revolution.

In 1970, Norman Borlaug received the Nobel Peace Prize for developing HYV wheat in Mexico in the 1950s. In the late 1960s, HYV wheat and rice became common in India. President Lyndon Johnson thought these "miracle seeds" held the key to food abundance for people in poor countries. So when India experienced food shortages due to a drought in 1966, Johnson "refused to commit food aid beyond one month in advance until an agreement to adopt the Green Revolution package was signed. . . ."[36] *Indian agriculture's use of the new seeds was initially considered successful. However, Shiva documents its ill effects on nature and on India, especially on its women and poor people.*

HYVs produce more of the desired cash crops of wheat and rice than other varieties, so experts who think narrowly consider them more productive. They produce more of the only things the experts care about. But HYVs require uniform, ideal conditions, such as lots of water, fertilizers, and pesticides. India, like many poor countries, has a water shortage due to insufficient rainfall. Under these conditions, HYVs require irrigation, usually from wells. Drawing extra water from wells for thirsty HYVs lowers the water table. We have noted already that water tables are dropping rapidly in India, especially in Green Revolution areas. So deeper wells must be dug. However, poor farmers cannot afford to dig deeper wells. Thus, when their wealthier neighbors lower the water table to irrigate HYVs, poorer farmers are put out of business.

The other requirements of HYVs have the same effect of disadvantaging the already poor, because required inputs—fertilizers, insecticides, herbicides, and seeds—all cost money. Traditional farming with non-miraculous seeds requires less money, primarily because farmers retain seeds from one harvest to plant the next year. HYV seeds, by contrast, are produced centrally by a seed company and must be bought each year.

The need to purchase seed is increased by the HYVs' susceptibility to disease and pests. Due to specialized thinking, HYVs are grown in **monocultures**, that is, fields in which only one crop is grown. This is the cash crop whose volume and value the experts want to maximize. But monocultures encourage the outbreak of dangerous pests. Given the uniformity and proximity of the pests' preferred food, they can quickly and easily devour one delicious plant after another without interruption. So they feed voraciously and multiply quickly. Because the plants are all the same, the insects or disease organisms that can eat and kill one plant, eat and kill them all. Diseases and pests therefore threaten the entire food supply when monocultures replace agricultural diversity.

This disease and pest problem increases the need for farmers to spend money. They must pay for insecticides and herbicides to keep the crop healthy. They must also pay for newer varieties of seed developed by seed companies to be resistant to insects or blight. Shiva quotes a textbook on HYVs: "The high-yielding varieties and hybrids have three to five years life in the field. Thereafter they become susceptible to the new races and biotypes of diseases and pests."[37] By contrast, "cropping systems based on diversity . . . have a built-in protection," Shiva writes:

> Indigenous varieties, or land races, are resistant to locally occurring pests and diseases. Even if certain diseases occur, some of the strains may be susceptible, while others will have the resistance to survive. Crop rotations also help in pest control. Since many pests are specific to particular plants, planting crops in different seasons and different years causes large reductions in pest populations.[38]

The specialized mentality that addresses one problem at a time and seeks uniform technological solutions to each one in turn does not blame modern agriculture for the pest problem. Instead, it assumes the problem to be eternal. And thank goodness we have experts today to help us! Shiva quotes a textbook on pest management:

> The war against pests is a continuing one that man must fight to ensure his survival. Pests (in particular insects) are our major competitors on earth and for the hundreds of thousands of years of our existence they have kept our numbers low and, on occasions, have threatened extinction. Throughout the ages man has lived at a bare subsistence level because of the onslaught of pests. . . . It is only in comparatively recent times that . . . we have . . . gained the upper hand over pests.[39]

This is baloney. As journalist Gregg Easterbrook points out in his 1995 book *A Moment on the Earth*, insecticide results have been poor even in the United States, where farmers spend huge sums on agricultural inputs:

> Department of Agriculture statistics show that in 1945 most corn in the United States was grown via rotation. Then using few pesticides, farmers saw annual 3.5 percent crop losses to insects. By 1992 most corn was grown without rotation but with lots of chemicals, and farmers saw an annual 12 percent crop loss to insects. . . . Obviously the higher rate of losses to insects suggests fewer chemicals and more rotation might be advised.[40]

Many monocultures of cash crops need herbicides as well as insecticides for normal growth. This is because they require large quantities of artificial fertilizers, and the fertilizers promote the growth of "weeds" as well as the desired crop. Isolating this problem from all others, experts develop and prescribe ever-stronger herbicides to fight the weeds. The herbicides must increase in strength because target plants evolve resistance. Geneticist Ricarda Steinbrecher gives this example from Australia:

> An Australian farmer in northern Victoria . . . recently discovered that ryegrass, the most common weed in Australia, on one of his fields was no longer affected

by Monsanto's herbicide, Roundup, after just 10 sprayings over 15 years. Researchers at Charles Sturt University in New South Wales showed that the ryegrass could tolerate nearly five times the recommended spraying dose.[41]

Again, poor farmers, especially the really poor farmers of the Third World, are at a disadvantage when increasing amounts of herbicide are needed. The system requires more inputs, that they lack money to purchase.

Herbicides associated with Green Revolution monocultures hurt many poor farmers in India also by eliminating useful plants that have little or no commercial value. In India, Shiva writes, one of these is bathua. It is:

An important leafy vegetable, with a very high nutritive value and rich in vitamin A, which grows as an associate of wheat. However, with intensive chemical fertilizer use, bathua becomes a major competitor of wheat and has been declared a "weed" that is killed with herbicides. . . . 40,000 children in India go blind each year for lack of vitamin A, and herbicides contribute to this tragedy by destroying the freely available sources of vitamin A.[42]

Herbicides kill other plants as well that women rely on for their livelihoods, Shiva reports: "Thousands of rural women who make their living by basket and mat making, with wild reeds and grasses, are . . . losing their livelihoods because the increased use of herbicides is killing the reeds and grasses.[43]

Biodiversity and Human Welfare

The problem for poor people is not just the Green Revolution. It is the expert mindset that fails to view situations holistically, and therefore misses the value of diversity. For example, modern forestry experts favor cash crops—tree species that can be grown for wood and sold for export. So they suggest cutting down forests of varied species composition and replacing them with tree monocultures. But this deprives poor people of the many free uses they traditionally make of forest plants. Shiva observes:

An important biomass output of trees that is never assessed by foresters who look for timber and wood is the yield of seeds and fruits. Fruit trees such as jack, jaman, mango, tamarind etc. have been important components of indigenous forms of social forestry as practiced over the centuries in India. . . . Other trees, such as, neem, pongamia and sal provide annual harvests of seeds which yield valuable non-edible oils. . . . The coconut, . . . besides providing fruits and oil, provides leaves used in thatching huts and supports the large coir industry. . . . [44]

John Tuxill, writing in State of the World 1999, gives these examples:

In northwest Ecuador, indigenous cultures that practice shifting agriculture use more than 900 plant species to meet their material, medicinal, and food needs;

halfway around the world, Dusun and Iban communities in the rainforests of central Borneo use a similar total of plants in their daily lives. . . . [45]

From the monetary perspective, these are unproductive uses because they generate no cash. Cutting down the forests to graze cattle for beef sold to McDonalds would increase the gross domestic product (GDP) of the countries involved. But this would not only reduce biodiversity, it would also deprive people of their livelihoods and contribute to the kind of desperate poverty that leads parents to kill infants or sell children for prostitution.

This is the general result of the Green Revolution and other attempts to help people of the Third World with economic development guided by experts who fail to think holistically and who equate progress with commerce. Environmental synergy is better. *Human beings thrive not by attempts to gain unlimited power over nature, but by working with nature. Much of that work takes place outside the cash economy, so GDP does not measure human well being. And much of that work succeeds by promoting biodiversity, so there is no real conflict between biodiversity and human flourishing.*

Many traditional Third World agricultural systems are synergistic. Berry recounts a study by Professor Stephen B. Bush, an anthropologist at the College of William and Mary, who studied the village of Uchucmarca in a valley in northern Peru. The valley is steep. People grow different crops at different elevations. Soil erosion is a problem on steep slopes, so the Peruvians keep their fields small, usually less than an acre, and surround them by a hedgerow. They ensure against food shortage due to crop failure partly by planting "several different fields of the same crop, hoping that if one field is destroyed, the others will survive."[46] Also, within extended families people exchange land, labor, and goods. They borrow from relatives in bad years. Berry notes:

> Against insects and diseases, the main weapon of the Andean peasants is genetic diversity: "Botanists estimate that there are well over 2,000 potato varieties in Peru alone. In single villages like Uchucmarca people identify some fifty varieties. . . ." Nearly all the methods of the Andean farmers are based upon the one principle of diversity.[47]

The Peruvians generate and maintain diversity on the margins of their fields. Professor Bush writes:

> New varieties are constantly being created through cross-pollination between cultivated, wild and semidomesticated (weedy) species. . . . These wild and semidomesticated species thrive in the hedgerows around fields, and birds and insects living there assist cross-pollination.[48]

Berry observes: "The farmer, in whose mind culture and agriculture are wedded, acts as both teacher-researcher and student, both extension agent and client." He finds this better than our reliance on specialized agricultural experts.

Bush points out: "One of the most important features of the local economy is that it is able to function as a largely nonmonetized economy. The average family in Uchucmarca needs less than $100 yearly." But this is not poverty, Bush writes:

> I calculate that with their "primitive" agriculture, the farmers of Uchucmarca pro-duce 2,700 calories and 80 grams of protein (vegetable) per capita per day. A very good diet and a well-fed population. The worst malnutrition occurs in cities where people must depend on "modern" agriculture.[49]

In contrast to this indigenous system, modern agriculture reduces diversity to promote the few varieties that yield the greatest cash crop. John Tuxill writes:

> In industrial countries, crop diversity has declined in concert with the steady com-mercialization and consolidation of agriculture this century: fewer family farmers, and fewer seed companies offering fewer varieties for sale, mean fewer crop vari-eties planted in fields or saved after harvest.[50] The proportion of varieties grown in the United States before 1904 but no longer present in either commercial agri-culture or any major seed storage facility ranges from 81 percent for tomatoes to over 90 percent for peas and cabbages. . . . China is estimated to have gone from growing 10,000 wheat varieties in 1949 to only 1,000 by the 1970s, while just 20 percent of the corn varieties cultivated in Mexico in the 1930s can still be found there. . . . [51]

This is dangerous for all of us, Tuxill contends. Diversity among agricultural varieties is necessary for food security. He gives this example:

> When grassy stunt virus began attacking high-yielding Asian rices in the 1970s, breeders located genetic resistance to the disease in only a single collection of one population of a wild rice species in Uttar Pradesh, India—and that population has never been found again since. Conserving and reinvigorating biodiversity in agri-cultural landscapes remains essential for achieving global food security.[52]

Another of Tuxill's examples relates directly to Andean farmers. In the 1840s, a fungus

> colonized and devastated the genetically uniform potato fields of Ireland, trigger-ing the infamous famine that claimed more than a million lives. The disease has been controlled this century largely with fungicides, but in the mid-1980s farmers began reporting outbreaks of fungicide-resistant blight. These new virulent strains have cut global potato harvests in the 1990s by 15 percent, a $3.25-billion yield loss; in some regions, such as the highlands of Tanzania, losses to blight have ap-proached 100 percent. Fortunately, scientists at the International Potato Center in Lima, Peru, have located genetic resistance to the new blight strains in the gene pools of traditional Andean potato cultivars and their wild relatives, and now see hope for reviving the global potato crop.[53]

So don't throw away that old potato! (Not really. Just checking your attention span.)

Biodiversity serves people not only by securing the food supply, but also by promising medical benefits, Tuxill notes:

> One quarter of the prescription drugs marketed in North America and Europe contain active ingredients derived from plants. Plant-based drugs are part of standard medical procedures for treating heart conditions, childhood leukemia, lymphatic cancer, glaucoma, and many other serious illnesses. . . . Major pharmaceutical companies and institutions such as the U.S. National Cancer Institute implement plant screening programs as a primary means of identifying new drugs.[54]

Tuxill writes of reductions in biodiversity due to modern agriculture:

> We are conducting an unprecedented experiment with the security and stability of our food supply, our health care systems, and the ecological infrastructure upon which both rest. To obtain the results we desire, we must conserve and protect the plant biodiversity that remains with us, and manage our use of natural systems in ways that restore biodiversity to landscapes worldwide.[55]

Tuxill is not alone in his thinking. The National Research Council (NRC), a prestigious group that advises the U.S. government on important scientific and technical matters, issued a report in 1989 entitled *Alternative Agriculture*. Their summary includes the following about American agriculture:

> Alternative systems are often diversified. Diversified systems, which tend to be more stable and resilient, reduce financial risk and provide a hedge against drought, pest infestation, or other natural factors limiting production. . . . [56] Wider adoption of proven alternative systems would result in . . . benefits to farmers and environmental gains for the nation.[57]

However, the report notes:

> As a whole, federal policies work against environmentally benign practices and the adoption of alternative agricultural systems, particularly those involving crop rotations, certain soil conservation practices, reductions in pesticide use, and increased use of biological and cultural means of pest control. These policies have generally made a plentiful food supply a higher priority than protection of the resource base.[58]

Anthropocentrism or Synergism?

According to the NRC, protecting the resource base would serve people better in the long run. Similarly, John Tuxill maintains that protecting biodiversity is in the human interest, and Vandana Shiva objects to the Green Revolution because it harms poor people. Perhaps, then, their views are simply anthropocentric. They advocate policies that maximize benefits to human beings. They may differ from other anthropocentrists only in their perception that people benefit more from the protection of biodiversity than from modern agriculture that reduces diversity in favor of monocultures.

On the other hand, they could be synergists who believe that we promote biodiversity only when we consider it good in itself. Only then will we, out of respect for nature, limit the power we wield. And only then will we maintain biodiversity adequately to derive maximum human benefits from it. This is the synergist paradox. But why should we believe it? Why can't people use scientific evidence to justify valuing and conserving biodiversity merely for the sake of humanity?

Synergists point first to the record. Anthropocentrically inspired actions continue to shrink rainforests, extinguish species, and reduce biodiversity, in spite of all that we know. Anthropocentric rationales for biodiversity are so far largely ineffective.

Second, it is hard to see how anthropocentric projects can incorporate the holistic perspective that environmental protection and long-term human well being require. Modern attempts to gain the most from nature use technologies created by specialized experts. The division of labor among experts makes holistic thinking unlikely.

Third, people are too ignorant to control nature in the human interest. Aldo Leopold, who is often considered a nonanthropocentrist because he appears to advocate caring about nature for itself, makes this point. (He may really be the first synergist, although that term was not used in his time). Leopold wrote:

> In short, a land ethic changes the role of *Homo sapiens* from conqueror of the land-community to plain member and citizen of it. It implies respect for his fellow-members, and also respect for the community as such.
>
> In human history, we have learned (I hope) that the conqueror role is eventually self-defeating. Why? Because it is implicit in such a role that the conqueror knows, *ex cathedra*, just what makes the community clock tick, and just what and who is valuable, and what is worthless, in community life. It always turns out that he knows neither, and this is why his conquests eventually defeat themselves.[59]

Arrogance concerning nature, often associated with anthropocentrism, blinds us to limitations and interferes with appropriate actions in the human interest.

Finally, arrogance concerning nature sometimes combines with arrogance concerning human beings to engender a **master mentality**. Would-be masters identify themselves as the true human beings and assign lesser status to women and subjugated people. Masters associate lower-status people with nature, which is to be conquered, so they tend to ignore much human suffering. If we value nature for itself, we are less likely to follow leaders of this sort and, therefore, less likely to harm fellow human beings. The next chapter discusses feminist critiques of the master mentality.

Judgment Calls

- In 1999, the Illinois State Legislature passed hog farm regulations that include new safety standards. But an editorial in Springfield's *The State Journal Register* noted:

  Rural residents . . . are still batting zero in two areas: regulation of odors from livestock facilities and local control over where the very largest facilities can locate. . . . For all other types of businesses, county board members—accountable to voters—have a final say on where an operation might fit with planned zoning. Increasingly, it makes less and less sense why modern livestock facilities, making significant demands on local water, roads and power usage, should not receive the same scrutiny as other businesses.[60]

  Livestock producers claim that they are trying to bring the best product possible to the American consumer at prices that meet foreign competition. Locally imposed land use restrictions jeopardize attainment of these goals, they say. What do you think?

- Wendell Berry quotes an article in the October 1974 issue of *American Farmer*. The subject is the "dream farm" of 2076 A.D.

  Livestock will be housed (and products processed) in a 15-story 150′ × 200′ building. . . . At capacity, the high-rise building will house 2,500 feeder cattle, 600 cow-calf units, 500 dairy cattle, 2,500 sheep, 6,750 finishing hogs, space for 150 sows and litters, 1,000 turkeys, and 15,000 chickens. . . . Crops will be grown year-round under plastic covers that provide precise climate control in three circular fields, each a mile in diameter. . . . Only a half-inch of water will be needed for each crop. That's because evapotranspiration from growing plants would be recycled under massive, permanent plastic enclosures. . . . If tillage is needed, it will be done by electromagnetic waves. . . . Recycling human, animal and crop wastes will be a key to the operation of the farm. . . . [61]

  What hopes and concerns do you have about this vision of the future?

- Here is an idea that comes from genetic engineering. The Associated Press reported in December 1998 the development of low-phytate corn. "Phytate is a plant compound that carries phosphorous but is difficult for some animals . . . to digest." Undigested phosphorous makes animal manure polluting and malodorous, so the new corn could address the problem of animal waste. "Rodney Weinzierl, executive director of the Illinois Corn Growers Association . . . said . . . that such corn could become an industry standard," the AP reports.[62] What do you think about this development regarding its effect on people living near hog farms, and on biodiversity and ecosystems? (We consider other examples of genetic engineering in Chapter 10.)

CHAPTER 9

Ecofeminism and Environmental Justice

From Feminism to Ecofeminism

In 1872, the United States Supreme Court denied Mrs. Myra Bradwell the constitutional right to practice law. Mrs. Bradwell lived in Chicago and had, according to the court, "been found to possess the requisite qualifications,"[1] but the State of Illinois had denied her a license on the sole ground of gender. The U.S. Supreme Court sided with the state. Concurring with the majority opinion, Mr. Justice Bradley wrote:

> Man is, or should be, woman's protector and defender. The natural and proper timidity and delicacy which belongs to the female sex evidently unfits it for many of the occupations of civil life. The constitution of the family organization, which is founded in the divine ordinance, as well as in the nature of things, indicates the domestic sphere as that which properly belongs to the domain and functions of womanhood. . . . The paramount destiny and mission of woman are to fulfil the noble and benign offices of wife and mother.[2]

In 1931, the Supreme Court of Massachusetts had to decide if the commonwealth's refusal to allow women to serve on juries violated a statute granting the right of jury service to all "persons." They decided: "The intent of the Legislature must have been, in using the word "person" in statutes concerning jurors and jury lists, to confine its meaning to men."[3] The good news: The court says in some contexts women are people.

In 1993, sociologist Steven Goldberg argued in *Why Men Rule: A Theory of Male Dominance*: "Men are more logical than women."[4] He claimed there has never been a woman of genius in disciplines that emphasize abstract reasoning, such as "mathematics, philosophy, legal theory, . . . composing music [and] chess." "Genius" refers to "a level of aptitude demonstrated by only twenty or thirty people in the history of each of the intellectual, scientific and artistic areas discussed."[5] For example, "As of January 1993, Judith Polgar, the highest-rated woman [chess] player *of all time*, tied for 53rd in the world ranking of *currently active* players. (Chess ratings are objective magnitudes derived by averaging recent results.)"[6] Goldberg claimed also that intelligence tests given to thousands of people "find a great difference in male and female aptitudes for this sort of abstraction,"[7] and noted promising research into physiological differences between the sexes to explain these results.

Thousands of miles away in Egypt, 10-year-old Nagla Hamza suffered female genital mutilation (FGM) by having her clitoris amputated. Why? Worldwatch Institute staff researcher Toni Nelson writes: "Most explanations relate in some way to male interest in controlling women's emotions and sexual behavior. One of the most common explanations is the need to lessen desire so women will preserve their virginity until marriage." In short, "FGM is meant to reinforce the power men have over women."[8]

Feminists, although they differ among themselves on many matters, generally oppose these and other manifestations and justifications of **patriarchy**, the rule of men over women. They advocate women having power over their own destinies. They want equal respect and opportunity for women.

But how does this relate to the environment and to power over nature? It might seem that as people gain power over nature, women and men both gain power, especially if gender equality is achieved. However, citing historical and contemporary examples, *some feminists claim that the exploitation of nature led by Western countries tends to harm many people. It tends to aggravate the already untoward effects of patriarchy, the power of men over women, in poorer countries. It also increases the oppression of many subordinated groups of human beings in both the developed and the developing world. Thinkers with these views are called* **ecofeminists**.

By why would exploiting nature tend to increase the oppression of women and other subordinated people? Ecofeminists point to the **master mentality** in Western thought, which associates many human beings with nature as something to be controlled. According to this mentality, certain men are superior to everyone else due to greater reasoning ability. These men should rule the world. Women, poor workers, indigenous people, racial minorities, and other humans, along with animals and ecosystems, are inferior because they lack reason or cannot reason well. Superior men should direct and mold their inferiors. The ancient Greek philosopher Aristotle defended slavery on this basis more than 2,300 years ago:

> It is clear that the rule of the soul over the body, and of the mind and the rational element over the passionate, is natural and expedient, whereas the equality of the two or the rule of the inferior is always hurtful. The same hold good for animals in relation to men; for tame animals have a better nature than wild, and all tame animals are better off when they are ruled by man; for then they are preserved. Again, the male is by nature superior, and the female inferior; and the one rules, and the other is ruled; this principle of necessity extends to all mankind. Where then there is [among men] such a difference as that between soul and body, or between men and animals, . . . the lower sort are by nature slaves, and it is better for them as for all inferiors that they should be under the rule of a master.[9]

Philosopher Karen Warren analyzes the master mentality, dividing it into three components. The first is **dualism**. Reality is divided into two mutually exclusive groups, such as men vs. women, human vs. animal, and master vs. slave. Second, the two groups are not accorded equal value. Instead, there is "value-hierarchical thinking, i.e., 'up-down' thinking which places higher value, status, or prestige on what is 'up' rather than on what is 'down.' "[10] Humanity, men, and masters are "up," whereas animals, women, and slaves are "down." Third, what is down should serve the needs and desires of what is up.

Patriarchy is rule by men with the master mentality. The Supreme Court's Justice Bradley believed that men make better lawyers than women. "The paramount destiny and mission of woman are to fulfil the noble and benign offices of wife and mother."[11] The administration of law requires "decision and firmness which are presumed to predominate in the sterner sex."[12] The judge no doubt thought this division of labor good for both sexes, but he left it to men alone to decide what is best.

Confidence in the superior male's ability to determine the right place for everyone and everything is part of the master mentality. Thus, men in Egypt prescribe FGM for women, and Steven Goldberg suggests that women concentrate on activities in which they excel, such as those requiring acute psychological perception.

Because people with the master mentality do not value nature for itself, they are anthropocentrists. They differ from other anthropocentrists, however, in their association of many human beings with denigrated nature. *Under patriarchy, which persists in our culture, certain masterful men believe that they should control the destinies of inferior beings, which include women, indigenous people, and many other humans, along with animals and ecosystems. Due largely to selfishness, prejudice, and misunderstanding, such masters tend to serve themselves at the expense of other people as well as nature.*

Ecofeminists support environmental synergism. They claim that much human oppression results from combining anthropocentrism's lack of respect for nature with patriarchy's association of many human beings with nature. Ecofeminists say that respect for nature generally promotes human welfare, and genuine respect for all human beings tends to protect nature. This is synergism.

Philosopher Val Plumwood finds five interrelated aspects of subordination in the master mentality: backgrounding, radical exclusion (or hyperseparation), incorporation (or relational definition), instrumentalism, and homogenization (or stereotyping).[13]

1) **Backgrounding**—What is "down" in the "up-down" classification is kept in the background and denied credit for its contributions.

2) **Radical exclusion** (or **hyperseparation**)—"Downs" are considered so different in potential from whatever is "up" that they cannot qualify for most positions of power and prestige.

3) **Incorporation** (or **relational definition**)—The identity of a "down" is tied to the identity of something that is "up."

4) **Instrumentalism**—A "down's" role in relation to something that is "up" is determined by the needs of whatever is "up."

5) **Homogenization** (or **stereotyping**)—"Downs" lack the individuality of "ups."

The present chapter shows that the master mentality in Western thought treats women, colonized people, and nature as "down" in these five ways. In this context, the masters' anthropocentrism often harms people along with nature.

Women as Subordinate

Consider *backgrounding*. We saw in the last chapter that in a world of specialists, people tend to evaluate things in monetary terms because they use money to buy almost everything they need. For example, my mother used to ask my father: "If you're so smart why aren't we rich?" She was evaluating my father's intelligence in monetary terms.

Such monetary evaluations undervalue the accomplishments and contributions of women because women do most of the unpaid housecleaning, cooking, and childcare. When "work" is defined to include only wage-earning labor, "women's work" disappears as work. This is what Plumwood calls backgrounding. What women do is kept in the background, whereas what men do is noticed, appreciated, and rewarded.

Because many women in the United States and other First World countries work outside the home for money, financially based backgrounding is worse in some Third World countries. More work there is unpaid and, like here, women do most of it. Worldwatch associate Jodi Jacobson gave this example in *State of the World 1993*:

> In India, conventional measures based on wage labor showed that only 34 percent of Indian females are in the labor force, as opposed to 63 percent of males. But a survey of work patterns by occupational categories including household production and domestic work revealed that 75 percent of females over age five are working, compared with 64 percent of males.[14]

Jacobson points out that this situation is common. Women work more than men, but are not given credit for their greater productivity because much of their work is unpaid. Philosopher James Sterba cites figures from the United Nations: "Although women do two-thirds of the world's work, they receive only 10 percent of the salaries. . . . Men own 99 percent of all the property in the world, and women only 1 percent."[15] Measuring social contributions in monetary terms perpetuates the backgrounding of women.

Such backgrounding helps to justify male dominance and disregard for women's needs. When women's contributions are unacknowledged, men can deny dependence on women and lose respect for them. The results can be lethal. Jacobson reports:

> In India, for instance, studies show that in many states sons consistently receive more and better food and health care than their sisters. . . . Harvard economist and philosopher Amartya Sen calculates that 100 million women in the developing world are "missing," having died prematurely from the consequences of such gender bias.[16]

In our society and many others, women are backgrounded in several ways, even when they work outside the home for money. Accounts of history, for example, emphasize the exploits of predominantly male soldiers, politicians, and scientists. Our understanding of education backgrounds women as well, Plumwood writes: "The immensely important physical, personal and social skills the mother teaches the child are merely the background to *real* learning, which is defined as the part of the male sphere of reason and knowledge."[17] We see backgrounding in employment, too. Most secretaries and nurses are women providing background services to more prominent executives and doctors who get public credit and higher salaries. This is one reason why in 1995, women in the United States earned on average only 72 cents for every dollar earned by men.[18]

In addition to backgrounding, women in many parts of the world still suffer from what Plumwood calls *"radical exclusion"* or *"hyperseparation."* Women are thought to be so different from men that common properties go unnoticed and women are excluded from the male, public sphere. In some Muslim societies, such as Saudi Arabia, women cannot vote or get drivers' licenses. Women were denied the vote in the United States until 1920, and were virtually excluded from many professions and occupations in law, politics, engineering, and the military until quite recently.

America is addressing, but has not entirely overcome, lingering effects of past radical exclusions. In many fields women still find placement more difficult than men. For example, there are only a handful of women in the 100-member U.S. Senate. One reason is that people still associate men more than women with traits needed in these fields. Like sociologist Steven Goldberg, they associate men more than women with impartial reason, and women more than men with emotional attachments. We want reason, not emotion, to guide our lawyers, judges, politicians, engineers, and soldiers.

Women are subordinate to men through what Plumwood calls *"incorporation"* or *"relational definition."* My wife gets mail addressed to "Mrs. Peter Wenz." This suggests that her identity is determined by her relationship to me.

It is not just a matter of whose name is used. When people initially meet a man they never ask him first, "What does your wife do for a living?" It is common, however, for people, women as well as men, to inquire of a woman what her husband does for a living before they ask what she does. The husband's work is considered important enough to define both him and his wife socially, but the wife's work is not.

❧   ❧   ❧

For Plumwood, *"instrumentalism"* applied to women means that they should concentrate on serving their partners. Women, much more than men, are called "helpmates." Women's magazines, much more than men's, concentrate on how to please the opposite sex and attain intimacy. Women spend more time and money on beauty care. I bet the vast majority of people reading this book who shave their legs, shave under their arms, and wear make-up are female. Women have largely internalized the view that they carry more of the burden of attracting and keeping a partner. The tradition that men propose marriage persists, so women must attract men.

Women still often judge themselves and other women by their attractiveness to men. In an address to a women's society in 1938, author Dorothy Sayers contrasts the roles of men and women by asking men to imagine what their lives would be like if roles were reversed and men were judged mostly by their attractiveness to women and by their ability to be stereotypically masculine. Although two generations have passed, and many feminist victories won, her satire still speaks to us:

> Probably no man has ever troubled to imagine how strange his life would appear to himself if it were unrelentingly assessed in terms of his maleness; if everything he wore, said, or did had to be justified by reference to female approval. . . . If he were vexed by continual advice about how to add a rough male touch to his typing, how to be learned without losing his masculine appeal, how to combine chemical research with seduction, how to play bridge without incurring the suspicion of impotence.
>
> If he gave an interview to a reporter, or performed any unusual exploit, he would find it recorded in such terms as these: Professor Bract, although a distinguished botanist, is not in any way an unmanly man. He has, in fact, a wife and seven children. Tall and burly, the hands with which he handles his delicate specimens are as gnarled and powerful as those of a Canadian lumberjack. . . .
>
> He would be edified by . . . irritable correspondence about men who . . . think about nothing but women, pretend an unnatural indifference to women, exploit their sex to get jobs, lower the tone of the office by their sexless appearance, and generally fail to please a public opinion which demands the incompatible.[19]

❧   ❧   ❧

In the sexist era that Western societies have to some extent transcended, greater uniformity was imposed on women than men. Good women could be housewives, nurses, teachers, or secretaries, whereas men could be everything else— a thousand different occupations. Plumwood calls this *"homogenization"* or *"stereotyping."*

When women's potentials were considered to be less than men's, and more uniform, women seemed to have less individuality than men. This helped to justify other features of sexist thinking. For example, it made backgrounding easier. Women's contributions could be more easily ignored, and male dependence on women more easily denied, because women were less specialized. Half of humanity was confined to half a dozen occupations, so what one woman could do, many others could do as well. There were fewer "indispensable women" than "indispensable men" at work.

Homogenization also reinforced incorporation or relational definition. If women are mostly like one another, then we must look to a women's male associate to determine her individuality. Homogenization reinforced instrumentalism as well. If women lack distinctive individuality, then they are not particularly interesting in themselves, so they derive worth by supporting a man's projects. Finally, homogenization validated radical exclusion. We know that some men are suited to the military and others the law. If women are relatively homogeneous, they are suited only to occupations that almost any woman can do, such as helping someone else who is an expert.

Even today, women's appearance and femininity are more standardized than male characteristics. Susan Faludi reports in her 1991 bestseller *Backlash* that women are much more likely than men to have plastic surgery to improve their looks. Because the ideal woman has large breasts, breast implants retain their popularity in spite of health concerns. Faludi discusses the medical practice of Dr. Robert Harvey, "the Breast Man of San Franscisco." He employed a female counselor to interview prospective breast implant patients. Faludi explains: "She had hers expanded from 34B to 34C a few years ago. She told the women, 'I can say that personally I feel more confident. I feel more like a woman.' "[20] Men, in contrast, can feel like men with less ideal looks. Dr. Harvey had never undergone plastic surgery himself, saying, "I guess my nose isn't great, but it just doesn't bother me."[21] Men can feel O.K. as men with more idiosyncratic features.

Indigenous People as Subordinate

Colonization typically included the subordination of native populations. The same five aspects of subordination by masters can be seen in the masters' treatment of indigenous people as in their treatment of women.

According to Dee Brown's *Bury My Heart at Wounded Knee*, when Christopher Columbus arrived on the island that we call San Salvador, the Taino people on the island "generously presented Columbus and his men with gifts and

"She's had so much done she's not even biodegradable."

treated them with honor."[22] This was their custom. But Columbus believed these people should be "made to work, sow and do all that is necessary and to adopt our ways." Accordingly, "The Spaniards looted and burned villages; they kidnapped hundreds of men, women, and children and shipped them to Europe to be sold as slaves. . . . Whole tribes were destroyed, hundreds of thousands of people in less than a decade after Columbus set foot on the beach of San Salvador, October 12, 1492."[23]

What could justify such treatment? The distinguished Spanish scholar Juan Gines de Sepulveda argued in 1547 that the Spanish could rightfully take the land and enslave natives because the Spanish were superior people:

> The man rules over the woman, the adult over the child, the father over his children. . . . This same relationship exists among men, there being some who by nature are masters and others who by nature are slaves. . . . Those who are dimwitted and mentally lazy, although they may be physically strong enough to fulfill all the necessary tasks, are by nature slaves.[24]

Sepulveda cites "the absence of gluttony and lasciviousness among the Spaniards" as a sign of their superiority. There were many signs of native inferiority: "These people possess neither science nor even an alphabet, nor do they preserve any monuments of their history except for some obscure and vague reminiscences depicted in certain paintings, nor do they have written laws, but barbarous institutions and customs."[25] Sepulveda concludes:

> It will always be just and in conformity with natural law that such people submit to the rule of more cultured and humane princes and nations. Thanks to their virtues and the practical wisdom of their laws, the latter can destroy barbarism and educate these [inferior] people to a more humane and virtuous life. And if the latter reject such rule, it can be imposed upon them by force of arms. Such a war will be just according to natural law.[26]

We see here the aspects of subordination that Plumwood highlights. There is hyperseparation—Indians and Spaniards are fundamentally different. There is instrumentalism—Indians should serve as slaves. There is homogenization—no individual Indians are considered different from the others so as to merit freedom. There is backgrounding—Indian accomplishments are ignored. In fact, rather than acknowledge that Spaniards benefit from the services of their Indian slaves, Sepulveda argues that the Indians receive most of the benefits:

> What is more appropriate and beneficial for these barbarians than to become subject to the rule of those whose wisdom, virtue, and religion have converted them from barbarians into civilized men (insofar as they are capable of becoming so), from being torpid and licentious to becoming upright and moral, from being impious servants of the Devil to becoming believers in the true God?[27]

Finally, there is incorporation—these lucky Indians are going to join Spanish civilization.

This is a common pattern. The British who settled North America also disregarded Native American claims to land and life. How could the British resettle (or just kill) Native Americans except on the assumption that the two groups were fundamentally different? This is hyperseparation. Attempts to enslave them are evidence of instrumentalism. The idea that the only good Indian is a dead Indian bespeaks homogenization—all Indians are uniformly bad. The forced enclosure of Indians on reservations until they adopt European ways, as well as attempts to teach them English and convert them to Christianity, are signs of incorporation.

Finally, Indian accomplishments are backgrounded. The seventeenth-century philosopher John Locke, for example, claimed that Indians failed to improve their land with their labor. They "are rich in land; . . . yet, for want of improving it by labour, have not one hundredth part of the conveniences we enjoy. . . ."[28] Locke apparently appreciated neither the Indian way of life nor such Indian accomplishments as the domestication of corn. In short, he thought that Europeans had nothing to learn from Indians.

British colonists treated Aboriginal Australians like this, too. Anthropologist Deborah Bird Rose calls attention to a statement in the South Australian Parliamentary Papers that during the gold rush of 1886, when Europeans were pouring across to the west, Aborigines were 'shot like crows'. . . . In the first three or four decades, which Aboriginal accounts identify as the time of the most intense killing, two language-identified groups—Karangpurru and Bilinara—were virtually annihilated.[29]

Of course, some Europeans were also killed. Rose reflects:

European death tolls loom large in the European Australian imagination. Aboriginal deaths are rarely counted; black deaths, like black lives, are most frequently acknowledged only to be consigned to the backdrop of historical pageantry. While European settlers, police, and travelers shot or poisoned nameless and countless blacks, . . . the silence with which whites have surrounded their actions, and their depictions of Aborigines as anonymous victims, has facilitated the outback myth of an empty, lonely, heartless country.[30]

When their power and culture were subdued, Aborigines proved useful to European settlers, who relied at first more on Aboriginal women than men. "During the early years women worked as trackers and guides, and as stockmen, riding, mustering, cooking." But they also supplied sex, as "there were few European women on the frontier." Rose quotes nineteenth-century Constable Wilshire: "Men would not remain so many years in a country like this if there were no women, and perhaps the Almighty meant them for use as He has placed them wherever the pioneers go."[31] God provides.

I leave to the reader relating this treatment of Aborigines to Plumwood's five aspects of subordination. The official status of Aborigines changed only recently:

Until 1967 Aborigines were not counted in official censuses, [and] were not allowed to vote or to travel away from the stations without permission. [They were] not allowed to marry Europeans without official permission, to manage their own money (if they had any), to raise their own children if those children were part-Aboriginal, to purchase alcohol, and subject to numerous other onerous restrictions. Aboriginal people's lives until 1967 were massively controlled.[32]

Nature as Subordinate

The same five aspects of subordination can be seen in early modern scientific attempts to harness nature for human benefit. The seventeenth century scientific revolution promoted the idea that nature is entirely mechanical. Rene Descartes, as we have seen, believed that the human soul or mind is spiritual, but that everything else on Earth is mechanical. Because we alone have minds, we alone have thought, reason, perception, joy, and pain. This is hyperseparation. Everything on Earth is entirely matter except for one, and this one's spirituality separates it radically from all others.

Plumwood's concept of homogenization comes in here too. All matter is essentially the same, because with sufficient knowledge people will be able to transform any kind of matter into any other kind. Each spiritual being, by contrast, is unique.

The dualism of matter and spirit is hierarchical as well. Spirit is better than matter, and the lower should serve the higher. All material beings exist on Earth to serve the one spiritual being—man. This is instrumentalism. Seventeenth-century jurist and philosopher Francis Bacon exhorted people to "endeavor to establish and extend the power and dominion of the human race itself over the universe [so] the human race [can] recover that right over nature which belongs to it by divine bequest."[33] One example of this attitude is vivisection, the use of animals in painful scientific explorations. Descartes' belief that nature is only a machine helped to justify such experiments.

The mechanical view justifies degrading nature also by considering it passive, rather than active. In the dualism "active vs. passive," "active" is "up," and "passive" is "down." In the mechanical view, nature must be passive because it is just machinery. Philosophers of the period assumed that matter is in motion only because God set it in motion at the time of creation. Left to itself, matter is inert. Self-moving people are superior to nature, so they have the right to conquer nature and make it serve their purposes. Historian Carolyn Merchant writes:

> The philosophy that the world was a vast machine made of inert particles in ceaseless motion appeared at a time when new and more efficient kinds of machinery were enabling the acceleration of trade and commerce. The development of transportation equipment, navigational techniques, [and] the building of roads and canals . . . could be realized by mining the earth for gold, copper, iron, and coal [and] by cutting its forests for fuel for the refining of ores. . . . The death of the world soul and the removal of nature's spirits helped to support increasing environmental destruction by removing any scruples that might be associated with the view that nature was a living organism.[34]

Writing in this period, John Locke backgrounded nature by ignoring its contributions to human welfare. He wrote:

> Labour . . . puts the difference of value on everything. . . . Of the products of the earth useful to the life of man, nine-tenths are the effects of labour. Nay, if we will rightly estimate things as they come to our use . . . what in them is purely owing to nature and what to labour—we shall find that in most of them ninety-nine hundredths are wholly to be put on account of labour. . . . Nature and the earth furnished only the almost worthless materials. . . . [35]

This backgrounding of nature supports its incorporation, that is, its assimilation to a superior who dominates it. Because nature is almost worthless until people mix their labor with it, unowned nature becomes the property of whoever improves it with labor. Locke writes: "As much as a man tills, plants, improves, cultivates, and can use the products of, so much is his property."[36] Once it is his property, he can do what he wants with it, so long as he does not jeopardize the interests of other people. Worthless nature is properly the handmaid or slave (we get to choose between sexist and racist metaphors) of masterful human beings, who are expected to manage it for human welfare.

Women and Nature

We have seen so far that women, colonized people, and nature are all subject to the five aspects of subordination identified by Plumwood as parts of the master mentality. Where nature is concerned, subordination includes failure to value nature for itself. Similar subordination of many human beings can lead psychologically to similar attitudes toward these people. Masters may fail, sometimes unwittingly, to value these people for themselves, because the up-down structure of their thinking about such people is the same as their thinking about subordinated nature. In the end, masters often feel equally free to control people and nature to realize their master plans. This is one reason why anthropocentrism does not result in maximum rewards for human beings. Efforts to use nature maximally in the human interest increase the influence of the master mentality, and actions guided by that mentality endanger many people.

The master mentality also includes specific "factual" claims that denigrate women. For example, according to some prominent religions (discussed in the next chapter), God, representing the highest good, is predominantly masculine, and only men can attain the highest levels of priesthood. Some "factual" claims denigrate women by associating them with nature. Sexists like Aristotle, for example, associate women with emotion, which people share with animals, and men with reason. When a woman is correct on some matter, she is said to have "women's intuition," which many consider more like animal instinct than human reason. Women are also considered naturally passive, like inert matter which, under the mechanical view, people are free to exploit. Superior men are more active. (Boy's dolls are called "action figures.")

Women are also associated symbolically with passive nature ripe for exploitation. For example, they often appear animal-like in advertisements. Susan Faludi recalls ads for Guess jeans "with cowgirls sucking on their fingers. They gazed into the camera with startled and vulnerable doe eyes, Bambis before the hunters."[37]

Women are often associated with animals, where meat eating is concerned. Women are sometimes referred to crudely as "pieces of meat." Feminist writer and activist Carol Adams points out in *The Sexual Politics of Meat* that "the bondage equipment of pornography—chains, cattle prods, nooses, dog collars, and ropes—suggest the control of animals. Thus, when women are victims of violence, the treatment of animals is recalled."[38] Adams notes the reverse, too. Breeders of animals for meat often artificially inseminate females after attaching them to what is called a "rape rack."[39]

Men's descriptions of their activities sometimes suggest that violence against women and animals can be substituted for one another. Adams writes:

In defense of the "Bunny Bop"—in which rabbits are killed by clubs, feet, stones and so on—sponsored by a North Carolina American Legion post, one organizer explained, "What would all these rabbit hunters be doing if they weren't letting off all this steam? They'd be drinking and beating their wives."[40]

Advertisements often associate butchering animals with violence against women. Adams offers these examples:

A woman is shown being ground up in a meat grinder as *Hustler* magazine proclaims: "Last All Meat Issue." Women's buttocks are stamped as "Choice Cuts" on an album cover entitled "Choice Cuts (Pure Food and Drug Act)". . . . Frank Perdue plays with images of sexual butchering in a poster encouraging chicken consumption: "Are you a breast man or a leg man?"

A popular poster in the butcher shops of the Haymarket section of Boston depicted a woman's body sectioned off as though she were a slaughtered animal, with her separate body parts identified.[41]

These are isolated examples. But they show that in our culture, there is a greater association of women than men with animals subjected to violence. When (white) men are associated with animals in our culture, they are usually lions, or studs, or cocks who rule the roost. Sexist non-white cultures, too, associate men more than women with animals that dominate.

Ecofeminists note that within the ruling Western culture, the master mentality tends to treat all subordinated groups alike. We have seen that women, Australian Aborigines, and American Indians are similarly backgrounded, hyperseparated, incorporated, instrumentalized, and homogenized. And just as women are associated with nature that is subject to control or aggression, so are members of other subordinated groups, whether male or female. For example, the phrase "wild Indian" suggests that Indians resemble wild animals that should be controlled or subdued. Racists today still refer disparagingly to African Americans as "jungle bunnies" and "coons" (short for raccoons). In sum, whatever would-be masters disdain and want to control is like nature, because basic to the master mentality is belief that nature should serve the masters' interests.

The association of women with nature is special in part because it was prominent at the dawn of the modern era, when the idea of progress through controlling nature for human welfare became popular. Francis Bacon, writing early in the seventeenth century, pioneered this view. He always referred to nature as female and as properly subjugated. He wrote in *The Masculine Birth of Time* (even his title was macho): "I am come in very truth leading to you nature with all her children to bind her to your service and make her your slave."[42] Historian Carolyn Merchant discusses some of Bacon's other works:

Much of the imagery he used in delineating his new scientific objectives and methods derives from the courtroom, and, because it treats nature as a female to be tortured through mechanical inventions, strongly suggests the interrogations of the witch trials and the mechanical devices used to torture witches.[43]

Bacon wrote: "For you have but to follow and as it were hound nature in her wanderings, and you will be able when you like to lead and drive her . . . for the further disclosing of the secrets of nature."[44] The result is that "she is put in constraint, molded, and made as it were new by art and the hand of man; as in things artificial."[45] "Human knowledge and power meet as one."[46] This power over nature is modeled on power over women. Nature's secrets are in her "womb." Bacon concludes: "There is therefore much ground for hoping that there are still laid up in the womb of nature many secrets of excellent use having no affinity or parallelism with anything that is now known. . . . [47]

Subordination of Minorities Encourages Pollution

Nature suffers due to disrespect for subordinated groups of human beings. In the United States, for example, poor people and members of some racial minority groups lack the prestige, economic resources, and political power to protect their communities from pollution-generating activities. The power of commercial interests to degrade the environment and jeopardize human health is relatively unchecked. Valuing natural ecosystems for themselves could restrain polluters and protect vulnerable people, just as respect for these people could restrain pollution and protect nature. Thus, pollution issues display synergy between respect for people and for nature.

Several studies indicate that in the United States, poor people and people of color are more likely than others to live in areas of health-impairing pollution. Consider Altgelt Gardens, a poor and predominantly African-American community of 10,000 on Chicago's far South Side. *The National Law Journal* reported in 1992 that a 36-square-mile area where steel factories and other heavy industries had helped people alter nature in the human interest is now horribly polluted. There are "50 abandoned dumps of toxic factory waste. . . . So potent are the discarded mixtures that stunned Illinois inspectors aborted one expedition in a dumping lagoon when their boat began to disintegrate."[48]

The area continues to receive toxic wastes because waste disposal is its major industry. The *Journal* writes: "An EPA study showed that 28 million pounds of toxic chemicals annually pour into South Side air, elevating the risk of cancer 100 to 1,000 times—but the study wasn't designed to trace the actual effects on health."[49]

Chicago's South Side is typical in its concentration of toxic pollution near people of color. Sociologist Robert Bullard reported in 1994:

In the Los Angeles air basin, 71 percent of African Americans and 50 percent of Latinos live in areas with the most polluted air, whereas only 34 percent of whites live in highly polluted areas. The "dirtiest" zip code in California (90058) is sand-wiched between South-Central Los Angeles and East Los Angeles. The one-square-mile area is saturated with abandoned toxic waste sites, freeways, smokestacks, and wastewater pipes from polluting industries. Some eighteen industrial firms in 1989 discharged more than 33 million pounds of waste chemicals into the environment.[50]

Indigenous people experience extraordinary pollution as well. When most of us think about nuclear power dangers, we imagine power plant explosions, as at Chernobyl. But mining uranium brings radioactive materials to the earth's surface, pulverizes it into powder, and leaves 85 percent of its radioactivity on the ground near the mine. Only the richest 1 percent of the material (which contains 15 percent of the radioactivity) is hauled away to be processed as nu-clear fuel. Mostly Native Americans worked in and continue to live near this hazardous by-product of the nuclear power industry. Dick Russell reported in *The Amicus Journal* in 1989: "2 million tons of radioactive uranium tailings have been dumped on Native American lands; reproductive organ cancer among Navajo teenagers is seventeen times the national average."[51]

This is the pattern worldwide. Uranium mining takes place mostly on lands that indigenous people occupy. This is true in Russia, Australia, Canada, China, and India.[52] Why? Is it just some cosmic coincidence that native peoples live on top of uranium deposits? Not likely. No one looks for uranium deposits un-der Manhattan, Moscow, or Beverly Hills. Instead, exploration concentrates on areas that could be exploited if uranium is found. This is land occupied by poor, subordinated people.[53]

The same reasoning explains the findings of a 1987 study conducted by the United Church of Christ. Russell reports:

> This study found that more than 15 million of the nation's 26 million blacks, and over 8 million of the 15 million Hispanics, live in communities with one or more un-controlled toxic-waste sites. The nation's largest hazardous-waste landfill, receiving toxics from forty-five states, is in Emelle, Alabama, which is 78.9 percent black.[54]

It is largely a matter of economics, explains Naikang Tsao in a 1992 article in *New York University Law Review*:

> In 1984, for example, a consulting firm advised the California Waste Management Board that it would meet less community resistance to the placement of garbage incinerators if it targeted low income rather than middle-class neighborhoods. The firm's report stated that "all socioeconomic groupings tend to resent the nearby siting of major facilities, but the middle and upper-socioeconomic strata possess better resources to effectuate their opposition."[55]

In short, exploiting nature in the human interest creates hazards for human beings. These hazards are most often foisted on poor people and members of minority groups because such people lack political clout. The result is unjust because wealthier people who benefit most from power over nature suffer least from negative by-products, whereas those who suffer most benefit least. Many benefits are too expensive for them.

This injustice to people fosters continued degradation of nature. *When people with the most clout are relatively unaffected by environmental pollution, and lack sufficient respect for all people, they pay little attention to pollution and allow those with the master mentality more freedom to degrade nature in the (supposed) human interest. So one way to protect the earth is to respect all people and treat them with justice. Environmental justice supports environmental protection.*

Subordination of Women, Environmental Degradation, and Overpopulation

Ecofeminists connect women's subordination to nature's degradation. Nature is degraded when people with the master mentality subordinate women, and women are harmed when attempts to control nature in the (supposed) human interest fail to respect biodiversity as valuable in itself.

Reprinted from Petricic. Cartoonists and Writers Syndicate.

The connection between women's subordination and nature's degradation is in one respect puzzling. The worst degradation of nature accompanies technologies developed and deployed initially in the industrialized world. These include most toxic chemicals, industrial agricultural methods, pollution-generating forms of transportation, and so forth. Yet the worst sexism seems to exist in the non-industrialized world. This includes selective infanticide of infant girls, female genital mutilation, and prohibitions on women owning property. So it seems that nature is degraded most by societies that subordinate women least. This casts doubt on the connection between subordinating women and degrading nature.[56]

A solution to this puzzle lies in the relationship between First World technologies and Third World sexism. We saw in the last chapter that specialization is part of the First World strategy to get the most for people from nature. But technical specialization requires that people trade with other specialists to get all they need and want, and this favors monetary transactions. In many Third World cultures, however, women's access to money and private property is severely limited. Even more than in our culture, in which women still do most of the unpaid housework and childcare, women in many Third World cultures are restricted to subsistence activities, such as growing crops, obtaining water, cooking, cleaning, and manufacturing household items for their families.

Jodi Jacobson, senior researcher at the Worldwatch Institute writes: "In much of sub-Saharan Africa, for instance, both men and women plant crops, but they do so with different goals. Men grow cash crops. . . . Women, by contrast, use their land primarily for subsistence crops to feed their families."[57] So when First World cash crop-oriented technologies are exported to the Third World, as in the Green Revolution or forestry for wood pulp alone, women are the major losers. These technologies favor monocultures of the relatively few crops that can be grown economically for cash in the area. From the cash crop perspective, all other plants are weeds. Killing these weeds reduces biodiversity and deprives many Third World women of the materials they need to perform culturally specific duties, for which they seldom receive monetary compensation.

Greater respect for women's culturally specific needs would restrict the spread of cash-oriented agriculture and promote biodiversity. Jacobson notes that women

> have played a leading role in maintaining crop diversity. In sub-Saharan Africa, for instance, women cultivate as many as 120 different plants in the spaces alongside men's cash crops. . . . Women in subsistence economies also are active managers of forest resources, and traditionally play the leading role in their conservation. Forests provide a multitude of products to households. They are, for example, a major source of fuel.[58]

Forests also provide medicines that many women use for their families. "Tribal women in India, for example, know of medicinal uses for some 300 forest species," Jacobson reports.[59] Tribal men are less knowledgeable. "A survey in

Sierra Leone found that women could name 31 products they gathered or made from nearby trees and bushes, while men could name only eight."[60]

In sum, the master mentality jeopardizes biodiversity by emphasizing cash crops and subordinating women, women's knowledge, and women's concerns. Men do not know or appreciate what they are sacrificing for cash. Respect for women, by contrast, would restrict such environmental degradation. By the same token, respect for biodiversity as good in itself would also restrict degradation, and benefit women the most. Thus, respect for women and protection of nature are mutually supporting when First World technologies are offered to Third World countries.

Another aspect of this synergy concerns population increases. *The degradation of nature gives women incentives to have additional children, and increases in human population strain ecosystems.* First, where men wield great power over women and do not have to do most of the day-to-day work caring for families, they do not have the same reasons as women to limit procreation.

But there is more. Partha Dasgupta, Professor of Economics at the University of Cambridge, contends in a 1995 article in *Scientific American* that, living with poverty and environmental degradation, women often desire more children. Dasgupta writes: "Parental demand for children rather than an unmet need for contraceptives in large measure explains reproductive behavior in developing countries."[61] Here is the reason:

> Third World countries are, for the most part, subsistence economies. The rural folk eke out a living by using products gleaned directly from plants and animals. Much labor is needed. . . . In semiarid and arid regions the water supply may not even be nearby. Nor is fuelwood at hand when the forests recede. . . . Members of a household may have to spend as much as five to six hours a day fetching water and collecting fodder and wood.
>
> Children, then, are needed as workers even when their parents are in their prime. . . . In parts of India, children between 10 and 15 years have been observed to work as much as one and a half times the number of hours that adult males do. By the age of six, children in rural India tend domestic animals and care for younger siblings, fetch water and collect firewood, dung and fodder.[62]

Jodi Jacobson notes also that "for women in Sudan, the average time required to collect a week's worth of fuelwood has quadrupled since the seventies."[63] Such women "are less likely to see the utility of having fewer children, even though population densities in the little land left for subsistence families are rapidly increasing."[64]

Distances to fuel and water increase when men dominate and favor cash crops over the biodiversity that women depend on to perform traditional roles. Thus, many policies designed to help poor people generate cash are counterproductive:

> This is the population trap: many of the policies and programs carried out in the name of development actually increase women's dependence on children as a

source of status and security. Moreover, environmental degradation triggered by misguided government policies is itself causing rapid population growth, in part as a result of women's economically rational response to increasing demands on their time caused by resource scarcity.[65]

In sum, *commercial development to alleviate poverty often degrades resources and encourages overpopulation, which further degrades resources, encourages increased fertility, and exacerbates poverty. One way out of this cycle is greater attention to women's roles, knowledge, perspectives, and needs. Respecting women and protecting nature are closely related. This is a central thesis of ecofeminism and synergism.*

Subordination of Native Peoples Reduces Biodiversity

Subordinating indigenous people also begets environmental degradation because such people, like women in many parts of the world, know, use, and appreciate biodiversity more than masters with commercial plans.

Commercial development has for centuries deprived native peoples of their land and their self-sufficient ways of life, creating tension between economic growth and indigenous cultural continuity. When native people gain all they want and need from the land without buying anything from outsiders, they are poor customers for commercial wares. When they use their land exclusively for their own needs, they deprive world trade of raw materials. So economic growth has come at the expense of native peoples. Worldwatch researcher Alan Durning quotes World Bank anthropologist Sheldon Davis:

> The creation of a . . . global economy . . . has meant the pillage of native peoples' lands, labor and resources and their enforced acculturation and spiritual conquest. Each cycle of global economic expansion—the search for gold and spices in the sixteenth century, the fur trade and sugar estate economics of the seventeenth and eighteenth centuries, the rise of the great coffee, copra and . . . tropical fruit plantations in the late nineteenth and early twentieth centuries, the modern search for petroleum, strategic minerals, and tropical hardwoods—was based upon the exploitation of natural resources or primary commodities and led to the displacement of indigenous peoples and the undermining of traditional cultures.[66]

This process coheres with the master mentality, which encourages power over nature through technological development. Such development requires specialists who tend to use money as their criterion of value and believe that economic growth automatically helps people. Specialists do not consider the destruction of cultural and biological diversity that has no monetary value. The result is harm to people and nature.

Today's indigenous (or native) peoples tend for the most part, and in the long run, to be the best guardians of biodiversity because they typically want to preserve traditional ways of life that depend on diversity in the areas where they live and hope to remain. Durning writes:

Native Americans are uncommonly careful with nature. Partly, it's a matter of . . . self-interest. Any people who know its children and grandchildren will live exactly where it does is likely to take a long view. Alaskan Eskimo Marie Adams explained her people's opposition to lucrative offshore oil drilling in their subsistence fishing and whaling area. "Oil and gas [are] only going to be here for 40 or 50 years. The resource we depend on, we want to be sure it's there when the oil's gone. . . ." Colombian anthropologist Martin von Hildebrand notes, "The Indians often tell me that the difference between a colonist [a non-Indian settler] and an Indian is that the colonist wants to leave money for his children and that the Indians want to leave forests for their children."[67]

Vandana Shiva, a physicist and environmental activist from India, comments on the greater importance of forest biodiversity to native than to commercial people:

> Most local knowledge systems have been based on the life-supporting capacities of tropical forests, not on their commercial timber value. These systems fall in the blind spot of a forestry perspective that is based exclusively on the commercial exploitation of forests. . . . Dominant forestry science has no place for the knowledge of the Hanunoo in the Philippines who divide plants into 1,600 categories, of which trained botanists can distinguish only 1,200. The knowledge base of the cropping systems based on 160 crops of the Lua tribe in Thailand is not counted as knowledge either by dominant forestry, which sees only commercial wood, or by dominant agriculture, which sees only chemically intensive agriculture.[68]

In sum, *native peoples are the best guardians of forests and other biologically diverse ecosystems because they know about and use them.* Worldwatch's Alan Durning writes: "Intact indigenous communities and little-disturbed ecosystems overlap with singular regularity, from the coastal swamps of South America to the shifting sands of the Sahara, from the ice floes of the circumpolar north to the coral reefs of the South Pacific." He quotes Geodisio Castillo, a Kuna Indian from Panama: "Where there are forests there are indigenous people, and where there are indigenous people there are forests."[69]

We jeopardize all human beings when we pursue projects guided by a commercially oriented master mentality that unjustly deprives indigenous people of their lands and cultures. Durning points out that when left undisturbed, native

> territories . . . provide important ecological services: they regulate hydrological cycles, maintain local and global climatic stability, and harbor a wealth of biological and genetic diversity. . . . Supporting indigenous survival is an objective necessity, even for those callous to the justice of the cause. As a practical matter, the world's dominant cultures cannot sustain the earth's ecological health—a requisite of human advancement—without the aid of the world's endangered cultures. Biological diversity is inextricably linked to cultural diversity.[70]

The "up-down" thinking of the master mentality ignores the knowledge of native people because, lacking money and modern technology, they are "down." Both the people and the biodiversity on which we all depend are *back-grounded*. Cultures are destroyed so that people and their resources can be *incorporated* into commercial culture where they can be *instruments* of economic growth. Durning notes the resulting simultaneous losses of cultural and biological diversity:

> Human cultures are disappearing at unprecedented rates. Worldwide, the loss of cultural diversity is keeping pace with the global loss of biological diversity. Anthropologist Jason Clay of Cultural Survival in Cambridge, Massachusetts, writes, "There have been more . . . extinctions of tribal peoples in this century than in any other in history." Brazil alone lost 87 tribes in the first half of the century. One third of North American languages and two thirds of Australian languages have disappeared since 1800—the overwhelming share of them since 1900.[71]

The best way to preserve the environment is to preserve native people, to learn from their knowledge and subsistence ways of life, and to develop something of their religious reverence for nature. Margaret Knox reported in *Sierra* in 1993 that religious attitudes pervade Native American discussions of the environment:

> Much of what mainstream environmentalists hold vital to their own battles—all the habitat maps and groundwater charts . . . plays only an incidental role in the reservation environmental politics. Indians speak otherwise, in terms outsiders would call religious, although they themselves say it isn't a question of religion as much as a question of "the way." Either you know all life to be sacred and intertwined, or you don't.[72]

Knox interviewed Gerald Clifford, an Oglala Lakota in South Dakota, where "despite their desperate financial needs, the Lakota are refusing a $300-million cash settlement from the government to relinquish their claim" to the Black Hills. Clifford said: "In Indian country you can talk all this dumbfounding talk about money. But then someone brings up that you're Lakota and the earth is sacred, and that ends the meeting."[73]

It is common for indigenous societies to maintain such an attitude toward the earth. John Tuxill reported in *State of the World 1999*: "Indigenous societies worldwide have traditionally protected prominent landscape features like sacred sites and ceremonial centers. In parts of West Africa, sacred groves hold some of the last remaining populations of important medicinal plants."[74]

Vandana Shiva notes that rural peasants also have religious as well as subsistence reasons for protecting biodiversity:

> At the social level, the values of biodiversity in different cultural contexts need to be recognised. Sacred groves, sacred seeds, sacred species have been cultural means for treating biodiversity as inviolable, and present us with the best examples of conservation.[75]

The next chapter explores religious sources of environmental values.

Judgment Calls

- Gary LaPlante is a member of the Dene Nation in Saskatchewan, Canada, and Communications Coordinator of Indigenous Survival International. He complained at an international meeting of environmentalists in 1992:

  The Animal Rights Movement . . . with their indiscriminate attacks on the fur trade . . . have had devastating negative impacts on our . . . indigenous communities in Canada. . . . We have had through our treaties with Canada as . . . recognition of aboriginal rights, some protection about our right to harvest as we have for centuries. . . . [But] it is not necessarily satisfying because of the decimation of basically the economic viability of carrying out these traditional activities such as fur harvesting. It's left our people and a lot of our communities virtually dependent on welfare from the state. . . . So, basically, what it comes down to is a loss of culture and a loss of use of indigenous languages.[76]

  What is your response to supporting indigenous people through purchase of leather and fur from their hunting? How do we balance animal rights and cultural survival?

- Many sports teams have names that refer to Native Americans, such as "Red Skins," "Indians," and "Braves." Some Native Americans criticize this practice, but most fans like the names and claim they mean no disrespect. What is the real issue?

- Monsanto Corporation plans to reduce pollution from herbicides through use of its newly developed line of crop varieties that resist applications of its popular herbicide Roundup. Roundup can then be sprayed directly on these cash crops to kill surrounding weeds. This makes spraying herbicides before weeds sprout (pre-emergent herbicides) unnecessary, and pre-emergents cause the worst pollution. What do you think? What more information would you want before deciding whether or not this is a positive development, all things considered?

- In 1999, the United States and the European Union threatened a trade war over beef. Much U.S. beef is grown with the aid of hormones produced by genetically engineered microorganisms. Many Europeans want to exclude hormone-treated beef from the European market as unsafe, but the U.S. government claims it is safe, and that Europeans are just trying to avoid foreign competition. How can we have free and fair world trade if countries can exclude products on the basis of fears that may not be justified? The World Trade Organization sided with the U.S. What do you think?

CHAPTER 10

Religion and Nature

Should People "Play God"?

On February 23, 1997, Ian Wilmut and his colleagues announced in the journal *Nature* that they had successfully cloned a sheep, whom they named Dolly. They started with a female's egg, or ovum, which contains only one-half the genes of a normal sheep. The other half comes in ordinary reproduction from a male's sperm. The researchers took the nucleus out of the ovum and replaced it with the nucleus of an ordinary sheep cell, which contains (almost) the full complement of the sheep's genes. The ovum then developed as though it had been fertilized normally, except that its genes were those of only one parent. The new sheep was a clone of that one parent. Should we do this with human beings?

Not yet, all agree, because it is still risky. Ethicist Dan Brock notes in an article commissioned by the National Bioethics Advisory Commission, "It took 276 failures by Wilmut and his colleagues to produce Dolly, their one success. . . ."[1] But what if the technique is perfected and made safe? Then should we clone human beings?

Brock recounts several arguments pro and con. Some reasons for cloning human beings are these: (1) Cloning could be used by couples who are infertile; (2) Some couples risk transmitting a serious genetic disease to their offspring because one member carries harmful genes. Cloning would enable them to reproduce safely with genes of the other member; (3) A cloned twin would be an ideal donor of bone marrow or other tissue that an individual may need to treat medical problems; (4) "Human cloning would enable individuals to clone someone who had special meaning to them, such as a child who had died"[2]; and (5) "Human cloning would enable the duplication of individuals of great talent, genius, [or] character . . . like Mozart, Einstein, Gandhi, and Schweitzer."[3]

Some arguments given by Brock on the other side are: (1) Human cloning would produce psychological distress in the cloned "twin" due to comparisons between him or her and the already known life history of the older "twin"; (2) "Human cloning would lessen the worth of individuals and diminish respect for human life"[4]; (3) "Human cloning might be used by commercial interests for financial gain. . . . One can imagine commercial interests offering genetically certified and guaranteed embryos for sale, perhaps offering a catalogue of different embryos cloned from individuals with a variety of talents, capacities, and other desirable properties"[5]; and (4) "Human cloning used on a very widespread basis could have a disastrous effect on the human gene pool by reducing genetic diversity and our capacity to adapt to new conditions."[6]

There are religious concerns as well. What is the proper role of people on Earth? The Bible says in Genesis 1:27 that "God created man in his own image . . . male and female. . . ."[7] What does this tell us about our rights and responsibilities? Does it mean that we have the right to rule the earth as God rules the universe? In that case cloning might be part of what God has in mind for people, because it gives people more power over, and responsibility for, human destiny.

On the other hand, the second chapter of Genesis has the story of Adam and Eve eating forbidden fruit. The serpent promises that by eating the fruit Adam and Eve will "be as gods, knowing good and evil." God punishes the couple for their offense. Many readers conclude that God does not want people to be godlike in knowledge and power. Perhaps cloning human beings, or even sheep, steps over the bounds.

Cloning critic Leon Kass wrote in a 1997 article in *The New Republic*:

> Human cloning would . . . represent a giant step toward turning begetting into making, procreation into manufacture. . . . Human nature becomes merely the last part of nature to succumb to the technological project, which turns all of nature into raw materials at human disposal. . . . [8]

Kass objects to the arrogance of people "who think they know who deserves to be cloned or which genotype any child-to-be should be thrilled to receive; the Frankensteinian hubris to create human life and increasingly to control its destiny; man playing God."[9]

Although he does not use the term, Kass is objecting to the master mentality, which, we saw in the last chapter, endangers both people and nature. *Some Christians adopt the master mentality and draw support for their views from the story of creation. Other Christians interpret the Bible differently.* This chapter looks generally at relationships between environmentalism and religion. It focuses on some views of biblically based Christianity because of their importance in Western industrial countries.

The Master Interpretation of Christianity

The **master interpretation** of Christianity receives support from the creation story in Genesis 1:26–28. God had created all creatures except human beings:

> And God said, "Let us make man in our image, after our likeness. They shall rule the fish of the sea, the birds of the sky, the cattle, the whole earth, and all the creep-

ing things that creep on earth." And God created man in His image . . . male and female. . . . God blessed them and God said to them, "Be fruitful and increase, fill the earth and master it; and rule the fish of the sea, the birds of the sky, and all the living things that creep on earth."[10]

Environmental historian Roderick Nash sees support for the master mentality here:

Hebrew linguists have analyzed Genesis 1:28 and found two operative verbs: *kabash*, translated as "subdue," and *radah*, rendered as "have dominion over" or "rule." Throughout the Old Testament *kabash* and *radah* are used to signify a violent assault or crushing. The image is that of a conqueror placing his foot on the neck of a defeated enemy, exerting absolute domination. Both Hebraic words are also used to identify the process of enslavement. It followed that the Christian tradition could understand Genesis 1:28 as a divine commandment to conquer every part of nature and make it humankind's slave.[11]

Lynn White, Jr. set off a firestorm of theological controversy in 1967 with an article in *Science* that accused Christianity of inspiring environmental degradation. He wrote in "The Historical Roots of Our Ecological Crisis" that Christianity is less earth friendly than the ancient religions it replaced:

In Antiquity every tree, every spring, every stream, every hill had its own . . . guardian spirit. . . . Before one cut a tree, mined a mountain, or dammed a brook, it was important to placate the spirit in charge of that particular situation, and to keep it placated. By destroying pagan animism, Christianity made it possible to exploit nature in a mood of indifference to the feelings of natural objects.[12]

White adds later in the same article:

To a Christian a tree can be no more than a physical fact. The whole concept of the sacred grove is alien to Christianity and to the ethos of the West. For nearly two millennia Christian missionaries have been chopping down sacred groves, which are idolatrous because they assume spirit in nature.[13]

In short, *people are permitted to master and enslave nature because it is not sacred.*
According to David Kinsley, Professor of Religious Studies at McMaster University, some people think that Christian emphasis on salvation devalues nature. Christians believe that God created people with free will to live an idyllic existence in the Garden of Eden. However, when Adam and Eve disobeyed God by eating fruit from the forbidden tree, they were cast out of the garden. They had fallen from God's grace. Jesus can save people from this fallen condition. Kinsley writes:

In this drama, human ethics and morality are central, as are certain historical events, such as the exodus from Egypt, the migration to the promised land, . . . and the coming of Jesus. . . . In this story, the relationship between human beings and nature is not important. . . . Offensive human action is almost invariably understood in the context of human-to-human or human-to-divine affairs.[14]

Also, Kinsley tells us, the early Christian theologian Origen (185–254) made salvation

primarily an ascent from the material to the spiritual. . . . It is absolutely clear in Origen that the material creation is not humankind's home. That home is in heaven, where matter has no place. . . . The material world, according to Origen, is created primarily by God as a kind of purgatory where fallen human beings are educated through trials and tribulations to return to the realm of pure spirit from which they have fallen."[15]

Worse than being unimportant, then, the material world, including the earth and all nonhuman species, is like a prison that humanity must learn to escape.

Western Christianity later replaced hostility toward nature with an instrumentalist attitude. We saw in the last chapter that Francis Bacon (1561–1626) claimed the technological mastery of nature to be a God-given right of humanity.

The master interpretation of the Bible was used also to interpret the story of Noah as justifying whites enslaving blacks. Historian Winthrop Jordan explains:

The original story . . . was that after the Flood, Ham had looked upon his father's nakedness as Noah lay drunk in his tent, but the other two sons, Shem and Japheth, had covered their father without looking upon him; when Noah awoke he cursed Canaan, son of Ham, saying that he would be a "servant of servants" unto his brothers.[16]

This story seems initially to explain why some people are slaves. They are slaves because they suffer from the curse laid on their ancestor Canaan. It may be unfair that Canaan and all his progeny should suffer for Ham's mistake, but that is the Bible's story.

But why are slaves black? If we take the story of the flood seriously, all human races are descended from Noah's sons. We know that some people are black, so they must be descended from one of Noah's sons. Winthrop Jordan notes, "the term *Ham* originally connoted both 'dark' and 'hot,'" so a son of Ham was assumed to be the ancestor of all black people. But why Canaan, rather than one of his brothers? Canaan was cursed. Some seventeenth-century theologians assumed that "blackness could scarcely be anything *but* a curse," Jordan writes, so Canaan was considered the ancestor of all black Africans.[17]

The great English Jurist Sir Edward Coke (1552–1634) used the Noah story to justify enslaving these black people: "This is assured, That Bondage or Servitude was first inflicted for dishonouring of Parents: For Cham the Father of Canaan . . . seeing the Nakedness of his Father Noah, and shewing it in Deri-

sion to his Brethren, was therefore punished in his Son Canaan with
Bondage."[18]

The master mentality, we saw in the last chapter, associates subordinated
groups with nature, so it is no surprise that slaves were considered less than
human. "So much was slavery a complete loss of liberty," Jordan adds, "that
it seemed to Englishmen somehow akin to loss of humanity. No theme was
more persistent than the claim that to treat a man as a slave was to treat him
as a beast."[19] People who thought the Bible endorses slavery thought on these
grounds that it implies blacks are beasts.

The biblical story of creation was later interpreted also to imply the bestiality
of blacks. The first book of Genesis describes people being made on the last of
the six days of creation. Historian George Fredrickson recounts the views of nineteenth-century Louisiana physician and pro-slavery writer Samuel A. Cartwright.
In 1860, Cartwright argued that "the Negro was actually referred to in the Bible
as a separately created and inferior creature . . . created before Adam and Eve
and . . . included among the 'living creatures' over which Adam was given dominion. . . . These pre-Adamite Negroes . . . were also the inhabitants of the Land
of Nod with whom Cain intermarried."[20] Blacks are beasts, on this interpretation, because they were created on the fifth day, before human beings.

Also in 1860, Jefferson Davis, who later became president of the Confeder-
ate States during the Civil War, combined the ideas of blacks as beasts and as
descended from cursed Canaan to argue in Congress against public education
for blacks in the District of Columbia:

> When Cain, for the commission of the first great crime, was driven from the face
> of Adam, no longer . . . fit . . . to exercise dominion over the earth, he found in the
> Land of Nod those to whom his crime degraded him to an equality; and when the
> low and vulgar son of Noah, who laughed at his father's exposure, sunk by de-
> basing himself and his lineage by connection with an inferior race of men, he
> doomed his descendants to perpetual slavery.[21]

*In sum, on these interpretations, the Bible approves of white people enslaving blacks.
In keeping with the master mentality, subordinated people (enslaved blacks) are associated in the masters' minds with nature (beasts), and the only purpose for subordinated people or nature is to serve masterful (white) human beings.*

*On such evidence as this, many people think the Christian message is anti-envi-
ronmental because it combines the master mentality with contempt for nature. They
claim that religious environmentalism must find non-Christian bases.*

Hermeneutics and the Constitution

*However, Christianity, like other religious traditions, is subject to different interpre-
tations.* **Hermeneutics** *is the study of interpretation that arose initially to help people interpret the Bible. Suitably (re-)interpreted, Christianity may be nature friendly.*

But biblical reinterpretation poses a problem. Many Christians believe the Bible records God's deeds and demands and tells us how to live our lives. Reinterpretation, these Christians think, leads to confusion and moral relativism, because it substitutes human judgment for God's revelations about right and wrong.

This view is often called **religious fundamentalism**. It is a version of **foundationalism**, the view that our knowledge should rest on firm foundations that no reasonable person would question. Fundamentalists think the Bible provides such firm foundations. Some philosophers have sought these foundations in mathematics, others in direct sense perception. In all these cases, *foundationalists seek knowledge that does not change with time and is immune to changing interpretations. Using these foundations, people can seek further knowledge without fear that their original assumptions are faulty.*

A full examination of foundationalism is beyond the scope of this book, which discusses only the religious version—fundamentalism.

Several years ago, the campus Christian Student Fellowship posted a notice around the university where I teach inviting anyone interested to come and talk about the Bible. It promised there would be no pressure, because they would let the Bible speak for itself. They implied that the Bible's meaning is plain enough, at least in parts, to give directions for life without potentially divergent interpretations.

I do not doubt the sincerity of the people who posted that notice, but I do doubt that any document as complex as the Bible can really speak for itself and give guidance without divergent interpretations. To see this, consider another document of importance in the United States—the Constitution. Where the Constitution is concerned, foundationalists call themselves "originalists." In the opinion of former judge Robert Bork, as explained in his 1990 book *The Tempting of America*, the Constitution means now and forever whatever it meant to the people who ratified it. He calls this "original understanding." It is supposed to provide firm foundations for constitutional interpretation the way literal readings of the Bible are supposed to give proper religious understanding.

Bork is reasonable enough to admit exceptions to his own rule. For example, the Fourth Amendment to the Constitution guarantees freedom from unreasonable searches and seizures. This was originally understood to protect the privacy of people in their homes. But what was originally understood about wiretapping telephones when this amendment was ratified in 1791? Obviously nothing, because telephones had not yet been invented. Does this mean the Fourth Amendment allows wiretapping? This would make people more vulnerable in their homes to government spying than may have been intended by those who ratified the amendment. So Bork endorses looking at the general principle that ratifiers were attempting to establish, and then interpreting the Constitution to maintain that principle under altered circumstances.

In this case, technology altered the circumstances. In other cases, changes in society and morality require new interpretations. Consider the 1892 Supreme

Court case *Church of the Holy Trinity v. United States.* The underlying issue was the legality at that time of the church paying its new pastor to immigrate to the United States. This seemed to violate an 1885 statute designed to reduce the influx of immigrant labor to the United States. The statute made it

> unlawful for any person, company, partnership, or corporation, in any manner whatsoever, to prepay the transportation, or in any way assist or encourage the importation or migration of any alien or aliens, any foreigner or foreigners, into the United States . . . under contract or agreement . . . to perform labor or service of any kind in the United States. . . . [22]

The Church of the Holy Trinity had paid someone to come to the United States to perform the service of church pastor. This seems a clear violation of the law.

However, the Supreme Court made an exception based on the man's religious vocation and the importance of Christianity to the United States. Writing for a unanimous court, Justice Brewer interpreted constitutional guarantees regarding speech and religion in ways we no longer accept. He declared: "This is a Christian nation."[23] He quoted with approval the opinion of "Chancellor Kent, the great commentator on American law, speaking as Chief Justice of the Supreme Court of New York."[24] Kent had written that free speech is a right, but because this is a Christian nation,

> to revile, with malicious and blasphemous contempt, the religion professed by almost the whole community, is an abuse of that right. Nor are we bound, by any expressions in the Constitution as some have strangely supposed, . . . to punish . . . the like attacks upon the religion of *Mahomet* or of the Grand *Lama*; and for this plain reason, that the case assumes that we are a Christian people, and the morality of the country is deeply ingrafted upon Christianity, and not upon the doctrines or worship of those impostors.[25]

Can you imagine the Supreme Court endorsing any such view today? Can you imagine them saying that Christianity, but not other creeds, limits free speech, because we are a Christian nation and other creeds were founded by *impostors*? Society and morality today favor religious toleration and ecumenism. We understand the First Amendment to incorporate these views regardless of how the amendment's ratifiers originally understood it. Again, Bork agrees in such cases.

What does this tell us about constitutional interpretation? It tells us that the Constitution can continue to guide and inspire our nation only if interpretations change over time. They must reflect changes in technology (telephones), society (greater variety of religions in the population), and morality (more respect for different religious traditions). Constitutional understanding cannot rest on unchanging foundations.

But then what guides our understanding of the Constitution? It is belief that the Constitution is a good document that provides appropriate guidance for the nation. Our assumption that the document is good leads us to impute to it many of our current beliefs about right and wrong. Regardless of the views of past generations, for example, we see the Constitution as outlawing racial discrimination in public schools and religious discrimination in the enforcement of free speech.

This approach to the Constitution agrees with a major tenet of hermeneutics, the study of interpretation: Preconceptions, often called "**pre-understanding**s," influence interpretations.[26] *People with different pre-understandings interpret the same text or situation differently. Interpretations of the Constitution change, while the text remains unchanged, because our pre-understandings have changed; for example, regarding religious toleration, which is viewed more positively today than it was 100 years ago. Changes in constitutional interpretation reflect such changes in pre-understanding.*

Hermeneutics and the Bible

Many of these considerations apply to biblical interpretations. Christians often use the Bible to guide their personal lives, but because the Bible is old and complex, many believe interpretations must change over time.

Consider, for example, Leviticus 19: 9 and 10: "When you reap the harvest of your land, you shall not reap all the way to the edges of your field, or gather the gleanings of your harvest. You shall not pick your vineyard bare, or gather the fallen fruit of your vineyard; you shall leave them for the poor and the stranger: I the Lord am your God."[27] I live in agricultural central Illinois where farmers do reap all the way to the edges of their fields. Does this mean that Christians among them are failing in their religious duty? Most people would not think so. Why? Because the underlying idea is to provide for the poor who subsist on charitable donations of food, and we now organize charity differently. We give food to the poor through tax-supported government programs as well as private charities that do not rely exclusively on contributions from farmers.

Because farmers constitute less than 2 percent of the working population in the United States, direct application of the Bible's method for feeding the poor would be unfair. It would place too great a burden on too few people. In biblical times most people were farmers so it was fair rely on farmers to contribute food for the poor.

The Bible provides good guidance here. It tells us to make sure that poor people have enough to eat. But a literal interpretation would not be so helpful as one that relates the Bible's underlying idea to the realities of contemporary life. People who accept this point do not interpret the Bible literally. Instead, they adapt their interpretations and understandings to make the Bible a good guide to conduct in today's world.

Some Old Testament verses engender more controversy. In Genesis 1:28, for example, God commands Adam and Eve to "be fruitful and multiply, and replenish the earth." He says the same to Noah after the flood (Genesis 9:1). Some Christians base opposition to birth control on these verses, because people use birth control primarily to limit "multiplying." Other Christians take a different view. They note that when God gave this command, the earth had few people. His point may therefore have been that when the human population is very low, people should be fruitful and multiply to avoid our species becoming extinct. In this interpretation, the verses do not forbid the use of birth control to reduce "multiplying" in a world already overpopulated by human beings.

Notice that neither side in this debate interprets the text literally. The text says nothing explicitly about birth control, nor does it say "multiply as much as possible" or "try to multiply whenever you have sex." A couple interpreting literally the command to be fruitful and *multiply* could have three children (so two would have "multiplied" to three) and then use birth control.

Concerning some other verses, many Christians reject, while others only partially accept, explicit advice in the New Testament as applying to our time. For example, St. Paul wrote to the church in Corinth: "Let your women keep silence in the churches: for it is not permitted unto them to speak; but they are commanded to be under obedience, as also saith the law. And if they will learn any thing, let them ask their husbands at home: for it is a shame for women to speak in the church."[28] Some Christians think this means women may not be ministers. Others disagree. Why?

We live in an age that rejects most traditional forms of sex discrimination. In order to hold the Bible in high enough esteem to justify patterning our lives on its model, we must understand it to reflect what we consider our highest ideals. Increasing gender equality is now one of those ideals. This may help to explain why some Christians say that St. Paul's statements merely reflect issues in Corinth at the time. My local Episcopal Bishop, Pete Beckwith, tells me that a competing religion in Corinth in Paul's time was the Cult of Aphrodite, which was run by prostitutes who sprinkled their spiritual message with carnal blessings. Paul advised the church to limit the public role of women to avoid confusion with this cult. On this reading, Paul's message to the Corinthians does not rule out full equality for women today.

These examples show that literal readings of the Bible do not provide firm, unchanging foundations for moral thought. The Bible, like all complex documents, is interpreted, and interpretations always reflect the readers' pre-understanding. People with generally negative attitudes toward sex, for example, may read God's command to "be fruitful and multiply" as condemning all birth control and recreational sex, even in marriage. People with more positive attitudes toward sex reject this interpretation. Similarly, people with patriarchal attitudes toward women may interpret Saint Paul's admonition, "it is a shame for women to speak in the church," to disallow equality for women. Others interpret Paul differently. Slave owners found in the story of Ham justification for enslaving black people. Few, if any, Christians would agree today.

This does not imply that people can interpret the Bible, the Constitution, or any other text to mean whatever they want it to mean. The United States Constitution cannot reasonably be interpreted to establish a monarchy, nor the New Testament to endorse child sacrifice. Nevertheless, *because interpretation is a meet-*

ing of individuals with texts, the meanings that reasonably emerge depend on both the individuals' pre-understandings and the text. So the Bible's environmental message for our time depends both on the Bible and on our pre-understanding. Two environmental interpretations of the Bible are considered near the end of this chapter.

Narratives, Grand Narratives, and Worldviews

How we interpret an event often depends on the story in which it is placed. Pre-understanding is often embedded in this story (or **narrative**). For example, boy meets girl. Is this event part of a story about everlasting romantic love, male/female friendship without sex, or casual sex on spring break? The general story line influences how the meeting is interpreted by participants and described to friends. Subsequent events, of course, may alter the story line. The romantic young man may have thought it was everlasting love until his idol's boyfriend showed up. Now he sees it as a story about a vulnerable, romantic, good-hearted young man whose love cannot be appreciated by shallow, fickle, dishonest women (with nice legs) whose only interest is. . . . Well, you get the point.

Setting our activities within stories is necessary for meaning. Meaning comes from connecting events, and the story tells how events are connected. The meaning of that first kiss, for example, depends on whether it is connected to casual sex or love.

We think of our lives in narrative form because this helps us interpret specific events and gives meaning to our lives. For the most part, the general story lines, like the ones surrounding boy meets girl, are established by our culture. We have the story of the faithful child taking care of parents in their old age; the story of the brash young person who shows the experts that they have much to learn; the story of the underdog competitor who overcomes great odds to win against fierce opposition; the story of the abused spouse, and so forth. Most people are engaged in more than one story at any given time. A person may be simultaneously spouse, parent, child, competitor, colleague, and employee, and different stories are appropriate to each role.

These personal narratives are set within **grand narratives**, *which are stories that start before the individual is born and are expected to extend beyond his or her death.* For example, a grand narrative in the Middle Ages was human salvation through *Christian* worship and practice. This motivated the Crusades of the eleventh to thirteenth centuries, which were wars aimed at defeating Mideastern Moslems so Jerusalem and other holy sites would return to Christian rule. A grand narrative in nineteenth-century America was "manifest destiny"—the story of progressive American rule from Atlantic to Pacific.

One twentieth-century grand narrative is the conquest of space. Here is what distinguished crystallographer J. D. Bernal wrote in 1929:

> Once acclimatized to space-living, it is unlikely that man will stop until he has roamed over and colonized most of the sidereal universe, or that even this will be

the end. Man will not ultimately be content to be parasitic on the stars, but will invade them and organize them for his own purposes. The stars cannot be allowed to continue in their old way, but will be turned into efficient heat-engines. . . . By intelligent organization, the life of the universe could probably be prolonged to many millions of millions of times what it would be without organization.[29]

A more common twentieth-century grand narrative is the story of economic progress. In his 1990 book *The Dream of the Earth*, Father Thomas Berry criticizes such progress:

"Progress" . . . remains the functional basis of our economy. The GNP must increase each year. Everything must be done on a larger scale. . . . However rational modern economics might be, the driving force of economics is not economic, but visionary, a visionary commitment supported by myth and a sense of having the magical powers of science to overcome any difficulty encountered from natural forces. . . . The tragedy is that our economy is being run by persons with good intentions under the illusion that they are bringing only great benefits to the world and even fulfilling a sacred task on the part of the human community. "We bring good things to life." "Progress is our most important product." [These are] dreams for moving into new frontiers of economic accomplishment, for the fulfillment of the high purposes of the universe itself.[30]

There is nothing wrong with needing a sense of destiny to give meaning to our lives. Philosopher Mary Midgley claims, in fact:

We . . . need a sense of destiny—a sense of a larger background, a context within which our own lives make sense. We need the idea of a drama in which we are acting. We have to have a sense of the sort of role that is expected of us. We need that sense whether or no we believe in God, whether or no we are important and influential people, whether or no we understand where it comes from.[31]

However, we should not deceive ourselves into thinking we are hardheaded realists who lack faith, because a sense of destiny resembles religious faith. Midgley writes:

A faith is not primarily a factual belief, . . . like "God exists". . . . It is rather the sense of having one's place within a whole greater than oneself, one whose larger aims so enclose one's own and give them point that sacrifice for it may be entirely proper. . . . This kind of faith is plainly something widespread and very important in our lives. . . . People have faith in humanity, in democracy, in art, in medicine, in economics or in western civilization. . . . [32]

Each faith is tied to a **worldview**, which Midgley calls a **world-picture**. These include assumptions about the nature of reality that support the grand narrative. The medieval grand narrative was tied to a worldview that included these beliefs: God exists, human beings suffer from original sin, Jesus is the Son of God, and so forth.

Nineteenth-century Americans had many beliefs supporting manifest destiny: Indians are inferior to white people, heathens are morally inferior to Christians, and technological mastery is a sign of superior civilization. The theory of evolution was later used to claim that Indians are less evolved, and so less fully human, than white people.

Faith in unlimited economic progress rests on several views. The first is anthropocentrism. Second, maximally converting the earth's resources to saleable commodities improves human welfare. Third, new technologies will enable people to surmount all difficulties—ozone depletion, global warming, increasing cancer rates, etc.

Worldviews often feature metaphors that enable people to make sense of remote or unfamiliar aspects of reality in terms that are more familiar. As we have seen, for example, because people in our society are so familiar with machines, many think of the larger (nonhuman) universe as just a gigantic machine.

A worldview featuring the machine metaphor can support anthropocentrism and technological optimism. If nonhuman reality is fundamentally like a machine, people alone are important because the only purpose of machines is to serve people. Also, if the world is like a machine, technological optimism is justified because people can learn how machines work and modify them as needed to produce desired results.

The mechanical metaphor, in turn, invites, but does not demand, belief in a world creator. Midgley writes, "The idea of a *machine* is essentially the idea of something planned and intended. The notion of an unplanned, independent spontaneous machine doesn't really make much sense."[33] So the Bible's story of creation by God coheres with a mechanical metaphor for the universe, anthropocentrism, and technological optimism to yield a worldview that underpins the grand narrative of economic progress.

Faith in the possibility and desirability of unlimited economic growth may account, for example, for Monsanto Corporation's development and marketing of Recombinant Bovine Growth Hormone (rBGH), also known as Bovine Somatotropin (BST). Through genetic engineering, Monsanto biologists have developed bacteria that produce a hormone that occurs naturally in cows. When extra amounts of the hormone are given to cows, they produce 10 to 20 percent more milk. In 1993, the United States Food and Drug Administration (FDA) declared milk produced in this way to be safe. Because cow's milk is generally an excellent food (especially when the cream is removed), Monsanto has used technological ingenuity to get more from the earth of what people want and need. And they can make a profit. Paul Kingsnorth writes in *The Ecologist* of "an estimated annual income for Monsanto of between $300 million and $500 million, and an estimated 12 percent increase in the nation's supply of milk."[34]

There are some problems, however. First, the United States usually produces more milk than it can use, and dairy farmers have been subsidized by government purchases of the excess. "In the period 1980–1985," Kingsnorth reports, "the U.S. government spent an average of $2.1 billion every year buying surplus milk."[35]

There are also negative health consequences for cows from Posilac, Monsanto's brand name for rBGH. The most serious is risk of mastitis, which is inflammation of the udder. Kingsnorth writes, "A cow with mastitis produces milk with pus in it," and dairies reject such milk. "Many farmers seek to treat the problem with antibiotics, but antibiotic residues in milk are suspected of causing health problems in humans who drink it, as well as contributing to the development of antibiotic resistance amongst bacteria."[36]

Humans may suffer additionally because rBGH in a cow's blood stimulates the production of another hormone called Insulin-Like Growth Factor 1 (IGF-1), a naturally occurring hormone-protein in both cows and people. Kingsnorth reports:

> The use of rBGH increases the levels of IGF-1 in the cow's milk. Because IGF-1 is active in humans—causing cells to divide—some scientists believe that ingesting high levels of it in rBGH-treated milk could lead to uncontrolled cell division and growth in humans—in other words, cancer.[37]

United States authorities consider such worries unjustified. Kingsnorth writes:

> In 1994, the FDA warned retailers not to label milk that was free of rBGH—thus effectively removing from consumers the right to choose what they drank . . . [because] in their words, there was 'virtually' no difference between rBGH-treated milk and ordinary milk. Labelling would thus unfairly discriminate against companies like Monsanto.[38]

Politics may have played a role in this FDA decision. Michael R. Taylor, the FDA official principally responsible for the decision, formerly worked for a law firm that represented Monsanto and has subsequently been employed by Monsanto.

In any case, although labeling rBGH-treated milk is still not required in the U.S., Monsanto will no longer sue companies, such as ice cream makers Ben and Jerry, who label their products "rBGH free." Regulators in some other countries, however, such as Canada and the nations in the European Union, have banned Posilac due to health concerns.

Monsanto could point out that people often fear new things, and economic motives for developing improved products without excessive government control fosters most technological advances that improve our standard of living. Their worldview: Progress that stems from mastering nature in the human interest is real and good. Cows are enough like machines to allow people morally and technologically to improve production and eliminate negative side effects as they arise. The master mentality and the grand narrative of progress underpin this view.

Naess' Deep Ecology

Deep Ecology presents a radically different worldview that rests on beliefs about cosmic unity and the nature of human maturity and fulfillment. Here we concentrate on one among several versions of deep ecology, that of the founder, Arne Naess. *Naess believes that as people mature they widen their sense of identification with others.* For example, small children on a playground may call others names or refuse to share toys because they do not identify with those whose feelings are hurt. More mature children avoid these actions out of concern for the pain of the other. People with even greater maturity care about those whom they will never meet, such as refugees from a war-torn country. Still greater maturity, Naess writes, brings identification with other life forms, such as hogs confined on a farm and wolves exterminated so hunters have deer to shoot.

Ultimate maturity brings identification with the entire universe. In an interview published in 1982, Naess said: *"We can be just as big as the cosmos, in a sense. We ourselves, as human beings, are capable of identifying with the whole of existence."*[39]

Naess maintains that many people experience movement toward greater maturity and identification

> when they see a death struggle—for instance when they see tiny animals like flies or mosquitoes fighting for their lives. When they see animals suffering, they may identify with a life form they usually don't identify with. Such situations offer us an opportunity to develop a more mature point of view. Insofar as this conversion, these deep feelings, are religious, then deep ecology [is] religious. . . . [40]

Naess calls identification with the whole of existence "Self-realization" (with a capital "S"), because he believes that the universe is fundamentally unified. When we identify with the entire universe, therefore, we realize our own, larger self.

Naess does not think this requires self-sacrifice, because he believes such identification enriches individual human life. But the riches are self-satisfaction, not material comforts. He believes that in rich countries "the material standard of living should be reduced and the quality of life, in the sense of basic satisfaction in the depths of one's heart or soul should be maintained or increased. This view is intuitive, as are all important views, in the sense that it can't be proven."[41] But we have reason to believe it, Naess says, when we "ask ourselves, 'In what situations do I experience the maximum satisfaction of my whole being?' and find that we need practically nothing of what we are supposed to need for a rich and fulfilling life."[42] He claims:

> I'm not for the simple life, except in the sense of a life simple in means but rich in goals and values. . . . I like richness, and I feel richer than the richest person when I'm in my cottage in the country with water I've carried from a certain well and with wood I've gathered. When you take a helicopter to the summit of a mountain, the view looks like a postcard. . . . But if you struggle up from the bottom, you have this deep feeling of satisfaction.[43]

Natural diversity enriches our lives because it enriches our extended selves. Naess says: "The self-realization we experience when we identify with the universe is heightened by an increase in the number of ways in which individuals, societies, and even species and life forms realize themselves. The greater the diversity then, the greater the Self-realization."[44] Deep ecologists therefore oppose economic development that extinguishes species and simplifies ecosystems. Instead, writes deep ecologist Warwick Fox, they favor an attitude of equality that "allows all entities (including humans) *the freedom to unfold in their own way unhindered by . . . human domination . . . .*"[45]

What makes deep ecology deep, according to Naess, is "the willingness to question, and an appreciation of the importance of questioning, every economic and political policy in public."[46] Such deep questioning yields "a realization of the deep changes which are required" in our lives and attitudes if we are to achieve Self-realization.[47] Because these changes enrich our lives as they protect the earth, deep ecology is a form of environmental synergism.

Deep ecologists have a platform of beliefs that includes the following affirmations:

> (1) The well-being and flourishing of human and non-human life forms on Earth have value in themselves; (2) Richness and diversity of life forms contribute to the realization of these values and are also values in themselves; (3) Humans have no right to reduce this richness and diversity except to satisfy vital needs; and (4) The flourishing of human life and cultures is compatible with a substantially smaller human population. The flourishing of non-human life *requires* a smaller human population.[48]

Thus, deep ecologists have a worldview and tell stories about their individual lives, about modern life in general, and about the universe, that are different from those of the proponents of unlimited economic growth. They participate in different narratives and grand narratives than those who seek maximum physical comfort or material wealth through controlling nature for exclusively human advantage in an ever-increasing economy.

As I use the term, these are differences of **religion**. A religion, in my usage, is a worldview that gives a meaning-oriented description of reality and of humanity's place within reality. Most religions include grand narratives about the origins and destiny of reality and humanity that connect people to a larger whole. An example is the Christian story of people falling out of favor with God and then being redeemed by His son Jesus. Another is the grand narrative of progress—people conquering the universe for human ends. A third is deep ecology's story of increasingly manifest universal unity amidst diversity made possible by the human mind's identification with all of reality.

As the religions of progress and deep ecology illustrate, not all religions, as I use the term, include belief in God. But all religions do include an element of faith. Beliefs about the general nature of reality and the destiny of humanity are tested in the life experiences of people living in accordance with those beliefs, and we cannot establish conclusively the greater fruitfulness of one kind of life over another.

Christian faiths sometimes differ profoundly from one another. At one time many Christians endorsed slavery, while others opposed it, on Christian grounds. Currently, many Christians believe in the grand narrative of progress and support maximum economic growth, whereas others condemn progress-oriented developments in genetic engineering. These Christians have importantly different worldviews and grand narratives. How, then, can they all be Christian? If Christianity is a religion and religions are specified by worldviews and grand narratives, it may seem that only some of these views are Christian whereas others are not.

To avoid concluding that some people who think they are Christian really are not, I consider Christianity to be a **religious tradition** rather than just a religion. It is an ongoing, culturally evolving tradition of religious inspiration and interpretation that encompasses many different worldviews and grand narratives. Other religious traditions include Judaism, Islam, and Hinduism. The present book cannot discuss all traditions. However, before returning to Christianity, let us look at Native American religions.

Native American Religions

Like deep ecology, Native American religions generally have worldviews that support nature-friendly grand narratives. These religions are many and various, because there are many distinct Native American cultures. Nevertheless, they all share, in the words of historian Calvin Martin, "genuine respect for the welfare of other life-forms."[49]

In *Black Elk Speaks*, John Neihardt relates an Indian shaman's autobiography as told to him in personal interviews in 1931. Black Elk was a second cousin of Crazy Horse and witnessed the 1890 battle at Wounded Knee that ended all Native American hopes for independence from white domination. He was a Lakota holy man who began:

> My friend, I am going to tell you the story of my life. . . . It is the story of all life that is holy . . . and of us two-leggeds sharing in it with the four-leggeds and the wings of the air and all green things; for these are children of one mother and their father is one Spirit. . . . Is not the sky a father and the earth a mother, and are not all living things with feet or wings or roots their children . . . ? For [it is] the earth . . . from whence we came and at whose breast we suck as babies all our lives, along with all the animals and birds and trees and grasses.[50]

Black Elk's worldview includes something like the Mother Earth metaphor associated with the Gaia Hypothesis. J. Baird Callicott notes in his 1994 book *Earth's Insights*:

> Sky and earth are father and mother; therefore, a filial piety should be exhibited in one's relations with one's cosmic parents. This mother-earth ethical precept was articulated by the Wanapum spiritual leader Smohalla, who was under pressure to cede territory and adopt a Euro-American lifestyle.

Smohalla said:

> You ask me to plow the ground. Shall I take a knife and tear my mother's bosom? You ask me to dig for stone. Shall I dig under her skin for bones? You ask me to cut grass and make hay and sell it, and be rich like white men. But how dare I cut off my mother's hair?[51]

Considering the earth to be one's mother still allows meeting vital needs by eating and otherwise using plants and animals, Callicott maintains. Like members of a family, species have relations of mutual care, dependency, and sacrifice. People sacrifice when they kill animals only in response to genuine need. They must show restraint and respect in other ways as well. Callicott reports the view of Wooden Leg, a nineteenth-century Cheyenne who shared the basic Lakota view:

> The old Indian teaching was that it was wrong to tear loose from its place on the earth anything that may be growing there. It may be cut off, but it should not be uprooted. The trees and the grass have spirits. Whenever one of such growths may be destroyed by some good Indian, his act is done in sadness and with a prayer for forgiveness because of his necessities, the same as we were taught to do in killing animals for food and skin.[52]

The Lakota maintain that other species are superior to human beings. Callicott writes: "Animals and plants, in permitting themselves to be taken for legitimate human needs, are said to 'pity' people and to voluntarily sacrifice themselves for the sake of their younger siblings, the human beings."[53]

❧ ❧ ❧

The Native American Ojibwa worldview depicts species more as different nations than as different branches of the same family. Callicott writes: "Animals are portrayed as enthusiastic partners with human beings. The animals willingly exchange their flesh and fur for the artifacts and cultivars that only human beings can produce."[54]

As in international relations, protocol and ceremony are important to the Ojibwa. For example, the bones of slain animals should be retained intact and then buried, because this enables the animals to come back to life. Callicott explains:

> The slain animals' spirits are imagined to come into the lodges of the people as dinner guests and to observe and partake of the feast made of their soft parts. Then their bones, returned whole to the forest or the stream, are re-clothed in flesh and fur and the literally reincarnated animals go back to their dens and lodges with warm memories of their visit to enjoy their "gifts."[55]

Failure to act appropriately leads to poor hunting results or other reprisals.

Protocol also includes tact. If people speak ill of another species, members of that species will not yield themselves to hunters. Ojibwa stories often include intermarriage between humans and members of other species. The humans come back to the tribe to share information on how to please the other species to ensure hunting success.

Both the extended family metaphor of the Lakota and the international relations metaphor of the Ojibwa result in worldviews that include respect for nonhuman nature. Because people and nature are thought to benefit mutually from this respect, these religions endorse environmental synergy. It is hard to imagine people who share the Lakota or Ojibwa worldview developing anything like rBGH, because the use of this hormone is intended to benefit people alone at the expense of other beings.

The Stewardship Interpretation of Christianity

Many Christians continue to understand their religion anthropocentrically, while others seek new, environmentalist interpretations. Catholic tradition, among others, makes explicit provision for new interpretations. It includes belief in continuing revelation through the third member of the Trinity, the Holy Spirit, who inspires new insights into the Bible's teaching. Lynn White, Jr., who was the first to accuse Western Christianity of responsibility for environmental degradation, made this point in 1971:

> Until about two hundred years ago the overwhelming body of Christians accepted slavery as a part of God's economy. So, if one points to the fact that historically Latin Christians have generally been arrogant toward nature, this does not mean that Scripture read with twentieth-century eyes will breed the same attitude. Perhaps the Holy Ghost is whispering something to us.[56]

But what statements in the Bible justify interpreting it environmentally? In the first place, the Bible clearly rejects reducing nature to mere mechanism, because nature is depicted as alive. Consider Psalm 96:11–13: "Let the heavens rejoice, and let the earth be glad; let the sea roar, and the fulness thereof. Let the field be joyful, and all that is therein; then shall all the trees of the wood rejoice before the Lord: for he cometh, for he cometh to judge the earth. . . ." Similarly, Psalm 148:7, 9,10 and 13: "Praise the Lord from the earth . . . : Mountains, and all hills; fruitful trees, and all cedars: Beasts, and all cattle; creeping things, and flying fowl: . . . Let them praise the name of the Lord."

In addition, the same story of creation that is quoted to justify the Master Interpretation can be used, instead, to justify the **Stewardship Interpretation**, which requires people to preserve nature. Genesis 1:24 describes the creation of animals before people: "And God made the beast of the earth after his kind, and cattle after their kind, and every thing that creepeth upon the earth after his kind: and God saw that it was good." Nonhuman creation is not only alive, but *good in the sight of God.*

How should people relate to this good creation? Genesis 2:15 says, "And the Lord God took the man [Adam], and put him into the garden of Eden to dress it and to keep it." This suggests to many Christians that people are meant by God to be stewards of creation. The American Baptist Churches, USA maintain: "The literal interpretation of steward is manager of the household. As such, we are all called to be managers of God's household, the earth and all that is in it." This means we should: "Promote an attitude affirming that all nature has intrinsic value and that all life is to be honored and reverenced." In addition, we should: "exert our influence in shaping public policy and insisting that industries, businesses, farmers and consumers relate to the environment in ways that are sensible, healthy and protective of its integrity."[57]

Evangelical Lutherans echo this sentiment: "Humans are part of nature, but with a special role on behalf of the whole. . . . Other creatures . . . have a value apart from what we give them. . . ."[58] Fourteen theologians from different Christian denominations came to similar conclusions in a 1988 report to the World Council of Churches. The report discusses the meaning of man being made in the image of God: "The image of God with its associated dominion is not for exploitation of animals but for responsible care. The plants that are good in themselves are given to both animals and human beings for their food. This is the integrity of creation in its ideal form."[59]

On the Stewardship Interpretation, the Bible endorses not anthropocentrism but environmental synergism. God created the world for the good of people and all other creatures. People should flourish as they care for creation. *Human domination of nature is meant to be for the good of the whole, not for anthropocentric mastery.* The report to the World Council of Churches is explicit: "The health of the ecosystem is essential for animals and human beings alike, and violence against ecosystems involves the oppression of human beings and the decimation of species. The need to preserve species is for the sake of the creatures themselves and at the same time for the sake of human purposes."[60]

❧ ❧ ❧

Father Thomas Berry expands the Christian understanding of stewardship by considering not just the Bible's particular account of creation, but the whole idea of creation. He considers creation, as understood through the theory of evolution, to have a sacramental quality. According to Catholic scholar John Haught, a **sacrament** is "any aspect of the world through which a divine mystery becomes present to religious awareness."[61] Berry thinks God reveals himself to us through cosmic evolution:

> The story of the universe is the story of . . . emergence . . . through . . . self-transcendence. Hydrogen in the presence of some millions of degrees of heat emerges into helium. After the stars take shape as oceans of fire in the heavens, they go through a sequence of transformations. Some eventually explode into the stardust out of which the solar system and the earth take shape. Earth gives unique

© Scott Willis/Copley News Service

expression of itself in its rock and crystalline structures and in the variety and splendor of living forms, until humans appear as the moment in which the unfolding universe becomes conscious of itself.[62]

This sequence of events leads Berry toward deep ecology. Like Arne Naess, Berry stresses the unity of the universe. He writes:

It is especially important . . . to recognize the unity of the total process [of evolution], from that first unimaginable moment of cosmic emergence through all its subsequent forms of expression until the present. This unbreakable bond of relatedness . . . makes . . . everything . . . intimately present to everything else in the universe. Nothing is completely itself without everything else.[63]

Human beings are special in part because we can reflect this unity through conscious awareness. Everything in the universe is related to everything else, but only human beings can display this unity through conscious awareness of it. Naess says we should identify with the universe to attain Self-realization. Berry considers this a two-way street. Not only do people attain Self-realization by identifying with the universe, the universe attains Self-realization as well. Through us the universe realizes its own unity. We are created (evolved) so the universe can reflect on itself and realize its unity.

Berry endorses the Gaia Hypothesis in this context. He writes: "One of the finest moments in our new sensitivity to the natural world is our discovery of the earth as a living organism."[64] Human beings are that part of Gaia (and of the entire universe) that gives Gaia (and the universe) self-awareness.

Berry considers people special also because we now have the power to direct evolution. He writes: "We now in large measure determine the earth process that once determined us. In a more integral way we could say that the earth that controlled itself directly in the former period now to an extensive degree controls itself through us."[65] This leads back to the idea of stewardship. We should use our power to further the goals of creation, which include the evolution of increasing complexity and awareness. We should protect diversity as the seedbed of evolution.

Some Christian environmentalists, however, attack the idea of stewardship. John Haught, for example, considers it unrealistic:

Stewardship . . . is . . . too managerial a concept to support the kind of ecological ethic we need today. Most ecologists would argue that the earth's life-systems were a lot better off before we humans came along to manage them. In fact, it is almost an axiom of ecology that these systems would not be in such jeopardy if the human species had never appeared in evolution at all.[66]

History suggests that people lack the knowledge and wisdom needed to manage nature well. Any God who would appoint us stewards would let Dracula guard the blood bank.

In addition to being unrealistic, the stewardship idea is anthropocentric, Haught claims. Stewardship "fails to accentuate that we belong to the earth much more than it belongs to us, that we are more dependent on it than it is on us."[67]

Haught makes some good points. The Stewardship Interpretation may not be the environmental ethic needed today. Yet, it seems clearly superior to the Master Interpretation. Let us now examine an even more environmentally friendly view.

The Citizenship Interpretation of Christianity

Daniel Quinn's award winning 1992 novel *Ishmael* analyzes the stories of Adam and Eve and Cain and Abel to support something like Aldo Leopold's land ethic. J. Baird Callicott calls this the **Citizenship Interpretation** of the Bible because the land ethic tells people to be "plain members and citizens" of the ecosystems they inhabit.

Quinn's novel is primarily a dialogue between a man and his tutor, a gorilla named Ishmael. (A gorilla? Don't ask.) Ishmael raises an issue that always puzzled me. Why did God forbid Adam and Eve to eat from the tree of the knowledge of good and evil? We usually think knowledge is a good thing, and the more we have the better. Knowledge of good and evil is especially helpful because it enables us to understand and do what is right and avoid what is wrong. Why deprive humanity of this knowledge?

Ishmael's answer begins by noting that people in different societies meet their needs in different ways. For example, the earliest humans were **foragers**, sometimes called hunter-gatherers. They did not raise livestock or plant fields. Instead, like most animals, they sought out and simply ate whatever was edible in their environment. They gathered fruits, nuts, and roots, and hunted animals for meat. Some people still live this way.

Herding is another way of life. People plant no fields, but raise livestock that they herd from place to place to graze on naturally occurring vegetation.

A third way of life is **agricultural**. Farmers plant fields to grow food. They must control what lives in and comes from those fields to ensure that the fields produce the food that people need. So they clear fields of unwanted vegetation (weeds), and protect the desired crop from animals and insects that would eat it before people have a chance to do so. Farmers, then, must decide which plants and animals shall live and which shall die.

Ishmael claims that the stories of Adam and Eve and Cain and Abel reflect the perspective of Semitic herders being displaced by farmers. About 4500 BCE (before the common era), farmers from the north started moving into areas used by Semitic herders. Adam and Eve represent the first wave of these farmers.

Why did they invade? The name "Eve" is a clue. It means "life." Eve represents the tendency of agricultural people to overpopulate. Ishmael explains: "What the Semites observed in their brothers from the north was that . . . if their population got out of hand, they didn't worry, they just put more land under cultivation."[68] They moved south, into the Semites' territory in search of new land to grow more food.

The Bible tells the story of Adam and Eve from the Semites' perspective. The Semites recognized that agriculture requires control over which animals and plants should live and which should die. Because farmers were the enemies of the Semites who originally told the story, knowledge of who should live and who should die is represented in the story as sinful. God told Adam and Eve not to eat of the tree of the knowledge of good and evil because this provides farmers' knowledge. If farming is bad, as herders being pushed off their land by farmers would think, then this knowledge is bad.

But why is it bad? The bad stems from people's inability really to know who should live and who should die. At most they can *think* they know. This leads them to *imagine* they can manage nature for the general good, when really they cannot. Farmers trying to exercise God's power over life and death mess things up for everyone.

The sin of eating the apple centers on Eve more than on Adam because women have the children that create overpopulation that motivates the farmers' invasion.

Another indication that the story was told by herders, Ishmael explains:

is the fact that agriculture is not portrayed as a desirable choice, freely made, but rather as a curse. It was literally inconceivable to the authors of these stories that anyone would *prefer* to live by the sweat of his brow. So the question they asked themselves was not, 'Why did these people adopt this toilsome life-style?' It was, 'What terrible misdeed did these people commit to deserve such a punishment?'[69]

The story of Cain and Abel reinforces this view. Cain is a farmer and Abel is a herder. God accepts Abel's sacrifice but not Cain's. God prefers herders to farmers. And then Cain kills Abel. This symbolizes what was happening. Farmers were killing herders so they could use the herders' land for agriculture, and God did not like it.

In this interpretation, God favors people who intervene less in Earth's life processes, people who make fewer decisions about who shall live and who shall die. The original sin, in this view, is anthropocentrism, because farmers tend to decide who shall live and who shall die from an entirely anthropocentric perspective. Foragers, on the other hand, require more biodiversity because they live primarily off the fruit of the land, like animals. They resemble "plain members and citizens" of the ecosystems they inhabit. Traditional herders manage their flock, but move the flock to eat off the fruit of the land, and so are more like foragers than farmers. The stories of Adam and Eve and Cain and Abel, then, can be interpreted to favor something like Leopold's land ethic. This is the Citizenship Interpretation of the Bible.

The interpretation also resembles the environmental ethics of many Native Americans. As we have seen, they disfavor massive manipulation of the earth. They portray relationships between people and the rest of the earth as family relationships or international relations, in which the ideal is satisfaction of everyone's needs. Unlike the stewardship idea, which gives extra responsibility and, therefore, pride of place, to human beings, Native American religions, like the Bible in the Citizenship Interpretation, make human beings "plain members and citizens" of a global community.

Judgment Calls

- Bobbi McCaughey was 28 years old. She and her husband had one child, Mikayla, who was 16 months old, but they were having trouble conceiving a second. So under the direction of fertility specialist, Dr. Katherine Hauser, Mrs. McCaughey took the fertility drug Metrodin. On November 19, 1997, she gave birth to seven babies, who were healthy enough to leave the hospital in January 1998. The family was showered with praise and gifts (a new house, a twelve-seat van, etc.), marking an event that was called a miracle.[70] How might different Christians view this "miracle" differently?

- A Virginia clinic has pioneered a process that enables couples to affect the sex of their child with a 65–90 percent chance of success. The man's sperm is collected and subjected to a process that separates sperm with a Y chromosome (which produces male offspring) from sperm with two X chromo-

somes (which results in a female child). The woman is artificially insemi-
nated with the sperm that will likely produce a child of the desired sex.[71]
What, if any, issues does this pose for religious people? How might religious
environmentalists differ from others of their faith on these issues?

- Deep ecologist Arne Naess opposes global competition in manufacturing,
  which requires efficient production methods that, he says, eliminate jobs and
  rob work of dignity and meaning. How might his alternative proposal be
  related to religion?

  What we need to do is to reduce our imports and therefore our exports, convert
  our big factories into small-scale, labor-intensive industry that makes products we
  need, and continue to sustain our culture as it has been, rather than to try to compete on the world market. Then we will have very little unemployment, and work
  will be much more meaningful.[72]

- In their 1984 book *The Creative Computer: Machine Intelligence and Knowledge*,
  artificial intelligence advocates Donald Michie and Rory Johnston express
  faith in computers. They write:

  The world is sliding precariously close to disaster. . . . In the face of this array of
  problems, we ask, from where might answers come? Could machines themselves
  conceive solutions that have eluded human minds? The message of this book is
  that they can. . . . We can foresee the day when poverty, hunger, disease and political strife have been tamed by the use of new knowledge, the product of computers acting as our servants. . . . In addition, the mental and artistic potential of
  man will be expanded in ways as yet undreamt of and the doors of the human
  imagination will be opened as never before.

  Mary Midgley thinks this sounds religious in tone and inspiration.[73] How
  does it relate to other religions in our society? How might computers have
  solved the problems in the Balkans that led to ethnocentrically and religiously inspired killing in Kosovo in 1999?

PART IV

APPLICATIONS

CHAPTER 11

Personal Choices, Consumerism, and Human Nature

Consumerism vs. Synergism

How should I live my life? No question is more important. The 1993 bestseller *Chicken Soup for the Soul* includes the following, found on a bulletin board:

> This life is a test.
> It is only a test.
> Had it been an actual life
> You would have received
> Further instructions on
> Where to go and what to do![1]

This is correct. In our actual lives we receive a lot of instructions on where to go and what to do. Much of it comes from advertisements telling us to buy something. Radio talk show host Dave Ramsey writes in his 1999 book *More Than Enough*:

> We live in the most marketed-to society in the history of the world. . . . Frogs selling beer, pantyhose hatching from eggs, Beanie Babies in McDonald's Happy Meals, sports figures pitching bill consolidation, and small dogs marketing tacos are enough to make you wonder what's next. Superstores that seem to be entire cities under one roof, warehouse stores with "great" buys, triple coupon days when Jupiter aligns with Mars, and billions and billions served—is there an end?[2]

Politicians generally favor economic growth and lower taxes so we have more money to spend. Economists credit people who can buy more with a higher standard of living, which they endorse. More is better.

The present chapter questions these ideas. It argues that most middle-class people may be better off with less money. Less money! How is that possible? This *contradicts the influential idea that life improves with increased spending power.*

We should be wary of influential, entrenched ideas, writes Alfie Kohn in *Punished by Rewards*:

> The time to worry is when the idea is so widely shared that we no longer even notice it, when it is so deeply rooted that it feels to us like plain common sense. At the point when objections are not answered anymore because they are no longer even raised, we are not in control: we do not have the idea; it has us.[3]

Today, an idea that has many of us confuses welfare with wealth, equating the better life with increased consumption. This idea underpins our consumer society.

Overcoming this idea supports environmental synergism, the view that human beings as a group fare best when they care about nonhuman nature for itself. Synergists reject any fundamental conflict between human beings and the rest of nature. Human flourishing generally goes hand in hand with healthy ecosystems and protected biodiversity. Native American religions, deep ecology, and some interpretations of Christianity endorse environmental synergism. However, *if the prevailing consumerist idea is correct, synergism is flawed. If human welfare requires increased consumption, then our welfare jeopardizes healthy ecosystems and protected biodiversity, because consumer lifestyles degrade nature.*

Increased consumption requires increased production. Organizational theorist David Korten points out in his 1995 book *When Corporations Rule the World*:

> About 70 percent of this productivity growth has been in . . . economic activity accounted for by the petroleum, petrochemical, and metal industries; chemical-intensive agriculture; public utilities; road building; transportation; and mining—specifically, the industries that are most rapidly drawing down natural capital, generating the bulk of our most toxic waste, and consuming a substantial portion of our nonrenewable energy.[4]

Worldwatch associate Alan Durning also notes that environmental degradation accompanies increases in consumption. Consumption is greatest in industrial countries, he writes: "Industrial countries, with one fourth of the globe's people, consume 40–86 percent of the earth's various natural resources. . . . The average resident of an industrial country consumes 3 times as much fresh water, 10 times as much energy, and 19 times as much aluminum as someone in a developing country." Such consumption hurts nature:

> Industrial countries' factories generate most of the world's hazardous chemical wastes. . . . And their air conditioners, aerosol sprays, and factories release almost 90 percent of the chlorofluorocarbons that destroy the earth's protective ozone layer. . . . The fossil fuels that power the consumer society are its most ruinous input. Wresting coal, oil, and natural gas from the earth permanently disrupts countless habitats; burning them causes an overwhelming share of the world's air pollution; and refining them generates huge quantities of toxic wastes.[5]

Consequently, Durning writes, "As people [enter] the consumer class, their impact on the environment makes a quantum leap. . . . Purchases of cars, gasoline, iron, steel, coal, and electricity, all ecologically . . . damaging to produce, multiply rapidly."[6] In sum, consumer lifestyles degrade nature. So if human flourishing depends on continued and increased consumption, environmental synergism is incorrect. People cannot flourish while valuing nature for itself and protecting ecosystems and biodiversity.

The present chapter supports synergism by challenging the link between human welfare and high levels of consumption. It challenges the view held by many economists that it is **human nature** for people to flourish through satisfaction of insatiable desires for consumer items. Gauging "human nature" by noting tendencies found in (almost) all human beings, this chapter argues that where consumption is already high, *people do best without growing economies or increased incomes, because high consumption frustrates needs rooted in human nature*. The next chapter discusses public policies that affect poorer countries as well as rich ones.

Justifications of Economic Growth

Some people in the United States are desperately poor and hungry. David Korten quotes a 1993 article featuring a CBS-TV interview of a sharecropper's child in Alabama:

"Do you eat breakfast before school?"
"Sometimes, sir. Sometimes I have peas."
"And when you get to school, do you eat?"
"No, sir."
"Isn't there any food there?"
"Yes, sir."
"Why don't you have it?"
"I don't have the 35 cents."
"What do you do while the other children eat lunch?"
"I just sits there on the side" (his voice breaking).
"How do you feel when you see the other children eating?"
"I feel ashamed" (crying).[7]

In 1998, the organization Bread for the World noted: "Hunger remains a pervasive reality for millions of people in the United States. . . . A U.S. Department of Agriculture (USDA) study reports that 11.2 million people live in households that are food insecure, meaning they cannot afford enough food for their families."[8]

How can we help such people? Many advocate improved educational opportunities and economic growth. Economic growth is needed, they say, to provide good jobs that pay well. An education without a job does not put food on the table.

Economic growth and related job opportunities require increased consumption. Vicki Robin and Joe Dominguez, experts in the field of simplified living, write in their 1992 bestseller *Your Money or Your Life*: "By the early 1920s a curious wrinkle had emerged in the U.S. economy. The astounding capacity of machinery to fill human needs had been so successful that economic activity was slowing down."[9] *When each worker can produce more of what people want, fewer workers are needed to fulfill human wants, and unemployment rises.* This is a problem, especially for poor people. *The solution is increased demand for goods and services.* Robin and Dominguez quote Victor Lebow, a U.S. retailing analyst, who maintained shortly after World War II:

> Our enormously productive economy . . . demands that we make consumption our way of life, that we convert the buying and use of goods into rituals, that we seek our spiritual satisfaction, our ego satisfaction, in consumption. . . . We need things consumed, burned up, worn out, replaced, and discarded at an ever increasing rate.[10]

Lebow's project of increasing consumerism was a success, write Robin and Dominguez:

> Americans used to be "citizens." Now we are "consumers"—which means (according to the dictionary definition of "consume") people who "use up, waste, destroy and squander."[11] If we don't consume, we're told, masses of people will be thrown out of work. Families will lose their homes. Unemployment will rise. Factories will shut down. Whole towns will lose their economic base. We *have* to buy widgets to keep America strong. . . . So . . . a day at the mall can be considered downright patriotic.[12]

Consumer demand not only keeps people working, the growing economy that it fosters increases tax revenues. This helps the government provide public education, school lunch programs, and other services for poor people.

Victor Lebow's call for people to seek "ego satisfaction" in consumption has been widely heard, reports Alan Durning: "Opinion surveys in the world's two largest economies—Japan and the United States—show that people increasingly measure success by the amount they consume."[13]

Besides satisfying the ego, buying and owning "stuff" can be functional and fun. I like to go to the movies. I need a car to get there, and to my work, because the streets in my town lack bicycle lanes and some drivers are aggressive when bicycles are in "their" lanes. Bicycling seems particularly dangerous after dark, when most movies are shown and many of my classes are over. My wife has her own car for the same reasons. When going greater distances, we sometimes fly. In 1997, I flew to a conference in Australia, and in 1999, I jetted to New Orleans, Louisiana, and Oxford, England to lecture.

I have many consumer items. I particularly like my hot-air popcorn popper because it lets me pop popcorn without oil. This saves calories so I can eat more. My wife and I have a kitchen with other gadgets, as well as a house with furniture in every room. You get the idea. We have a lot of "stuff," and most of what we have we enjoy. It seems to improve the quality of our lives. Our purchases also help the economy grow, encourage employment in the United States and elsewhere, and raise tax revenues.

But what about the environment? Most of what I own is made of wood, metal or plastic. The wood comes from cutting down trees. This may harm forest ecosystems. Energy is used to cut and transport the wood. Metal comes from rocks that are often mined in environmentally destructive ways and then smelted using enormous amounts of (usually) fossil fuel energy. This adds to global warming. Smelting creates toxic byproducts as well. Plastics are petrochemicals whose manufacture uses a lot of energy and produces health-damaging toxic wastes. I consume additional energy when I use many of my items—microwave, popcorn popper, lawnmower, automobile, etc.

What a mess! It seems that our "good life" harms nature. Consider energy consumption alone. David Korten notes that averting the worst of global warming seems to require eventually lowering per capita carbon dioxide emissions to the equivalent of "one liter of carbon-based fuel per day."[14] This allows going about 15 miles by car, 31 by bus, 40 by train, or just over 6 by plane. I would have to save up for more than 6 years to fly to Australia and back, and would not be able to drive my car, use the toaster, or buy any new "stuff" during all that time, to avoid using more than my share of energy. This seems unrealistic. How can synergism be correct? How can people flourish while valuing nature for itself and living in ways that preserve ecosystems and biodiversity? *It appears to be human nature to want comforts, conveniences, and travel that harm the rest of nature. Fortunately, this appearance is deceiving.*

High Consumption and Human Welfare

Economic growth and increased personal consumption do not always improve people's sense of well being. In *The Battle for Human Nature,* psychologist Barry Schwartz discusses the work of economist Tibor Scitovsky. Schwartz writes:

> Scitovsky cites the results of surveys of how happy Americans thought they were over a twenty-five-year period from 1946 to 1970. During this period, real (inflation-adjusted) income in the United States rose 62 percent. So people on the whole were much better off in 1970 than they were in 1946. Yet this large change in material welfare had absolutely no effect on happiness ratings. People were no happier in 1970 than they were in 1946, although if you had asked them, in 1946, how happy they would be if they had the standard of living that they actually did have in 1970, nearly everyone would have been ecstatic.[15]

The disconnect between happiness and overall consumption continues in the United States. Writing in 1992, Alan Durning notes:

> Regular surveys by the National Opinion Research Center of the University of Chicago reveal . . . that no more Americans report they are "very happy" now than in 1957. The "very happy" share of the population has fluctuated around one-third

[between 31 and 35 percent of people reporting themselves to be "very happy"] since the mid-fifties, despite near-doublings in both gross national product and personal consumption expenditures per capita.[16]

The same phenomenon exists internationally as well, Durning reports:

A landmark study in 1974 revealed that Nigerians, Filipinos, Panamanians, Yugoslavians, Japanese, Israelis, and West Germans all ranked themselves near the middle on a happiness scale. Confounding any attempt to correlate material prosperity with happiness, low-income Cubans and affluent Americans both reported themselves considerably happier than the norm. . . . [17]

What accounts for these results? *It is human nature for the happiness people derive from consumption to be largely comparative.* First, *people compare their current consumption unfavorably with increased consumption,* writes Lewis Lapham:

No matter what their income . . . Americans believe that if only they had twice as much, they would inherit the estate of happiness. . . . The man who receives $15,000 a year is sure that he could relieve his sorrow if he had only $30,000 a year; the man with $1 million a year knows that all would be well if he had $2 million a year.[18]

Yet increased income seldom brings long-term benefits because the higher income becomes a new basis for comparison. It seems that for most people the initial happiness diminishes as comparisons are made to even greater affluence.

This may result from what psychologists call affective contrast, which is used to explain drug addiction. The pleasure that people experience with drugs diminishes over time as they get used to it. For a time people can take increasing doses to get the pleasure they had at first. But when they reach the limit of their body's ability to tolerate the drug, increasing doses are no longer possible. Then they are addicted not because the drug continues to bring pleasure, but because doing without the drug is painful.

Barry Schwartz compares this to the transformation of consumer luxuries— "air conditioners, cars, telephones, televisions, washing machines, and the like"[19]—into necessities. Air conditioning, for example, gives pleasure at first. But as we become habituated to it individually and it becomes the social norm, we take it for granted, no longer notice it, and no longer get pleasure from it. At that point we "need" it to avoid the unusual (to us) discomfort of experiencing prolonged heat in the summer.

A second reason increased consumption does not make people happier concerns comparisons people make between themselves and others. *People feel deprived when others with whom they compare themselves have more than they do.* Durning observes:

Psychological data from diverse societies such as the United States, the United Kingdom, Israel, Brazil, and India show that the top income strata tend to be slightly happier than the middle strata, and the bottom group tends to be least happy. The upper classes [in rich countries] . . . are no more satisfied than the upper classes of much poorer countries.[20]

Because of such comparisons, Durning reports, some Wall Street dealmakers during the 1980s boom suffered anxiety and self-doubt when they earned only $600,000 per year. Most of us can think of talented sports figures who would be insulted by contract offers of $1 or $2 million per year because others earn more.

In sum, human nature prevents overall increases in affluence through a growing economy from increasing general happiness. People become used to, "addicted" to, higher levels of consumption, and their increased affluence disappoints due to invidious comparisons they make between themselves and those who are wealthier still.

Worse yet, the gap between rich and poor is increasing. The rich are getting richer, the poor are getting poorer, and the middle class is losing ground in the United States. Bread for the World policy analyst Lynette Engelhardt reported in 1998:

Over the past two decades, the gap between rich and poor in the United States has increased dramatically. The wealthiest 1 percent of Americans have more wealth than the bottom 90 percent combined. . . . A 1997 study by the Center on Budget and Policy priorities found that since the mid-1970s, the income of the richest fifth of Americans grew by 30 percent while that of the poorest fifth fell by 21 percent.

Over the last five years, corporate profits have risen by about 62 percent in real terms. CEO salaries have increased dramatically as well. In 1978, CEOs earned about 60 times the pay of the average worker. In 1989, the ratio had increased to 122. By 1995, CEOs were paid at a rate 173 times higher than the average worker in the U.S.[21]

Tax laws also increase the income gap. Sociologist Walden Bello reports in *Dark Victory* that tax "reform" in the early 1980s "reduced . . . the tax share of the top 1 per cent of the population . . . by 14 per cent, while that of the bottom 10 per cent rose by 28 per cent."[22] In August 1999, Congress passed a tax bill, later vetoed by the president, that also favored the rich. Eighty percent of its benefits were for the top 10 percent of taxpayers.[23]

The poor also lose government help as welfare and food-assistance programs are cut to balance the federal budget in the face of diminished contributions from the rich. Think again about that poor child in Alabama who lacked 35 cents for a school lunch. Does our economy as a whole have to grow to feed that child? The problem is not the size of the economy or the presence of food, but the availability of jobs and the distribution of money and food. *In general, an increasing percentage of people suffer genuine deprivation as gaps between rich and poor increase, and they suffer less when the gap is reduced.*

David Korten gives this example from history, illustrating the misery that befalls most people, even when the economy is growing, if inequality increases:

Economists estimate that between 1750 and 1850, Britain's per capita income roughly doubled, but the quality of life for the majority of people steadily declined.

Before 1750, travelers to the British countryside reported little evidence of deprivation. For the most part, people had adequate food, shelter, and clothing, and the
countryside had a prosperous appearance.[24]

By 1850, common people lived in the squalor that Charles Dickens described in
his novels. But then the reverse took place, Korten tells us: "Conditions for ordinary people in Britain improved from 1914 . . . through the end of World War
II . . . when there was no overall growth in Britain's national income. . . . The
real purchasing power of most wage-earner households improved."[25] The United
States experienced the same pattern, Korten maintains: "The imperatives of the
depression of the 1930s and World War II galvanized political action behind measures that resulted in a significant redistribution of income and built the strong
middle class. . . ."[26] Continued economic growth since the early 1970s, however,
has resulted in growing inequality that leaves most Americans behind.

The greater importance of equality than of economic growth to human well
being is illustrated internationally as well. For example, Korten writes: "Saudi
Arabia's literacy rate is lower than Sri Lanka's, despite the fact that its per capita
income is fifteen times higher. Brazil's child mortality rate is four times that of
Jamaica, even though its per capita income is twice as high."[27] By the end of
the 1980s, the infant mortality rate for African Americans in the U.S. was higher
than for people in much poorer Cuba.[28]

In sum, human beings, like all living things, need to consume to live. However, economic growth, as currently conceived and measured, is unnecessary
in the U.S. to meet material needs or foster happiness. And when policies that
promote growth increase inequality of income, the results are unhappiness and
serious material deprivation.

Marketing Discontent

*The nature of marketing and advertising helps to explain why economic growth leads
to unhappiness.* Economic growth and high employment require that people consume more. But what motivates people to consume more, especially when additional consumption strains budgets or creates debt? We have looked at two
reasons so far: Increased consumption can be addictive, and people want what
others already have. Both of these are tied to another factor—marketing and
advertising.

Political scientist Benjamin Barber notes in his 1995 book *Jihad vs. McWorld*:
"Global advertising expenditures have climbed a third faster than the world
economy and three times faster than world population, rising sevenfold from
1950 to 1990 from a modest $39 billion to $256 billion."[29] David Korten adds
that corporations spent "another $380 billion . . . on packaging, design, and
other point-of-sale promotions. Together, these expenditures amounted to $120
for every single person in the world." This is "well over half as much per capita
. . . as the $207 per capita . . . the world spends on public education."[30]

Korten remarks:

Today, television is the primary medium through which corporations shape the culture and behavior of Americans. The statistics are chilling. The average American child between the ages of two and five watches three and a half hours of television a day; the average adult, nearly five hours. . . . At this rate, the average American adult is seeing approximately 21,000 commercials a year, most of which carry an identical message: "Buy something—do it now!"[31]

Ads can be enormously effective. Alan Durning quotes a "specialist in marketing to children [who] told the *Wall Street Journal*, 'Even two-year-olds are concerned about their brand of clothes, and by the age of six are full-out consumers.' "[32] Dave Ramsey cites a study that links television viewing with consumer spending:

Juliet B. Schor, in her book *The Overspent American*, states that her research shows that each added hour of television viewing increases a consumer's spending by roughly $200 per year. So an average level of TV watching of fifteen hours per week equals nearly $3000 extra spent per year. When you consider a study by A. C. Nielsen Co. that says in 1996 Americans watched 250 billion hours of TV, the overspending as a culture is incredible.[33]

Far from leading to happiness, purchases stemming from advertisements rest on creating discontent. Ramsey writes:

Professional marketers and advertisers understand that they have to point out a need to you so you will recognize a need you didn't know you had. When you recognize that need, [a] process . . . has started [that] will end in frustration and finally purchase. . . . If you are a good marketer or advertiser your job is to bring dissonance or a disturbance to the person receiving your message. . . . That is the essence of marketing, to create an emotional disturbance.[34]

Alan Durning agrees: "Many ads offer little information, trafficking instead in images evoking sexual virility, eternal youth, existential fulfillment, and infinite other variations on the 'wouldn't-you-like-to-be-like-this' theme." The ads work when they convince people to be dissatisfied with their current lives and selves. Durning notes:

Advertisers especially like to play on the personal insecurities and self-doubt of women. As B. Earl Puckett, then head of the Allied Stores Corporation, put it 40 years ago, "It is our job to make women unhappy with what they have." Thus for those born with short, skinny eyelashes, the message mongers offer hope. For those whose hair is too straight, or too curly, or grows in the wrong places, for those whose skin is too dark or too light . . . advertising assures us that synthetic salvation is close at hand.[35]

Advertisers invent so many ways people can be unhappy with themselves that few people who heed their messages can ever be content. There are always more flaws to overcome.

Advertising leads to discontent also when it rests on unrealistic associations that create unfulfilled expectations. Political Scientist Benjamin Barber notes that Nike sells an image more than anything: "Humankind walked the globe for millennia without the specialty items developed in the last few decades for professional athletes," Barber writes. "Today . . . 40 percent of all shoes sold are already athletic shoes. . . ." Nike's success depends, according to Liz Dolan, corporate communications vice president, on being "not a shoe company . . . [but] a sports company." Nike CEO, Phillip H. Knight, wrote in his 1992 annual report: "How do we expect to conquer foreign lands? We will simply export sports, the world's best economy." Barber comments:

> Well, not exactly sports and not just sports, but the image and ideology of sports: health, victory, wealth, sex, money, energy. . . . If actual athletes were the only consumers of athletic shoes, there would be far too few of them to keep sales perking . . . , so the object becomes to make those who watch athletics believe that in wearing Nikes they too are athletes, even if they [just sit in] armchairs. . . . [36]

But most people can fool themselves for only so long. Convinced that athletes are the highest form of humanity, they are distraught when they eventually look in the mirror.

Barber makes similar comments about soft drink ads that associate consumption

> with new "needs," new tastes, new status. You must drink because it makes you feel (your choice): young, sexy, important, "in," strong, sporty, smart, with it, cool, hot (as in cool), athletic, right on, part of the world as in we-are-the-world . . . : in sum, like a winner, like a hero, like a champion, like an American, which is to say, above all, fun-loving (as in blondes have more).[37]

Obviously, people whose lives are really not that much fun will be frustrated by attempts to sweeten their sourpusses with soft drinks. And then there really is a new need. ("It's down that hall and to the left." "Thank goodness.")

Syndicated columnist Dave Barry gives an amusing account of disappointment stemming from expectations raised by marketing. American Airlines announced that Barry's flight would have "bistro service." Barry writes:

> I honestly wasn't sure what "bistro" meant but it sounded French, which I thought was a good sign. . . .
>
> When the plane took off, I opened my "bistro" sack. Here are the items it contained: 1) a container of yogurt, 2) a "breakfast bar" made from compressed dried wood chips, and 3) the greenest, coldest, hardest banana I have ever touched in my life.

Why did the airline call it "bistro service?" The image it conjures up is of a cozy little place on a picturesque little street in Paris, with candlelit tables for two occupied by lovers kissing, drinking wine [and] enjoying French food. . . .

Why [call it "bistro service"]? The answer is marketing. . . . "Bistro service" . . . sounds a LOT better, from a marketing standpoint, than "a sack of inedible objects."[38]

Similar logic leads marketers of sport utility vehicles to suggest that each of us is the rugged type ready to take our chances off road, going over the mountain rather than around it. Have my neighbors with SUVs in central Illinois not noticed the absence of mountains? When they go off road, whose corn or soybean fields do they go through?

Succumbing to marketing hype breeds discontent also because it strains budgets. SUVs are between two and four times the price of my little car. Families that pay together may not stay together. Divorce often follows financial troubles.

Debt compounds the problem. (I take credit for all word play.) Vicki Robin and Joe Dominguez write that young people are particularly at risk: "Young Americans currently spend an average of $1.20 for every $1 that they make." Credit cards promote debt. "A survey reported in *The People's Almanac* indicates that people spend 23 percent more when they buy with credit cards than when they buy with cash."[39] Debt, in turn, breeds bankruptcy, which became so common in Illinois that in 1998 the state passed tougher bankruptcy laws to discourage the practice. (This is Chapter 11.)

Dave Ramsey sums it up this way:

The more we are pummeled with ads the more we buy, chasing that brass ring of happiness around our own little gerbil wheel. Living in the most marketed-to civilization in history means we are systematically having our contentment stolen. All of this disturbance has led us to be very discontented people. This discontent is taking our wealth and our relationships.[40]

Extrinsic Motivations and Their Limits

One of the ideas we have been critiquing is that consumption is good because it creates jobs. Slacking consumer demand would throw people out of work. So advertisers perform a valuable service when they sow discontent. A different justification for the consumer society is that consumer discontent among workers is needed to keep them productive. In this view, people work primarily or exclusively for a paycheck. When they have unmet consumer "needs," they compete with one another to earn more money, and are forced in the process to improve efficiency and productivity.

Notice that the second justification for consumerism clashes with the first. The first assumes that technological innovation makes workers too productive. Over-consumption is needed to mop up excess productivity. The second as-

Courtesy of Adbusters Media Foundation. www.adbusters.org

sumes, by contrast, that greater productivity is needed. Why is it needed? Maybe to meet consumer demand! (You see, ideas do not have to make sense to be accepted by most of us most of the time. Familiarity with the ideas and their acceptance by others often substitute for logic. This applies to all of us and justifies vigilant social criticism and frequent self-examination.)

In any case, this justification for consumerism rests on the idea that extrinsic motivation is needed to keep people working. **Extrinsic motivators** are reasons for engaging in an activity that stem from the activity, like a paycheck for work, but are not part of that activity. **Intrinsic motivators**, by contrast, are reasons that not only stem from the activity but are part of it. Unpaid singers in a community or church choir, for example, typically participate for intrinsic reasons. They like music, want to sing, enjoy socializing, value the arts, and so forth. Engaging in the activity is rewarding in itself. A paid singer may be motivated intrinsically in all of these ways, too, but to the extent that she is motivated by pay, she is motivated extrinsically as well.

Behaviorism, a psychological theory, says that our social actions are shaped by their external results. *Behaviorists believe that it is human nature for people to work* *for the benefit of others only if they receive extrinsic rewards. Society can be assured of sufficient labor only by arranging rewards to motivate laborers. Enticing people to work for a paycheck, which they need to buy consumer items made attractive by advertising, secures the labor needed to maintain civilization and secure human well being.*

This is another rationale for claiming that consumerism is needed for human flourishing. But because consumerism degrades nature, this idea contradicts the synergist thesis that humans fare best when they value nature for itself and protect biodiversity.

Fortunately for environmental syngergism, much evidence contradicts behaviorism. Psychologist Alfie Kohn claims in *Punished by Rewards* that much human motivation is intrinsic, and that extrinsic motivators often actually interfere with intrinsic motivation. He cites a host of studies. Here is one:

> Take smoking cessation. A very large study, published in 1991, recruited subjects for a self-help program designed to help people kick the habit. Some were offered a prize for turning in weekly progress reports; some got feedback designed to enhance their motivation to quit; everybody else (the control group) got nothing. What happened? Prize recipients were twice as likely as the others to return the first week's report. But three months later, they were lighting up again more often than those who received the other treatment—and even more than those in the control group. . . . Not only were rewards unhelpful; they actually did harm.[41]

Similarly, Kohn reports:

> More research has been done on applying behaviorism to the promotion of seat belt use. The result: programs that rewarded people for wearing seat belts were the *least* effective over the long haul. In follow-up measures ranging from a month to more than a year later, programs that offered prizes or cash for buckling up found changes in seat belt use ranging from a 62 percent increase to a 4 percent decrease. Programs without rewards averaged a 152 percent increase.[42]

Such *studies suggest that people often have intrinsic motivations unrelated to extrinsic rewards.* What are these motivations and how do they relate to human welfare?

Some Intrinsic Motivations

One intrinsic motivation that benefits society is *curiosity*. Kohn writes: "All of us start out in life intensely fascinated by the world around us and inclined to explore it without any extrinsic inducement. It is not part of the human condition to depend on rewards" to motivate curiosity.[43]

Kohn notes, too, several other psychological theories at odds with behaviorist assumptions that people are unproductive except when motivated extrinsically:

> All the work showing that we are motivated by a need to attain a sense of competence (Robert White), to be self-determining (Richard deCharms, Edward Deci,

and others), . . . or to "actualize" our potential in various ways (Abraham Maslow) implicitly refutes the idea that it is natural to do as little as possible.[44]

Philosopher Alasdair MacIntyre's concept of a **practice** *helps explain productive behavior that is independent of extrinsic rewards. A practice is a socially created form of cooperative activity with built-in standards of excellence.* Consider, MacIntyre writes:

> the practice of portrait painting as it developed in Western Europe from the late middle ages to the eighteenth century. The successful portrait painter is able to achieve many goods which are . . . external to the practice of portrait painting— fame, wealth [and] social status. . . . But those external goods are not to be confused with the goods which are internal to the practice. The internal goods are those which result from an extended attempt to show . . . how the face at any age may be revealed as the face that the subject of the portrait deserves.[45]

Socially created standards of excellence internal to the practice motivate dedicated painters and give them a sense of connection to one another and to an ongoing tradition.

MacIntyre gives chess as another example. He imagines that a child might originally be attracted to chess by external rewards, such as money for winning or quality time with a parent. But the child may later enter the practice of chess. Then she will

> find in those goods specific to chess, in the achievement of a certain highly particular kind of analytical skill, strategic imagination and competitive intensity, a new set of reasons, now not just for winning on a particular occasion, but for trying to excel in whatever way the game of chess demands.[46]

The difference is significant. For example, if the child just wants money, she may be tempted to cheat, but after immersing herself in the practice of chess, if she cheats, she cheats herself.

Science, too, is a practice for those genuinely interested in knowledge. Doing good research is internally rewarding. People who research merely for profit or external recognition, however, may be tempted to fudge their data and fake significant results.

In sum, where practices are concerned, internal rewards are not only effective, but in some ways superior to the external rewards that behaviorists emphasize. People engaged in practices are motivated to actually do the job well, not just look like they are doing it well. They are motivated to be honest with themselves and others.

Practices help people to find meaning in life. Meaning in life, according to philosopher Mary Midgley "begins from the group one belongs to having a satisfactory communal life, and then the individual achieving [in that community] whatever aims are currently most needed and valued."[47] People engaged in practices integrate their sense of self with a set of activities that a social group has defined and declared worthwhile. Being a fine chef, musician, farmer, teacher, or scientist becomes part of the way the individual conceives of himself. It enters (without necessarily dominating) the narrative or story that the individual tells about his life. Excellence in the chosen area becomes one of his goals in life and progress toward that goal is one area of activity that gives his life meaning.

Meaning often increases with faith in the practice's goals and future. Midgley equates faith with "the sense of having one's place within a whole greater than oneself, one whose larger aims so enclose one's own and give them point that sacrifice for it can be entirely proper."[48] Engaging in a practice often elicits such faith. Imagine a doctor who not only gains internal satisfaction from contributing to the health of her patients, but sees her work of information gathering as contributing to improved health care in the future. Midgley notes: "Even in quite unpretentious groups such as trades or professions, there is often a strong sense of a greater purpose transcending individual wishes, a purpose which carries everyone forward and which all must serve."[49]

Vicki Robin and Joe Dominguez make the same point: "It's fairly easy to know what fulfillment is in terms of food or other temporary pleasures," they write. "But to have fulfillment in the larger sense, to have a fulfilled life, you need to have a sense of purpose, a dream of what a good life might be."[50] They tell a story about three stonecutters to illustrate purpose, which they define as "the meaning you give to actions."

> A passerby approaches the first stonecutter and asks, "Excuse me, what are you doing?" The stonecutter replies rather gruffly, "Can't you see? I'm chipping away at this big hunk of stone." Approaching the second craftsman, our curious person asks the same question. This stonecutter looks up with a mixture of pride and resignation and says, "Why, I'm earning a living to take care of my wife and children." Moving to the third worker, our questioner asks, "And what are *you* doing?" The third stonecutter looks up, his face shining, and says with reverence, "I'm building a cathedral!"[51]

Looking for Love

Motivation by lofty ideals not only gets the job done, but contributes more than external rewards to a sense of meaning and personal fulfillment. Love, family and *community* are also essential for human flourishing, but are unattainable principally through external motivation. This, too, is part of human nature. Dave Ramsey writes:

> A workaholic gerbil in a wheel invented the stupid phrase "quality time." There is no question that quantity time is what is needed to develop strong fruitful relationships. We are failing miserably in this culture by not slowing down enough to enjoy each other. . . .
>
> When I was growing up in the sixties, my mom would often be at a neighbor's kitchen table having a cup of coffee at midmorning while the kids played. . . . The evenings would find half the neighborhood gathered on a deck or patio to enjoy a night of interaction. We camped together, the men fished together, and as a kid

you could get your butt busted by any adult in the neighborhood. There was a real sense of community.

What has stolen our ability to find those luxurious hours to invest in family and friends? Several things have stolen that time. We are so marketed to that we have started to believe that more stuff will make us happy. But in this country, more stuff has resulted in more debt. What debt means is that we end up spending our every waking hour working to pay off our bills.[52]

Robin and Dominguez echo this view:

It would seem that the primary "thing" many people have sacrificed in "going for the gold" is their relationships with other people. Whether you think of that as a happy marriage, time with the children, neighborliness, a close circle of friends, shopkeepers who know you, civic involvement, community spirit, or just living in a place where you can walk to work and the beat cop is your friend, it's disappearing across the country.[53]

What is more, much of the stuff we buy separates us from one another. Ramsey cites a study showing that "the typical house in 1960 was 1,375 square feet, 1 story, with 3 bedrooms and 1.5 baths while the typical house in the 1990s is 1,940 square feet, 2 stories, 4 bedrooms, and 2.5 baths."[54] Because family size has not increased, each family member now has more room at home. Now children are less likely to share a bedroom, and the single-occupancy bedroom is more likely to contain its own television, stereo, and computer (with software for games). This tempts children to stay isolated in their rooms. In 1960, most houses had only one television and no computer.

Other aspects of affluence also contribute to social isolation. Most houses built before World War II had front porches, which were the coolest places to be on hot summer days. Neighbors would converse from porch to porch, especially in urban and suburban areas where houses were closer together than is typical today. Now larger lawns and yards separate houses and central air conditioning keeps people indoors during hot weather. *Much of our stuff contributes to a loss of community.*

The resulting loss of a sense of connection with others sets the stage for a vicious circle. Increased consumerism weakens personal bonds that people need to feel whole and good about themselves. Influenced in part by advertising, people try to compensate for feelings of emptiness through higher incomes and more purchases. Alfie Kohn notes: "As a number of psychologists and social critics have argued, when a sense of meaning or deep connection to others is absent . . . from one's life: a plump bank account is made to substitute for authentic fulfillment."[55] Additional work hours away from friends and family are needed to build that bank account and pay for stuff. This increases the sense of isolation and emptiness, so people buy even more, and so on. Kohn adds:

That we are dealing with a substitute satisfaction here seems clear from the fact that no sum ever suffices: such people always "need" more than they are currently making—or buying. Add one more pair of shoes, a new electronic gizmo, or a higher salary, . . . and it is still not enough. It is never enough.[56]

Such *compulsive consumerism harms the environment and frustrates people. Here, too, what is bad for nature is also bad for people.* Alan Durning writes that for most people "the main determinants of happiness in life . . . are satisfaction with family life, especially marriage, followed by satisfaction with work, leisure to develop talents, and friendships."[57] *So people would fare better with a sense of connection to one another and to nature than with high-consumption life styles that degrade the environment.*

Of course, people cannot ignore money altogether. In our society we need money to live. But *those who want to flourish need to examine their relationships to money and consumer goods to find the best path toward personal fulfillment.* Almost always, Robin and Dominguez argue, that path will involve less money, fewer purchases, and a lighter burden on ecosystems. Let us examine their views.

Your Money or Your Life

Robin and Dominguez say that we get the most out of life when we have fulfilling work and meaningful relationships. Working for money interferes with leading such a life when it channels our limited time and energy to less internally rewarding tasks. So most people can improve their lives by reducing their need for money. We should aim at maximum fulfillment from each expenditure. This requires developing an internal yardstick that shows when we have had just enough of something. They write:

> Being fulfilled is having just enough. Think about it. Whether it's food or money or things, if you don't know, from an internal standard, what is enough, then you will pass directly from "not enough" to "too much". . . . Having an internal yardstick for fulfillment is actually one part of what we call Financial Integrity. You learn to make your financial choices independently of what advertising and industry have decided would be good for their business. You are free of the humiliation of being manipulated into spending your life energy on things that don't bring you fulfillment.[58]

They suggest beginning the discovery of what is enough by organizing expenditures into categories. This helps people whose paychecks seem to disappear without a trace get a realistic picture of where their money is going. The categories include such things as transportation, clothing, groceries, travel, and so forth. Robin and Dominguez tell the story of a man who could not account for 20 percent of his income until he discovered that he had a penchant for buying shoes:

> He had golf shoes, tennis shoes, running shoes, boating shoes, walking shoes, hiking shoes and climbing shoes, as well as cross-country-ski shoes, downhill-ski boots

and after-ski boots. Just having a category for shoes helped him find some of that missing income—and face the fact that he rarely wore anything but comfortable around-the-house shoes. He wasn't alone in his shoe fetish. . . . Eighty percent of the athletic shoes in this country are never used for the activity for which they've been designed.[59]

Robin and Dominguez have a term for the kinds of items we tend to buy without thinking clearly about fulfillment. They call them gazingus pins:

A gazingus pin is any item that you just can't pass by without buying. Everybody has them. They run the gamut from pocket calculators and tiny screwdrivers to pens and chocolate kisses. So there you are in the mall, a shopping robot on your weekly tour of the stations of the crass. You come to the gazingus-pin section and your mind starts cranking out gazingus-pin thoughts: Oh, there's a pink one . . . I don't have a pink one . . . Oh, that one runs on solar cells . . . That would be handy . . . My, a waterproof one . . . If I don't use it I can always give it away. . . . [60]

The result is a waste of money and clutter in the home. Robin and Dominguez recommend discovering what your gazingus pins are and avoiding them.

They make other suggestions for saving money as well. Here are a few examples that point in the right direction. Avoid credit card debt:

You pay from 16 percent to over 20 percent interest on your credit card debt. That's like working a five-day week and getting paid for four. If your employer announced such a downward revision in salaries, you and your coworkers would be up in arms. People who see debt as endless and just pay down as little as possible are actually opting for that lower income.[61]

Here is another idea. Do not go shopping unless there is a specific item you have decided you want and need. Robin and Dominguez write:

About 53 percent of groceries and 47 percent of hardware-store purchases are "spur of the moment." When 34,300 mall shoppers across the country were asked the primary reason for their visit, only 25 percent said they had come in pursuit of a specific item. About 70 percent of all adults visit a regional mall weekly.[62]

Other suggestions include taking care of what you have, using what you have until it is worn out, anticipating your needs so you can buy needed items when they are on sale, comparison shopping by telephone, and buying things used.

I would add vegetarianism, or at least reduced meat consumption, to the list. It saves money, makes it easier to control weight, improves the diet of most Americans, enables more people to be fed from diminishing supplies of good topsoil and fresh water, leaves more uncultivated land for use by other species, and reduces the cruel treatment of animals. *People whose reasons to reduce meat consumption, or become vegetarians, include concern about other species illustrate environmental synergy. People and nature are better off due to (at least some aspects of) nature being valued for itself.*

Robin and Dominguez give about 100 tips for **frugality**. "Frugality," they write:

> is . . . getting good *value* for every minute of your life energy and from everything you *have the use of*. . . . Waste lies not in the number of possessions but in the failure to enjoy them. . . . To be frugal means to have a high joy-to-stuff ratio. If you get one unit of joy for each material possession, that's frugal. But if you need ten possessions to even begin registering on the joy meter, you're missing the point of being alive.[63]

And you can't take it with you, Dave Ramsey points out: "He with the most toys when he dies is dead. . . . You never see a Ryder truck following a hearse."[64]

Because frugal people get more bang for the buck, they need fewer bucks to have fulfilling lives. So they may be able to pass up a distasteful job for one they find more satisfying; or they may work for money only part-time; or they may retire early. The key, write Robin and Dominguez, is to separate in your mind productive work from paid employment. *Financial freedom enables people to follow their dreams and be productive to their greatest capacity with diminished concern about pay.* Such people can work for grand causes they believe in, volunteer in local organizations, or spend more time with family, friends, and neighbors.

Of course, frugal people may reduce paid employment opportunities for others. *When consumer demand diminishes, fewer paid workers are needed.* Alan Durning quotes Harvard economist Juliet Schor, who wrote in *The Overworked American*:

> Since 1948, the level of productivity of the U.S. worker has more than doubled. In other words, we could now produce our 1948 standard of living in less than half the time. Every time productivity increases, we are presented with the possibility of either more free time or more money. We could have chosen the four-hour day. Or a working year of six months. Or every worker in the United States could now be taking every other year off from work—with pay.[65]

These same choices exist when fewer worker hours are needed due to declining consumer demand. However, unlike the lifestyle choices discussed above, these societal arrangements are not choices people can make individually. Employment policies affect these matters. The next chapter discusses these and other policies.

This chapter concludes with observations by Robin and Dominguez that support environmental synergism:

> Your health, your pocketbook and the environment have a mutually enhancing relationship. If you do something good for one, it's almost always good for the other two. If you walk or bicycle to work to reduce your contribution to greenhouse gases you are also saving money and getting great exercise at the same time. If you compost your kitchen scraps to improve your soil (the environment) you are also improving the quality of your vegetables (your health)—and saving money on your garbage bill. . . .

It isn't just an odd coincidence that saving money and saving the planet are connected. In fact, in some sense your money *is* the planet. Here's how.

Money is a lien on earth's resources. Every time we spend money on anything, we are consuming not only the metal, plastic, wood or other material in the item itself, but also all the resources it took to extract these from the earth, transport them to the manufacturer, process them, assemble the product, ship it to the retailer and bring it from the store to your home. . . . [66]

Synergists claim that valuing nature for itself, which motivates reducing our exploitation of it, is generally necessary for the best human life. Critics of synergism may think that reducing our consumption to lessen our environmental impact detracts from the quality of human life. This chapter answers critics by claiming that less consumption by middle-class people enhances human life. Caring about biodiversity for itself, goes together with saving money and increasing personal fulfillment. That is synergy.

Judgment Calls

- Journalist Douglas Martin reported in *The New York Times Sunday* that inventor and manufacturer Gregg A. Miller is doing a booming business selling artificial testicles for pets. Some pet owners who have their animals neutered want that natural look, and Mr. Miller claims that neutered pets need artificial testicles to avoid "post-neutering trauma." What do you think?[67]

- We saw in Chapter 3 that Mark Sagoff makes a distinction between our roles as citizens and as consumers. He contends that consumer choices are unaffected by ideals about what is needed to make the world a better place. He claims to drive a car with an "Ecology Now" sticker on it that leaks oil wherever it is parked. How does this chapter relate to his views?

- Ecologist Aldo Leopold suggests that human nature makes some personal choices more satisfying than others. He writes that young children "do not tremble when they are shown a golf ball, but I should not like to own the boy whose hair does not lift his hat when he sees his first deer."[68] What effect might this observation reasonably have on parents who are helping their children develop values that will guide consumer choices?

- My wife and I both need cars, in part because bicycling after dark is dangerous where we live. How might the government expand transportation possibilities so that we would have more choices and would need, perhaps, only one car?

- Poor workers in Third World countries make most of the sports shoes that would go unsold if people in the United States started buying only the shoes they really needed. How might our knowledge of this work force reasonably affect consumer choices in our country? (See the next chapter for more on government policies and globalization.)

CHAPTER 12

Public Policies, Efficiency, and Globalization

The Need for Collective Action

According to a 1997 article in *U.S. News and World Report*, road rage—"events in which an angry or impatient driver tries to kill or injure another driver after a traffic dispute—has risen by 51 percent since 1990." Consider these examples:

> In Salt Lake City, . . . 75-year-old J.C. King—peeved that 41-year-old Larry Remm, Jr. honked at him for blocking traffic—followed Remm when he pulled off the road, hurled his prescription bottle at him, and then—smashed Remm's knees with his '92 Mercury. In . . . Potomac, Md., Robin Ficker—an attorney and ex-state legislator—knocked the glasses off a pregnant woman after she had the temerity to ask him why he bumped her Jeep with his.[1]

About 40,000 people are killed in car accidents every year in the United States and "the U.S. Department of Transportation estimates that two-thirds of fatalities are at least partially caused by aggressive driving."[2]

Why is road rage increasing? The answer is related to the limits of individual action. *Individuals can do many things to save money, improve the quality of their lives, and reduce their negative impact on nature. But many other improvements in life require collective action. Improvements in transportation are among these.*

"Traffic is getting worse," write journalists for *U.S. News and World Report*:

> Since 1987, the number of miles of roads has increased just 1 percent while the miles *driven* have shot up by 35 percent. According to a recent Federal Highway Administration study of 50 metropolitan areas, almost 70 percent of urban freeways today—as opposed to 55 percent in 1983—are clogged during rush hour. . . . A study by the Texas Transportation Institute last year [1996] found that commuters in one-third of the largest cities spent well over 40 hours a year in traffic jams.[3]

Americans often equate cars with freedom. The bald eagle might not be the national symbol if cars had been invented earlier. Yet driving can also be frustrating. My physics professor defined an instant as the time between the light turning green and the person behind you honking. And claims of freedom can be challenged. Organizational theorist David Korten notes that between 1950 and 1990 the number of miles driven by Americans rose two-and-a-half times. But this count included longer commutes to work, greater distances between home and shopping areas, and increased chauffeuring of children to schools, churches, and doctors. "Social and recreational travel actually declined by 1 percent, perhaps because we had less time left for it. Korten adds on the topic of overcrowding: "It is estimated that in the largest U.S. urban areas, 1 billion to 2 billion hours a year are wasted due to traffic congestion."[4]

There is little that most of us individually can do about the situation. Most of us have to use cars because distances between work, home, shopping, and other activities are too great for walking, bicycling is dangerous, and public transportation is poor. But this does not mean we are helpless. *We often can do collectively as citizens what we cannot do individually to promote environmental synergy, human flourishing in harmony with an environment valued for itself.* This chapter considers public policies promoting synergy in transportation, agriculture, unemployment, politics, and world trade.

Subsidizing Inefficiency

Most people value efficiency because it allows us to get more of what we want from the means at our disposal. The free market often fosters efficiency. Producers compete with one another to provide goods and services of greater quality at lower prices. A lower price typically represents a smaller drain not only on our individual financial resources, but also on the resources of the planet. For example, telephone communication with fiber optics is cheaper than with copper wire, and it is cheaper at least in part because fiber optics takes up less space and uses more readily available materials. The lower price corresponds to reduced environmental impact. Free market competition within the profit-oriented telecommunications industry results in efficiencies that benefit both customers and ecosystems. Long distance rates keep coming down.

We saw in Chapter 1 that this logic does not work with public goods, such as clean air and water. These are goods that no one owns individually, so no one has a financial incentive to use them efficiently. They tend to be wasted unless society imposes regulations, such as required pollution permits, which make degradation costly.

Another limit to efficiency from profit-oriented competition stems from subsidies. *If the government pays part of the cost of engaging in an activity, it will be cheaper for consumers. But this does not make it cheaper for society or less destructive of nature. People unaware of subsidies may look at the price and consider the activity efficient, but this will be an illusion. The efficiency of automotive transport is just such an illusion.*

Consider parking, for example. It is not cheap. In 1991, Deborah Gordon of the Union of Concerned Scientists reported figures from the United States Department of Transportation and other sources:

An above-grade space can cost up to $18,000 to build, and underground parking is at least twice that much. . . . Moreover, a 500-car parking lot requires an estimated 170,000 gallons of gasoline to construct and 1,200 gallons of gasoline for annual maintenance. . . . Cost savings per parking space eliminated can range from $1,000–$15,000 depending on land cost and type of parking facility.[5]

The typical commuter does not pay a fair share of these costs, Gordon notes: "Seventy-five percent of all commuters park in free, employer-provided, off-street spaces. . . ."[6] Commuting to work by car appears cheaper than it really is due to employers' subsidies.

Taxpayers subsidize the car commute as well. Employees do not have to pay taxes on the monetary worth of the parking subsidies they receive from employers, but they do have to pay taxes when employers give them more than $15 per month to take mass transit. Additionally, Gordon writes: "Employers can deduct their parking maintenance and operating costs for tax purposes."[7] So employers make the car commute seem cheap by subsidizing it, and taxpayers subsidize employer generosity.

This is just the tip of the iceberg. We subsidize automotive transport when we pay doctors' bills and insurance premiums, Gordon maintains: "The annual cost to human health and the environment from vehicle pollution has been estimated at between $4 and $93 billion. . . . As many as 120,000 deaths each year can be linked to air pollution."[8] Most comes from cars and light trucks, the most common means of transportation. They "have the highest emission levels per passenger mile for all principal pollutants. In fact, a single-occupancy car emits twice as much NOx, three times as much CO_2, 10 times as many hydrocarbons, and 17 times as much CO as mass transit."[9] So it may be cheaper for me to drive than take the bus from Springfield, Illinois, to Denver, Colorado to visit my brother, but that is because my trip expenses do not include compensation for ill health and premature death due to air pollution created by highway driving.

That is not all. The trip is cheaper also because it does not reflect military costs incurred to secure a steady supply of imported oil. Because we use cars so much, we have to import most of our crude oil. Unfortunately for national security, Gordon writes, "the U.S. is importing an increasing amount of oil from politically unstable sources, including the Persian Gulf countries and Nigeria."[10] Consider the Gulf War. It "cost the equivalent of an average 40 cents per gallon of imported gasoline. . . . Furthermore, the cost will be a continuing one, since even if future wars are avoided, the U.S. is expected to maintain a constant military presence in the Middle East."[11]

General tax revenues also subsidize highways and other infrastructures that cars require, writes Worldwatch senior associate Marcia Lowe:

Drivers in the United States . . . are often surprised to learn that gasoline taxes, vehicle taxes, and road tolls typically cover less than two-thirds the total capital and operating costs of highways. These costs include what all levels of government spend on administration, traffic services, and interest and debt retirement. The amount not covered by user fees—in 1992, more than $32 billion—comes from local property taxes, general fund appropriations and other sources.[12]

Automotive transport is thus much less efficient than most people imagine because it degrades public goods, such as clean air, and receives massive government subsidies. It also inefficiently performs its primary function—getting people where they need to go. One major reason is traffic congestion, which not only frays nerves and provokes road rage, but is also expensive. Again, Marcia Lowe:

> The United States General Accounting Office (GAO) reports that productivity losses from highway congestion cost the nation some $100 billion annually.[13] The Texas Traffic Institute estimates that, in 1988, traffic congestion in U.S. urban areas cost more than $400 per vehicle. In cities in the Northeast, the figure rose to $750 per vehicle.[14]

And the situation is expected to get worse, Lowe reports: "A calculation by the U.S. General Accounting Office found that at the current rate of growth, traffic congestion on roads will triple in 15 years—even if road capacity is increased by 20 percent. And such a massive expansion of capacity is unlikely. . . ."[15]

Deborah Gordon explains some implications:

> What these figures mean is that by 2005 the average commuter from one suburb of a metropolitan area to another suburb could spend up to five times as long in traffic as in 1990. This could mean moving at five miles per hour over a 10-mile trip—a two-hour commute. Not only time but fuel would be wasted; the FHWA [Federal Highway Administration] projects that by 2005, 7.3 billion gallons of fuel will be wasted each year—7 percent of projected oil use for highway passenger transport.[16]

Besides wasting time, gasoline, and money, *driving in congested traffic harms the environment and human health.* Gordon writes:

> Congestion is extremely destructive to the environment. The inefficient operation it causes—reduced speed, frequent acceleration, stop-and-go movement, and longer trips—increases air pollution and greenhouse-gas emissions. For example, carbon dioxide emissions double when average speed drops from 30 to 10 mph, and hydrocarbon and carbon monoxide emissions triple at speeds of less than 35 mph compared with a constant speed of 55 mph. . . . [17]

Stop-and-go driving is particularly health impairing. It adds more pollution to the air, and people stuck in traffic have longer exposure to this highly concentrated pollution. Maybe this is why lung cancer increases as cigarette smoking declines.

Altogether, enormous subsidies lower the direct cost of using a car, Lowe concludes. Considering " 'free' parking . . . smog, accidents, and traffic jams— the total U.S. subsidy paid to drivers is estimated to range from $300 billion–$600 billion per year."[18] But this is not all. Consider subsidies for suburban sprawl that promote the use of automobiles. Worldwatch research associate David Roodman put it this way:

Today's buildings would be useless without the pipes, cables, and roads that splay out to them to provide water, gas, electricity, and mobility. Yet when governments bury the costs of these connectors, which vary with length, they encourage sprawl. . . . Unless the people who decide to live far from city or town centers are asked to pay the higher costs of the infrastructure they need, suburban sprawl will appear artificially cheap. Like other factors that encourage car-dependent development, . . . making infrastructure appear cheap to its users contributes to pollution, oil dependence, and traffic jams that chew up billions of hours of people's time.[19]

No wonder cars symbolize freedom. Much of their use is free.

More Efficient Transportation

Rail is more efficient than cars. Rail travel reduces energy use and air pollution, Marcia Lowe reports:

For every kilometer of travel, an intercity passenger train consumes only one-third as much energy per rider as a commercial airplane, and one-sixth as much as a car carrying only the driver. Commuters who take light rail or the subway to work instead of driving solo slash their contribution to urban smog, cutting nitrogen oxide emissions from each trip by 60 percent and nearly eliminating carbon monoxide and particulate emissions.[20]

Rail saves time and space as well. When more people use rail there is more room for the cars that remain on roads. Their speed increases, Roodman writes, "more than proportionally, so that in total, vehicles cover more kilometers in less time."[21] Lowe points out savings of space: "Two railroad tracks can carry as many people in an hour as 16 lanes of highway."[22] This saves money in urban areas where property values are high.

Rail saves space indirectly by encouraging more compact residential and commercial development, the opposite of suburban sprawl. Because these communities are more compact, people can more easily walk or bicycle. This provides health-preserving exercise, forestalls health-impairing pollution, and reduces congestion. The result is improved prospects for economic development, Lowe writes:

Montgomery County, Maryland—a county of 740,000 people near Washington, D.C.—is a case in point. A long-range planning study for the county found that if urban growth continued in the usual auto- highway-oriented pattern—even at a slower pace—the resulting traffic congestion would stifle further economic development. In contrast, focusing most new urban growth in pedestrian- and bicycle-friendly clusters along an expanded rail and bus system—and revising commuter subsidies to discourage the use of cars—would enable the county to double its current number of jobs and households without exacerbating traffic congestion.[23]

Another benefit of rail is safety, Lowe adds:

> In the United States, the risk of death in an auto accident is roughly 18 times that for rail. . . . In addition to incalculable health damage and loss of human life, road accidents impose financial burdens. . . . A recent study for the U.S. Federal Highway Administration included estimates of the monetary worth of pain, suffering, and lost quality of life in its tally of costs of U.S. road accidents in 1988. It arrived at a total of $358 billion, 8 percent of GNP.[24]

Expanding mass transit rail and bus service tends to evoke anxiety about public subsidies. People often imagine that if the service were genuinely efficient and helpful, people would ride trains and buses enough for mass transit to pay for itself in user fees. Subsidies should not be necessary. However, this line of thinking makes sense only if the alternative to riding trains and buses—which is the car in most cases—were also subsidy free. But it is not. The practical issue now is not whether to subsidize transportation, but which transportation alternatives to subsidize when, and how much. *Given that rail and buses are safer, carry more people per lane, use less fuel per passenger mile, reduce costly congestion, encourage efficient, compact development, and add less health-impairing pollution to the air than cars, it is no surprise that subsidies for public transportation are more rewarding financially than subsidies for cars.* Lowe reports:

> A recent U.S. study looked at the impact of government transport expenditures on worker productivity. A 10-year, $100-billion increase in public transport spending was estimated to boost worker output by $521 billion—compared with $237 billion for the same level of spending on highways. Moreover, public transport investments began returning net benefits nearly three times as quickly as highway expenditures. Other studies have drawn similar conclusions. . . . A 1991 study . . . compared the economic effects of investing in rehabilitation and continued operation of SEPTA (the light rail, subway, and commuter rail system in the Philadelphia metropolitan area) with cutting or eliminating its services. The study found that for every dollar of public spending on rebuilding and operating SEPTA, $3 would accrue to the state and the region as a direct result of improved transport.[25]

Compact development through subsidized mass transit does more than save tax dollars. It also helps poor people avoid welfare. James Kunstler writes in his 1993 book *The Geography of Nowhere* about low-income wage earners in upstate New York:

> They commute to Saratoga, Glens Falls, Albany—an expense that only puts a further drain on their finances. The $4500 it costs to own and operate a car each year could cover a year's payments on a $30,000 mortgage. Often, it is absolutely necessary to keep two cars operating in a family so that two adults can drive long distances to work low-wage jobs. The cost of driving everywhere . . . makes it impossible for them to own their own home.[26]

Many Americans work extra hours and see their families less to pay car expenses. Car travel is so inefficient that it drains budgets even after massive government subsidies.

Why, then, do people love their cars so much, condemn public transportation for requiring subsidies, and fail to perceive subsidies for automotive transport? MONEY and PROPAGANDA. People with money misrepresent the situation to the public. David Korten writes: "It is not difficult to figure out who benefits from this damage to the quality of our living. In terms of sales, the three largest companies in America are General Motors Corporation (cars), Exxon Corporation (oil), and Ford Motor Company (cars). Mobil Corporation (oil) is number seven."[27] Car companies use money to advertise their products and associate them with freedom. Together with oil and road-building enterprises, they have the money to support political candidates who oppose subsidies for mass transit. They use their money also to oppose candidates who favor mass transit and dare to point out subsidies for cars.

Of course, it is convenient for most people in the United States at this time to use their cars. Cars help us go wherever we want, whenever we want. When we think of public transportation we imagine waiting in the rain for half an hour at a bus stop, travelling ever so slowly on the bus, and then walking half a mile at the other end. We know also that many places are simply inaccessible by public transportation. So we think that cars give us freedom and save us time.

We tend to think this way because most of us have never lived where society supports public instead of private transportation. Where urban public transport is good, light rail and subways pick people up every three to five minutes and move them much faster than buses or cars can move in traffic. People are let off near their destinations, even destinations in the suburbs. They go where they want, when they want, just as with cars, but at greater speed, in greater safety, at less total cost, and without the need to find parking. Transportation in Manhattan approximates these conditions closely enough that most New Yorkers use public transportation there.

The proposal here is to extend these conditions from a few large cities to medium-size cities and the suburbs of all cities. Then most people would have real freedom, which includes the freedom to choose public over private transportation. Up to now, automotive-related interests have used the political system to reduce this freedom. I suggest different government transportation policies to increase freedom and save money.

Subsidies for cars should be reduced gradually and the money saved devoted to mass transit and inter-urban rail systems. When enough of these are in place to give people genuine alternative modes of transportation, all subsidies for automotive transport should be removed by gradually increasing the tax on a gallon of gasoline to reflect the full social cost of using that gallon to power a car or truck. People will still have the freedom to own and drive cars and trucks, but they will not have the freedom to make others share the cost.

We will all have greater freedom to use our transportation dollars as we wish, not as automotive interests determine.

This is environmentally synergistic. People save time, money, and live more safely. More compact human living leaves more space for other species. All species benefit from cleaner air and a reduced threat of global warming.

Agricultural Policies

Subsidies also bedevil agriculture, making it less efficient and more costly than necessary. David Roodman starts with this example:

> In California's Central Valley, some farmers can buy a thousand cubic meters of water from a federal project—enough to irrigate a few hundred square meters of vegetables—for $2.84, even though it costs the government $24.84 to deliver it. Thanks to fertile soil and favorable climate, however, the water is actually worth at least $80–160 in the valley, based on what farmers pay for water from the state government. . . . In a region where this precious resource is scarce and salinization and other side effects of improper irrigation are becoming increasingly serious, low prices are encouraging farmers to squander water rather than husband it.[28]

Many subsidies for agriculture in the United States have been justified as needed to save the family farm. But most have had the opposite effect, Roodman observes:

> Most payments are based on how much food farmers grow, not on how small their farms are. Not surprisingly, the number of U.S. farms fell by two-thirds between 1930 and 1990, even as grain elevators bulged with millions of tons of surplus food. As a result of this concentration in ownership, 58 percent of the agricultural support payments—$6.5 billion—went to the top 15 percent of farms in 1991, those grossing over $100,000 per year.[29]

The poorest 60 percent of farmers received only 17 percent of government support. *Farms got larger not because large farms are more efficient, but because the government gave more money to large farms than to small ones, making them appear more efficient.*

Worse yet, Roodman writes:

> In western industrial nations . . . production subsidies have also encouraged environmentally destructive farming, including the use of chemical fertilizers and pesticides and the abandonment of traditional practices such as rotating crops and fallowing fields. These shifts have accelerated soil erosion and the accumulation of chemicals in land and water, threatening the sustainability of agriculture even as global population continues to expand.[30]

Roodman here agrees with the National Research Council:

> As a whole, federal policies work against environmentally benign practices and
> the adoption of alternative agricultural systems, particularly those involving crop
> rotations, certain soil conservation practices, reductions in pesticide use, and in-
> creased use of biological and cultural means of pest control.[31]

In other words, from the long-term environmental perspective, governments
have subsidized particularly inefficient agricultural practices.

Large agribusinesses that sell artificial fertilizers and pesticides used extensively on large, government-subsidized farms, claim that such farming is
needed to feed the world. One of the largest companies, Archer Daniels Midland (ADM), calls itself "supermarket to the world," and suggests that its products will help feed hungry people worldwide. United States Senator Richard
Lugar, Republican from Indiana and head of the Senate Agriculture Committee, makes the same claim for genetically altered varieties of corn and soybeans
produced by Monsanto Corp. Roger Cohen of *The New York Times* summarizes
Lugar's argument for such products: "The population of the world will probably grow to nine billion from six billion by 2050. Available acreage for planting has already been identified. So, unless food productivity is increased—
which will not happen without scientific intervention—people are going to go
hungry."[32]

ADM and Monsanto are profit-oriented corporations attempting to increase
the value of shareholder stocks. They can afford to advertise their products'
benevolent effects on the world's poor. However, no organization dedicated to
serving the poor *without profit* endorses such corporate claims. Organizations
such as Care, Save the Children, Bread for the World, and Oxfam stress the
need for poor people around the world to grow their own food, not buy it from
overseas.

Why? For one thing, many people around the world are expected to remain
too poor to buy seed or food from overseas companies trying to make a profit.
Second, the importation of food from overseas is largely responsible for the
collapse of local agriculture and the hunger of poor people. Roodman explains
that when rich countries subsidize their own farmers, the result is overpro-
duction. Much of this surplus is sold cheaply for a time in developing countries, where tax revenues are insufficient to allow governments to give local
farmers equivalent subsidies. Local farmers go broke, local sources of food decline, and poor people are at the mercy of price fluctuations in food sold on
the world market. Then when food prices go up, many go hungry. The export
of American agricultural products to the Third World helps create the problem of hunger. It is not part of the solution.

Other reasons favoring local production worldwide and smaller farms in the
U.S. are given in Chapter 8. They relate to the values of home, community, and
work, as well as species diversity, pollution abatement, cultural diversity, and
food self-sufficiency.

What should our government do? Its *policies should favor small American farms owned by the farmers who work them. Policies should also help family farmers pass the farm down to the next generation.* These policies would help revive rural communities, because more people would live on the land. They would also provide incentives for soil conservation and other measures needed for sustainable agriculture. When people own their land and can realistically expect to pass it on to the family's next generation, they are more motivated to protect its long-term productivity. Policies of this sort include crop support payments that favor smaller farms; reductions in the capital gains tax when large farms are broken up and sold to farm families; and revisions in inheritance laws that permit tax-free inheritance of smaller family farms.

The government should also phase out water subsidies and buy only sustainably grown food for the military and for food assistance programs. Sustainable agriculture would then have a ready market for its products. In addition, the government could phase out not only direct, but also indirect support for large, chemically dependent agriculture. For example, the government should reduce subsidies for motorized transport. Large, centralized agricultural enterprises use artificially cheap transportation by truck to get their products to market.

Corporate Welfare and Campaign Finance Reform

Changes like those described above threaten wealthy corporations that benefit from the status quo. *Seed and chemical companies such as Monsanto and ADM flourish when government policies favor large, chemically dependent farms at home, production for export, and food dependency overseas. These corporations use their political clout to influence public policy.*

Consider subsidies for ethanol, a fuel currently manufactured primarily from corn. Advocates point out that it is a renewable source of energy: we can grow more corn. Because the United States produces a lot of corn, advocates insist, the more ethanol we use, the smaller our dependence on foreign sources of oil. This helps national security. In addition, ethanol is somewhat cleaner burning than ordinarily gasoline, so its use can help improve air quality and human health.

Ethanol cannot be used as a fuel in today's cars because it corrodes engines, but it can be used in a 10-percent mixture with normal gasoline to make what is called gasohol. "In 1988," Deborah Gordon writes, "about 800 million gallons of ethanol were sold in the United States, . . . nearly all of it domestically produced. It was used to make over eight billion gallons of gasohol, enough to fuel 7 percent of U.S. automobiles. Ninety-five percent of U.S. ethanol was made from corn. . . ."[33]

So far this looks good, but appearances are deceiving. First, ethanol is not price competitive with ordinary gasoline. Gordon notes: "Estimates of the cost to produce, distribute, and market ethanol from corn range from $1.75 to $2.07 per gallon of gasoline-equivalent. Because this price is too high to compete with gasoline, commercial viability will depend on government subsidies, mandates, and incentives."[34] Beginning in 1978, the U.S. government has supported gasohol with a tax exemption worth about 6 cents a gallon. "Since gasohol is 10 percent ethanol, the equivalent tax subsidy for ethanol itself is 60 cents per gallon of pure ethanol or 90 cents per gallon of gasoline equivalent."[35] Is this a good use of taxpayer money?

No. The United States Office of Technology Assessment concluded in 1990 that ethanol made from corn adds little, if anything, to the country's energy supplies because current methods of growing corn use enormous amounts of petroleum for fertilizer, harvesting, transport, and so forth. Petroleum is being put into agriculture at one end to produce ethanol at the other end that barely replaces the original petroleum. Imagine someone wanting to drink a cola beverage. He has Coca-Cola, which is just fine, but instead of drinking the Coke he engages in a costly process of transforming it into Pepsi. Then he drinks the Pepsi. Seems crazy, right? How crazy would you have to be to pay for this? Well, American taxpayers are paying to transform petroleum through corn into ethanol for cars.

Any reductions in air pollution from burning ethanol instead of gasoline are overwhelmed by gasoline emissions released in the process of producing that ethanol. Worse yet, current methods of growing corn are environmentally harmful. For example, plowing results in soil erosion. Fertilizer and pesticide runoff pollutes water supplies. In terms of the cola example, imagine that besides everything else, the person is using your kitchen, leaving it a mess, and ruining your appliances. Now how much would you pay?

In 1998, Congress extended the ethanol subsidy until 2007. Why? According to Jennifer Loven, reporting for the Associated Press:

> agribusiness giant Archer Daniels Midland Co. [is] the nation's largest ethanol producer [and] counts the tax break as a key component of its bottom line. . . . Pro-ethanol groups spent more than $5.6 million in 1997 and the first half of 1998 to persuade Congress to preserve ethanol's special status in the tax code, lobbying reports show. Adding more firepower were $23,540 in campaign contributions this election cycle from many of the about three dozen lobbyists deployed to canvass Capitol Hill by those groups. Another $527,255 was poured into the system by ADM employees and the family of the company's politically connected chairman, Dwayne Andreas, according to federal campaign financial records and data compiled by the Center for Responsive Politics.[36]

This is perfectly legal influence peddling that makes good economic sense from corporate and industry perspectives. David Roodman points out that in the United States:

> Candidates for Congress and the presidency spent $1.6 billion campaigning in 1996. . . . Though this is a huge sum to spend on electing fewer than 500 people, it is trivial compared with the roughly $1.6 trillion at stake each year in federal spending and tax decisions. Ten-thousand-dollar or even million-dollar donations may

make politicians' mouths water, but they are peanuts for large corporations, and excellent investments even if they only sway legislators occasionally.[37]

ADM, for example, has spent many millions on lobbyists and campaign contributions in the last two decades. But, Roodman reports, the ethanol subsidy "has cost the government $6.3 billion [between 1983 and 1996], much of that going to ADM, which holds half the market."[38] *Campaign contributions and lobbying expenditures often yielded 1,000 percent return or more within a year. Better investments are hard to find.*

ADM and ethanol are not unique, Roodman explains:

> Between 1993 and mid-1996, oil and gas companies gave $10.3 million to protect special tax breaks worth roughly $4 billion over the same period. Timber lobbies donated $2.3 million in order to keep the subsidized timber coming. Mining firms handed out $1.9 million to members of Congress to fend off royalty charges on public hardrock minerals, something they have succeeded in doing since 1872. Ranching interests contributed too, in order to keep federal grazing fees low, as they have been since 1906. . . . Almost all succeed in keeping their subsidies. . . .[39]

Automotive and oil interests keep subsidies for automotive transportation and block most funding for efficient public transportation. None of these subsidies (and there are many more) makes any more sense environmentally or economically than the one for ethanol.

Reprinted by permission of John Jonik

Politicians need money to run their campaigns, and these groups have the money to give. Roodman reports, "During the same period [between 1993 and mid-1996], environmental groups gave only $1.6 million" in political contributions.[40] What should be done? David Korten recommends the following "sweeping campaign reforms":

> In return for their right to use public airways, television and radio stations should be required to provide exposure for candidates for public office on issues-oriented interview programs and debates on an equal-time basis.
>
> Political advertising on television should be prohibited. It is enormously expensive, often misleading, and rarely informative.
>
> Total campaign expenditures should be limited.
>
> Campaign costs should be covered by a combination of public funding and small individual tax-deductible contributions. Political action committees should be abolished, and corporations should be prohibited from making any kind of political contribution or using corporate resources to favor any candidate. . . . [41]

Many people would resist such reforms in the name of free speech. According to their argument, we should be able to use our resources to communicate with others about important public issues, and this is what people do when they pay for political ads either individually or as members of political action committees.

There is some truth to this. But it is not the whole truth. Another important point is that *democracy is valuable, and democracy increases as people have more equal access to political speech. The current system fosters extremely unequal access,* which harms not just the environment, but democracy itself. If a major reason for free speech is to foster democracy, then limits like those Korten recommends seem worthwhile.

Others object to using taxpayers' money to fund campaigns. Tax money should be reserved for more important matters, they think.

These people seem to forget two things. First, the amount of money is trivial compared to what could be saved through avoiding costly and unnecessary subsidies. Failure to spend tax dollars to finance campaigns is penny wise and pound foolish. Second, under the current system, taxpayers fund campaigns anyway. Corporations with government subsidies use some of the money they get from the government to fund candidates favorable to the continuation of the subsidies. This, too, is taxpayers' money funding campaigns, but for special interests, not the common good.

The Promise of Globalization

Proponents of **globalization** support public policies that many environmentalists oppose. *Globalization is a movement to create a worldwide free market in which job opportunities, products, and investment capital can move as freely among nations as they currently do within them.* In this section, the nature and advantages of globalization are explained, with special attention to the views that *The New York Times* correspondent Thomas Friedman expresses in his 1999 bestseller *The Lexus and the Olive Tree*. Criticisms of globalization follow in the next section.

Globalization involves aiding international competition by lowering or removing tariff barriers and facilitating international investing by allowing all currencies to be traded freely in international currency markets, so investors can decide when to put money into or take money out of any country. It also requires lowering or eliminating government subsidies of local industries. Such subsidies are unfair to unsubsidized foreign competitors and, as we have seen, tend to create the kinds of inefficiencies that free markets are supposed to eliminate. *Globalization attempts to extend free market efficiencies worldwide.*

Globalization requires uniform, international standards regarding such matters as intellectual property rights, workplace safety, and environmental protection. Uniform intellectual property rights improve incentives for firms to invest in innovation. They gain the right to receive royalties when their product is used anywhere in the world.

Uniform standards on such matters as workplace safety and environmental protection are needed to prevent countries from using employment or environmental standards as pretexts for restricting international trade. For example, a country wanting to protect local producers may claim that foreign competitors have an unfair advantage because they do not give their employees paid vacations or because they are not required to treat wastewater before it enters the environment. Globalization requires what they call "harmonization" on such matters, and a court where disputes can be resolved.

Thomas Friedman claims that globalization is the only route to prosperity:

> The centrally planned, nondemocratic alternatives [to free-market capitalism] . . . *didn't work*. And the people who rendered that judgment were the people who lived under them. So with the collapse of communism in Europe, in the Soviet Union and in China . . . those people who are unhappy with . . . free-market capitalism don't have any ready ideological alternative now. When it comes to the question of which system today is the most effective at generating rising standards of living, the historical debate is over. The answer is free-market capitalism. . . . In the end, if you want higher standards of living in a world without walls, the free market is the only ideological alternative left.[42]

Global free market capitalism, according to Friedman, can foster worldwide prosperity. Free flows of technology, capital, and information around the world mean:

> Countries . . . can now increasingly choose to be prosperous. They don't have to be prisoners of their natural resources, geography or history. In a world where a country can plug into the Internet and import knowledge, in a world where a country can find shareholders from any other country to invest in its infrastructure . . ., where a country can import the technology to be an auto producer or computer

maker even if it has no raw materials, a country can more than ever before opt for prosperity or poverty, depending on the policies it pursues.[43]

Those policies, which Friedman calls "the Golden Straitjacket," include the following:

Making the private sector the primary engine of . . . economic growth, . . . shrinking the size of [the] state bureaucracy, maintaining as close to a balanced budget as possible . . . , eliminating and lowering tariffs on imported goods, removing restrictions on foreign investment, getting rid of quotas and domestic monopolies, increasing exports, privatizing state-owned industries and utilities, . . . making [the] currency convertible, [and] opening . . . industries, stock, and bond markets to direct foreign ownership and investment. . . . [44]

Friedman admits that "this Golden Straitjacket is pretty much 'one size fits all'," and not everyone is pleased by this. "But," he claims, "it's here and it's the only model on the rack this historical season."[45]

The two results of putting on the straitjacket are prosperity and shrinking politics. "The Golden Straitjacket narrows the political and economic policy choices of those in power to relatively tight parameters. . . . Governments . . . which deviate too far from the core rules will see their investors stampede away, interest rates rise and stock market valuations fall."[46] Friedman quotes Monmohan Singh, India's former Finance Minister: "In a world in which capital is internationally mobile, you cannot adopt rates of taxation that are far from the rates that prevail in other countries, and when labor is mobile you also can't be out of line with others' wages."[47]

This applies to rich countries as well as poor ones. Friedman recalls visiting Canada in February 1995, when all the talk was about a recent visit of

"the Man from Moody's." Canada's Parliament at the time was debating the country's budget. The team from Moody's [an organization that rates credit risks that affect interest rates] . . . had just read the riot act to the Canadian Finance Ministry and legislators. The Moody's team told them that if they did not get their deficit-to-GDP ratio more in line with international norms and expectations, Moody's would downgrade their triple-A credit rating, and therefore Canada and every Canadian company would have to pay higher interest rates to borrow abroad.[48]

This loss of local control over such matters as wages, working conditions, foreign investment, environmental protection, budget deficits, and government subsidies is worth it, Friedman contends, because it results in prosperity, and the only alternative is poverty. He claims, too, that this is what ordinary people want. He cites the example of a Vietnamese woman in the heart of Hanoi "crouched on the sidewalk with her bathroom scale. She was offering to weigh people for a small fee." Friedman adds: "To me, her unspoken motto was: 'Whatever you've got, no matter how big or small—sell it, trade it, barter it, leverage it, rent it, but do something with it to turn a profit, improve your standard of living and get into the game.' " He concludes:

> Globalization emerges from below, from street level, from people's very souls and from their very deepest aspirations. . . . , [from] the basic human desire for a better life—a life with more choices as to what to eat, what to wear, where to live, where to travel, how to work, what to read, what to write and what to learn.[49]

Globalization and Human Misery

Friedman is concerned that inequalities between rich and poor are increasing:

> According to the 1998 United Nations Human Development Report, in 1960 the 20 percent of the world's people who live in the richest countries had 30 times the income of the poorest 20 percent. By 1995, the richest 20 percent had 82 times as much income. . . . Today the wealthiest one-fifth of the world's people consume 58 percent of total energy, while the poorest fifth consume less than 4 percent. The wealthiest one-fifth now have 74 percent of all telephone lines, the poorest fifth 1.5 percent. . . . The wealthiest one-fifth consume 45 percent of all meat and fish, while the poorest fifth consume less than 5 percent.[50]

Income gaps are increasing within nations, too, especially within developing countries. "In Brazil, for instance, the poorest 50 percent of the population received 18 percent of the national income in 1960. By 1995, they received only 11.6 percent, while the richest 10 percent of Brazil's population were taking home 63 percent of the national income."[51]

Friedman observes: "there is something inherently unstable about a world that is being knit together tighter and tighter by technology, markets and telecommunications, while splitting apart wider and wider socially and economically."[52] The UN report notes:

> A host of consumption options have been opened for many consumers—but many are left out in the cold through lack of income. And pressures for competitive spending mount. "Keeping up with the Joneses" has shifted from striving to match the consumption of a next-door neighbor to pursue the lifestyles of the rich and famous depicted in movies and television shows.[53]

Permanently disappointing such dreams can be dangerous. It can foment discontent, disruptive behavior, terrorism, and revolution. In a world in which atomic bombs can be made small enough to fit into a large backpack, discontent is more dangerous than ever.

Friedman and other advocates of globalization seem to think, however, that free market capitalism will unleash so much productivity that people in poor countries will eventually be able to live like Americans. He writes, you will recall, "Countries . . . can now increasingly choose to be prosperous,"[54] and he associates prosperity with the American lifestyle, including our penchant for McDonalds.[55] *But this is pure fantasy that soothes the conscience and dulls the mind.* Here is where we must criticize globalization.

Everyone around the world cannot, for example, eat the way Americans do. We saw in the introductory chapter to this book that the world's freshwater sources are diminishing. In Chapter 1, we saw that world grain production per capita has been falling since 1984. The American meat-oriented diet consumes too much grain, and producing that grain requires too much water, to be extended to more than about 2.5 billion people. But there are already more than 6 billion people in the world. Free market globalization cannot result in diets worldwide like those enjoyed in the United States.

The same is true of timber usage. David Korten writes:

> The allowable timber usage, based on an assumption that . . . existing nonprimary forestlands will be used on a sustained-yield basis, would be 0.4 cubic meters per person per year—including wood used for paper. To bring consumption in line with equitable sustainable use . . . the United States . . . would have to reduce its timber consumption by 79 percent.[56]

Or consider the use of fossil fuels. As pointed out in the last chapter, *avoiding the worst global warming scenario requires people in the United States eventually to cut drastically their use of fossil fuels if they are to share equitably with people around the globe. But developing countries tend to increase the use of fossil fuels to (you guessed it) "fuel" their economies. Such development, which is what globalization has so far produced, is a recipe for disaster.* Korten sums up this way:

> If the earth's sustainable natural output were shared equally among the earth's present population, the needs of all could be met. But it is . . . clear that it is a physical impossibility, even with the most optimistic assumptions about the potential of new technologies, for the world to consume at levels even approximating those in North America, Europe, and Japan. Furthermore, each time the world's population doubles, the allowable per capita consumption share is reduced by half.[55]

Globalization enthusiasts appear to confuse "anyone can" with "all of us together can." If they are correct about technological possibilities, then *any* nation can become rich. But this does not mean that *every* nation together can become rich. Consider this example. Suppose I order 25 textbooks for a class, and 30 students enroll. I can tell any student that the book was available for her. *Any* student could have been among the 25 who showed up early enough to get the textbook. But obviously *every* one among the 30 students could not have been among the first 25. Similarly, even if it is true that *any* nation can become rich, limited natural resources make it impossible for *every* nation to follow this path. In fact, few can do so. Korten cites a study by William Rees, an urban planner at the University of British Colombia:

> Rees estimates that four to six hectares of land are required to maintain the consumption of the average person living in a high-income country—including the land required to maintain current levels of energy consumption using renewable

sources. Yet in 1990, the total available ecologically productive land area (land capable of generating consequential biomass) in the world was only an estimated 1.7
hectares per capita.[58]

Since 1990, world population has increased and productive land area decreased.

The actual results of globalization are worse than simply leaving some countries behind. For the most part *globalization further impoverishes the already poor.*
Korten gives the example of Japan reducing domestic pollution from smelting
copper. They financed the Philippine Associated Smelting and Refining Corporation (PASAR):

> The plant occupies 400 acres of land expropriated by the Philippine government
> from local residents at give-away prices. Gas and wastewater emissions from the
> plant contain high concentrations of boron, arsenic, heavy metals, and sulfur com-
> pounds that have contaminated local water supplies, reduced fishing and rice
> yields, damaged the forests, and increased the occurrence of upper-respiratory dis-
> eases among local residents. Local people . . . are now largely dependent on the
> occasional part-time or contractual employment they are offered to do the plant's
> most dangerous and dirtiest jobs.
>
> The company has prospered. The local economy has grown. . . . The Philippine
> government is repaying the foreign aid loan from Japan that financed the con-
> struction of supporting infrastructure for the plant. And the Japanese are con-
> gratulating themselves for . . . their generous assistance to the poor of the Philip-
> pines.[59]

Korten claims that this case is typical. He offers this summary:

> Rapid economic growth in low-income countries brings modern airports, televi-
> sion, express highways, and air-conditioned shopping malls . . . for the fortunate
> few. It rarely improves living conditions for the many. This kind of growth re-
> quires gearing the economy toward exports to earn the foreign exchange to buy
> the things that wealthy people desire. Thus, the lands of the poor are appropri-
> ated for export crops. The former tillers of these lands find themselves subsisting
> in urban slums on starvation wages paid by sweatshops producing for export. Fam-
> ilies are broken up, the social fabric is strained to the breaking point, and violence
> becomes endemic.[60]

The UN statistics cited by Friedman concerning income gaps between rich and
poor support this analysis. Friedman's Golden Straightjacket points in the same
direction. It requires selling public lands to profit-oriented businesses, and profits usually come by kicking peasants off the land and using the land to generate foreign exchange income.

Friedman cites the example of the Vietnamese woman on a sidewalk in Hanoi
offering to weigh people for a small fee. Living so long inside the money-
beltway, he imagines she is bullish on globalization. Korten's analysis suggests
she is more likely a displaced victim of globalization. Friedman is probably
correct that such people must adopt the motto, in his words: "Whatever you've

got, no matter how big or small—sell it, trade it, barter it, . . . rent it. . . . " Friedman, a man who seems to mean well, appears not to realize that the Golden
Straightjacket makes people so desperate that they have to rent their bodies in
prostitution, sell their children into bondage, and barter family ties for food. It
seems the larger the money-belt, the more likely it is worn over the eyes.

The World Trade Organization, Environmental Protection, and Democracy

As noted already, free market globalization requires "harmonization" of standards regarding such matters as intellectual property rights, workplace rules,
and environmental protection. The current process of generating such standards began in 1947 with establishment of the **General Agreement on Tariffs
and Trade (GATT)**. It provided a forum for more specific agreements and for
the establishment in 1995 of the **World Trade Organization (WTO)**, which now
oversees compliance with relevant treaties.

The WTO discourages trade restrictions among its more than 100 member
countries by imposing sanctions on those found guilty of restricting trade.
Heavy duties are placed on their exports to compensate other countries hurt
by restrictions. Offending countries thus lose exports, jobs, and money. So WTO
rulings have financial clout.

This system endangers many environmental and safety standards, Korten
notes:

> The WTO's global health and safety standards relating to food are set by a group
> known as the Codex Alimentarius Commission, or Codex. . . . Critics of Codex ob-
> serve that it is heavily influenced by industry and has tended to harmonize stan-
> dards downward. For example, a Greenpeace USA study found that Codex safety
> levels for at least eight widely used pesticides were lower than current U.S. stan-
> dards by as much as a factor of twenty-one. The Codex standards allow DDT
> residues up to fifty times those permitted under U.S. law.[61]

If a member country wants to export to the United States crops with the Codex-
allowed level of DDT, we cannot legally stop them. WTO rulings take prece-
dence over state and federal law. If we block the food's importation, we face
stiff fines. Korten reports that "Clayton Yeutter, in his capacity as U.S. secretary of agriculture under George Bush," welcomed this result. He "stated pub-
licly that one of his main goals was to use GATT [WTO's predecessor] to over-
turn strict local and state food safety regulations."[62]

According to Hilary French, writing in *WorldWatch* in 1993, GATT was used
to undermine environmental regulations before it was replaced by the more
powerful WTO:

> For instance, Austria was recently forced to abandon plans to introduce a 70 per-
> cent tax on tropical timber, as well as a requirement that tropical timber be labeled

as such, when the Association of Southeast Asian Nations (ASEAN) complained that the law violated GATT. . . . The European Union . . . formally challenged two U.S. automobile taxes intended to promote fuel efficiency—the Corporate Average Fuel Economy Law and the gas-guzzler tax.[63]

National attempts to save tropical forests, reduce oil consumption, and lessen global warming can all be disallowed as undue restrictions on trade.

GATT and WTO rulings tend to ignore environmental concerns because the judges are mostly "industry experts" trying to promote world trade. Consumer and environmental groups have little representation. Also, the panels' deliberations are secret, further isolating judges from public opinion or any other dissenting voice.[64]

The results can be tragic. Consider dolphins. They can be killed or fatally injured when caught in nets designed to capture tuna. Dolphin-safe tuna nets were designed to eliminate or drastically reduce dolphin deaths, writes Frederic Frommer in the fall 1999 issue of *Animal Watch* magazine: "In 1992, Congress passed legislation banning the import of tuna to the United States that wasn't dolphin-safe. . . . Last year, some 2,000 dolphins were killed by tuna fishermen compared to about 133,000 in 1986."[65]

Is this important? Dolphin deaths in old-fashioned tuna nets represent needless killing. What is more, if we think human beings have more rights than animals, in part because of our greater intellectual potential, then we should give dolphins special treatment among animals, because dolphins may be smarter than human beings! One measure of mental capacity is the size of the brain and the complexity of brain folds compared to total weight. On this measure, for example, chimpanzees are about 33 percent as brainy as people. *Dolphins* are 110 percent as brainy. Yes, they *seem to have more mental capacity than we do*. However, our methods of communication are so different that it is difficult for us to know much about what they do with their brainpower.

Except sometimes. The bestseller *Chicken Soup for the Soul* contains the true story of Elizabeth Gawain, who almost drowned when she got stomach cramps while scuba diving. As she sank, unable to remove her weight belt, she thought:

"I can't go like this! I have things to do! Somebody, something, help me!" Suddenly I felt a prodding from behind me under the armpit. . . . My arm was being lifted forcibly. Around into my field of vision came an eye. . . . I swear it was smiling. It was the eye of a big dolphin . . . [who] moved forward, nudging under and hooking its dorsal fin below my armpit with my arm over its back . . . lifting me toward the surface. . . . At the surface it drew me all the way into shore. It took me into water so shallow that I began to be concerned that it might be beached. . . . When I took off the weight belt and oxygen tank, I . . . went . . . back into the ocean to the dolphin . . . [who] played around in the water with me. I noticed that there were a lot of dolphins there, farther out. After a while it brought me back to shore. . . . Then he turned sideways with one eye looking into mine. We stayed that way for what seemed like a very long time. . . . Then he made just one sound and went out to join the others. And all of them left.[66]

There are many true stories of untamed, untrained dolphins helping human strangers.

The U.S. Congress legislated dolphin-safe tuna to help dolphins, while ensuring a steady supply of tuna for consumers. However, as *Public Citizen News* reported in early 1999, *"the World Trade Organization (WTO) has forced the U.S. to abandon its dolphin-protection law which bans sale of domestic and imported tuna caught with nets that kill dolphins.* Now the imports must be allowed."[67] Our law was deemed an unacceptable barrier to free trade.

Democracy and national sovereignty suffer along with dolphins. The American people are no longer able to express all their values in their laws. The value of free trade is, according to the WTO, more important than dolphins, American food-safety standards, and many other factors affecting the health and conscience of the American people.

This does not mean that the United States should isolate itself from world affairs. International cooperation is needed to support human rights and to combat worldwide environmental problems such as global warming and ozone depletion. But where we can improve our country in a way that is consistent with human rights and without depriving people in other lands, we should be free to do so. People in other countries should be equally free.

Consider agriculture, for example. Suppose we adopt national policies that favor sustainable agriculture on small family farms. We do this to provide satisfying jobs, improve the quality of food, revitalize rural areas, reduce our country's contribution to global warming, and assure food supplies for the future. But, at least initially, most food grown this way will cost more than food grown without attention to long-term environmental degradation. Farmers in countries growing cheap food in unsustainable ways can use the WTO to force the U.S. to allow their food to compete on the American market. But the importation of this cheap food could force many family farms out of business and impair our farm policy's effectiveness. With the WTO, much of democracy and national sovereignty go down the drain, while topsoil goes down river.

What should we do about this situation? Only someone with the master mentality would think he has all the answers, so the following are just suggestions to consider. First, *perhaps we should give up membership in the World Trade Organization.* This does not mean giving up worldwide trade. It means merely taking back the right to decide when other values are more important than trade. We can then tailor individual treaties accordingly.

A second suggestion is that we subject prospective treaties to the full process of congressional debate. *We should not give our presidents what is called* **fast track authority**. This is the authority to negotiate trade agreements that Congress must either accept or reject as written. Amendments are not allowed. This authority reduces democracy and diminishes the chances that agreements will incorporate a plurality of relevant values. Presidents of both parties have claimed, however, that they need this authority to avoid government gridlock that stems from lobbyists seeking incompatible treaty modifications for opposing special interests. Without fast track authority, they say, the United States may miss some treaty opportunities. I suggest that, on balance, missing such opportunities is better than having treaties narrowly focused on some values to the exclusion of others. Presidents had fast track authority for a time, but it was not extended when its time limit ran out. This is good, and should remain so.

What results should we expect from such policies? Again, only someone with the master mentality would imagine that he knows for sure, so I venture only some educated guesses. Leaving the WTO and refusing to give presidents fast track authority will probably slow globalization, encourage more national self-sufficiency, and generate employment opportunities to serve local markets. At least in the short run, in poorer countries such "employment" opportunities for many people will be simply to live as peasants in traditional ways. This is better, however, than being displaced from the land so outsiders can use it to provide luxury goods for rich people in big cities and foreign countries. Employees in rich countries will likely have less job competition from displaced peasants overseas who work for pennies a day.

Paying a decent wage to workers in rich countries will probably raise the price of many goods, so public policies must improve efficiency in transportation and other areas. For example, with efficient mass transportation, a family of four may need just one car instead of two or three. This helps the environment as well as the family budget.

More generally, people in rich countries should be able to use some of their technology-enhanced productivity to spend time with family and friends, build community organizations, participate in politics, develop talents, save money as do-it-yourselfers, participate in job sharing to provide work for the unemployed, and just relax. Most people will have more freedom, but less "stuff." People may buy less but savor more of life's inexpensive, enduring values.

Total corporate profits will likely decrease, and stock prices with them, if workers earn more and consumer demand declines. This could reduce opportunities to make money without working, and narrow the income gap between the rich and the middle class.

Such changes are synergistic when human welfare and environmental quality improve together due to policies adopted at least in part because people value for themselves such nonhuman aspects of nature as dolphins and biodiversity.

Judgment Calls

- David Korten writes that Nike shoes selling in the United States or Europe for $73 to $135 a pair are produced in Indonesia for about $5.60 by 75,000 girls and young women who are "independent contractors" paid as little as 15 cents an hour:

  The $20 million that basketball star Michael Jordan reportedly received in 1992 for promoting Nike shoes exceeded the entire annual payroll of the Indonesian factories that made them. . . . When asked about conditions at plants where Nikes are produced, John Woodman, Nike's general manager in Indonesia [said] although he knew that there had been labor problems . . . , he had no idea what they had been about. Furthermore, he said, "I don't know that I need to know. It's not within our scope to investigate."[68]

What do you think?

• Archer Daniels Midland (ADM) calls itself "supermarket to the world" and claims its products are needed to avoid human starvation as population increases. How does this claim relate to their support for using corn to make ethanol fuel for cars?

• Benjamin Barber notes that many corporations attempt deliberately to alter Third World cultures to increase consumer demand. For example, Coca-Cola CEO Roberto C. Goizueta favors "aggressive investment" to alter "societies that have traditionally consumed beverages like tea" so they will make "the transition to sweeter beverages like Coca-Cola."[69] But people drink tea as part of larger local customs, so Coke is attempting to alter some basic patterns of social interaction. This is not an isolated case, Barber reports:

Long-lunch traditions obstruct the development of fast-food franchises, and successful fast-food franchises inevitably undermine Mediterranean home-at-noon-for-dinner rituals. . . . Agricultural lifestyles (rise at daylight, work all day, to bed at dusk) are inhospitable to television watching. People uninterested in sports buy fewer athletic shoes.[70]

What moral issues arise from deliberate attempts to alter other people's cultures? What difference does it make if commercial interests are just manipulating *our* culture?

Is Optimism Justified?

Conflicting Trends

Journalist Gregg Easterbrook claims in his 1995 book *A Moment on Earth* that environmentalism has already saved us. Dire predictions were wrong, he reports:

> Paul Ehrlich's *The Population Bomb*, released in 1968, predicted that general crop failures would "certainly" result in mass starvation in the United States by the 1980s. Instead the leading American agricultural problem of that decade was over-supply. . . . *The Limits to Growth*, a . . . 1972 volume, . . . projected that petroleum would be exhausted by the 1990s. Instead oil prices hover near postwar lows, reflecting ample supply.[1]

Predicted extinctions of species were also wrong, Easterbrook notes: "*Silent Spring*, published by Rachel Carson in 1962, foretold such a widespread biological wipeout that today robins should be extinct. . . . Instead the robin is today one of the two or three most prolific birds in the United States."[2] In fact,"of the 40 birds Carson said might by now be extinct or nearly so, . . . half . . . have shown no change; 35 percent are going up, about 15 percent are going down. This sounds like business as usual for nature."[3]

Birds are not alone, Easterbrook maintains: "*The Sinking Ark*, published in 1979 by the biologist Norman Myers [projected] . . . thousands of species to become extinct during the 1980s. Instead there were at worst a handful of confirmed extinctions globally in that decade."[4] Consider whales, for example:

> Fin and humpback whales are gaining in numbers. A decade ago about 1,400 humpback whales were observed annually off Hawaii; currently the annual number is running around 3,400. The blue whale, largest known creature ever to live, was hunted to the brink of extinction until 1968, when whaling of blues was banned internationally. Now the blue is plentiful again off California.[5]

Similarly, "Sea otters and brown pelicans, both said near extinction a few decades ago, are recovering nicely in and near the United States."[6] And the trend continues. In August 1999, the Peregrine falcon was taken off the endangered species list because its reproduction is now sufficient to assure species survival.[7]

None of this means that environmentalism was or is unnecessary, according to Easterbrook. It means that environmentalism and the measures it inspires, such as the Endangered Species Act and the Marine Mammal Protection Act, have worked.

But there is another side to the success story. Easterbrook is correct that relatively few known species have become extinct in recent decades. However, he overlooks what biologists stress. *Most of the world's species are unknown, and many inhabit the tropics. Rapid destruction of tropical rainforests extinguishes thousands of species annually, biologists estimate, before they ever become known and classified.*

Easterbrook points out that other environmentalist initiatives are also working to make the environment more healthful. For example, the air is getting cleaner:

> Underlying trends in air pollution were positive throughout the 1980s. In that decade ambient smog in the United States declined a composite 16 percent. . . . In the beginning of the 1980s there were about 600 air-quality-alert days each year in major cities. By the end of the 1980s there were about 300 such days annually.[8]

But some of our initiatives create health problems. Consider the story of two-year-old Dalton Canterbury whose "flu" in February 1999 got so bad that his parents took him to the hospital. There, *U.S. News and World Report* journalist Amanda Spake tells us:

> a spinal tap showed cloudy fluid, a sign of bacterial meningitis. . . . Dalton had a seizure, caused by the infection in the membranes surrounding his brain. . . . Dalton's best chance . . . was to fly him immediately to Johns Hopkins Hospital in Baltimore, 50 miles away. Susan Canterbury suddenly grasped what the doctor was trying to tell her. "You mean," she asked, "he could *die*?"[9]

This was a real possibility because "the strain of pneumococcus infecting the fluid around Dalton's brain was resistant to penicillin. It was also partly resistant to ceftriaxone, a powerful drug used to treat penicillin-resistant meningitis."[10] Nevertheless, massive doses of that drug, along with another, vancomycin, finally killed the bacteria. However, the bug had damaged the part of Dalton's brain that processes visual images. Dalton could not see in early March, but had regained most of his vision by mid-April.

His case is not unique. Many children are permanently injured or killed by

> common microbes easy to treat just a few years ago. There's Shaunna Littlejohn, 10, now blind and in a vegetative state due to drug-resistant meningitis; Christine

Girata, 3, who contracted multidrug-resistant meningitis at 2 months and was left profoundly deaf; Ariana Broadway, 4, who nearly died from a bloodstream infection and pneumonia when she was 2.[11]

Our use of antibiotics promotes the growth of antibiotic-resistant organisms. Due to chance variations among bacteria, some are naturally resistant to any given antibiotic. When antibiotics are used to kill all bacteria susceptible to them, resistant strains live, multiply, and quickly spread worldwide, Spake reports:

> The first penicillin-resistant pneumococcal strain was reported in New Guinea in 1967. By 1992, about 5 percent of U.S. samples tested by the CDC [Centers for Disease Control] were resistant to penicillin. Now, seven years later, an average of 25 percent of cases are resistant; in some areas the rate tops 40 percent.[12]

Spake notes this worrisome fact: "Bugs that have become resistant to one antibiotic also seem to find it easier to build resistance to others."[13] Dr. Rebecca Goldburg, an ecologist for the Environmental Defense Fund, points out:

> More than 90% of strains of *staphylococcus aureus* bacteria, a common cause of hospital Staph infections, are now resistant to penicillin. More that 30% are resistant not only to penicillin but also to every other antibiotic used to treat Staph infections—except one, vancomycin [the drug that helped save Dalton Canterbury's life]. Now a vancomycin-resistant strain of Staph has emerged, which is untreatable (but, luckily, still rare).[14]

We do not know how long it will remain rare.

The problem is that we use antibiotics too much. Spake cites these figures: "Forty-four percent of kids are prescribed antibiotics for colds and 46 percent for upper-respiratory infection—both conditions usually caused by viruses, against which antibiotics are useless."[15] Why are they prescribed? Anxious parents, who often need their children well so they can get back to work, prevail upon doctors to prescribe antibiotics just in case they might help. As a result, "The rate of antibiotic use among children has jumped more than 48 percent since 1980, according to the CDC."[16] Many doctors believe, often with justification, that if they do not write the prescription, some other doctor will, and they may lose a patient. Most medicine is still commercial in the United States so doctors depend on patient loyalty for their livelhihood.

Spake notes that this actually puts wealthier people at greater risk than the poor, because the poor are less likely to get inappropriate antibiotics. For example, in affluent

> Anne Arundel County . . . 27 percent of patients with invasive pneumococcol disease . . . were infected with penicillin-resistant strains in 1998. By comparison, downtown Baltimore, with a lower-income population that sees doctors less often, had more invasive infections, but only 12 percent were resistant.[17]

Agriculture is another area of antibiotic overuse. Goldburg reports: "Farmers actually use more than 40% of all antibiotics sold in the United States today." Most is "added to poultry, hog, and cattle feed, not to treat sick animals but to promote growth and prevent disease." This practice "dangerously increases the possibility that these antibiotics (and other closely related ones) will be ineffective when needed to treat people." In 1997, the World Health Organization recommended ending this practice. "The use of four antibiotics in animal feed was banned throughout Europe last year," Goldburg writes. In the U.S., however, "legislators representing agribusiness interests" have prevented the issue from even coming up after they defeated a similar proposal in the 1970s.[18]

New classes of drugs and vaccines will be available soon, but with job pressures on parents, consumer pressures on doctors, and financial pressures on politicians, it is likely that these, too, will be overused and become ineffective. *Should we be optimistic about the ability of science to stay ahead of the bugs, or pessimistic about widespread epidemics provoked by our inability to use drugs wisely?*

Fragmenting Societies

The New York Times correspondent Thomas Friedman reports in his 1999 bestseller *The Lexus and the Olive Tree* that human life is improving around the globe. He writes: "The ranks of the middle class in countries like Thailand, Brazil, India and Korea have swelled. . . . "[19] This results largely from industrialization and production for export.

However, there are clouds over such developments. One is composed of carbon dioxide. Steven Yearley writes in *Sociology, Environmentalism, Globalization*: "Since, typically, industrializing countries have sought to develop their economies in part through encouraging heavy industry—shipbuilding, heavy engineering, vehicle manufacture and so on—it is likely that they will be relatively large-scale emitters of CO_2."[20] For example, *India will have to emit more CO_2 than Germany, Japan, and the United Kingdom combined long before most Indians reach the middle class. The situation is similar for China and other developing countries.*

But according to a report issued by the Environmental Defense Fund: "Uncontrolled global warming and the resulting sea-level rise could lead to repeated flooding of New York City's roads, subways, and airports during the next century." And, the report continues: "New Yorkers have reason to sweat. The year 1998 was the warmest on record globally, and seven of the hottest years of the century have occurred since 1990."[21] Higher temperatures could also impair health by increasing levels of ambient ozone and by promoting mosquito-borne infectious diseases. "Other low-lying port cities, including New Orleans and Miami, may be at even more risk. Experts say that, nationwide, a one-foot or greater rise in sea level could eliminate 20 to 40 percent of remaining U.S. wetlands, causing severe damage to vital fisheries and wildlife habitat."[22]

Social disruption and war provoked by deteriorating Third World environments also becloud the future, writes Robert Kaplan in "The Coming Anarchy":

> For a while the media will continue to ascribe riots and other violent upheavals abroad mainly to ethnic and religious conflict. But as these conflicts multiply, it will become apparent that something else is afoot, making more and more places like Nigeria, India, and Brazil ungovernable. . . . The political and strategic impact of surging populations, spreading disease, deforestation and soil erosion, water depletion, air pollution, and, possibly, rising sea levels in critical, overcrowded regions like the Nile Delta and Bangladesh—developments that will prompt mass migrations and, in turn, incite group conflicts—will be the core foreign-policy challenge.[23]

One response to this upheaval will be dictatorial regimes in such countries as Indonesia, Brazil, and Nigeria. "Democracy is problematic; scarcity is more certain" Kaplan observes. After all, "95 percent of the population increase will be in the poorest regions of the world, where governments now—just look at Africa—show little ability to function." As a result, "an increasingly large number of people will be . . . living in shantytowns where attempts to rise above poverty, cultural dysfunction, and ethnic strife will be doomed by a lack of water to drink, soil to till, and space to survive in."[24]

There will still be enclaves of affluence, but outside those enclaves will be "a rundown, crowded planet of skinhead Cossacks and *juju* warriors, influenced by the worst refuse of Western pop culture and ancient tribal hatreds, battling over scraps of overused earth."[25] They will fight because, Kaplan maintains, "a large number of people on this planet, to whom the comfort and stability of a middle-class life is utterly unknown, find war and a barracks existence a step up rather than a step down."[26] Such people will readily join terrorist organizations.

States will no longer be the only war-making entities: "Loose and shadowy organisms such as Islamic terrorist organizations suggest why borders will mean increasingly little and sedimentary layers of tribalistic identity and control will mean more."[27] This will break down the distinction between crime and war, as we see already in Colombia. As a result, Kaplan predicts, "to the average person, political values will mean less, personal security more.[28]

Does this picture seem more realistic than Friedman's rosy outlook, or is it too pessimistic? Since it was written in 1994, examples abound that support Kaplan's vision of the twenty-first century. The years 1995–1999 saw upheaval in many "emerging" Asian economies, political and military brutality in Indonesia, the conflict over Kosovo in the Balkans, war in the Republic of Congo, continuing military conflict over the drug trade in Colombia, and heightened concern about terrorism in the United States. Income gaps between the rich and poor increased in the United States and in most developing countries, as did the income gap between rich and poor countries.

Environmentalist Jeff Gersh states in a 1999 article in *The Amicus Journal*:

According to the United Nations, 20 percent of the populations of the world's poorest countries lack access to the most basic modern health care; 25 percent do not have adequate housing; 30 percent lack access to clean water. . . . Since 1980, 100 nations have been either economically stagnant or in decline. On average, an African household today consumes one-fifth less than it did a quarter-century ago. . . . Because hunger and misery cannot afford to make the distinctions of the well-fed—to choose between cutting a tree or saving it—poverty is among the greatest environmental threats in the world.[29]

So rainforests continue to diminish, water tables decline, and species disappear. Poverty and environmental degradation reinforce one another.

Organizations dedicated to promoting Third World development still lack environmental sensitivity. Gersh cites the Environmental Defense Fund's Stephanie Freed concerning Indonesian forest fires and the International Monetary Fund (IMF):

In 1997, a fact-finding mission led by U.S. Senator Max Baucus revealed that the extraordinary forest fires of that year, which blackened the skies over six countries and resulted in $1.3 billion in damages (not including the catastrophic loss of trees), were "caused largely by Indonesian and Malaysian timber companies clearing land for palm oil plantations." Yet in 1998, the IMF pressed Indonesia to attract new investment by removing barriers to foreign financing for palm oil plantations.[30]

We Are the World

There is a brighter side. Thomas Friedman points out that the United States leads the world: "We send our culture, values, economics, technologies and lifestyles everywhere. . . ."[31] I find hope in the possibility of altering those exports.

To do so we must alter our own values, personal behaviors, and public policies. Value change alone is insufficient, but necessary.

Values change all the time, often for the better. In the 1930s, for example, racial segregation was valued by many people in the United States and required by law in several states. The majority also accepted racial discrimination in employment. By the end of the century, more people saw value in racial integration and equal employment opportunity. Gender relations changed in similar ways starting in the 1960s. These are not just liberal values. I know politically and religiously conservative men who expect their daughters to get equal pay for equal work.

Values have changed regarding cigarette smoking. A generation ago smokers, as they reached for cigarettes, would ask rhetorically if anyone minded their smoking. Objections were rare. Really! Today it is often considered impolite to ask if you can smoke, and it is illegal to smoke in most public indoor environments.

Value changes regarding work, leisure, and consumption in the United States could make our country an environmental leader. Vicki Robin and Joe Dominguez report in their 1992 book *Your Money or Your Life*: "A recent poll conducted by John Robinson for the Hilton Hotels Corporation found that 70 percent of those earning $30,000 a year or more would give up a day's pay each week for an extra day of free time. Even among those earning $20,000 a year or less, 48 percent would do the same."[32] Robin and Dominguez also found evidence that many "upwardly mobile professionals . . . are voluntarily taking cuts in pay and responsibility in order to live saner, more balanced and more contributory lives."[33]

This suggests that values are changing away from environmentally destructive overworking and over-consuming lifestyles. However, there are countertrends as well. Steven Greenhouse reports in *The New York Times*:

> A new study by the International Labor Organization found that the number of hours Americans work each year has climbed skyward in recent years. . . . [34] Even as many stressed-out workers are deliberately reducing their hours, the Bureau of Labor Statistics has found that 19 percent of Americans report working more than 49 hours a week, up from 16 percent in 1985.[35]

This shows that value change alone is not enough. Labor legislation is needed as well. Such legislation will come when public pressure is strong enough to overcome the clout of large campaign contributors. It was the same with smoking. For years many people disliked breathing other people's smoke. Then statistics showed breathing second-hand smoke to be health impairing. Finally, voters impelled legislators to defy the powerful tobacco lobby and pass laws restricting the right to smoke.

Work rules are similar. In Europe, where laws governing campaign finances limit industry clout, the workweek is shrinking. *Americans concerned about family values and the quality of life may eventually impel legislators to defy industry demands and pass appropriate labor legislation. This will include laws limiting the amount of overtime that employers can demand, limiting the ability of employers to classify employees as outside contractors, and requiring more benefits for part-time workers. Such laws give people more freedom to act on their values. People who value family, contentment, and leisure can work less without being unemployed, and can work part-time without losing benefits.* This could happen, but campaign finance reform may be necessary first.

Optimism is justified regarding foods genetically modified to contain the pesticide Bt, because Europeans reject them. Kenneth Klee reports in a September 1999 issue of *Newsweek* that Archer Daniels Midland (ADM) sent "a fax to grain elevators throughout the Midwest" telling them to "start segregating their genetically modified crops from conventional ones because that's what foreign buyers want."[36] In July 1999, "Heinz and Gerber . . . announced . . . that they'll go to the considerable trouble of making their baby foods free of genetically modified organisms."[37] Another reason to reject GM crops is that their Bt can kill beneficial insects, such as the caterpillar of the monarch butterfly.[38]

There are glimmers of hope, but not much more, that rainforests can be saved. These glimmers stem from, for example, increasing Brazilian protection of rainforests (assuming that Brazil avoids political chaos), and from increasing commercial uses of intact forests. In Chiapas, Mexico, for example, some coffee is now grown in the forest shade, which is the natural habitat of the coffee plant, rather than in open fields created by deforestation. In 1999, Starbucks began selling this "Mexican Shade-Grown" coffee. I am optimistic that many consumers will prefer products that save rainforest, but I am uncertain that such preferences will be sufficient to save them.

More *troubling is the inability of many Americans to see beyond the status quo to a better future.* In 1998, my friend and colleague, Management Professor Joe Wilkins, wrote an opinion piece for the local paper opposing the Kyoto Protocol. This is an international agreement, not yet ratified by the United States, designed to reduce greenhouse gas emissions and avert the worst effects of global warming.

Wilkins claims the accord is unfair to the United States and harmful to Illinois. It is unfair to the U.S., he maintains, because "while we would be required to reduce greenhouse gas emissions by 7 percent [below 1990 levels], China, Mexico, India and 126 other nations would not."[39] He neglects to mention that in 1990 our per capita emissions of carbon dioxide were nine times China's and twenty-four times India's.[40] So even after we reduce emissions as the Protocol requires, we will still be emitting many times the carbon dioxide per capita that most other nations emit. Should we fight global warming by requiring those who already emit little CO_2 to emit less, or should we start with rich countries that now emit the most? Our position as cultural leader, as well as largest emitter, requires that we reduce first.

The Kyoto Protocol is bad for Illinois, Wilkins maintains, because it will reduce job opportunities in Illinois industries that emit greenhouse gases, such as coal production, oil refining, and automobile manufacture. He does not consider that, with proper national leadership, Illinois could retool to produce fast inter-city trains. Jobs could increase also in sustainable agriculture. It is hard to be optimistic when a smart and good man advises us to walk ahead with eyes fixed on our toes. Yet I am optimistic that eventually we will recognize the harm we do to ourselves and the planet by subsidizing automotive instead of mass transit, just as we came to realize the dangers of smoking cigarettes. I am unsure how bad global warming will be by then.

Value Nature and Limit Human Power

A necessary component of the will to make changes that protect species diversity and natural ecosystems is love or respect for nature itself. For example, Wilkins would never suggest that if child slavery exists in India or China then we should enslave children here to remain internationally competitive. Like most Americans, Wilkins values children for themselves, so enslaving them is out of the question. Our child labor laws reflect this value. When we similarly value nature for itself, we will forgo the short-term economic advantages provided by, for example, membership in the World Trade Organization, because the planet-harming effects will be simply unacceptable.

Ecologist Aldo Leopold recognized the importance of valuing nature for itself. He advocated an ecological conscience among farmers of his day who, he observed ruefully, participated in government programs designed to conserve nature, but then abandoned conservation practices as soon as government payments stopped. He wrote:

> The existence of obligations over and above self-interest is taken for granted in such rural community enterprises as the betterment of roads, schools, churches, and baseball teams. . . . [But] the farmer who clears the woods off of a 75 per cent slope, turns his cows into the clearing, and dumps its rainfall, rocks, and soil into the community creek, is still (if otherwise decent) a respected member of society.[41]

Leopold advocated seeing nature preservation as an obligation. "Obligations," Leopold wrote, "have no meaning without conscience."[42] To save nature we must value species and ecosystems, much as we value human individuals and communities, for themselves. Then, harming nature will bother our conscience, and we will not revert to harmful practices as soon as the government stops subsidizing better behavior.

A troubled conscience does not by itself help the environment, but is usually necessary to spur appropriate collective action, such as the Endangered Species Act and the Marine Mammal Protection Act. Such legislation exists because extinguishing species gnaws at the conscience of most Americans. I am optimistic that our conscience and ethics will expand further as we recognize additional ways we harm nature and additional connections between the degradation of nature and of humanity.

Enlightened anthropocentrism that concentrates solely on improving the human condition is insufficient. *Unless we care about nature for itself, we are likely to attempt increasing control over nature to serve human interests, even though experience shows many such attempts to be counterproductive. Environmental synergism, unlike anthropocentrism, includes concern for nature itself. This puts many power grabs beyond consideration, thereby protecting both people and nature.*

Consider, for example, successful attempts through genetic engineering to improve the intelligence of mice. An enlightened anthropocentrist may welcome the opportunity, as this may eventually provide a way to treat human disease. Michael Lemonick notes in his September 1999 *Time* magazine article the possibility of "therapies to treat learning and memory disorders, including Alzheimer's disease, a condition likely to afflict more and more people in an increasingly aging population."[43] But Nancy Gibbs' article in the same issue points out the dangers. She writes:

> Correcting is one thing, perfecting is another. If doctors can some day tinker with a gene to help children with autism, what's to prevent them from tinkering with other genes to make "normal" children smarter? Technology always adapts to de-

mand; prenatal sex-selection tests designed to weed out inherited diseases that strike one gender or the other—hemophilia, for instance—are being used to help families have the son or daughter they always wanted. Human-growth hormone was intended for children with a proven severe deficiency, but came to be used on self-conscious short kids—if their parents could afford as much as $30,000 for a year's injections.[44]

In a competitive society that values height, beauty, and intelligence, parents may feel morally compelled to secure for their children all medically possible enhancements. Gene therapies for intelligence could accelerate the already increasing gap between rich and poor, as the rich alone can afford to make their children smarter. Will they do this even if the treatment tends to make their children more nervous, or shy, or mean? The answer may be "yes" in a society that places highest value on competitive production and consumption, rather than, for example, on non-competitive leisure and contentment. Intelligence, even in a nervous, shy, or mean person, promotes competitive success.

In sum, power over human intelligence is dangerous in a competitive society. The synergist's respect for nature puts attempts to gain such power out of the question, regardless of some undoubtedly beneficial applications. Optimism is justified if environmental synergism becomes America's common value assumption.

© Steve Kelley/Copley News Service

How likely is this? Science is venerated in our society, and modern theories of evolution and genetics imply our kinship with all other life forms. Sensing this kinship at the deepest level dissolves the master mentality. Most people already oppose cruelty to animals and want to save species from extinction. They know that we are, in Aldo Leopold's words, but "fellow-voyagers with other creatures in the odyssey of evolution."[45] How can we think the entire ship, this blue planet, is for us alone?

In addition, life is richer when varied leisure pursuits replace compulsive consumption and competition. We flourish with more connections to family, community, and nature. Most people know this upon a moment's reflection, so we are ripe for a sea change in environmental ethics.

Worldwatch Institute president Lester Brown, writing in *State of the World 2000*, compares dramatic changes in environmental thought to political change in Eastern Europe. "It almost seemed that people woke up one morning and understood that the era of the one-party political system and the centrally planned economy was over. Even those in power at the time realized this. . . . Although we do not understand the process well, we do know that at some point a critical mass had been reached. . . ."[46] Brown cites current environmental examples of dramatic change. Some oil companies, including Royal Dutch Shell and ARCO, now plan to abandon fossil fuels. The United States Forest Service now opposes road building in national forests, and China is trying to save its trees.[47]

These are impressive, positive developments. But encouraging responses from ordinary people are also needed. I am optimistic when readers of this book discuss its message with family, colleagues, and friends in respectful, serious conversations. I am optimistic when bearers of this message illustrate their commitment with lifestyle choices (that place no great burdens on themselves or others). I am optimistic when environmentalists vote for like-minded politicians. I am optimistic when you do these things, because I believe that what you do, many others will do as well. Together we can make a difference. The title of a book about social activism gives me hope:

We Make the Road by Walking.[48]

Glossary

adaptation—a species' evolution over generations to maintain or improve its fitness.

altruistic—the disposition to be concerned about the welfare of every being affected by an action or policy, one's self neither more nor less than others.

agriculture—the process by which people live by deliberately fostering the germination and growth of plants and animals for human consumption or other use.

anthropocentric—centered on human beings. Anthropocentrists consider human beings alone to be of value in themselves, and assume that animals, species, and ecosystems must typically be sacrificed for people to attain maximum well being.

aquifer—an underground reservoir of water. The water in many aquifers is pumped to the surface of the earth for human use.

backgrounding—denying credit for accomplishments to whatever is lower on a dualistic hierarchy.

behaviorism—a psychological theory according to which our social actions are shaped by their external results; that is, that all social actions are extrinsically motivated.

biodiversity—the variety of species in a given ecosystem, or on Earth as a whole.

biota—living organisms.

biotic pyramid—categorized by how directly organisms receive and use energy from the sun; life forms are more abundant in total mass the more direct their use of the sun's energy. So green plants are most abundant, then whatever eats green plants directly, and so forth.

category mistake—the kind of mistake you make when you predicate one concept of another that makes no sense in relation to it, such as claiming that the square root of two is blue.

citizenship interpretation—an interpretation of the Bible according to which God wants people to be plain members and citizens of the ecosystems they inhabit, much as prescribed by Aldo Leopold's land ethic.

cornucopian view—due to human ingenuity, there are no inherent limits to the human use of natural resources.

cost-benefit analysis—a method of calculating the best policy or course of action that puts all costs and benefits of each alternative in monetary terms, so all alternative proposals can be compared mathematically.

cost-effectiveness analysis—a method of calculating how to achieve with the least monetary cost a goal chosen by other means.

culling—the systematic, professional killing of the members of a species to maintain the welfare of the species and its ecosystem. In the case of elephants, this may include killing an entire herd at one time.

decommissioning—as related to nuclear power plants, it is the conversion of the plant and its site from one where electricity is generated to one that is safe for other uses. Decommissioning can involve, for example, dismantling or burial. ,

discount rate—the annual percentage used to calculate the current dollar equivalent of a benefit or cost that will not materialize until some future time. It is like an interest rate, but it is called a discount rate because the current worth of a future benefit or cost is less than its dollar equivalent will be in the future, when it actually exists.

dualism—the division of reality into pairs of mutually exclusive groups, such as men vs. women, and human vs. animal.

ecofeminism—the view that both human and nonhuman beings will fare best when women, other subordinated human beings, and nonhuman nature are valued as good in themselves and are permitted more self-determination than is allowed by the plans of (mostly) men with the master mentality.

economic anthropocentrism—an anthropocentric view that holds that all values of importance to people, at least in relation to the nonhuman environment, can be expressed adequately in terms of monetary equivalents.

ecosystem—living organisms as they interact systematically with one another and with their nonliving surroundings.

environmental ethics—a reasoned reconsideration of how people should interact with one another and with nonhuman nature in the light of human-created environmental problems that arose (mostly) during the twentieth century.

environmental synergism—see "synergistic environmental ethics."

ethics—a reasoned account of how people should live their lives.

exotics—species introduced into ecosystems by human beings.

externality—the good or bad effects on others of actions taken by agents whose decision procedure does not include consideration of these effects.

extrinsic motivators—reasons for engaging in an activity that stem from the activity, like a paycheck for work, but are not an intrinsic part of that activity.

factory farming—current large-scale farming methods that use high inputs of pesticides and fertilizers instead of crop rotation to raise grains and vegetables, and that crowd large numbers of farm animals indoors where their movements are restricted. Animal behavior is controlled, for example, by cutting the beaks off of laying hens and the tails off of hogs.

fast track authority—the authority of the president of the United States to negotiate international agreements that Congress can accept or reject, but cannot amend.

fitness—a species' ability, through its members' activities, to remain in the environment indefinitely.

food chains—see "trophic relationships."

foragers—people who live by hunting and gathering whatever grows or lives wild in nature.

foundationalism—the view that our knowledge should and can rest on firm foundations that no reasonable person would question.

free markets—rule-governed institutions for the exchange of goods and services, in which consumer demand significantly influences the nature, quantity, and price of what is produced.

free rider—someone who benefits from the cooperation of others, while not engaging in the cooperative behavior that generates these benefits.

frugality—getting maximum benefit in life from everything you have use of.

futurity problem—a puzzle about the justification of leaving a good environment for future generations. It seems it cannot be the right of people who will exist in the future that a good environment be left to them, because the very existence of those particular people in the future depends on what we do now about environmental problems. If we leave a polluted Earth, those people cannot reasonably complain, unless they prefer non-existence to living in a polluted world.

General Agreement on Tariffs and Trade (GATT)—an agreement to standardize conditions of trade to promote globalization.

global warming—a general heating of the earth due to emissions of greenhouse gases.

globalization—a movement to create a worldwide free market in which job opportunities, products, and investment capital can move as freely among nations as they currently do within them.

grand narrative—a story that starts before an individual is born and is expected to extend beyond that individual's death, which the individual uses to place his or her life in a meaningful context.

greenhouse gases—atmospheric gases that trap heat in the earth's atmosphere. The most important are water vapor, carbon dioxide, methane, nitrous oxide, and chlorofluorocarbons.

Green Revolution—the adoption of high-yield varieties (HYVs) of grains that have been bred to place about half of the product of photosynthesis in the part of the plant that people eat. Traditional varieties may put only 20 percent in that part of the plant.

hedonic calculus—mathematical calculation of pleasure and pain that hedonistic utilitarians are supposed to be able to perform to determine the right course of action.

hedonic paradox—the best way to attain happiness is to work for some goal other than happiness and forget about trying to be happy.

hedonism—the belief that pleasure is the only good.

herding—a way of life in which people live from raising livestock. Traditionally, they move from place to place so the livestock can graze on naturally occurring vegetation.

hermeneutics—the study of interpretation that arose originally to help people interpret the Bible.

high-yield varieties (HYVs)—grains, usually with short stems, bred to maximize the percentage of photosynthate, the product of photosynthesis, that goes into production of the seeds that people eat. These are central to the green revolution. They often require greater inputs of water, fertilizer, and pesticides than traditional varieties.

holistic entities—beings that we ordinarily identify as individuals, but that are composed of more than one thing. States and corporations composed of many individual human beings are holistic entities. Species and ecosystems are holistic entities that can include nonhuman individuals as constituents.

holistic nonanthropocentric concerns—concerns for the existence and condition of such holistic entities as species, ecosystems, and the biosphere.

homeostasis—the tendency toward constancy in all living things.

homogenization—recognizing less individuality in whatever is lower on a dualistic hierarchy than is recognized in whatever is higher on that hierarchy.

human nature—tendencies found in (almost) all human beings.

hyperseparation—see "radical exclusion."

incorporation—tying the identity of whatever is lower on a dualistic hierarchy to something that is higher on that hierarchy.

individualistic nonanthropocentric concerns—concerns for the welfare of individual nonhuman animals.

instrumentalism—belief that whatever is lower on a dualistic hierarchy should serve the needs of whatever is higher on that hierarchy.

internalize externalities—have the effects on others from an agent's action affect the agent instead of others, as when polluters of the air or water pay for the damage they cause to the environment. This is often done in the case of negative externalities by the agent compensating others for bad effects on them of the agent's activities.

intrinsic motivators—reasons for engaging in an activity that stem not only from the activity but are part of it, such as the motive of mastery in solving puzzles intrinsic to chess.

intrinsic value—the kind of value we attribute to something when we think the world is just a better place when that thing exists.

malthusian—Related to the eighteenth century thinker Thomas Malthus who is known for believing that people, like many other animals, tend to overpopulate to the point of exhausting natural resources. Ultimately, only lack of food and starvation limit human populations.

master interpretation—an interpretation of the Bible according to which human beings should control the rest of nature as much as possible and for the exclusive welfare of humanity.

master mentality—the anthropocentric view, held mostly by white males, who believe that they are superior to the rest of humanity in knowing how to manage everyone and everything for the overall good.

monoculture—field where only one crop variety is grown.

moral pluralism—the guidance of human conduct by a variety of competing moral principles that cannot all be boiled down to any one principle.

narrative—a story.

niche—the role played by a species in circulating the energy that comes ultimately from the sun.

nonanthropocentric—not centered on human beings. Nonanthropocentrists believe that other beings, in addition to human beings, have value in themselves. They assume that, typically, human beings should sacrifice some of their well being out of consideration for the value of animals, species, and ecosystems.

non-economic anthropocentrism—an anthropocentric view that holds that some values of importance to people, even in relation to the nonhuman environment, cannot be expressed in terms of monetary equivalents. There are a plurality of values of importance to people, and they cannot all be expressed adequately in monetary terms.

patriarchy—the rule of men over women.

pollution permits—certificates that allow companies to pollute in a certain way and in a given amount during a specified time period in a given geographical location. These can be traded among companies whose pollution is relevantly similar.

practice—a socially created form of cooperative activity with built-in standards of excellence that can serve as intrinsic motivators.

preference utilitarianism—the utilitarian view that holds preference satisfaction to be the good that utilitarians should attempt to maximize.

pre-understanding—the beliefs and assumptions a person holds that influence his or her interpretation of texts and events.

privatization—the transformation of some public amenity or asset that was generally available free into private property, whose owners can limit public access.

psychological egoism—the view that everyone always behaves selfishly all the time.

public goods—goods whose benefits cannot be limited to a single owner. If anyone benefits, many others benefit as well.

radical exclusion—the exclusion of whatever is lower on a dualistic hierarchy from the possibility of attaining equality in value, prestige, or power, with whatever is higher on that hierarchy.

reflective equilibrium—the state of consistency among one's beliefs, especially among one's general principles, and between general principles and particular applications.

relational definition—see "incorporation."

religion—a worldview that gives a meaning-oriented description of reality and of humanity's place within reality. Most religions include grand narratives about the origins and destiny of reality and humanity, which connect people to a larger whole.

religious fundamentalism—the belief that the Bible records God's deeds and demands in a form that supplies people with clear guidance that should be taken as firm, unchanging foundations for ethics.

religious tradition—an ongoing, culturally evolving tradition of religious inspiration and interpretation that encompasses many different worldviews and grand narratives. Example are Christianity, Judaism, Islam, and Hinduism.

replacement argument—the argument that on hedonistic utilitarian grounds the right behavior is to eat the meat of animals raised humanely so long as the animals are killed painlessly and replaced by additional animals raised humanely. The idea is that in this way herds of happy farm animals will remain large, adding that much happiness to the world.

sacrament—any aspect of the world through which a divine mystery becomes present to religious awareness.

sentiment-based ethics—ethics based on the sentiments that people experience, such as sympathy and loyalty.

shadow pricing—estimating the monetary equivalent of something, such as a human life, that has no market price because it is not traded in markets. This is needed in cost-benefit analysis so all factors can be compared mathematically.

social contract view of justice—belief that a society's basic rules are just if they are the ones people would accept contractually when they are free, well-informed, and rationally guarding their own interests.

speciesism—a prejudice or attitude of bias in favor of the interests of members of one's own species and against those of members of other species.

stereotyping—see "homogenization."

stewardship interpretation—an interpretation of the Bible according to which God has given people the role of caring for the rest of creation as good in itself, not merely as a means to human satisfaction.

subjects-of-a-life—living beings with awareness, self-awareness, and plans for the future. This includes all normal human beings and at least all other mature mammals.

synergistic environmental ethics—the view that simultaneous respect for people and nature improves outcomes for both. In general, people benefit from valuing nature for itself because this helps people avoid oppressing one another. It also helps people attain their own highest good. In general, nature benefits when all people are respected, because then the biologically diverse environment that many poor people depend on will be spared, out of respect for those people. Also, toxic pollution will be reduced when all people are respected, because no person's exposure to this pollution will be considered acceptable.

technological optimist—someone who believes that people will always be able to develop satisfactory technological solutions to environmental and other problems stemming from modern technology.

trophic relationships—relationships among living things of eating and being eaten.

utilitarianism—an ethical theory according to which the right action is the one with the best overall, long-term consequences for everyone. The most common forms are hedonistic utilitarianism, which counts pleasure or happiness as the good to be maximized, and preference utilitarianism, which counts preference satisfaction as the good to be maximized.

vegan—a person whose diet excludes animal products, such as dairy products and eggs, as well as animals killed for their meat or other parts.

vegetarian—a person whose diet excludes animals killed for their meat or other parts.

veil of ignorance—the (hypothetical) ignorance of people about their own circumstances in life so when they make a (hypothetical) social contract establishing the basic rules of society, they will be motivated to establish rules that are fair to everyone.

vivisection—the cutting up of live animals in biology experiments.

World Trade Organization (WTO)—the organization created under GATT that oversees compliance with specific agreements designed to foster globalization.

world-picture—see "worldview."

worldview—beliefs about the nature of reality that support a grand narrative.

Notes

Introduction

[1]*Newsweek*, September 7, 1998, p. 38.

[2]*Newsweek*, September 7, 1998, p. 43.

[3]*The New York Times Book Review*, August 23, 1998, p. 28.

[4]*The New York Times Book Review*, August 23, 1998, p. 25.

[5]Julian L. Simon, *The Ultimate Resource* (Princeton: Princeton University Press, 1981), pp. 137–138. For pollution issues in general, see Chapter 9.

[6]Simon, p. 140, where he quotes an article in *Newsweek*, November 16, 1970, p. 67.

[7]Simon, p. 140, quoting from *Newsweek*.

[8]Simon, p. 136.

[9]Simon, p. 130.

[10]Simon, pp. 130–131.

[11]Edward Goldsmith, "Are the Experts Lying?" *The Ecologist*, Vol. 28, No. 2 (March/April 1998), pp. 51–53, at 51.

[12]Samuel Epstein, "Winning the War Against Cancer? . . . Are They Even Fighting It?" *The Ecologist*, Vol. 28, No. 2 (March/April 1998), pp. 69–80, at 71.

[13]Epstein, p. 71.

[14]Quoted in Zac Goldsmith, "Cancer: A Disease of Industrialization," *The Ecologist*, Vol. 28, No. 2 (March/April 1998), p. 93

[15]Zac Goldsmith, p. 93.

[16]Quoted in Zac Goldsmith, p. 94.

[17]Epstein, p. 73.

[18]Epstein, p. 76.

[19]Epstein, p. 75.

[20]Sandra Steingraber, *Living Downstream* (New York: Addison-Wesley, 1997), p. xvi.

[21]Mark Purdey, "Anecdote and Orthodoxy: Degenerative Nervous Diseases and Chemical Pollution," *The Ecologist*, Vol. 24, No. 3 (May/June 1994), pp. 100–105, at 100. Emphasis added.

[22]Jennifer D. Mitchell, "Nowhere to Hide: The Global Spread of High-Risk Synthetic Chemicals," *WorldWatch*, Vol. 10, No. 2 (March/April 1997), pp. 26–36, at 28.

[23]Mitchell, p. 28.

[24]Mitchell, p. 30.

[25]Mitchell, p. 31.

[26]Mitchell, p. 31

[27]Ann Misch, "Chemical Reaction," *WorldWatch*, Vol. 6, No. 2 (March/April 1993), pp. 10–17, at 13.

[28]See Peter S. Wenz, "Environmental Health," *Encyclopedia of Bioethics* (New York: Macmillan, 1995).

[29]Vyvyan Howard, "Synergistic Effects of Chemical Mixtures—Can We Rely on Traditional Toxicology?" *The Ecologist*, Vol. 27, No. 5 (September/October 1997), pp. 192–195, at 192.

[30]Gary Gardner, "From Oasis to Mirage: The Aquifers That Won't Replenish," *WorldWatch*, Vol. 8, No. 3 (May/June 1995), pp. 30–36, at 34.

[31]Gardner, pp. 34–35.

[32]Charles V. Blatz, "General Introduction," *Ethics and Agriculture* (Moscow, Idaho: University of Idaho Press, 1991), p. 11.

[33]For more on these matters, see Gary Gardner, "Shrinking Fields: Cropland Loss in a World of Eight Billion," *Worldwatch Paper # 131* (July1996), especially pp. 6–7, and 26–31.

[34]Daniel Quinn, *Ishmael* (New York: Bantam, 1993), pp. 105–106.

[35]Sandra Postel, *The Last Oasis* (New York: W.W. Norton, 1997), p. xiv. See also, for an emphasis on China, Lester R. Brown, "Challenges of the New Century," *State of the World 2000*, Lester R. Brown, ed. (New York: W.W. Norton, 2000), pp. 3–21, at 14.

[36]Postel, p. xiv.

[37]Lester R. Brown, "Can We Raise Grain Yields Fast Enough?" *WorldWatch*, Vol 10, No. 4 (July/August 1997), pp. 8–17, at 8.

[38]John Tuxill and Chris Bright, "Losing Strands in the Web of Life," *State of the World 1998* (New York: W.W. Norton, 1998), pp. 41–58, at 41.

[39]Tuxill and Bright, p. 46.

[40]Tuxill and Bright, p. 48.

[41]Tuxill and Bright, p. 52.

[42]Tuxill and Bright, p. 43.

[43]Aldo Leopold, "On a Monument to the Pigeon," *A Sand County Almanac with Essays on Conservation from Round River* (New York: Ballantine, 1970), pp. 116–117.

Chapter 1

[1]Gregg Easterbrook, *A Moment on the Earth* (New York: Penguin Books, 1995), p. 473.

[2]Clement A. Tisdell, *Natural Resources, Growth, and Development: Economics, Ecology, and Resource-Scarcity* (New York: Praeger Publishers, 1990), pp. 1–2.

[3]William F. Baxter, "People or Penguins: The Case for Optimal Pollution," in *Environmental Ethics: Readings in Theory and Application*, Louis P. Pojman, ed. (Boston: Jones and Bartlett, 1994), pp. 339–343, at 340.

[4]Baxter, p. 340. Baxter's anthropocentrism is egalitarian. Each human being represents one unit of importance. Presumably, each unit is equal. The defining belief of anthropocentrists, however, is that in the last analysis, *only* human beings are important. Some anthropocentrists may not consider all people to be of equal importance.

[5]Julian L. Simon, *The Ultimate Resource* (Princeton: Princeton University Press, 1981), pp. 43–44.

[6]Simon, p. 5.

[7]Garrett Hardin, "The Tragedy of the Commons," *Science*, Vol. 162 (December 1968), pp.1243–1248. It is widely reprinted. The quote here is taken from *Population and Ethics*, Michael D. Bayles, ed. (Cambridge, MA: Schenkman Publishing, 1976), pp. 3–18, at p. 7.

[8]Hardin, "Tragedy," p. 7.

[9]Hardin, "Tragedy," pp. 7–8.

[10]Hardin, "Tragedy," p. 8.

[11]Hardin, "Tragedy," p. 9.

[12]Hardin, "Tragedy," p. 9.

[13]Hardin, "Tragedy," p. 14.

[14]Thomas Michael Power and Paul Rauber, "The Price of Everything," *Sierra* (November/December 1993), pp. 87–88.

[15]Power and Rauber, p. 88.

[16]Herman E. Daly and John B. Cobb, Jr., *For the Common Good* (Boston: Beacon Press, 1994), p. 245.

[17]Daly and Cobb, p. 245.

[18]"Civil War, Drought Create Famine in Sudan," *Bread*, Vol. 10, No. 6, (September 1998), p.4.

[19]Garrett Hardin, "Lifeboat Ethics," in *World Hunger and Morality*, 2nd ed. William Aiken and Hugh LaFollette, eds. (Upper Saddle River, NJ: Prentice Hall, 1996), pp. 5–15, at 6. This article appeared originally in *Psychology Today Magazine* in 1974.

[20]Hardin, "Lifeboat," p. 10.

[21]Hardin, "Lifeboat," p. 12.

[22]Hardin, "Lifeboat," p. 13.

[23]Hardin, "Lifeboat," p. 12.

[24]Bill McKibben, "A Special Moment in History," *The Atlantic Monthly* (May 1998), pp. 55–78, at 56.

[25]Jennifer D. Mitchell, "Before the Next Doubling," *WorldWatch*, Vol. 11, No. 1 (January/February 1998), pp. 20–27, at 22–23.

[26]Gary Gardner, "Shrinking Fields: Cropland Loss in a World of Eight Billion," *Worldwatch Paper #131* (July 1996), p. 40.

[27] Alan B. Durning and Holly B. Brough, "Taking Stock: Animal Farming and the Environment," *Worldwatch Paper #103* (July 1991), pp. 17–18.

[28]Sandra Postel, "Dividing the Waters: Food Security, Ecosystem Health, and the New Politics of Scarcity," *Worldwatch Paper #132* (September 1996), p. 63.

[29]Durning and Brough, pp. 40–41.

[30]Robert L. Bartley, Editorial, *The Wall Street Journal Europe* (February 15, 1993).

[31]Terry L. Anderson and Donald R. Leal, "Free Market Environmentalism," in *Environmental Ethics: Divergence and Convergence*, 2nd ed. Richard G. Botzler and Susan J. Armstrong, eds. (Boston: McGraw-Hill, 1998), pp. 527–539, at 528. This selection is from the authors' book *Free Market Environmentalism* (Boulder: Westview Press, 1991), pp. 4–23 and 169–172.

[32]See *Poverty and Hunger: Issues and Options for Food Security in Developing Countries* (Washington, D.C.: World Bank, 1986).

[33]*Bread*, p. 1.

[34]Michael Pollan, "Playing God in the Garden," *The New York Times Magazine* (October 25, 1998), pp. 44–51, 62–63, 82 and 92–93.

Chapter 2

[1]Paul Rauber, "Heat Wave," *Sierra* (September/October 1997), p. 34.

[2]Colum F. Lynch, "Global Warning," *The Amicus Journal* (Spring 1996), p. 20.

[3]Lynch, p. 23.

[4]Gregg Easterbrook, *A Moment on Earth* (New York: Penguin Books, 1995), pp. 301–302.

[5]Simon Retallack, "Kyoto: Our Last Chance," *The Ecologist*, Vol. 27, No. 6 (November/December 1997), p. 230.

[6]Retallack, p. 231.

[7]Quoted in Lynch, p. 23.

[8]Reprinted in Retallack, p. 232.

[9]Easterbrook, pp. 303–306.

[10]Robert Heilbroner, "What Has Posterity Ever Done for Me?" *The New York Times Magazine*, January 19, 1975, found in *Environmental Ethics: Readings in Theory and Application*, 2nd ed. Louis P. Pojman, ed. (Belmont, CA: Wadsworth, 1998), pp. 276–278, at 277.

[11]Lewis Carroll, *Alice's Adventures in Wonderland and Through the Looking-Glass* (New York: Macmillan, 1965), p. 62.

[12]Derek Parfit, "Energy Policy and the Further Future: The Identity Problem," in Pojman, ed., pp. 289–296, at 290.

[13]Parfit, p. 295.

[14]John Rawls, *A Theory of Justice* (Cambridge, MA: Harvard University Press, 1971).

[15]Rawls, Section 44, pp. 284–293.

[16]William F. Baxter, "People or Penguins: The Case for Optimal Pollution," in Pojman, pp. 393–396, at 395–396.

[17]Baxter, p. 396.

[18]42 U.S.C. Paragraph 5877 © (1976).

[19]42 U.S.C. Paragraph 4332 (2) (B) (1976).

[20]46 Federal Register 13,193 (1981).

[21]National Public Radio, "Morning Edition," May 20, 1999.

[22]The GDP often excludes the monetary worth of some items, such as clean air and other public goods, when shadow pricing has not been used to assign a dollar value to them.

[23]This point was made first by economist James M. Lauderdale, *An Inquiry into the Nature and Origin of Public Wealth and into the Means and Causes of Its Increase*, 2nd ed. (Edinburgh: Constable, 1819). I found it in Herman E. Daly and John B. Cobb, Jr., *For the Common Good* (Boston: Beacon Press, 1994), pp. 147–148.

[24]Lester R. Brown, *Who Will Feed China?* (New York: W.W. Norton, 1995), p. 131.

[25]Nicholas Lenssen, "Confronting Nuclear Waste," *State of the World 1992* (New York: W.W. Norton, 1992), p. 52.

[26]Philip A. Greenberg, "Dreams Die Hard," *Sierra* (November/December 1993), p. 85.

[27]Sam Schurr, et al., *Energy in America's Future: The Choices Before Us* (Baltimore: Johns Hopkins University Press, 1979), p. 355. I found this in Daly and Cobb, p. 153.

[28]Peter Unger, *Living High and Letting Die: Our Illusion of Innocence* (New York: Oxford University Press, 1996), p. 6.

[29]Lenssen, p. 50.

[30]Lenssen, pp. 56–57.

[31]Lenssen, p. 58.

[32]Konrad B. Krauskopf, "Disposal of High-Level Nuclear Waste: Is It Possible?" *Science* (September 14, 1990). This was found in Lenssen, p. 55.

[33]William Poole, "Gambling with Tomorrow," *Sierra* (September/October 1992), p. 52.

[34]Morning Edition–Marketplace Report, National Public Radio, November 6, 1998.

[35]Bill McKibben, "A Special Moment in History," *The Atlantic Monthly* (May 1998), pp. 55–78, at 72–73.

Chapter 3

[1]Claude Alvares, "A Walk Through Bhopal," in David Weir, ed. *The Bhopal Syndrome* (San Francisco: Sierra Club Books, 1987), pp. 159–180, at 165–166.

[2]Ward Morehouse, "Unfinished Business: Bhopal Ten Years After," *The Ecologist*, Vol. 24, No. 5 (September/October 1994), pp. 164–168, at 165.

[3]David Weir, *The Bhopal Syndrome*, (San Francisco: Sierra Club Books, 1987), p. 31.

[4]Weir, p. 32.

[5]Weir, p. 36.

[6]Weir, p. 33.

[7]Weir, pp. 40–42.

[8]Weir, p. 59.

[9]Weir, p. 60.

[10]Jodi L. Jacobson, "Abandoning Homelands," *State of the World 1989*, Lester R. Brown, ed. (New York: W.W. Norton, 1989), pp. 59–76, at 70.

[11]Aaron Sachs, "Upholding Human Rights and Environmental Justice," *State of the World 1996*, Lester R. Brown, ed. (New York: W.W. Norton, 1996), pp. 133–151, at 144.

[12]Morehouse, p. 168.

[13]Sachs, p. 148.

[14]Morehouse, p. 167.

[15]*The Guardian*, 14 February 1992, p. 29. Emphasis in original. Reprinted in Steven Yearly, *Sociology, Environmentalism, Globalization* (Thousand Oaks, CA: Sage Pubications, 1996), pp. 75–76.

[16]Quoted in Weir, p. 60.

[17]*The Economist*, 11-17 (March 1995), p. 73. Reprinted in Yearly, p. 76.

[18]Yearley, p. 141, footnote #4, reporting on an article in *The Guardian*, 1 November 1995, pp. 6–7.

[19]Bill McKibben, "A Special Moment in History," *The Atlantic Monthly* (May 1998), pp. 55–78, at 72.

[20]Gregg Easterbrook, *A Moment on the Earth* (New York: Penguin Books, 1995), p. 314.

[21]Easterbrook, p. 313.

[22]Jacques Thiroux, *Ethics: Theory and Practice*, 5th ed. (Englewood Cliffs, NJ: Prentice Hall, 1995), p. 359.

[23]George F. Will, "Prostitution Should Be Decriminalized," *The Washington Post* (August 26, 1974). Reprinted in Robert Baum, ed., *Ethical Arguments for Analysis*, 2nd ed. (New York: Holt, Rinehart and Winston, 1976), p. 80.

[24]Mark Sagoff, *The Economy of the Earth* (New York: Cambridge University Press, 1988), p. 8.

[25]Sagoff, pp. 16–17.

[26]Sagoff, pp. 52–53.

[27]Sagoff, p. 93.

[28]Sagoff, pp. 94–95.

[29]Hugh H. Macauley and Bruce Yandle, *Environmmental Use and the Market* (Lexington, Mass.: Lexington Books, 1977), pp. 120–121. I found it in Sagoff, p. 231, note #44.

[30]405 U.S. 727 (1972). Reprinted in part in *Green Justice: The Environment and the Courts*, Thomas More Hoban and Richard Oliver Brooks, eds. (Boulder, CO: Westview, 1987), pp. 143–154, at 145.

[31]Hoban and Brooks, p. 150.

[32]Hoban and Brooks, p. 146.

[33]Hoban and Brooks, p. 144.

[34]Aldo Leopold, "The Green Lagoons," *A Sand County Almanac with Essays on Conservation from Round River* (New York: Ballantine Books, 1970), pp. 150–151.

[35]Leopold, p. 155.

[36]Leopold, p. 157.

[37]Eugene C. Hargrove, *Foundations of Environmental Ethics* (Englewood Cliffs, NJ: Prentice Hall, 1989), pp. 82–83.

[38]Hargrove, p. 127.

[39]Hargrove, p. 169.

[40]Hargrove, p. 82.

[41]Sagoff, p. 133.

[42]Sagoff, p. 135.

[43]Perry Miller, *Errand into the Wilderness* (New York: Harper and Row, 1964), p. 207. Found in Sagoff, p. 140.

[44]Sagoff, p. 142.

[45]Sagoff, p. 51.

[46]Sagoff, pp. 59–60.

[47]Bryan G. Norton, *Why Preserve Natural Variety?* (Princeton: Princeton University Press, 1987), pp. 189–190.

[48]Norton, p. 209.

[49]Norton, p. 210.

[50]Sagoff, p. 63.

[51]J. Baird Callicott, "The Case against Moral Pluralism," *Environmental Ethics*, Vol. 12, No. 2 (Summer 1990), pp. 99–124. See especially pp. 109–113.

[52]414 U.S. 218.

[53]*Knowles v. Iowa*, No. 97-7597 (Decided December 8, 1998).

[54]*The United States Law Week*, "Arguments Before the Court," Vol. 67, No. 18 (November 17, 1998), pp. 3329–3330, at 3330.

[55]*Knowles v. Iowa*, No. 97-7597.

[56]No. A-091133 (Los Angeles Cty. Super. Ct. filed April 24, 1985), cited in an Unsigned Note: "The Cultural Defense in the Criminal Law," in *Philosophical Problems in the Law*, David M. Adams, ed. (Belmont, CA: Wadsworth, 1996), pp. 391–398, at 391.

[57]Unsigned Note, p. 391.

[58]Unsigned Note, p. 391–192.

Chapter 4

[1]In this book I use the word "animal" to mean "nonhuman animal."

[2]*Illinois Revised Statutes*, Chapter 8, Sections 703 and 704.

[3]I have changed this quote from present to past tense.

[4]From the American Humane Association's Fall 1998 letter, put into the past tense.

[5]Immanuel Kant, "Duties to Animals and Spirits," in *Lectures on Ethics*, trans. Louis Infield (New York: Harper and Row, 1963), and reprinted in part in *Animal Rights and Human Obligations*, Tom Regan and Peter Singer, eds. (Englewood Cliffs, NJ: Prentice-Hall, 1976), pp. 122–123, at 122.

[6]Peter Singer, *Animal Liberation*, New Revised Edition (New York: Avon Books, 1990), p. 6. Emphasis added.

[7]Jeremy Bentham, *The Principles of Morals and Legislation*, Chapter XVII, Section 1 (1789), in Regan and Singer, eds., pp. 129–130, at 130.

[8]Singer, p. 129.

[9]Singer, p. 120.

[10]Singer, p. 123.

[11]In Singer, p. 121.

[12]Singer, p. 121.

[13]Singer, p. 122.

[14]Singer, p. 124.

[15]Singer, p. 126.

[16]Singer, p. 127.

[17]Singer, p. 128.

[18]Singer, pp. 125–126. Emphasis added.

[19]Gail A. Eisnitz, *Slaughterhouse* (Amherst, NY: Prometheus Books, 1997), p. 24.

[20]Eisnitz, p. 101.

[21]Eisnitz, p. 102.

[22]Eisnitz, p. 68.

[23]Eisnitz, p. 68.

[24]Eisnitz, p. 70.

[25]Singer, pp. 107–108.

[26]Singer, pp. 109–110.

[27]The National Census Bureau estimates the U.S. population at the end of this century will be 571 million, as reported on National Public Radio's "Morning Edition" on January 13, 2000.

[28]Friends of Animals, Inc., reprinted in Robert Baum, ed., *Ethical Arguments for Analysis*, 2nd ed. (New York: Holt, Rinehart and Winston, 1976), p. 333.

[29]*Pennsylvania S.P.C.A. v. Bravo Enterprises, Inc.* (1968) 237A 2d 342. Bravo Enterprises eventually won the case because a higher court denied that the PSPCA had the required judicial standing in the matter to sue in the first place.

[30]For some discussions of this issue, see L. W. Sumner, "Classical Utilitarianism and the Population Optimum," in *Obligations to Future Generations*, R. I. Sikora and Brian Barry, eds. (Philadelphia: Temple University Press, 1978), pp. 91–111; Jan Narveson, "Moral Problems of Population," in *Ethics and Population*, Michael D. Bayles, ed. (Cambridge, MA: Schenkman Publishing, 1976), pp. 59–80; Peter Singer, "A Utilitarian Population Principle," in Bayles, pp. 81–99.

[31]William Shakespeare, "Hamlet, Prince of Denmark," Act II, Scene II, in *The Complete Works of William Shakespeare*, Hardin Craig, ed. (Fair Lawn, NJ: Scott, Foresman and Company, 1961), pp. 901–943, at 919.

[32]William Shakespeare, "Othello, the Moor of Venice," Act IV, Scene I, in Craig, ed., pp. 943–979, at 969.

[33]Aldous Huxley, *Brave New World* (New York: Bantam Books, 1962), p. 149.

[34]*The Christian Century* (March 4, 1970), reprinted in Baum, ed., p. 56.

[35]Mark Sagoff, *The Economy of the Earth* (New York: Cambridge University Press, 1988), p. 102.

[36]Clinton was impeached also for allegedly obstructing justice, but that part of the case does not illustrate the point made here.

[37]Jane Goodall, *Through a Window: My Thirty Years with the Chimpanzees of Gombe* (Boston: Houghton Mifflin Company, 1990), p. 206.

Chapter 5

[1]Robert J. White, "The Facts about Animal Research," *Reader's Digest* (March 1988), reprinted as "Animal Experimentation Is Adequately Regulated," in *Animal Rights: Opposing Viewpoints*, Janelle Rohr, ed. (San Diego: Greenhaven Press, 1989), pp. 77–82, at 78.

[2]Leo Katz, *Ill-Gotten Gains* (Chicago: University of Chicago Press, 1996), pp. 53–54.

[3]Rene Descartes, "Animals Are Machines," in *Animal Rights and Human Obligations*, Tom Regan and Peter Singer, eds. (Englewood Cliffs, NJ: Prentice Hall, 1976), pp. 60–66, at 64.

[4]Descartes, p. 65. In Descartes' time, philosophers did not often use the terminology of rights as we do today, but his point is captured well by our notion of rights.

[5]Ovid, "The Teachings of Pythagoras," *Metamorphosis*, reprinted in *Ethical Vegetarianism: From Pythagoras to Peter Singer*, Kerry S. Walters and Lisa Portmess, eds. (Albany: SUNY Press, 1999), pp. 16–22, at 22.

[6]Steven Pinker, *The Language Instinct* (New York: HarperPerrenial, 1995), pp. 68–69.

[7]Pinker, p. 69.

[8]Mary Midgley, *Animals and Why They Matter* (Athens, GA: The University of Georgia Press, 1983), pp. 57–58.

[9]Jane Goodall, *Through a Window: My Thirty Years with the Chimpanzees of Gombe* (Boston: Houghton Mifflin Company, 1990), p. 169.

[10]For a more detailed account see Stanley Milgram, *Obedience to Authority: An Experimental View* (London: Tavistock, 1974).

[11]James Rachels, *Created from Animals: The Moral Implications of Darwinism* (New York: Oxford University Press, 1990), p. 150.

[12]Rachels, p. 149.

[13]Carl Cohen, "The Case for the Use of Animals in Biomedical Research," *The New England Journal of Medicine*, Vol. 135 (1986), pp. 865–870, reprinted as "The Case Against Animal Rights," in Rohr, ed., pp. 23–28.

[14]Peter Carruthers, *The Animals Issue* (New York: Cambridge University Press, 1992), pp. 98–99.

[15]Carruthers, p. 103.

[16]For a more inclusive critique of Carruthers's book, see Peter S. Wenz, "Contracts, Animals, and Ecosystems," *Social Theory and Practice*, Vol. 19, No. 3 (Fall 1993), pp. 315–344.

[17]Midgley, p. 84.

[18]Midgley, pp. 84–85.

[19]Tom Regan, *The Case for Animal Rights* (Berkeley: University of California Press, 1983), p. 243.

[20]Goodall, p. 44.

[21]Goodall, pp. 47–48.

[22]Frans de Waal, *Good Natured: The Origins of Right and Wrong in Humans and Other Animals* (Cambridge, MA: Harvard University Press, 1996), p. 67.

[23]De Waal, p. 68.

[24]De Waal, pp. 68–69.

[25]Rohr, p. 61.

[26]Sidney Gendin, "The Use of Animals in Science," *Animal Sacrifices: Religious Perspectives on the Use of Animals in Science*, Tom Regan, ed. (Philadelphia: Temple University Press, 1986), pp. 15–60, at 18.

[27]Jane McCabe, *Newsweek* (December 28, 1988), quoted in "The Ability to Empathize," by Rohr in Rohr, pp. 101–102, at 101.

[28]American Medical Association, "Use of Animals in Biomedical Research: The Challenge and Response," reprinted in Rohr, ed., pp. 59–67, at 62.

[29]AMA in Rohr, p. 65.

[30]Stephen Kaufman, "Most Animal Research Is Not Beneficial to Human Health," reprinted in Rohr, ed., pp. 68–76, at 69.

[31]Paul Beeson, "Growth of Knowledge about a Disease: Hepatitis," *American Journal of Medicine*, Vol. 67 (1979), pp. 366–370, in Kaufman, p. 70.

[32]Kaufman, p. 69.

[33]Kaufman, p. 75. For a more complete account see Hugh LaFollette and Niall Shanks, *Brute Science: Dilemmas of Animal Experimentation* (New York: Routledge, 1996).

[34]Gendin, p. 28.

[35]Goodall, p. 226.

[36]Goodall, p. 227.

[37]Kaufman, pp. 71–72.

[38]Peter Singer, *Animal Liberation* (New York: Avon Books, 1990), p. 68.

[39]Singer, p. 62.

[40]The American Anti-Vivisection Society, *The Case Book of Experiments with Living Animals* (August 1988), reprinted as "Animal Experimentation is Unethical" in Rohr, pp. 54–58, at 57.

[41]Richard C. Simmonds, "Should Animals Be Used in Research and Education?" *The New Physician* (March 1986). Reprinted as "Animal Experimentation is Ethical" in Rohr, pp. 50–53, at 52.

[42]Goodall, pp. 249–250.

[43]Aldo Leopold, *A Sand County Almanac with Essays on Conservation from Round River* (New York: Ballantine Books, 1970), pp. 4–5.

[44]Gendin, p. 30.

[45]Paul Recer, "Studies Continue Stem Cell Revelations," *The State Journal-Register* (January 22, 1999), p. 4.

Chapter 6

[1]Douglas Adams and Mark Carwardine, *Last Chance to See* (New York: Ballantine Books, 1990), pp. 203–204.

[2]See Paul Rauber, "An End to Evolution," *Sierra* (January/February 1996), pp. 28–32 and 123, at 31.

[3]John Tuxill, "Losing Strands in the Web of Life: Vertebrate Declines and the Conservation of Biological Diversity," *Worldwatch Paper #141* (May 1998), p. 61.

[4]Gregg Easterbrook, *A Moment on the Earth* (New York: Penguin Books, 1995), p. 552.

[5]Tuxill (1998), p. 9.

[6]Tuxill (1998), p. 7.

[7]John Tuxill, "Death in the Family Tree," *WorldWatch*, Vol. 10, No. 5 (September/October 1997), pp. 13–21, at 13.

[8]Susan Middleton and David Liittschwager, "Parting Shots: Species Your Grand-children May Never Have a Chance to See?" *Sierra* (January/February 1996), pp. 40–45, at 43.

[9]Middleton and Liittschwager, p. 41.

[10]Tuxill (1997), p. 14.

[11]Adams, p. 111.

[12]Adams, p. 115.

[13]Adams, pp. 114–115.

[14]Adams, pp. 119–120. Emphasis added.

[15]Adams, p. 116.

[16]Easterbrook, pp. 553–555.

[17]Tuxill (1998), p. 9.

[18]Tuxill (1998), p. 10.

[19]Bryan G. Norton, *Why Preserve Natural Variety?* (Princeton: Princeton University Press, 1987), pp. 189–190 and 209–210.

[20]Norton, p. 210.

[21]Adams, p. 124.

[22]Adams, pp. 188–189.

[23]Adams, p. 190.

[24]Adams, p. 195.

[25]Lawrence E. Johnson, *A Morally Deep World: An Essay on Moral Significance and Environmental Ethics* (New York: Cambridge University Press, 1991), p. 156. Emphasis added.

[26]Holmes Rolston, III, *Environmental Ethics: Duties to and Values in the Natural World* (Philadelphia: Temple University Press, 1988), p. 105.

[27]Paul W. Taylor, *Respect for Nature: A Theory of Environmental Ethics* (Princeton: Princeton University Press, 1986), p. 122.

[28]David Hull, "Kitts and Kitts and Caplan on Species," *Philosophy of Science* 48 (1981), pp. 141–152, at 146. Found in Johnson, p. 154. Actually, species are also classes, so Hull's point could more accurately be put as involving a distinction between "mere classes" and "classes that are species."

[29]Johnson, p. 155.

[30]Rolston, p. 143.

[31]Rolston, pp. 149–150.

[32]Rolston, p. 147.

[33]J.E. Lovelock, *Gaia: A New Look at Life on Earth* (New York: Oxford University Press, 1979, 1987), p. 19.

[34]Lovelock (1979), p. 23.

[35]Lovelock (1979), p. 20.

[36]James Lovelock, *The Ages of Gaia: A Biography of Our Living System* (New York: W.W. Norton, 1988), p. 37.

[37]Lynn Margulis, *Symbiotic Planet: A New View of Evolution* (New York: Basic Books, 1998), p. 127.

[38]Margulis, pp. 127–128.

[39]Lovelock (1988), p. 39.
[40]Lovelock (1979), p. 70.
[41]Lovelock (1979), p. 71.
[42]Lovelock (1979), p. 72.
[43]Lovelock (1979), p. 73.
[44]Lovelock (1979), p. 74.
[45]Lovelock (1988), p. 19.
[46]Lovelock (1988), p. 39.
[47]Margulis, p. 125.
[48]*Webster's New Collegiate Dictionary*, 2nd ed., p. 361.
[49]George Lakoff, *Women, Fire, and Dangerous Things: What Categories Reveal about the Mind* (Chicago: The University of Chicago Press, 1987), pp. 276–278.
[50]Lakoff, p. 209.
[51]In Garrett Hardin, "Lifeboat Ethics," in *World Hunger and Morality*, 2nd ed., William Aiken and Hugh LaFollette, eds. (Upper Saddle River, NJ: Prentice Hall, 1996), p. 12.
[52]Rolston, p. 105.
[53]Rolston, pp. 99–100.
[54]Lovelock (1988), p. 56.
[55]*World Report: A Newsletter for Friends of Care*, No. 101 (Winter 1999), p. 3.

Chapter 7

[1]Lynn Margulis, *Symbiotic Planet* (New York: Basic Books, 1998), p. 120.
[2]Some hunters may be anthropocentrists whose justification for hunting centers exclusively on the welfare of human beings. The present chapter, however, concentrates on nonanthropocentric concerns.
[3]In *Ethical Arguments for Analysis*, 2nd ed., Robert Baum, ed. (New York: Holt, Rinehart and Winston, 1976), p. 331.
[4]Aldo Leopold, *A Sand County Almanac with Essays on Conservation from Round River* (New York: Ballantine Books, 1970), pp. 139–140.
[5]Leopold, p. 252.
[6]Leopold, p. 252.
[7]Leopold, p. 253.
[8]Leopold, p. 253. Emphasis added.
[9]Leopold, p. 7.
[10]This example is drawn from Leopold, pp. 29–32.
[11]Leopold, p. 272–273.
[12]Leopold, p. 274.
[13]*Archery World*, "The Hunter's Story," reprinted as "Hunting Helps Animal Conservation," in *Animal Rights: Opposing Viewpoints*, Janelle Rohr, ed. (San Diego: Greenhaven Press, 1989), pp. 158–165, at 159.
[14]Rohr, p. 159.
[15]Margaret L. Knox, "In the Heat of the Hunt," *Sierra* (November/December 1990), pp. 48–59, at 53.
[16]Patrick F. Scanlon, "Humans as Hunting Animals," in *Ethics and Animals*, Harlan B. Miller and William H. Williams, eds. (Clifton, NJ: Humana Press, 1983), pp. 199–205, at 199–200 and 204.

[17]See Knox, p. 55 for figures for the 1988–1989 season.

[18]Robert W. Loftin, "The Morality of Hunting," *Environmental Ethics* Vol. 6, No. 3 (Fall 1984), pp. 241–250, at 244.

[19]Knox, p. 55.

[20]Loftin, p. 245.

[21]Loftin, p. 246.

[22]Leopold (1970), p. 268.

[23]John Tuxill, *Losing Strands in the Web of Life: Vertebrate Declines and the Conservation of Biological Diversity*, Worldwatch Paper #141 (May 1998), p. 25.

[24]Tuxill (1998), p. 26.

[25]Tuxill (1998), p. 26.

[26]Tuxill (1998), p. 27.

[27]Tuxill, "Death in the Family Tree," *WorldWatch*, Vol. 10, No. 5 (September/October 1997), pp. 13–21, at 17.

[28]Ann S. Causey, "On the Morality of Hunting," *Environmental Ethics*, Vol. 11, No. 4 (Winter 1989), pp. 327–343, at 341.

[29]Leopold, pp. 219–220 and 288–290.

[30]Aldo Leopold, *The River of the Mother of God and Other Essays*, Susan L. Flader and J. Baird Callicott, eds. (Madison: University of Wisconsin Press, 1991), p. 280.

[31]Charles R. Darwin, *The Descent of Man and Selection in Relation to Sex* (New York: J. A. Hill and Company, 1904), p. 111. Found in J. Baird Callicott, "The Conceptual Foundations of the Land Ethic," *Companion to A Sand County Almanac: Interpretive and Critical Essays*, J. Baird Callicott, ed. (Madison: University of Wisconsin Press, 1987), pp. 186–217, at 192.

[32]Callicott (1987), pp. 192–193.

[33]Leopold (1970), p. 239.

[34]Leopold (1970), p. 240. Emphasis added.

[35]Leopold (1970), p. 262. Ecological investigation since Leopold's time reveals that ecosystems typically lack the integrity and stability that Leopold attributes to them. They change more rapidly than Leopold thought, and they do not tend to return to a single climax condition. Their complement of species is unstable. Often species disappear, and their ecological "services" are performed just as well by different species. Callicott argues convincingly, however, that these facts do not affect the land ethic. The land ethic's cogency does not depend on the exact nature of the ecological communities we inhabit, but on the fact of our dependence on them and on the plausibility of analogizing this dependence to the kind of interdependence within human communities. See J. Baird Callicott, "Do Deconstructive Ecology and Sociobiology Undermine the Leopold Land Ethic?" in *Beyond the Land Ethic: More Essays in Environmental Philosophy* (Albany: State University of New York Press, 1999), pp. 117–139, especially pp. 125 and 130–139.

[36]Callicott (1987), p. 194.

[37]For more on this see Peter S. Wenz, "Alternate Foundations for the Land Ethic: Biologism, Cognitivism, and Pragmatism," *Topoi*, Vol. 12, No. 1 (March 1993), pp. 53–67.

[38]Tom Regan, "Ethical Vegetarianism and Commercial Animal Farming," in *Today's Moral Problems*, 3rd ed., Richard Wasserstrom, ed. (New York: Macmillan, 1985), pp. 475–476.

[39]Callicott (1987), p. 208. For more on this issue see Peter S. Wenz, *Environmental Justice* (Albany: State University of New York Press, 1988), especially Chapter 14, "The Concentric Circle Theory," pp. 310–335.

[40]Holmes Rolston, III, "Feeding People versus Saving Nature?" in *World Hunger and Morality*, 2nd ed., William Aiken and Hugh LaFollette, eds. (Upper Saddle River, NJ: Printice Hall, 1996), pp. 248–267, at 261–262.

[41]Rolston, p. 266.

[42]Rolston, p. 250.

[43]Rolston, p. 252.

[44]Rolston, p. 261.

[45]Rolston, p. 261.

[46]Ramachandra Guha, "The Authoritarian Biologist and the Arrogance of Anti-Humanism: Wildlife Conservation in the Third World," *The Ecologist*, Vol. 27, No. 1 (January/February 1997), pp. 14–20, at 16–17.

[47]Guha, p. 17.

[48]Guha, p. 17.

[49]R. Sukumar, "Wildlife-Human Conflict in India: An Ecological and Social Perspective," in *Social Ecology*, R. Guha, ed. (New Delhi: Oxford University Press, 1994), quoted in Guha, p. 18.

[50]Cheri Sugal, "The Price of Habitat," *WorldWatch*, Vol. 10 No. 3 (May/June 1997), pp. 18–27, at 20.

[51]Sugal, p. 19.

[52]Sugal, p. 18.

[53]Sugal, p. 22.

[54]Wayne Pacelle, letter about Sugal's article, *WorldWatch*, Vol. 10 No. 5 (September/October 1997), p. 5.

[55]Sugal, p. 24.

[56]See J. Baird Callicott, "Animal Liberation: A Triangular Affair," in *In Defense of the Land Ethic* (Albany: State University of New York Press, 1989), pp. 15–38; originally published in the journal *Environmental Ethics*, Vol. 2 (1980), pp. 311–328.

[57]This case is taken from Christopher D. Stone, *Earth and Other Ethics: The Case for Moral Pluralism* (New York: Harper and Row, 1987), pp. 155–156.

Chapter 8

[1]John Ward Anderson and Molly Moore, "The Burden of Womanhood," in *Global Issues 96/97*, Robert M. Jackson, ed. (Guilford, CT: Dushkin, 1996), pp. 162–165, at 162.

[2]Germaine W. Shames, "The World's Throw-Away Children," in *Global Issues 94/95*, Robert M. Jackson, ed. (Guilford, CT: Dushkin, 1994), pp. 229–232, at 229.

[3]Aaron Sachs, "The Last Commodity: Child Prostitution in the Developing World," *WorldWatch*, Vol. 7, No. 4 (July/August 1994), pp. 24–30, at 26.

[4]Sachs, p. 25.

[5]Anderson and Moore, p. 163.

[6]Sachs, pp. 26–27.

[7]Jodi L. Jacobson, "Out of the Woods," *WorldWatch*, Vol. 5, No. 6 (November/December 1992), pp. 26–31, at 26.

[8]Brian Murphy in *The State Journal-Register* (April 7, 1999), pp. 1 and 5.

[9]Lester R. Brown, "Feeding Nine Billion," *State of the World 1999*, Lester R. Brown, ed. (New York: W.W. Norton, 1999), pp. 115–132, at 115.

[10]Brown, p. 119.

[11]Brown, p. 118.

[12]Brown, p. 123.

[13]Brown, p. 116.

[14]Brown, p. 226.

[15]Brown, p. 125.

[16]Wendell Berry, *The Unsettling of America: Culture and Agriculture* (San Francisco: Sierra Club Books, 1977, 1996), p. 19.

[17]W. Berry, p. 42.

[18]W. Berry, p. 21.

[19]W. Berry, pp. 34-35.

[20]W. Berry, pp. 35.

[21]From W. Berry, p. 34.

[22]Quoted in *EDF Letter*, Vol. XXX, No. 1 (January 1999), p. 2.

[23]*EDF Letter*, p. 2.

[24]Donald L. Barlett and James B. Steele, "The Empire of the Pigs," *Time* (Novermber 30, 1998), pp. 52–64, at 58 and 60.

[25]W. Berry, p. 53.

[26]W. Berry, p. 52

[27]W. Berry, p. 62.

[28]Brown, p. 124.

[29]Brown, p. 124.

[30]Brown, pp. 120–121.

[31]Gary Gardner, "Shrinking Fields: Cropland Loss in a World of Eight Billion," *Worldwatch Paper #131* (July 1996), p. 6.

[32]Gardner, p. 7.

[33]Gardner, p. 27.

[34]Brown, pp. 126–127.

[35]Brown, p. 117.

[36]Vandana Shiva, *The Violence of the Green Revolution* (Atlantic Highlands, NJ: Zed Books 1991), pp. 31–32.

[37]Shiva, p. 89.

[38]Shiva, p. 93.

[39]Shiva, p. 96.

[40]Gregg Easterbrook, *A Moment on the Earth* (New York: Penguin, 1995), p. 393.

[41]Ricarda A. Steinbrecher, "From Green to Gene Revolution: The Environmental Risks of Genetically Engineered Crops," *The Ecologist*, Vol. 26, No. 6 (November/December 1996), pp. 273–281, at 274.

[42]Shiva, p. 206.

[43]Shiva, p. 206.

[44]Vandana Shiva, *Monocultures of the Mind* (London: Zed Books, 1993), p. 36.

[45]John Tuxill, "Appreciating the Benefits of Plant Biodiversity," *State of the World 1999*, Lester R. Brown, ed. (New York, W.W. Norton, 1999), pp. 96–114, at 103.

[46]From W. Berry, p. 177.

[47]W. Berry, p. 177.

[48]From W. Berry, p. 178.

[49]From W. Berry, p. 176.

[50]Tuxill, p. 101.

[51]Tuxill, p. 100.

[52]Tuxill, p. 101.

[53]Tuxill, p. 96.

[54]Tuxill, p. 102.

[55]Tuxill, p. 106.

[56]National Research Council, "Executive Summary," *Alternative Agriculture* (1989), reprinted in *Global Resources: Opposing Viewpoints*, Matthew Polesetsky, ed. (San Diego, CA: Greenhaven Press, 1991), pp. 188–195, at 191.

[57]NRC, p. 192.

[58]NRC. p. 192.

[59]Aldo Leopold, *A Sand County Almanac with Essays on Conservation from Round River* (New York: Ballantine Books, 1970), p. 240.

[60]"Editorial," *The State Journal-Register* (March 28, 1999), p. 18.

[61]W. Berry, p. 68.

[62]Found in *The State Journal-Register* (December 30, 1998), p. 9.

Chapter 9

[1]*Bradwell v. The State* 16 Wall. 130, at 130.

[2]*Bradwell*, p. 141.

[3]*Commonwealth v. Welosky* 177 N.E. 656, at 660.

[4]Steven Goldberg, *Why Men Rule: A Theory of Male Dominance* (Chicago: Open Court, 1993), p. 199.

[5]Goldberg, p. 200.

[6]Goldberg, p. 201.

[7]Goldberg, p. 205.

[8]Toni Nelson, "Violence Against Women," *WorldWatch*, Vol. 9, No. 4 (July/August 1996), pp. 33–38, at 33.

[9]Aristotle, *Politics*, book 1, chapters 4–5. Found in Val Plumwood, *Feminism and the Mastery of Nature* (New York: Routledge, 1993), p. 46.

[10]Karen J. Warren, "The Power and the Promise of Ecological Feminism," in *Environmental Philosophy: From Animal Rights to Radical Ecology*, Michael E. Zimmerman, ed. (Englewood Cliffs, NJ: Prentice Hall, 1993), pp. 320–341, at 322.

[11]*Bradwell*, p. 141.

[12]*Bradwell*, p. 142.

[13]Plumwood, p. 60.

[14]Jodi L. Jacobson, "Closing the Gender Gap in Development," *State of the World 1993*, Lester R. Brown, ed. (New York: W.W. Norton, 1993), pp. 61–79, at 66–67.

[15]James P. Sterba, *Justice for Here and Now* (New York: Cambridge University Press, 1998), p. 88.

[16]Jacobson (1993), p. 65.

[17]Plumwood, p. 22.

[18]Sterba, p. 87.

[19]Dorothy L. Sayers, *Are Women Human?* (Grand Rapids, MI: William B. Eerdmans Publishing, 1971), pp. 39–42.

[20]Susan Faludi, *Backlash: The Undeclared War Against Amercan Women* (New York: Anchor Books, 1991), p. 215.

[21]Faludi, p. 216.

[22]Dee Brown, *Bury My Heart at Wounded Knee* (New York: Bantam Books, 1970), p. 1.

[23]Brown, p. 2.

[24]Juan Gines de Sepulveda, in *1492: Discovery, Invasion, Encounter*, Marvin Lunenfeld, ed. (Lexington, MA: C.C. Heath and Company, 1991), pp. 218–221, at 218.

[25]Sepulveda, p. 219.

[26]Sepulveda, p. 218.

[27]Sepulveda, pp. 220–221.

[28]John Locke, *Two Treatises of Government*, in *Social and Political Philosophy*, James P. Sterba, ed. (Belmont, CA: Wadsworth, 1995), pp. 163–184, at 170.

[29]Deborah Bird Rose, *Dingo Makes Us Human* (New York: Cambridge University Press, 1992), p. 11.

[30]Rose, p. 13.

[31]Rose, p. 14.

[32]Rose, pp. 17–18.

[33]Carolyn Merchant, *The Death of Nature* (New York: HarperCollins, 1980), p. 172.

[34]Merchant, pp. 226–227.

[35]John Locke, *Two Treatises of Government*, Chapter V, paragraphs 40 and 43, in Sterba, ed. (1995), p. 170.

[36]Locke, p. 169.

[37]Faludi, p. 199.

[38]Carol J. Adams, *The Sexual Politics of Meat* (New York: Continuum, 1990), p. 43.

[39]Adams, p. 54.

[40]Adams, p. 45.

[41]Adams, p. 58.

[42]Found in Carolyn Merchant, *The Death of Nature* (New York: HarperCollins, 1980), p. 170.

[43]Merchant, p. 168.

[44]Merchant, p. 168.

[45]Merchant, p. 170.

[46]Merchant, p. 171.

[47]Merchant, p. 169.

[48]*The National Law Journal* (September 21, 1992), p. s3.

[49]*The National Law Journal*, p. s3.

[50]Robert D. Bullard, "Decision Making," in *Faces of Environmental Racism*, Laura Westra and Peter S. Wenz, eds. (Lanham, MD: Rowman and Littlefield, 1995), pp. 3–28, at 7.

[51]Dick Russell, "Environmental Racism," *The Amicus Journal* (Spring 1989), pp. 22–31, at 24.

[52]Peter S. Wenz, *Nature's Keeper* (Philadelphia: Temple University Press, 1996), pp. 89–90.

[53]For more on this see Wenz (1996), especially Chapter 6.

[54]Russell, pp. 24–25.

[55]Naikang Tsao, "Ameliorating Environmental Racism: A Citizen's Guide to Combatting the Discriminatory Siting of Toxic Waste Dumps," *New York University Law Review*, Vol. 67 (May 1992), pp. 366–418, at 367.

[56]I owe this point to David Schmidtz.

[57]Jacobson (1993), p. 64.

[58]Jacobson (1993), p. 68.

[59]Jodi L. Jacobson, "Out of the Woods," *WorldWatch*, Vol. 5, No. 6 (November/ December 1992), pp. 26–31, at 30.

60Jacobson (1992), p. 30.

61Partha S. Dasgupta, "Population, Poverty and the Local Environment," in *The Environmental Ethics and Policy Book*, 2nd ed., Donald VanDeVeer and Christine Pierce, eds. (Belmont, CA: Wadsworth, 1998), pp. 404–409, at 409.

62Dasgupta, p. 407.

63Jacobson (1993), p. 74.

64Jacobson (1993), p. 75.

65Jacobson (1993), p. 76.

66Alan Thein Durning, "Supporting Indigenous Peoples," in *State of the World 1993*, Lester R. Brown, ed. (New York: W.W. Norton, 1993), pp. 80–100, at 85–86.

67Alan Thein Durning, "Native Americans Stand Their Ground," *WorldWatch*, Vol. 4, No. 6 (November/December 1991), pp. 10–17, at 11–12.

68Vandana Shiva, *Monocultures of the Mind* (Atlantic Highlands, NJ: Zed Books, 1993), pp. 14–15.

69Durning (1993), p. 85.

70Durning (1993), pp. 80–81.

71Durning (1993), p. 83.

72Margaret L. Knox, "Their Mother's Keepers," *Sierra*, Vol. 78, No. 2 (March/April 1993), pp. 50–57 and 80–84, at 53.

73Knox, pp. 53–54.

74John Tuxill, "Appreciating the Benefits of Plant Biodiversity," *State of the World 1999*, Lester R. Brown, ed. (New York: W.W. Norton, 1999), pp. 96–114, at 109.

75Shiva, p. 89.

76Gary LaPlante, "Testimony," in *Poison Fire-Sacred Earth*, Sibylle Hahr and Uwe Peters, eds. (Munich: The World Uranium Hearing, 1993), pp. 80–81, at 80.

Chapter 10

1Dan W. Brock, "Cloning Human Beings: An Assessment of the Ethical Issues Pro and Con," in *Ethical Issues in Modern Medicine*, 5th ed. John D. Arras and Bonnie Steinbock, eds. (Mountain View, CA: Mayfield, 1999), pp. 484–496, at 485.

2Brock, p. 489.

3Brock, p. 489.

4Brock, p. 494.

5Brock, p. 495.

6Brock, p. 495.

7*The Scofield Reference Bible*, Rev. C. I. Scofield, ed. (New York: Oxford University Press, 1945). Authorized Version (AV).

8Leon R. Kass, "The Wisdom of Repugnance," in Arras and Steinbock, pp. 496–510, at 506.

9Kass, p. 500.

10"From the Hebrew Bible," in Roger S. Gottlieb, ed., *This Sacred Earth: Religion, Nature, Environment* (New York: Routledge, 1996), p. 72, quoting *The TANAKH: The New JPS Translation According to the Traditional Hebrew Text* (New York: Jewish Publication Society, 1985).

11Roderick Frazier Nash, *The Rights of Nature: A History of Environmental Ethics* (Madison: University of Wisconsin Press, 1989), p. 90.

[12]Lynn White, Jr., "The Historical Roots of Our Ecological Crisis," in Gottlieb, pp. 184–193, at 189.

[13]White, p. 191.

[14]David Kinsley, "Christianity as Ecologically Harmful," in Gottlieb, ed., pp. 104–116, at 107.

[15]Kinsley, p. 109.

[16]Winthrop D. Jordan, *White over Black: American Attitudes Toward the Negro, 1550–1812* (Chapel Hill: University of North Carolina Press, 1968), p. 17.

[17]Jordan, p. 19.

[18]Sir Edward Coke, *The First Part of the Institutes of the Laws of England: or, a Commentary upon Littleton . . .* , 12th ed. (London, 1738), Lib. II, Cap. XI. Found in Jordan, p. 54.

[19]Jordan, p. 54.

[20]George M. Fredrickson, *The Black Image in the White Mind: Debate on Afro-American Character and Destiny, 1817–1914* (Middletown, CT: Welseyan University Press, 1971), p. 87.

[21]Fredrickson, p. 89.

[22]*Church of the Holy Trinity v. United States* 143 U.S. 457, at 458.

[23]*Church of the Holy Trinity*, p. 471.

[24]*Church of the Holy Trinity*, p. 470.

[25]*Church of the Holy Trinity*, p. 471.

[26]See Richard E. Palmer, *Hermeneutics* (Evanston: Northwestern University Press, 1969), especially pp. 4 and 22–26.

[27]In Gottlieb, p. 76.

[28]I Corinthians, Chapter 14, verses 34–35. AV.

[29]J. D. Bernal, *The World, the Flesh and the Devil* (Bloomington: Indiana University Press, 1969), pp. 35–36. Found in Mary Midgley, *Utopias, Dolphins and Computers* (New York: Routledge, 1996), p. 143.

[30]Thomas Berry, *The Dream of the Earth* (San Francisco: Sierra Club Books, 1990), pp. 75–77.

[31]Midgley (1996), p. 104.

[32]Mary Midgley, *Evolution as Religion: Strange Hopes and Stranger Fears* (New York: Methuen, 1985), pp. 14–15.

[33]Midgley (1996), pp. 139–140.

[34]Paul Kingsnorth, "Bovine Growth Hormones," *The Ecologist*, Vol. 28, No. 5 (September/October 1998), pp. 266–269, at 266.

[35]Kingsnorth, p. 266.

[36]Kingsnorth, p. 266–267.

[37]Kingsnorth, p. 267.

[38]Kingsnorth, p. 268.

[39]Stephen Bodian, "An Interview with Arne Naess," in *Environmental Philosophy: From Animal Rights to Radical Ecology*, Michael E. Zimmerman, *et. al.*, eds. (Englewood Cliffs, NJ: Prentice-Hall, 1993), pp. 182–192, at 182–183. Emphasis added.

[40]Bodian, p. 186.

[41]Bodian, p. 189.

[42]Bodian, p. 184.

[43]Bodian, pp. 191–192.

[44]Bodian, p. 185.

[45]Warwick Fox, "The Deep Ecology-Ecofeminist Debate and Its Parallels," in Zimmerman, ed., pp. 213–232, at 214. Emphasis added.

⁴⁶Arne Naess, "The Deep Ecological Movement: Some Philosophical Aspects," in Zimmerman, ed., pp. 193–212, at 203.

⁴⁷Naess, p. 204.

⁴⁸Naess, p. 197.

⁴⁹Calvin Martin, *Keepers of the Game: Indian-Animal Relationships and the Fur Trade* (Berkeley: University of California Press, 1978), p. 186. Found in J. Baird Callicott, *Earth's Insights: A Multicultural Survey of Ecological Ethics from the Mediterranean Basin to the Australian Outback* (Berkeley: University of California Press, 1994), p. 119.

⁵⁰John G. Neihardt, *Black Elk Speaks: Being the Life Story of a Holy Man of the Oglala Sioux* (New York: Pocket Books, 1971), pp. 1–2. The Lakota were called Sioux by the French, but most now prefer to be called Lakota, because that is their traditional name. The Oglala are a band of the Lakota.

⁵¹Callicott, p. 121.

⁵²Callicott, p. 122.

⁵³Callicott, p. 124.

⁵⁴Callicott, p. 127.

⁵⁵Callicott, p. 127.

⁵⁶Lynn White, Jr., "Continuing the Conversation," in Ian G. Barbour, ed., *Western Man and Environmental Ethics* (Reading, MA: Addison-Wesley, 1973), pp. 55–64, at 61.

⁵⁷American Baptist Churches, USA, "Creation and the Covenant of Caring," in Gottlieb, pp. 238–242, at 238, 241, and 243.

⁵⁸Evangelical Lutheran Churches in America, "Basis for Our Caring," in Gottlieb, pp. 243–250, at 246–247.

⁵⁹"Liberating Life: A Report to the World Council of Churches," in Gottlieb, pp. 251–269, at 255.

⁶⁰"Liberating Life," p. 259.

⁶¹John F. Haught, "Christianity and Ecology," in Gottlieb, pp. 270–285, at 276.

⁶²T. Berry, p. 132.

⁶³T. Berry, p. 91.

⁶⁴T. Berry, p. 18.

⁶⁵T. Berry, p. 133.

⁶⁶Haught, p. 277.

⁶⁷Haught, p. 277.

⁶⁸Daniel Quinn, *Ishmael* (New York: Bantam/Turner, 1992), p. 180.

⁶⁹Quinn, p. 177.

⁷⁰See Bonnie Steinbock, "The McCaughey Septuplets: Medical Miracle or Gambling with Fertility Drugs?" in Arras and Steinbock, eds., pp. 375–377.

⁷¹See Christopher Joyce, "Special Delivery," in *USA Weekend: The State Journal Register* (of Springfield, Illinois) (May 14–16, 1999), pp. 6–7.

⁷²Bodian, pp. 190–191.

⁷³Found in Midgley (1996), p. 145.

Chapter 11

¹Jack Canfield and Mark Victor Hansen, *Chicken Soup for the Soul* (Deerfield, FL: Health Communications, 1993), p. 279.

²Dave Ramsey, *More Than Enough* (New York: Viking Penguin, 1999), p. 232.

³Alfie Kohn, *Punished by Rewards* (New York: Houghton Mifflin, 1993), p. 3.

⁴David C. Korten, *When Corporations Rule the World* (West Hartford, CN: Kumarian Press, 1995), pp. 37–38.

[5]Alan Thein Durning, *How Much Is Enough?* (New York: W.W. Norton, 1992), pp. 50–52.

[6]Durning, pp. 51–52.

[7]Korten, p. 105.

[8]James V. Riker, "The Changing Politics of Hunger," *Bread for the World Background Paper Number 144* (November 1998), p. 5.

[9]Vicki Robin and Joe Dominguez, *Your Money or Your Life* (New York: Penguin Books, 1992), p. 15.

[10]Robin and Dominguez, p. 17.

[11]Robin and Dominguez, p. 15.

[12]Robin and Dominguez, p. 18.

[13]Durning, p. 22.

[14]Korten, p. 34.

[15]Barry Schwartz, *The Battle for Human Nature* (New York: W.W. Norton, 1986), p. 164.

[16]Durning, pp. 38–39.

[17]Durning, p. 39. More recent studies show people in poorer countries generally to be less satisfied than those in richer countries. The difference from earlier times seems to be more global advertising. People in poorer countries are more likely now to compare their level of affluence not to the level of others in their own countries, but to the level in wealthier countries as depicted in ads. This finding supports the thesis given below that satisfaction from consumption rests largely on the comparisons people make between their level of consumption and that of others in a group with whom they compare themselves. See Benjamin M. Friedman, "The Power of the Electronic Herd," *The New York Review of Books*, Vol. XLVI, No. 12 (July 15, 1999), pp. 40–44, at 40.

[18]Lewis H. Lapham, *Money and Class in America: Notes and Observations on Our Civil Religion* (New York: Weidenfeld and Nicolson, 1988), found in Durning, p. 38.

[19]Schwartz, p. 163.

[20]Durning, p. 39.

[21]Lynette Engelhardt, *Bread for the World Background Paper Number 142* (September 1998), p. 6.

[22]Walden Bello, *Dark Victory* (London: Pluto Press, 1994), p. 90.

[23]Daniel Schor, "Sunday Weekend Edition," National Public Radio (August 15, 1999).

[24]Korten, p. 46.

[25]Korten, p. 47.

[26]Korten, p. 47.

[27]Korten, p. 41.

[28]Bello, p. 97.

[29]Benjamin R. Barber, *Jihad vs. McWorld* (New York: Ballantine Books, 1995), p. 62.

[30]Korten, pp. 152–153.

[31]Korten, p. 152.

[32]Durning, p. 120.

[33]Ramsey, pp. 234–235.

[34]Ramsey, p. 234.

[35]Durning, pp. 119–120.

[36]Barber, p. 66.

[37]Barber, p. 69.

[38]Dave Barry, "Recycling Yogurt in the Sky," *International Herald Tribune* (Saturday-Sunday, July 24–25, 1999), p. 20.

[39]Robin and Dominguez, p. 160.

[40]Ramsey, p. 235.

[41]Kohn, p. 40.

[42]Kohn, p. 40.

[43]Kohn, p. 91.

[44]Kohn, p. 297, endnote #45.

[45]Alasdair MacIntyre, *After Virtue* (Notre Dame, IN: University of Notre Dame Press, 1981), p. 176.

[46]MacIntyre, pp. 175–176.

[47]Mary Midgley, *Evolution as a Religion* (London: Methuen and Co., 1985), p. 59.

[48]Midgley, p. 14.

[49]Midgley, p. 60.

[50]Robin and Dominguez, p. 109.

[51]Robin and Dominguez, p. 121.

[52]Ramsey, pp. 22–23.

[53]Robin and Dominguez, p. 142.

[54]Ramsey, p. 24.

[55]Kohn, p. 132.

[56]Kohn, pp. 132–133.

[57]Durning, p. 41.

[58]Robin and Dominguez, pp. 116–117.

[59]Robin and Dominguez, p. 84.

[60]Robin and Dominguez, p. 27.

[61]Robin and Dominguez, p. 160.

[62]Robin and Dominguez, p. 171.

[63]Robin and Dominguez, pp. 167–168.

[64]Ramsey, p. 237.

[65]Juliet Schor, *The Overworked American: The Unexpected Decline of Leisure* (New York: Basic Books, 1992). Found in Durning, p. 113.

[66]Robin and Dominguez, p. 213.

[67]Douglas Martin, "If Dogs Could Talk, They'd Say, 'Are You Crazy?'" *The New York Times Sunday*, News of the Week in Review (August 8, 1999), p. 2.

[68]Aldo Leopold, *A Sand County Almanac with Essays on Conservation from Round River* (New York: Ballantine Books, 1970), p. 227.

Chapter 12

[1]Jason Vest, Warren Cohen, and Mike Tharp, "Road Rage," *U.S. News and World Report*, Vol. 122, No. 21 (June 2, 1997), pp. 24–30, at 24.

[2]Vest, p. 25.

[3]Vest, p. 28.

[4]David C. Korten, *When Corporations Rule the World* (West Hartford, CN: Kumarian Press, 1995), p. 284.

[5]Deborah Gordon, *Steering a New Course: Transportation, Energy, and the Environment* (Washington, D.C.: Island Press, 1991), p. 147.

[6]Gordon, p. 147.

[7]Gordon, p. 149.

[8]Gordon, p. 63.

[9]Gordon, p. 64.

[10]Gordon, p. 40.

[11]Gordon, pp. 41–42.

[12]Marcia D. Lowe, "Back on Track: The Global Rail Revival," *Worldwatch Paper #118* (Washington, D.C., April 1994), p. 35.

[13]Lowe, p. 6.

[14]Lowe, p. 13.

[15]Lowe, p. 13.

[16]Gordon, pp. 42–43.

[17]Gordon, p. 25.

[18]Lowe, p. 35.

[19]David Malin Roodman, "Paying the Piper: Subsidies, Politics, and the Environment," *Worldwatch Paper #133* (Washington, D.C., December 1996), p. 41.

[20]Lowe, p. 6.

[21]Roodman, p. 43.

[22]Lowe, p. 7.

[23]Lowe, p. 15–16.

[24]Lowe, p. 16.

[25]Lowe, pp. 41–42.

[26]James Howard Kunstler, *The Geography of Nowhere* (New York: Simon and Schuster, 1993), p. 183.

[27]Korten, p. 284.

[28]Roodman, p. 6.

[29]Roodman, p. 28.

[30]Roodman, p. 30.

[31]National Research Council, "Executive Summary," *Alternative Agriculture* (1989), reprinted in *Global Resources: Opposing Viewpoints*, Matthew Polesetsky, ed. (San Diego, CA: Greenhaven Press, 1991), pp. 188–195, at 192.

[32]Roger Cohen, "Heartburn: Fearful Over the Future, Europe Seizes on Food," *The New York Times*, "The News of the Week in Review" (Sunday, August 29, 1999), pp. 1 and 3, at 3.

[33]Gordon, p. 89.

[34]Gordon, p. 87.

[35]Gordon, p. 90. It takes a gallon-and-a-half of ethanol to produce the power of only a gallon of gasoline. So a subsidy of 60 cents a gallon of ethanol equals a subsidy of 90 cents per gallon of gasoline equivalent. Roodman (p. 56) estimates the subsidy at only about 82 cents per gallon of gasoline equivalent.

[36]Jennifer Loven, "Farmers' Clout Wins in Battle over Ethanol," *The State Journal-Register* of Springfield, Illinois (November 16, 1998), p. 12.

[37]Roodman, p. 54.

[38]Roodman, p. 56.

[39]Roodman, pp. 54–55.

[40]Roodman, p. 55.

[41]Korten, p. 310.

[42]Thomas L. Friedman, *The Lexus and the Olive Tree* (New York: Farrar, Straus and Giroux, 1999), pp. 85–86.

[43]Friedman, p. 167.

[44]Friedman, pp. 86–87.

[45]Friedman, p. 87.

[46]Friedman, pp. 87–88.

[47]Friedman, p. 89.
[48]Friedman, pp. 91–92.
[49]Friedman, p. 285.
[50]Friedman, p. 259.
[51]Friedman, p. 259.
[52]Friedman, p. 258.
[53]Friedman, p. 259.
[54]Friedman, p. 167.
[55]Friedman, especially pp. 197–207.
[56]Korten, p. 34.
[57]Korten, p. 35.
[58]Korten, p. 33.
[59]Korten, pp. 31–32.
[60]Korten, p. 42.
[61]Korten, p. 179.
[62]Korten, p. 179.
[63]Hilary F. French, "GATT: Menace or Ally?" *WorldWatch*, Vol. 6, No. 5 (September/October 1993), pp. 9–13, at 12.
[64]Korten, pp. 176–179.
[65]Frederic J. Frommer, "Caught in the Net," *Animal Watch* (Fall 1999), pp. 29–31, at 29.
[66]Elizabeth Gawain, "The Dolphin's Gift," in *Chicken Soup for the Soul*, Jack Canfield and Mark Victor Hansen, eds. (Deerfield Beach, FL: Health Communications, Inc., 1993), pp. 291–292.
[67]*Public Citizen News*, Vol. 19, No. 4 (January/February 1999), p. 1. Emphasis added.
[68]Korten, p. 111.
[69]Benjamin Barber, *Jihad vs. McWorld* (New York: Ballantine Books, 1995), p. 70.
[70]Barber, p. 71.

Final Reflections

[1]Gregg Easterbrook, *A Moment on the Earth* (New York: Penguin, 1995), p. xiv.
[2]Easterbrook, p. xiv.
[3]Easterbrook, p. 82.
[4]Easterbrook, p. xiv.
[5]Easterbrook, p. 568.
[6]Easterbrook, p. 569.
[7]CNN (August 20, 1999).
[8]Easterbrook, pp. xiv-xv.
[9]Amanda Spake, "Losing the Battle of the Bugs," *U.S. News and World Report* (May 10, 1999), pp. 52–60, at 52.
[10]Spake, p. 55.
[11]Spake, p. 54.
[12]Spake, p. 55.
[13]Spake, p. 54.
[14]Rebecca J. Goldburg, "Antibiotic Resistance: A Grave Threat to Human Health," *EDF Letter*, Vol. XXX, No. 3 (June 1999), p. 4.
[15]Spake, p. 58.
[16]Spake, p. 58.

[17]Spake, p. 58.

[18]Goldburg, p. 4.

[19]Thomas L. Friedman, *The Lexus and the Olive Tree* (New York: Farrar, Straus, and Giroux, 1999), p. 287.

[20]Steven Yearley, *Sociology, Environmentalism, Globalization* (Thousand Oaks, CA: Sage, 1996), p. 82.

[21]*EDF Letter*, Vol. XXX, No. 4 (September 1999), pp. 1 and 3, at 1.

[22]*EDF Letter*, p. 3.

[23]Robert D. Kaplan, "The Coming Anarchy," *The Atlantic Monthly*, Vol. 273, No. 2 (February 1994), pp. 45–76, at 57–58.

[24]Kaplan, p. 59.

[25]Kaplan, p. 62.

[26]Kaplan, p. 72.

[27]Kaplan, p. 73.

[28]Kaplan, p. 74.

[29]Jeff Gersh, "Seeds of Chaos," *The Amicus Journal*, Vol. 21, No. 2 (Summer 1999), pp. 36–40, at 37.

[30]Gersh, p. 39.

[31]Friedman, p. 312.

[32]Vicki Robin and Joe Domingues, *Your Money or Your Life* (New York: Penguin Books, 1992), p. 227.

[33]Robin and Dominguez, p. 235.

[34]Steven Greenhouse, "So Much Work, So Little Time," *The New York Times Sunday*, "News of the Week in Review" (September 5, 1999), p. 1 and 4, at 1.

[35]Greenhouse, p. 4

[36]Kenneth Klee, "Frankenstein Foods?" *Newsweek* (September 13, 1999), pp. 33–35, at 33.

[37]Klee, p. 34.

[38]Klee, p. 35.

[39]Joe Wilkins, "Kyoto Accord Bad for Illinois," *The State Journal-Register* of Springfield, Illinois (December 20, 1998), p. 16.

[40]In Yearley, p. 82.

[41]Aldo Leopold, *A Sand County Almanac with Essays on Conservation from Round River* (New York: Ballantine Books, 1970), p. 245.

[42]Leopold, p. 246.

[43]Michael D. Lemonick, "Smart Genes?" *Time*, Vol. 154, No. 11 (September 13, 1999), pp. 54–58, at 55.

[44]Nancy Gibbs, "If We Have It, Do We Use It?" *Time*, Vol. 154, No. 11 (September 13, 1999), pp. 59–60, at 59.

[45]Leopold, p. 117.

[46]Lester R. Brown, "Challenges of the New Century," in *State of the World 2000*, Lester R. Brown, ed. (New York: W.W. Norton, 2000), pp. 3–21, at 10–11.

[47]Brown, pp. 11–12.

[48]It is a book of conversations between social activists Miles Horton and Paulo Friere, found in David C. Korten, *When Corporations Rule the World* (West Hartford, CT: Kumarian Press, 1995), p. 10.

Index